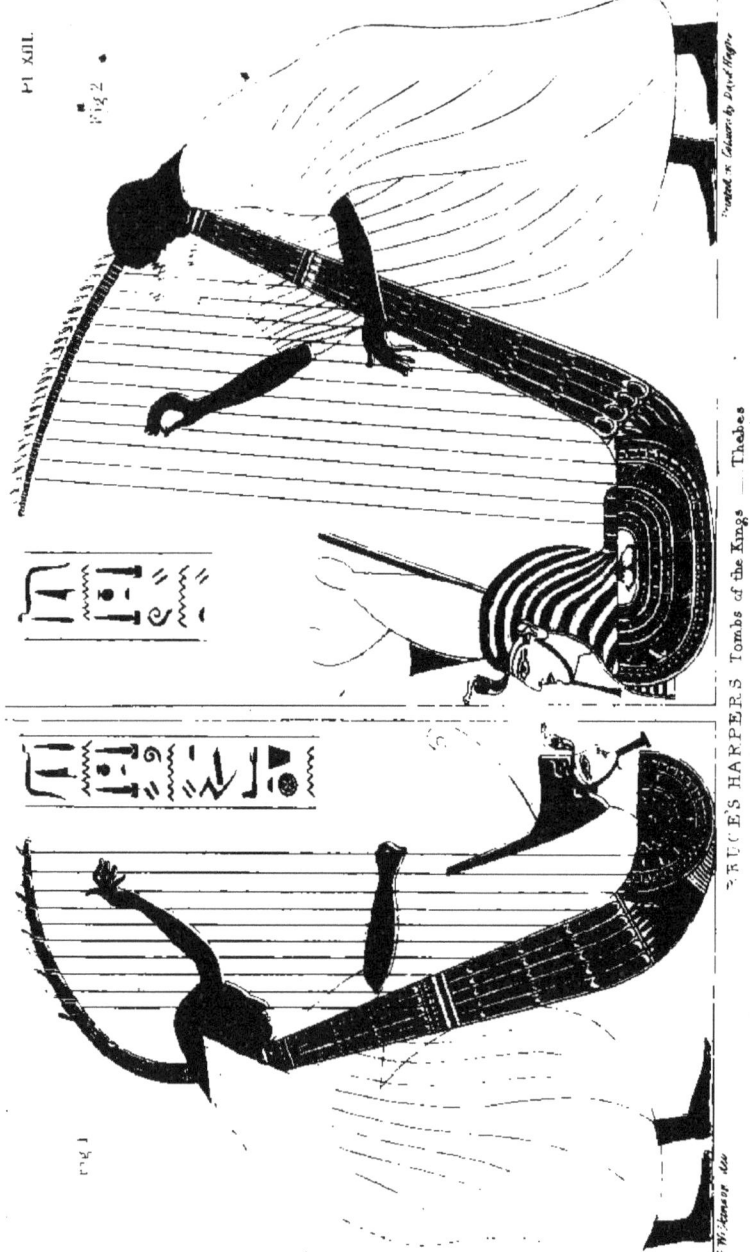

BRUCE'S HARPERS   Tombs of the Kings — Thebes

Pl. XIII.

Fig 2.

Fig 1.

Printed & Coloured by David Hughes

J. G. Wilkinson del.

MANNERS AND CUSTOMS

OF

THE ANCIENT EGYPTIANS,

INCLUDING

THEIR PRIVATE LIFE,
GOVERNMENT, LAWS, ARTS, MANUFACTURES,
RELIGION, AND EARLY HISTORY;

DERIVED FROM A COMPARISON OF

THE PAINTINGS, SCULPTURES, AND MONUMENTS STILL EXISTING,
WITH THE ACCOUNTS OF ANCIENT AUTHORS.

Illustrated by Drawings of those Subjects.

By J. G. WILKINSON, F.R.S. M.R.S.L. &c.

AUTHOR OF "A GENERAL VIEW OF EGYPT, AND
TOPOGRAPHY OF THEBES," &c.

IN THREE VOLUMES.

VOL. II.

LONDON:

JOHN MURRAY, ALBEMARLE STREET.

MDCCCXXXVII.

London:
Printed by A. Spottiswoode,
New-Street-Square.

CONTENTS

OF

THE SECOND VOLUME.

CHAPTER IV.

A 2

CHAP. V.

* This distinction between Egypt and the Thebaïd confirms what I have
observed in Vol. I. p. 12.

* There was another Monochordium said to have been invented by
Pythagoras to measure geometrically, or by lines, the proportion of sounds.
It was a ruler divided into many parts, with a string placed over it, a bridge
at each end, and a moveable one which traversed the whole length, and
whose place indicated the proportions of the sounds to the length of the
chords which gave them.

CHAP. VII.

VASES.

a 3

LIST AND EXPLANATION

OF THE

PLATES, WOOD-CUTS, AND VIGNETTES OF VOL. II.

CHAP. V.

CHAP. VI.

CHAP. VII.

* The cut of page 337. should have been marked 240. and 241.; that of 338. No. 242.

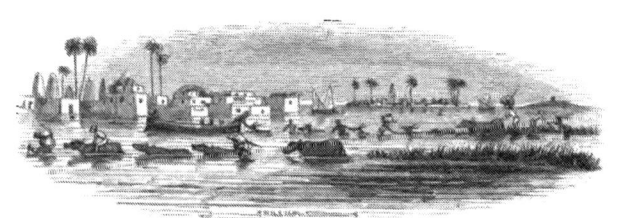

Cattle during the inundation, in the Delta.

MANNERS AND CUSTOMS

OF THE

ANCIENT EGYPTIANS.

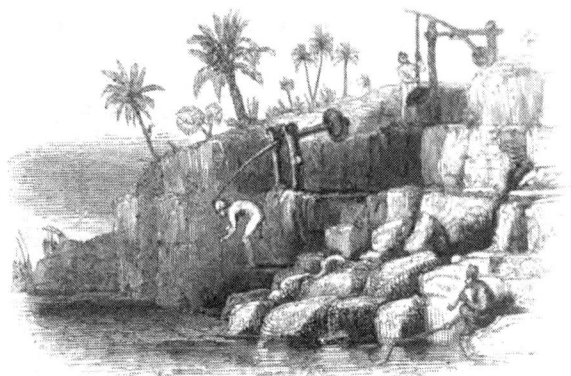

CHAPTER IV.

*The other Members of the Second Caste: The Peasants, Hunts-
men, and Boatmen. — The Lands farmed. — Irrigation. —
Third Caste: Tradesmen, Artificers, Public Weighers and
Notaries. — Money. — Writing. — Fourth Caste: Pastors,
Fishermen, and common People. — Legislative Rights of the
King. — Judges. — Laws. — Passports. — The Bastinado.*

I HAVE concluded the foregoing chapter with an
account of the military order, which, as it holds a

rank so far above all the other subdivisions of the second caste, I may be excused for treating almost as if distinct from it.   We now proceed to notice the other members of this caste ; the principal subdivisions of which consisted of the military just mentioned, the farmers, husbandmen, gardeners, huntsmen, and boatmen.

The statement of Diodorus, who says, the husbandmen were hired to till the estates of the kings, priests, and soldiers, is so strongly confirmed by the scriptural account of the cession of all the landed property to the government on the occasion of Joseph's famine, that we are reduced to the necessity of concluding, the husbandman had no rights in the soil, the richer peasants farming the land from the proprietor, while the poor were hired as labourers for the cultivation of the ground.   The wages paid them were trifling *, and it may be inferred that the farmer received the land on very moderate terms. The cattle, flocks, or herds, which were tethered in the clover, appear also to have belonged to the land-owner; but those employed in the plough, and for other agricultural purposes, were usually the property of the farmer. In extensive domains, the peasants frequently acted as superintendents of the herdsmen, and were obliged to give an account to the steward of the number and condition of the cattle on the estate, the direct care of them being the office of an inferior class of people : the clover was also let, as at the present day, to any person who had cattle, which

* Diodor. i. 74.

were tethered in the meadows about the close of autumn, and, at other seasons of the year, particularly during the period of the inundation, were fed in the villages and farm-yards on hay, which had been dried and preserved for the purpose.*

If the farmer had no right in the soil, it is still reasonable to suppose, that the choice of the crop depended chiefly on his decision, care being taken, as is still the custom in Egypt, as well as in other countries, that the land should not be injured by an imprudent repetition of similar crops †: and, indeed, from what Diodorus says, it is evident the farmers were not only permitted to choose the grain they intended to cultivate, but were justly deemed the only persons of sufficient experience to form a judicious opinion on the subject; and so skilful were they, says the historian, about these matters, in the study of which they were brought up from their youth, that they far excelled the agriculturists of every other nation.   They carefully considered the nature of the soil, the proper succession of crops, and the mode of tilling and irrigating the fields; and by a constant habit of observation, and by the lessons received from their parents, they were acquainted with the exact season for sowing and reaping, and with all the peculiarities of each species of produce.

The gardeners were employed by the rich in cultivating trees and flowers in the parterres at-

---

* Diodor. i. 36.   Like the *drees*, dried clover of modern Egypt.
† M. Macaire has shown the reason of this, and proved by experiments that the noxious matter thrown out by roots of vegetables unfits the soil for the growth of the same plant, though it may be beneficial to another kind.

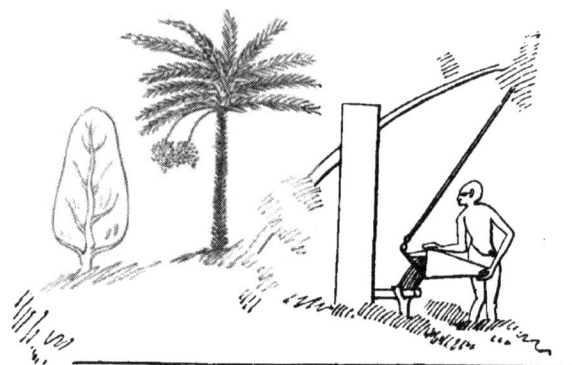

No. 74. Shadoof, or pole and bucket, for watering the garden. *Thebes.*

tached to their houses; and the vineyard, orchard, and tanks which served for ornament as well as for the purposes of irrigation, were under their superintendence and direction. In Egypt, the garden, and the fields, were both watered by the *shadóof**,

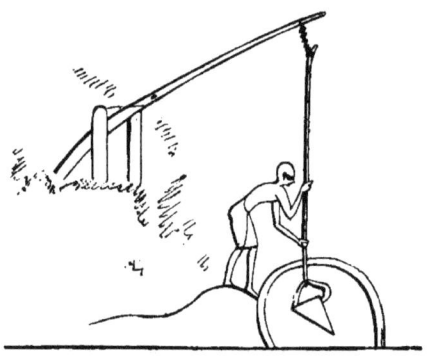

No. 75. Shadóof for watering the lands. *Thebes.*

* The pole and bucket still used in Egypt. This is the Arabic name. *Vide* Vignette D.

or by buckets, carried on a yoke across the
shoulders; but there is no appearance of their

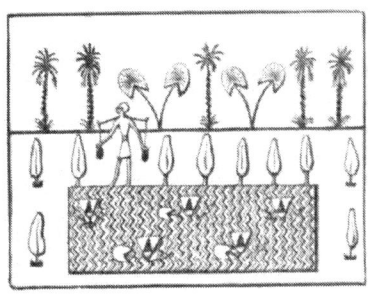

No. 76.   Water buckets carried by a yoke on the shoulders.   *Thebes.*

having used any hydraulic machine similar to the
Persian wheel, now so common in the East; nor do
the sculptures represent the foot machine mentioned
by Philo, which is supposed to be referred to in
the sacred writings. *   It is, however, not a little
remarkable that an Arab tradition still records the
use of the shadoof in the time of the Pharaohs:
and I have found a part of one in an ancient tomb
at Thebes, consisting of an angular piece of wood,
on which the pole turned, and the rope that secured it to the cross bar.

The hunstmen constituted another subdivision
of this caste, many of whom were employed to
attend and assist the chiefs, during their excursions
in pursuit of the wild animals of the country; the

---

* Deut. xi. 40. " Egypt . . . . where thou sowedst thy seed, and
wateredst it with thy *foot,* as a garden of herbs." Some think that
this alludes to the mode of stopping the small watercourses with mud
by the foot, and turning off the water into another channel, still adopted
in their gardens and fields. *Vide infrà* on the gardens.

scenes of which amusements were principally in
the deserts of Upper Egypt. They conducted
the dogs to the field, they had the management
of them in loosing them for the chase, and they
secured and brought home the game, having generally contributed with their own skill to increase
the sport of the chasseur. They also followed this
occupation on their own account, and secured for
themselves considerable profit, by catching those
animals that were prized for the table, by the rewards given for destroying the hyæna and other
noxious animals, and by the lucrative chase of the
ostrich, which was highly valued for its plumes
and eggs *, and was sold to the wealthier Egyptians.

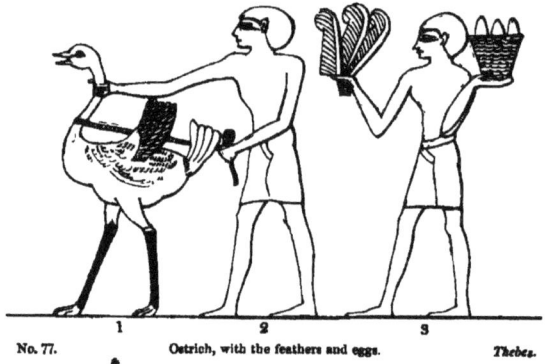

No. 77.   Ostrich, with the feathers and eggs.   *Thebes.*

The boatmen, like others who composed the
subdivisions of each caste, were of different grades :
some belonged to the private sailing or pleasure

---

* That ostrich eggs were also highly prized, is evident from their
forming part of the tributes brought to the kings.

boats of the grandees; others to those of burden;
and the rank of each depended on the station he
held.   The office of steersman seems to have been
the most important, and to have ranked above all
the other grades; but it is reasonable to suppose
that when the Egyptians undertook naval expeditions, the more warlike occupation of the sailor
raised that class of people in the estimation of their
countrymen, and the pilots of ships of war bore the
highest station in the class of boatmen. The officers
of their fleet were probably selected from the army*,
and the marines, or fighting men, who served on
board, were all of the military order.†

THE THIRD CASTE.

The third caste consisted of artificers, tradesmen
or shopkeepers, musicians, builders, masons, carpenters, cabinet-makers, potters, public weighers,
and an inferior class of notaries.

Among the artificers may be reckoned bra-
ziers and smiths of all kinds, in short, all who
pursued any handicraft occupation not included
among those which I have distinctly mentioned;
and the leather cutters, many of whom are said
to have lived at Thebes in the quarter of the
Memnonia‡, were doubtless a branch of the same
class.   Their skill in stamping leather was very remarkable; and many specimens of unusual thinness

---

* The Austrian admirals at the present day are military men.
† Sculptures at Medeenet Haboo.
‡ In the papyrus of Mr. Grey.   *Vide* Dr. Young on Egyptian
Lit. p. 65.

and delicacy, presenting figures and other devices, show how well they understood the art of tanning, and of turning it to an ornamental purpose.

The workers in linen, and other manufacturers, were comprehended under the same general head; but each class had its peculiar branch, and no one presumed to interfere with the occupation of another. Indeed it is probable that certain portions of the city, in which they dwelt, were set apart for, and exclusively belonged to, each of the different trades (as is still the case in a great degree at Cairo*): and this may be inferred from the mention of "the leather cutters of the Memnonia," above alluded to, who appear to have been a body of workmen living in a particular part of Thebes.

All trades, says Diodorus†, vied with each other in improving their own peculiar branch, no pains being spared to bring it to perfection; and to promote this object more effectually, it was enacted that no artisan should follow any other trade or employment, but that which had been handed down to him from his parents‡, and defined by law. Nor was any one permitted to meddle with political affairs, or to hold any civil office in the state, lest his thoughts should be distracted by the inconsistency of his pursuits, or by the jealousy and displeasure of the master in whose business he was employed. They foresaw that without such a law

* As the Seroogëéh, or saddlers; the Harrateen, turners; the Warakeen, paper-sellers, and others, which are the names of the streets of Cairo where they have their shops.
† Diodor. i. 74.
‡ Like many other things, this is plausible in theory, but bad in practice.

constant interruptions would take place, in consequence of the necessity, or the desire, of becoming conspicuous in a public station; that their proper occupations would be neglected, and that many would be led by vanity and self-sufficiency to interfere in matters which were out of their sphere. Moreover, they considered that to follow more than one occupation would be detrimental to their own interests, and to those of the community at large; and that when men, from a motive of avarice, are induced to engage in numerous branches of art, the result generally is, that they are unable to excel in any. Such, adds Diodorus, is the case in some countries, where artists occupy themselves in agricultural pursuits, or in commercial speculation, and frequently in two or three different arts at once. Many, again, in those communities which are governed according to democratical principles, are in the habit of frequenting popular assemblies, and, dreaming only of their own interests, receive bribes from the leaders of parties, and do incredible mischief to the state. But with the Egyptians, if any artisan meddled with political affairs, or engaged in any other employment than the one to which he had been brought up, a severe punishment was instantly inflicted upon him; and it was with this view that the regulations, respecting their public and private occupations, were instituted by the early legislators of Egypt.

It is unnecessary to enter into any detail of the peculiar employments of the various members of the class of artificers and tradesmen, as mention will be made of them in noticing the manufactures of the country; I therefore confine myself to a few remarks on the office of the public weighers or *qabbáneh*, and notaries. The business of the former was to ascertain the exact weight of every object presented to them in the public street, or market *, where they temporarily erected their scales, and to adjust the sale of each commodity with the strictest

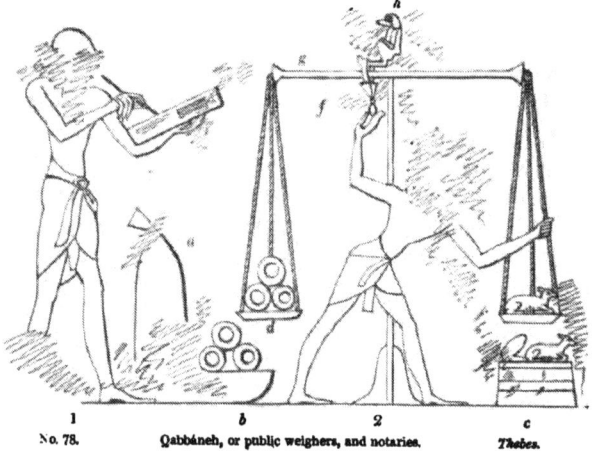

1   *b*   2   *c*
No. 78.   Qabbáneh, or public weighers, and notaries.   *Thebes.*

regard to justice, without favouring either the buyer or seller. All things sold by weight were submitted to this test†; and even the value of the

---

* " The *superintendence* of weights and measures " belonged to the priests, until the Romans took away that privilege. Conf. the banquet of Xenophon, " as the civil magistrate weighs bread in the market-place."

† Small objects were, no doubt, weighed at the shop by the seller; but if any question arose, it was decided by the public scales; larger goods being always weighed by the *qabbáneh*, as in Modern Egypt.

money paid for them was settled by the same unquestionable criterion.   It was owing to this custom that the money paid by the sons of Jacob for
the corn they purchased, and which had been
returned into their sacks, was said to be found of
"full *weight* *;" and it is highly probable that the
purity of gold and silver was subjected to the trial
of fire.†

Their money, as I shall have occasion to observe, was in rings of gold and silver; and it is remarkable that the same currency is to this day
employed in Sennár, and the neighbouring countries.   But whether those rings had any government stamp to denote their purity, or to serve as a
test of their value, I have not been able to deter-

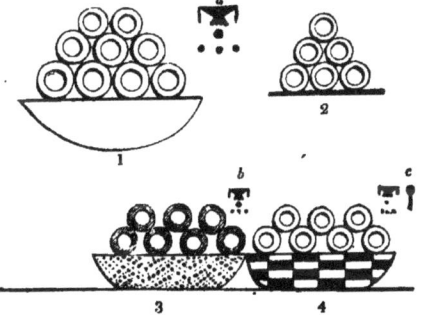

No. 79.   Rings of gold and silver.   *Thebes.*

* Exod. xliii. 21. " Our money in full weight." The Jews also
weighed their money. Their weights were of stone; and the word
weight, in Hebrew, אבן, also means a stone. Deut. xxv. 13. 15. They
had certain standard weights, as the shekel of the sanctuary. Roman money was also weighed in ancient times. Liv. iv. 60. The
Egyptian mode of weighing and of noting down the account frequently
occurs in the sculptures.

† As with the modern Ethiopians. Conf. Zech. xiii. 9., and 1 Pet.
i. 7.

mine; and it is singular that none have yet been discovered in the ruins or tombs of Thebes, though so frequently represented in the sculptures.

A scribe or notary marked down the amount of the weight, whatever the commodity might be ; and this document, being given or shown to the parties, completely sanctioned the bargain, and served as a pledge that justice had been done them.

The same custom is still retained by the modern Egyptians, the scales of the public *qabbáneh* in the large towns being a criterion to which no one can object ; and the weight of meat, vegetables, honey, butter, cheese, wood, charcoal, and other objects, having been ascertained, is returned in writing on the application of the parties.

The scribes or notaries were probably public writers, like the Arab *kátebs* of the present day, or the *scrivani* of Italy, who, for a small trifle, compose and pen a petition to government, settle accounts, and write letters, or other documents, for those who are untaught, or for those who are too idle to do so for themselves. These persons, however, must not be confounded with the royal and priestly scribes, who were of a very different grade, and who ranked among the principal people of the country : though it is sometimes difficult to distinguish them from an inferior class of scribes, of the sacerdotal order.

Most of the shopkeepers, and of the master tradesmen, learned to write * : but the workmen were contented to occupy their time in acquiring

* Diodor. i. 81.

from their parents or friends that art to which they were brought up; and the common people, as might be supposed, were entirely ignorant of the art of writing.

EGYPTIAN WRITING.

The characters used by the Egyptians consisted of three different kinds, — the hieroglyphic *, the hieratic, and enchorial ; the first and last known to all who received a good education ; the hieratic confined more particularly to the priests.   There is reason to believe the enchorial did not exist at a very remote period ; the earliest inscriptions written in that character, hitherto discovered, not dating prior to the accession of the Ptolemies ; and some of the hieratic in the time of Darius seems to be undergoing a transition to this new form.   Indeed, the appearance of the letters proves them to have been derived from the hieratic, which is itself directly taken from the hieroglyphic ; and it is probable that this last was the sole mode of writing known to the Egyptians in the earliest periods of their history, though the hieratic, a much earlier invention than the enchorial, dates from a very remote era.

Clement of Alexandria† says, those who are educated among the Egyptians learn three different modes of writing, one of which is the epistolary

* The hieroglyphic has been called the monumental, but it is also used in papyri, and for all the purposes for which the other two are employed.
† Stromat. lib. v.

(enchorial), the other, the sacerdotal (hieratic), and the third, the hieroglyphic; and though Porphyry, in his life of Pythagoras, gives to the hieratic the name of symbolic, it is evident he alludes to the same modes of writing, when he says that the philosopher, during his stay in Egypt, learnt the three different kinds of letters, — the epistolic, the hieroglyphic, and the symbolic. Herodotus[*] mentions two, — the sacred and demotic; but as he speaks of their writing from right to left, it is possible that he only here alludes to the two cursory characters, the hieratic and enchorial, without comprehending the hieroglyphics under the head of writing.

FALSE WEIGHTS.

The great confidence reposed in the public weighers rendered it necessary to enact suitable laws in order to bind them to their duty; and considering how much public property was at their mercy, and how easily bribes might be taken from a dishonest tradesman, the Egyptians inflicted a severe punishment as well on the weighers as on the shopkeepers, who were found to have false weights and measures, or to have defrauded the purchaser in any other way. Scribes who kept false accounts, made erasures from public documents, forged a signature, or altered any agreements without the consent of the parties, were punished, like the preceding offenders, with the loss of both their hands; on the principle, says

[*] Herodot. ii. 36.

Diodorus, that the offending member should suffer*, and, while the culprit expiated the crime with a most signal punishment, that the severity of the example might deter others from the commission of a similar offence.

FOURTH CASTE.

The fourth caste was composed of pastors, poulterers, fowlers, fishermen, labourers, servants†, and common people.

PASTORS.

The pastors, who were divided into different classes, consisted of oxherds, shepherds, goatherds, swineherds, and others, whose occupation was to tend the herds of the rich in the pastures, during the grazing season, and to prepare the provender, required for them, when the waters of the Nile covered the irrigated lands.   They were looked upon by the rest of the Egyptians as a degraded class, who followed a disgraceful employment; and it is not surprising that Pharaoh should have treated the Jews with that contempt which it was customary for every Egyptian to feel towards shepherds.   Nor can we wonder at Joseph's warning his brethren, on their arrival, of this aversion of the Egyptians, who, he assured them, considered " every shepherd an abomination‡;" and from

---

* Diodor. i. 78. This *lex talionis* is a very primitive mode of punishing crime.   *Vide* Deut. xix. 21.

† Gen. xii. 16.   Exod. ii. 5.

‡ Gen. xlvi. 34.   According to Herodotus (ii. 46.) goatherds were much honoured in the Mendesian nome.

his recommending them to request they might dwell in the land of Goshen, we may conclude it was with a view to avoid as much as possible those who were not shepherds like themselves, or to obtain a settlement in the land peculiarly adapted for pasture *; and it is probable that much of Pharaoh's cattle was also kept there, since the monarch gave orders that if any of the Jews were remarkable for skill in the management of herds, they should be selected to overlook his own cattle†, after they were settled in the land of Goshen.

The hatred borne against shepherds by the Egyptians, was not owing solely to their contempt for that occupation; this feeling originated in another and a far more powerful cause, — the previous occupation of their country by a pastor race, who had committed great cruelties during their possession of the country; and the already existing prejudice against shepherds, when the Hebrews arrived, plainly shows their invasion to have happened previous to that event.‡ As if to prove how much they despised every order of pastors, the artists, both of Upper and Lower Egypt, delighted on all occasions in representing them as dirty and unshaven; and at Beni Hassan and the tombs near the Pyramids of Geezeh, we find them caricatured as a deformed and unseemly race.

The swineherds were the most ignoble, and of

---

* The Delta and those lands lying to the east of the Damietta branch of the Nile are still preferred for grazing cattle.
† Gen. xlvii. 6.
‡ *Vide* p. 20. and 38.

all the Egyptians the only persons who are said not to have been permitted to enter a temple[*]; and even if this statement is exaggerated, it tends to show with what contempt they were looked upon by the individuals from whom Herodotus received his information, and how far they ranked beneath any others of the whole order of pastors.   Like the other classes, their office descended from father to son, and the same occupation was followed by successive generations.

The skill of these people, in rearing animals of different kinds, was the result, says Diodorus[†], of the experience they had inherited from their parents, and subsequently increased by their own observation; and the spirit of emulation, which is natural to all men, constantly adding to their stock of knowledge, they introduced many improvements unknown to other people.   Their sheep were twice shorn, and twice brought forth lambs in the course of one year[‡]; and though the climate was the chief cause of these phenomena, the skill and attention of the shepherd were also necessary; nor, if the animals were neglected, would unaided nature alone suffice for their continuance.

But of all the discoveries to which any class of Egyptians attained, the one, says the historian, which is most worthy of admiration, is their mode

---

[*] Herodot. ii. 47. The swineherds in India are the very lowest class, and are so despised that no others will associate with them.
[†] Diodor. i. 74.
[‡] Diodor. i. 36. This happens now, but not unless the sheep are properly fed and attended to.

of rearing fowls* and geese; and by a process
their ingenuity has devised, they hatch the eggs,
and thereby secure an abundance of poultry, without the necessity of waiting for the incubation of
the hens.

POULTERERS, FOWLERS, AND FISHERMEN.

The poulterers may be divided into two classes, —
the rearers, and those who sold poultry in the
market; the former living in the country and villages, and the latter in the market towns. They
fed them for the table; and, independent of the
number required for private consumption, a great
many were exclusively fattened for the service of
the temple, as well as for the sacred animals[†], and
for the daily rations[‡] of the priests and soldiers, or
others who lived at the government expense, and
for the king himself.[§]

Their geese were the *vulpanser* of the Nile, and
others of the same genus still common on its banks,
many of which were tamed and fed like ordinary
poultry. Those in a wild state were caught in
large clap nets, and being brought to the poulterers, were salted and potted in earthenware
vases.[||] Others were put up in the shop for im-

---

* The modern Egyptians (particularly the Copts) have borrowed
this custom from their predecessors, and eggs are annually hatched in
the towns of Upper and Lower Egypt. *Vide* my Egypt and Thebes,
p. 246., where the process is described.

† Diodorus (i. 84.) says, " Some were fed with the meat of geese,
both boiled and roast, and others, which lived on raw food, were provided with birds caught by the fowlers."

‡ Herodot. ii. 37.   Gen. xlvii. 22.   § Diodor. i. 70.

|| Such I suppose to be the subject of the wood-cut in the opposite
page.

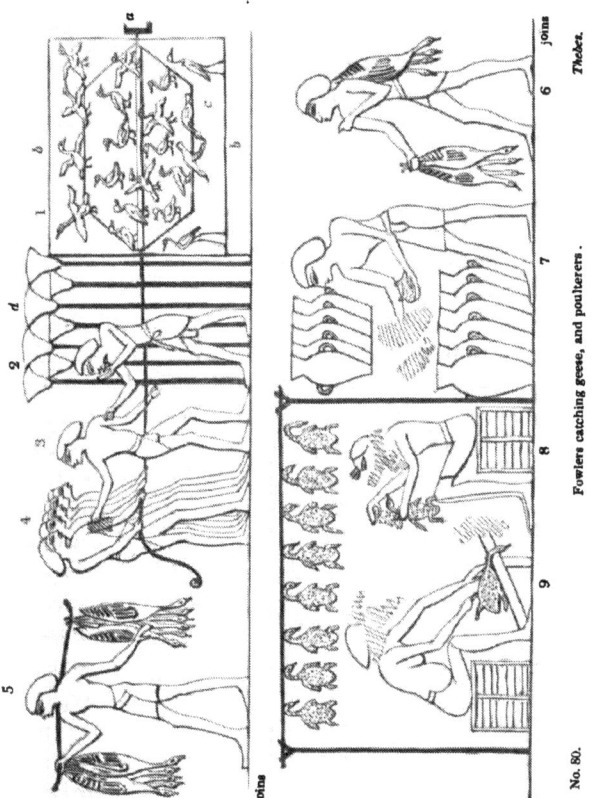

mediate sale; and whenever eggs could be procured they carefully collected them, and submitted
them to the management of the rearers, who
thereby increased the more valuable stock of tame
fowl. The same care was taken to preserve the
young of gazelles, and other wild animals of the

c 2

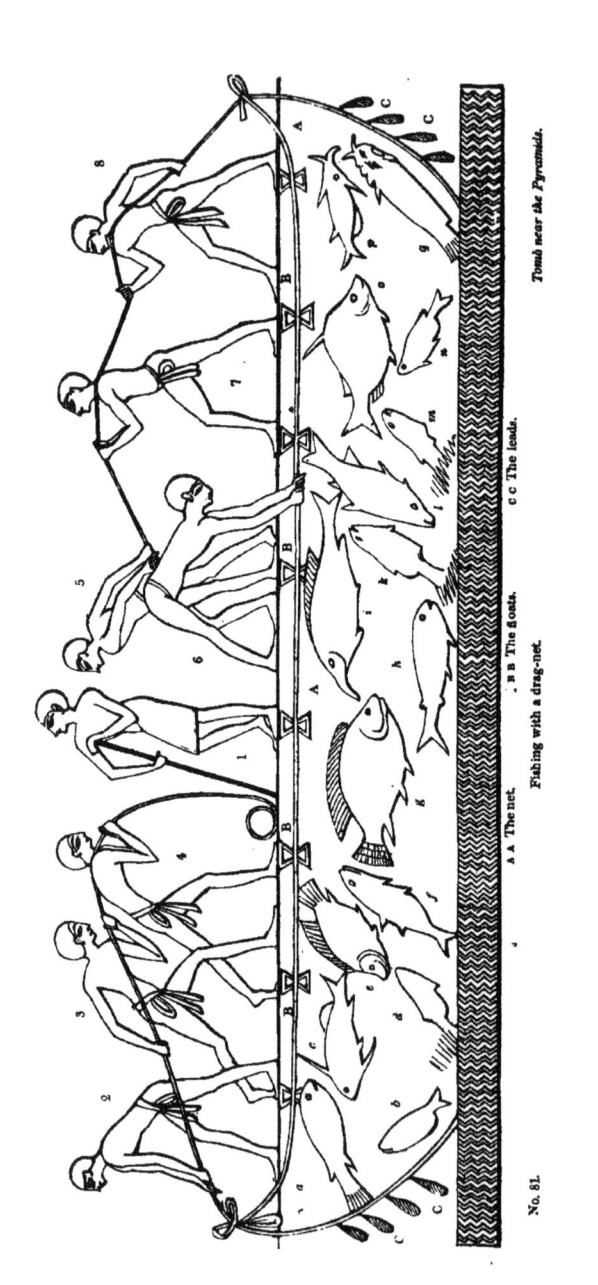

No. 81.   Fishing with a drag-net.   Tomb near the Pyramids.

A A The net.   B B The floats.   c c The leads.

desert, whose meat was reckoned among the dainties of the table; and by paying proper attention
to their habits, they were enabled to collect many
head of antelopes, which frequently formed part of
the herds of the Egyptian nobles.   And in order to
give an idea of the pains they took in rearing these
timid animals, and to show the great value of the
possessions of the deceased, they are introduced
with the cattle, in the sculptures of the tombs.

   The fishermen mostly used the net: it was of a
long form, like the common drag-net, with wooden
floats on the upper, and leads on the lower, side * ;
but though it was sometimes let down from a boat,
those who pulled it generally stood on the shore,
and landed the fish on a shelving bank.   The
leads were occasionally of an elongated shape,
hanging from the outer cord or border of the net,
but they were more usually flat, and, being folded
round the cord, the opposite sides were beaten
together ; a satisfactory instance of which is seen
in the ancient net preserved in the Berlin Museum,

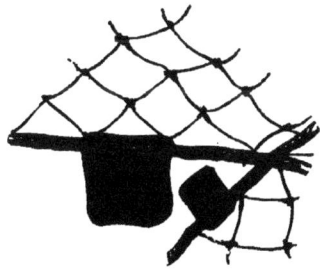

No. 82.   Leads, with part of a net.   *Berlin Museum.*

* *Vide* wood-cut, No. 81., opposite page.

c 3

and this method still continues to be adopted by the modern Egyptians.

In a country where fish will not admit of being kept, the same persons who caught them were the sole venders, and the fishermen may be considered an undivided body. The class of labourers, on the contrary, consisted of several different subdivisions, according to their occupation ; among whom we may, perhaps, include the workers in mud and straw, and brickmakers*, as well as those who performed various drudgeries in the field and in the town : but as I shall have occasion to speak of them hereafter, I now content myself with these general remarks, and pass on to the consideration of the government and laws of the country.

THE LEGISLATIVE RIGHTS OF THE KING.

The king had the right of enacting laws†, and of managing all the affairs of religion and of the state ; and so intimate was the connection of these two, that the maintenance of the one was considered essential for the very existence of the other. This notion has, indeed, always been cherished in the East ; and we find Khandemir and other Moslem writers give it as a received opinion, that the state cannot exist without religion, and that " it is of minor consequence if the former perishes, provided

---

* Many of those who made bricks, and worked in the field, were foreign slaves, as I have already observed ; and on them, no doubt, fell the most arduous portion of these laborious tasks. But it was not only the Jews who were so treated : other captives were similarly employed, as we see in the sculptures at Thebes, where the Jews never lived, and where people of other conquered nations are mentioned. *Vide* Chap. V., wood-cut, No. 93.

† Herodot. ii 136. 177. Diodor. i. 79.

the latter survives, since it is impossible that the state can survive if religion is subverted."

We are acquainted with few of the laws of the ancient Egyptians; but the superiority of their legislature has always been acknowledged as the cause of the duration of an empire, which lasted with a very uniform succession of hereditary sovereigns, and with the same form of government, for a much longer period than the generality of ancient states. Indeed the wisdom of that people was proverbial, and was held in such consideration by other nations, that we find it taken by the Jews as the standard to which superior learning* in their own country was willingly compared; and Moses had prepared himself for the duties of a legislator by becoming versed " in all the wisdom of the Egyptians."†

Besides their right of enacting laws, the kings administered justice to their subjects on those questions which came under their immediate cognisance‡, and they were assisted in the management of state affairs by the advice of the most able and distinguished members of the priestly order.§ With them the monarch consulted upon all questions of importance, relating to the internal administration of the country; and previous to the admission of Joseph to the confidence of Pharaoh, the opinion of his ministers was asked, as to the expediency and propriety of the measure.||

* Of Solomon. 1 Kings, iv. 30.   † Acts, vii. 22.
‡ Diodor. i. 71. Herodot. ii. 173.   § Diodor. i. 73.
|| Gen. xli. 38. " And Pharaoh said unto his servants (ministers), Can we find such a one as this is?" Gen. l. 7. " The elders of his (Pharaoh's) house." And Isaiah, xix. 11. " The wise counsellors of Pharaoh."

Their edicts appear to have been issued in the form of a *firmán**, or written order, as in all Oriental countries; and from the expression used by Pharaoh in granting power to Joseph, we may infer, that the people who received that order adopted the usual Eastern mode† of acknowledging their obedience and respect for the sovereign. Nor can there be any doubt that, besides the custom of *kissing* the signature attached to those documents, they were expected to " bow the knee‡ " in the presence of the monarch and chiefs of the country, and even to prostrate themselves to the earth before them. §

JUDGES.

Causes of ordinary occurrence were decided by those who held the office of judges; and the care with which persons were elected to this office is a strong proof of their regard for the welfare of the community, and of their earnest endeavours to promote the ends of justice. None were admitted to it but the most upright and learned individuals; and, in order to make the office more select, and more readily to obtain persons of known character, ten only were chosen from each of the three cities, — Thebes, Memphis, and Heliopolis; a body of

---

* Like the Khot è Shereef, " handwriting of the Shereef," or order of the soltans of Constantinople.

† The expression in the Hebrew is, " according to thy word shall all my people" *kiss* (" be ruled "), alluding evidently to the custom of kissing a *firmán*. Gen. xli. 40.

‡ Gen. xli. 43. The word abrek אברך is very remarkable, as it is used to the present day by the Arabs when requiring a camel to kneel and receive its load.

§ Joseph's brethren bowed to the earth. Gen. xliii. 26. 28. These prostrations are frequently represented in the sculptures.

men, says Diodorus, by no means inferior either to the Areopagites of Athens, or to the senate of Lacedæmon.

These thirty individuals constituted the bench of judges ; and at their first meeting they elected the most distinguished among them to be president, with the title of Arch-judge. His salary was much greater than that of the ·other judges, as his office was more important; and the city to which he belonged enjoyed the privilege of returning another judge, to complete the number of the thirty from whom he had been chosen. They all received ample allowances from the king; in order that, possessing a sufficiency for their maintenance and other necessary expenses, they might be above the reach of temptation, and be inaccessible to bribes: for it was considered of primary importance, that all judicial proceedings should be regulated with the most scrupulous exactitude, sentences pronounced by authorised tribunals* always having a decided influence, either salutary or prejudicial, on the affairs of common life. They felt that precedents were thereby established, and that numerous abuses frequently resulted from an early error, which had been sanctioned by the decision of some influential person, and for this reason they weighed the talents as well as the character of the judge.

The first principle was that offenders should be discovered and punished, and that those who had been wronged should be benefited by the interposition of the laws; since the least compensation

* Diodor. i. 75.

which can be made to the oppressed, and the
most effectual preventative of crime, are the speedy
discovery and exposure of the offender. On the
other hand, if the terror which hangs over the
guilty in the· hour of trial could be averted by
bribery or favour, nothing short of distrust and
confusion would pervade all ranks of society; and
the spirit of the Egyptian laws was not merely to
hold out the distant prospect of rewards and
punishments, or merely threaten the future ven-
geance of the gods *, but to apply the more persuasive stimulus of present retribution.

Besides the care taken by them that justice
should be administered according to the real merits
of the case, and that before their tribunals no
favour or respect of persons should be permitted,
another very important regulation was adopted,
that justice should be gratuitously administered:
and it was consequently accessible to the poor,
as well as to the rich. The very spirit of their
laws was to give protection and assistance to the
oppressed†, and every thing that tended to promote an unbiassed judgment was peculiarly commended by the Egyptian sages.‡

When a case was brought for trial, it was customary for the arch-judge to put a golden chain round
his neck, to which was suspended a small figure of

---

* Diodor. i. 93. " ου μυθωδους αλλ' ορατης . . . της κολασεως."
† Diodor. loc. cit. " των αδικουμενων βοηθειας τυγχανοντων."
‡ When consulted by the Eleans respecting their games, their objec-
tion was founded on the persuasion that no unbiassed judgment could
be given when the Eleans themselves were admitted to the contest.
Herodot. ii. 160., Diodor. i. 95. The former says, in the reign of
Psammis, the latter, of Amasis. *Vide supra*, p.167.   ʼ

Truth, ornamented with precious stones. This
was, in fact, a representation of the goddess who
was worshipped under the double character of
Truth and Justice, and whose name, Thmei*, ap-

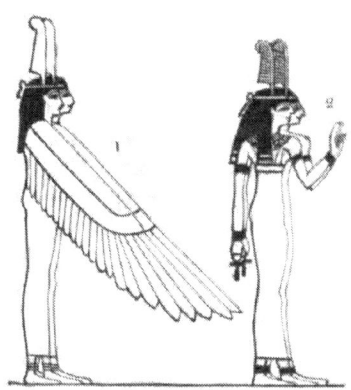

The goddess of Truth and Justice.   *Thebes.*

pears to have been the origin of the Hebrew
Thummim †; a word, according to the Septuagint
translation, implying truth ‡, and bearing a further analogy § in its plural termination.   And what
makes it more remarkable is, that the chief priest
of the Jews, who before the election of a king
was also the judge of the nation, was alone entitled

* The Egyptian or Coptic name of Justice or Truth. We do not
yet read it in the hieroglyphics, as the characters are still uncertain.
Hence the θεμις of the Greeks.

† Lord Prudhoe has very ingeniously suggested that the Urim is
derived from the *two* asps or basilisks, *urei*, which were the emblems of
royalty in Egypt.   Ouro is the Egyptian word implying a king.

‡ Exod. xxviii. 30.

§ The goddess frequently occurs in the sculptures in this double capacity, represented by two figures exactly similar.

to wear this honorary badge; and the Thummim, like the Egyptian figure, was studded with precious stones of various colours. The goddess was represented * " having her eyes closed," purporting

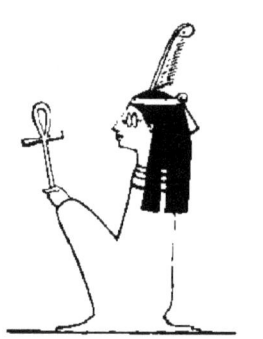

No. 84. The goddess of Truth, " with her eyes closed." *Thebes.*

that the duty of a judge was to weigh the question according to the evidence he had heard, and to trust rather to his mind than to what he saw; and was intended to warn him of that virtue which the Deity peculiarly enjoined: an emblematic idea, very similar to "those statues at Thebes of judges without hands, with their chief or president at their head having his eyes turned downwards," signifying, as Plutarch observes, " that Justice ought neither to be accessible to bribes, nor guided by favour and affection." †

It is not to be supposed that the president and the thirty judges above mentioned were the only house of judicature in the country; each city or

* Diodor. i. 48. † Plut. de Is. s. x.

capital of a nome had no doubt its own court, for the trial of minor and local * offences; and it is probable that the assembly returned by the three chief cities resided wherever the royal court was held, and performed many of the same duties as the senates of ancient times. And that this was really the case, appears from the account of Diodorus†, who mentions the thirty judges and their president, represented at Thebes in the sculptures of the tomb of Osymandyas.

The president, or arch-judge having put on the emblem of Truth, the trial commenced, and the eight volumes which contained the laws of the Egyptians were placed close to him‡, in order to guide his decision, or to enable him to solve a difficult question, by reference to that code, to former precedents, or to the opinion, of some learned predecessor. The complainant stated his case. This was done in writing; and every particular that bore upon the subject, the mode in which the alleged offence was committed, and an estimate of the damage, or the extent of the injury sustained, were inserted.

The defendant then, taking up the deposition of the opposite party, wrote his answer to each of the plaintiff's statements, either denying the charge, or endeavouring to prove that the offence was not of a serious nature, or, if obliged to admit his guilt,

* I should rather think that those who had committed any very grave offence were sent to the capital, than that the Egyptian judges performed any circuits for the administration of justice.

† Diodor. i. 48.   ‡ Diodor. i. 48. 75.

suggesting that the damages were too high, and in-
compatible with the nature of the crime.   The
complainant replied in writing; and the accused
having brought forward all he had to say in his
defence, the papers were given to the judges;
and if no witnesses* could be produced on either
side, they decided upon the question according to
the deposition of the parties.   Their opinion only
required to be ratified by the president, who then
proceeded, in virtue of his office, to pronounce
judgment on the case; and this was done by touching the party who had gained the cause with the
figure of Truth.   They considered that this mode
of proceeding was more likely to forward the ends
of justice than when the judges listened to the statements of pleaders; eloquence having frequently
the effect of fascinating the mind, and tending to
throw a veil over guilt and to pervert truth.   The
persuasive arguments of oratory, or those artifices
which move the passions and excite the sympathy
of the judges, were avoided, and thus neither did
an appeal to their feelings, nor the tears and dissimulation of an offender, soften the just rigour
of the laws.†   And while ample time was afforded
to each party to proffer or to disprove an accusation, no opportunity was given to the offender to
take advantage of his opponent, but poor and rich,
ignorant and learned, honest and dishonest, were

---

* This is omitted by Diodorus; but from the great pains they took
to discover false accusers, and from every kind of probability, we may
conclude they were examined whenever they could be produced.
Diodor. i. 77. 92.
† Diodor. i. 76.

placed on an equal footing; and it was the case, rather than the persons, upon which the judgment was passed.

LAWS.

The laws of the Egyptians were handed down from the earliest times, and looked upon with the greatest reverence.   They had the credit of having been dictated by the gods themselves, and Thoth * (Hermes or Mercury) was said to have framed them for the benefit of mankind.

The names of many of the early monarchs and sages who had contributed to the completion of their code were recorded and venerated by them ; and whoever at successive periods made additions to it was mentioned with gratitude as the bene-factor of his country. †

Truth or justice was thought to be the main cardinal virtue among the Egyptians, inasmuch as it relates more particularly to others ; prudence, temperance, and fortitude being relative qualities, and tending only to the immediate benefit of the individual who possesses them.   It was, therefore, with great earnestness that they inculcated the necessity of fully appreciating it ; and falsehood was not only considered disgraceful, but when it en-tailed an injury on any other person was punishable by law.   A calumniator of the dead was condemned to a severe punishment‡ ; and a false accuser was

---

* The priests, of course, understood the allegorical meaning of this fable, referring to an intellectual agency : the people received it literally.
† Diodor. i. 94.
‡ Diodor. i. 92.   " μεγαλοις περιπιπτει προστιμοις."

doomed to the same sentence which would have
been awarded to the accused, if the offence had
been proved against him * ; but to maintain a falsehood by an oath was deemed the blackest crime,
and one which, from its complicated nature, could
be punished by nothing short of death.   For they
considered that it involved two distinct crimes, — a
contempt for the gods, and a violation of faith towards man ; the former the direct promoter of
every sin, the latter destructive of all those ties
which are most essential for the welfare of society.

In order more effectually to protect the virtuous,
and detect the wicked, it was enacted† that every
one should at certain times present himself before
the magistrates or provincial governors, and give
his name, his place of abode, his profession or
employment, and, in short, the mode in which he
gained his livelihood ; the particulars being duly
registered by the official scribes.   The time of
attendance was fixed, and they proceeded in bodies
to the appointed office, accompanied with their
respective banners‡; each member of the body
being introduced singly to the registering clerks.
In approaching these functionaries, it was required

* Conf. Deut. xix. 19.
† Herodotus (ii. 177.) attributes it to Amasis : Diodorus (i. 77.)
mentions it merely as an Egyptian law.   They both agree that Solon
adopted and introduced it at Athens.   I am inclined to think it
much more ancient than Amasis; and it appears to be represented in
the sculptures, and those, too, of a very early epoch.   Perhaps it was a
law of Amosis or Ames I.   Amasis, in hieroglyphics, is the same name
as Ames, Amosis, or Ames II. ; but Ames I. was the leader of the 18th
dynasty.   The subjects of the following wood-cuts, Nos. 85. and 86.,
relate, I believe, to this custom : they are of the time of Thothmes IV.
‡ *Vide* wood-cut, No. 85., opposite page.

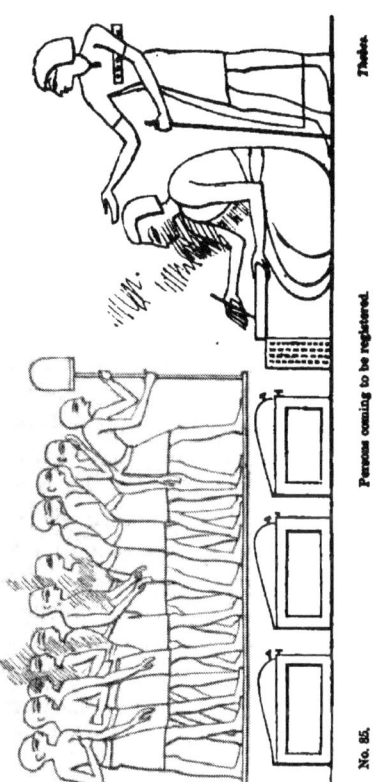

that the individual should make a profound bow, which was similar to that described by Herodotus[*], the hand falling down to the knee; and this mark of deference was expected from every one, as

* Herodot. ii. 80.

a token of respect to the court, on all occasions, both when accused before a magistrate, and when attending at the police office to prefer a complaint, or to vindicate his character from an unjust imputation.

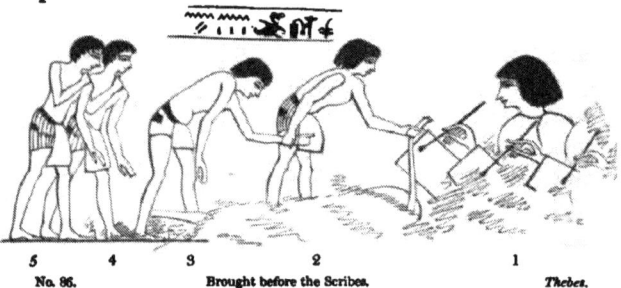

5   4   3   2   1

No. 86.   Brought before the Scribes.   *Thebes.*

Whether they received a passport from the magistrates, or merely enrolled their names and the other particulars required of them, does not appear, nor can we come to any conclusion on this head, either from the sculptures, the accounts of ancient writers, or even from the mode of describing persons, who were parties to the sale of estates, and other private or public contracts: but the formula much resembles that adopted in the passport offices of modern Europe.

In a deed of the time of Cleopatra Cocce and Ptolemy Alexander I., written in Greek, and relating to the sale of a piece of land at Thebes, the parties are thus described* : — " Pamonthes, aged about forty-five†, of middle size, dark com-

---

* Papyrus of S. d'Anastasy. *Vide* Dr. Young on Hieroglyphical Literature, p. 65.

† It is remarkable that, in the East, no one knows his exact age; nor do they keep any registers of births or deaths.

plexion, and handsome figure, bald, round faced
and straight nosed; Snachomneus, aged about
twenty, of middle size, sallow complexion, round
faced and straight nosed; Semmuthis Persineï, aged
about twenty-two, of middle size, sallow complexion, round faced, flat nosed, and of quiet de-
meanour; and Tathlyt Persineï, aged about thirty,
of middle size, sallow complexion, round face and
straight nose, — the four being children of Pe-
tepsais, of the leather cutters of the Memnonia;
and Nechutes the less, the son of Asos, aged about
forty, of middle size, sallow complexion, cheerful
countenance, long face and straight nose, with a
scar upon the middle of his forehead." Even if the
mode of registering the names, which is noticed by
Diodorus, and the sculptures of Thebes, does not
in reality refer to passports, it is at least very similar
in spirit and intent, and may be considered the
earliest indication of a custom so notoriously un-
pleasant to modern travellers.

During their examination, if any excesses were
found to have been committed by them, in consequence of an irregular mode of life, they were
sentenced to the bastinado; but a false statement*, or the proof of being engaged in unlawful
pursuits, entailed upon them the punishment of a
capital crime.

MURDER.

The wilful murder of a freeman, or even of a
slave, was punished with death, from the conviction

* Diodor. i. 77. " τον εν τουτοις ψευσαμενον."

that men ought to be restrained from the commission of sin, not on account of any distinction of station in life, but from the light in which they viewed the crime itself; while at the same time it had the effect of showing, that if the murder of a slave was deemed an offence deserving of so severe a punishment, they ought still more to shudder at the murder of one who was a compatriot and a free-born citizen.

In this law we observe a scrupulous regard to justice and humanity, and have an unquestionable proof of the great advancement made by the Egyptians in the most essential points of civilisation, affording a pleasing comment on their character; and it is a striking fact, that neither Greece[*] nor Rome[†], proud as they both were of their superiority, and of their skill in jurisprudence, had the good sense to adopt or imitate this wise regulation.[‡] Indeed, the Egyptians considered it so heinous a crime to deprive a man of life, that to be the accidental witness of an attempt to murder, without endeavouring to prevent it, was a capital offence, which could only be palliated by bringing proofs of inability to act. With the same spirit they decided, that to be present when any one

---

[*] I must do the Greeks the justice to say they acknowledged the superior wisdom and equity of the Egyptians, and were in the habit of consulting them, and of visiting Egypt to study their institutions.

[†] Masters had an absolute power of life and death over their slaves, and they generally crucified them, when convicted of a capital offence. Juv. Sat. vi. 219. Constantine abolished this punishment.

[‡] The Athenian lawgiver did, however, institute a very proper custom, that the funerals of slaves should be properly solemnised by the magistrates (demarchs). Demosth. Or. in Macart. And slaves received much better treatment at Athens than at Sparta.

inflicted a personal injury on another, without interfering, was tantamount to being a party, and was
punishable according to the extent of the assault;
and every one who witnessed a robbery was bound
either to arrest, or, if that was out of his power, to
lay an information, and to prosecute the offenders:
and any neglect on this score being proved against
him, the delinquent was condemned to receive a
stated number of stripes, and to be kept without
food for three whole days.

Although, in the case of murder, the Egyptian
law was inexorable and severe, the royal preroga-
tive might be exerted in favour of a culprit, and
the punishment was sometimes commuted by a
mandate from the king. Sabaco, indeed, during
the fifty years of his reign, "made it a rule* not to
punish his subjects with death," whether guilty of
murder or any other capital offence, but, "according to the magnitude of their crimes, he condemned
the culprits to raise the ground about the town to
which they belonged. By these means the situation of the different cities became greatly elevated
above the reach of the inundation, even more than
in the time of Sesostris;" and either on account
of a greater proportion of criminals, or from some
other cause, the mounds of Bubastis† were raised
considerably higher than those of any other city.

---

* Herodot. ii. 137.
† The mounds of Bubastis (Tel Basta) are of very great height, and
are seen from a considerable distance.

RIGHT OF FATHERS.

Among the Romans, a father had the right of life and death over his son, and could sell him as a slave to a free-born citizen; no child was therefore free until his parent had emancipated* him, in the presence of the prætor. The Greeks permitted the same right to fathers; and the Spartans even prevented a parent from nourishing his children: and having submitted them to a certain court, it was there decided whether they were to be preserved, or to be left to die in a cavern of Taygetus. But far from adopting so barbarous a custom as the exposure of infants, or allowing a father any right over the life of his offspring, the Egyptians deemed the murder of a child an odious crime, that called upon the direct interposition of the laws. They did not, however, punish it as a capital offence, since it appeared inconsistent to take away life from one who had given it to the child†, but preferred inflicting such a punishment as would induce grief and repentance. With this view they ordained that the corpse of the deceased should be fastened to the neck of its parent, and that he should be obliged to pass three whole days and nights in its embrace, under the surveillance of a public guard.

But parricide was visited with the most cruel of chastisements; and conceiving, as they did, that the murder of a parent was the most unnatural of

---

* Unless he was in any public office.
† Diodor. i. 77.

crimes, they endeavoured to prevent its occurrence by the marked severity with which it was avenged. The criminal was therefore sentenced to be lacerated with sharpened reeds, and after being thrown on thorns he was burnt to death.

WOMEN.

When a woman was guilty of a capital offence, and judgment had been passed upon her, they were particularly careful to ascertain if the condemned was in a state of pregnancy; in which case her punishment was deferred till after the birth of the child, in order that the innocent might not suffer with the guilty *, and thus the father be deprived of that child to which he had at least an equal right.

But some of their laws regarding the female sex were cruel and unjustifiable ; and even if, which is highly improbable, they succeeded by their severity to enforce chastity, and to put an effectual stop to crime, yet the punishment rather reminds us of the laws of a barbarous people than of a wise and civilised state.   A woman who had committed adultery was sentenced to lose her nose, upon the principle that being the most conspicuous feature, and the chief, or, at least, an indispensable, ornament of the face, its loss would be most severely felt, and be the greatest detriment to her personal charms ; and the man was condemned to receive a bastinado of one thousand blows.   But if it was proved that

* A law adopted also by the Athenians.

force had been used against a free woman, he was doomed to a cruel and inhuman punishment.*

The object of the Egyptian laws was to preserve life, and to reclaim an offender. Death took away every chance of repentance, it deprived the country of his services, and he was hurried out of the world when least prepared to meet the ordeal of a future state. They, therefore, preferred severe punishments, and, except in the case of murder, and some crimes which appeared highly injurious to the community, it was deemed unnecessary to sacrifice the life of an offender.

THE BASTINADO.

Some of the laws and punishments of the Egyptian army I have already noticed: and in military as well as civil cases, minor offences were generally punished with the stick; a mode of chastisement still greatly in vogue among the modern inhabitants of the valley of the Nile, and held in such esteem by them, that convinced of (or perhaps by) its efficacy, they relate " its descent from heaven as a blessing to mankind."†

If an Egyptian of the present day has a government debt or tax to pay, he stoutly persists in his inability to obtain the money, till he has withstood a certain number of blows, and considers himself compelled to produce it; and the ancient inhabitants, if not under the rule of their native princes, at least in the time of the Roman emperors, gloried equally in the obstinacy they evinced, and the difficulty the go-

---

* Προσεταξαν αποκοπτεσθαι τα αιδοια. Diod. i. 77. With the Jews it was punished by death. Deut. xxii. 22.

† The Moslems say, " Nézel min e'semma e'nebóot, báraka min Allah." " The stick came down from heaven, a blessing from God."

vernors of the country experienced in extorting
from them what they were bound to pay ; whence
Ammianus Marcellinus tells us, " an Egyptian
blushes if he cannot show numerous marks on
his body that evince his endeavours to evade the
duties." *

The bastinado was inflicted on both sexes †, as
with the Jews.‡   Men and boys were laid prostrate

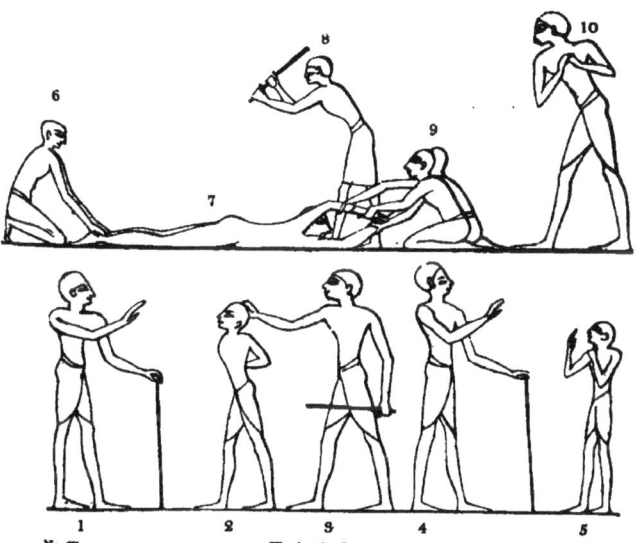

No. 87.   The bastinado.   *Beni-Hassan.*

on the ground §, and frequently held by the hands
and feet while the chastisement was administered;

* Amm. Marcel. life of Julian.
† Sculptures at Beni-Hassan.
‡ Exodus, xxi. 20.
§ As with the Jews. Deut. xxv. 2.

but women, as they sat, received the stripes on their

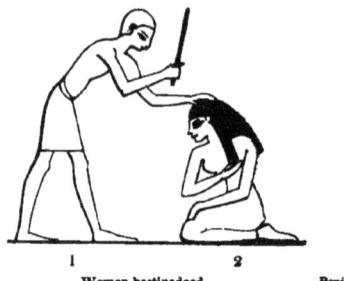

No. 88.   Women bastinadoed.   *Beni-Hassan.*

back, which were also inflicted by the hand of a
man.   Nor was it unusual for the superintendents
to stimulate labourers to their work by the persuasive powers of the stick, whether engaged in
the field or in handicraft employments; and boys

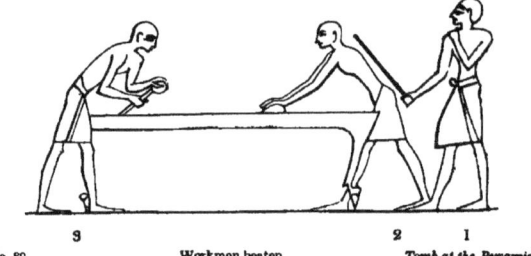

No. 89.   Workmen beaten.   *Tomb at the Pyramids.*

were sometimes beaten without the ceremony of
prostration, the hands being tied behind their back,
while the punishment was applied.

It does not however appear to have been from
any respect to the person, that this less usual method

was adopted; nor is it probable that any class of
the community enjoyed a peculiar privilege on
these occasions, as among the modern Moslems:
who, extending their respect for the Prophet to his
distant descendants of the thirty-sixth and ensuing
generations, scruple to administer the stick to a
Shereef until he has been politely furnished with a
mat, on which to prostrate his guilty person. Among
other amusing privileges in modern Egypt, is that
conceded to the grandees, or officers of high rank.
Ordinary culprits are punished by the hand of
persons usually employed on such occasions; but
a Bey, or the governor of a district, can only
receive his chastisement from the hand of a Pasha,
and the genteel *daboss* (mace) is substituted for
the vulgar stick. This is no trifling privilege: it
becomes fully *impressed* upon the sufferer, and
renders him, long after, *sensible* of the peculiar
honour he has enjoyed; nor can any one doubt
that an iron mace, in form not very unlike a cho-
colate mill, is a *distingué* mode of punishing men
who are proud of their rank.

Having noticed the pertinacity of the modern
Egyptians in resisting the payment of their taxes,
I shall introduce the following story as remarkably
illustrative of this fact. In the year 1822, a Copt
Christian, residing at Cairo, was arrested by the
Turkish authorities for the non-payment of his
taxes, and taken before the Kehia, or deputy of
the Pasha. "Why," inquired the angry Turk,
" have you not paid your taxes?"—" Because," replied the Copt, with a pitiable expression, per-

fectly according with his tattered appearance, " I
have not the means." He was instantly ordered
to be thrown upon the floor, and bastinadoed.
He prayed to be released, but in vain : the stick
continued without intermission, and he was scarcely
able to bear the increasing pain.   Again and again
he pleaded his inability to pay, and prayed for
mercy : the Turk was inexorable ; and the tor-
ments he felt at length overcame his resolution :
they were no longer to be borne.   " Release me,"
he cried, "and I will pay directly."—" Ah, you
Giower ! go."   He was released, and taken home,
accompanied by a soldier, and the money being
paid, he imparted to his wife the sad tidings.
" You coward, you fool," she exclaimed ; " what,
give them the money on the very first demand ! I
suppose after five or six blows, you cried, ' I will
pay, only release me ; ' next year our taxes will
be doubled through your weakness ; shame !"—
" No, my dear," interrupted the suffering man, " I
assure you I resisted as long as it was possible :
look at the state I am in, before you upbraid me.
I paid the money, but they had trouble enough
for it ; for I obliged them to give me at least a
hundred blows before they could get it."   She was
pacified ; and the pity and commendation of his
wife, added to his own satisfaction in having shown
so much obstinacy and courage, consoled him for
the pain, and, perhaps, in some measure, for the
money thus forced from him.

HANGING.

Hanging * was the customary mode of punishment for many capital crimes; and the criminals were kept "bound" in prison† till their fate was decided; whether it depended on the will of the sovereign, or the decision of the judges; and these places of confinement were under the immediate superintendence, and within the house, of the chief of the police. ‡

The character of some of the Egyptian laws was quite consonant with the notions of a primitive age. In those cases punishment was directed more particularly against the offending member; and adulterators of money, falsifiers of weights and measures, forgers of seals or signatures, and scribes who altered any signed document by erasures or additions, without the authority of the parties, were condemned to lose both their hands.

But their laws do not seem to have sanctioned the gibbet, or the exposure of the body of an offender; since the conduct of Rhampsinitus, in the case of the robbery of his treasure, is mentioned by Herodotus § as a singular mode of discovering an accomplice, and not as an ordinary punishment.

---

* Gen. xl. 22.

† Gen. xxxix. 20. " The prison, a place where the king's prisoners were bound."

‡ Gen. xl. 3. " In the house of the captain of the guard," who was probably the same as the captain of the watch, the *zábut* of modern Egypt. He is called " an officer of Pharaoh." Gen. xxxix. 1.

§ Herodot. ii. 121.

Thefts, breach of trust, and petty frauds were punished with the bastinado; but robbery and

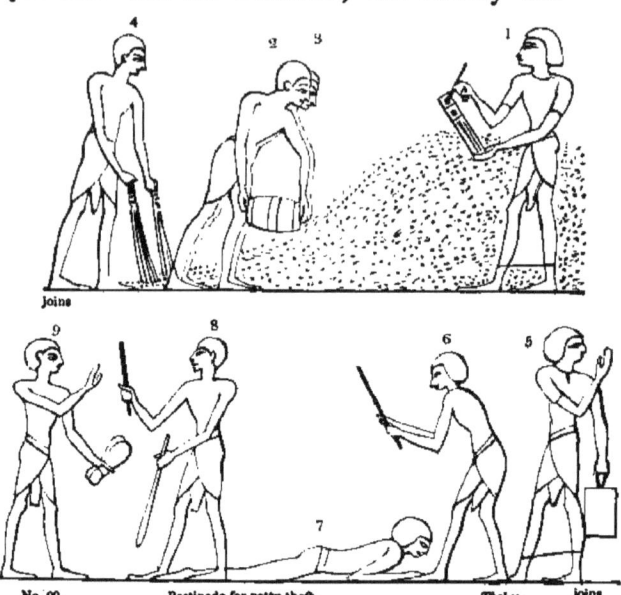

No. 90. Bastinado for petty theft. *Thebes.* Joins

housebreaking were sometimes considered capital crimes, and deserving of death; as is evident from the conduct of the thief, when caught by the trap in the treasury of Rhampsinitus, and from what Diodorus * states respecting Actisanes. This monarch, instead of putting robbers to death †, instituted a novel mode of punishing them, by cutting off their noses, and banishing them to the

---

* Diodor. i. 60.
† Implying that other monarchs did.

confines of the desert, where a town was built, called Rhinocolura, from the peculiar nature of their punishment*; and thus, by removing the bad, and preventing their corrupting the good, he benefited society, without depriving the criminals of life; at the same time that he punished them severely for their crimes, by obliging them to live by their industry in a barren and inhospitable region.

THIEVES.

The Egyptians had a singular custom respecting theft and burglary. Those who followed the *profession* of thief gave in their names to the chief of the robbers †; and agreed that he should be informed of every thing they might thenceforward steal, the moment it was in their possession. In consequence of this the owner of the lost goods always applied by letter to the chief for their recovery; and having stated their quality and quantity, the day and hour when they were stolen, and other requisite particulars, the goods were identified, and, on payment of one quarter of their value, they were restored to the applicant, in the same state as when taken from his house.

For being fully persuaded of the impracticability of putting an entire check to robbery, either by the dread of punishment, or by any method that

---

* From what he afterwards says, we may conclude that the king punished great and petty cases in the same manner; his object being to prevent the contamination of bad example.

† The same as the Shekh el Harameéh, or Shekh of the robbers in modern Egypt, and at Constantinople. Diodor. i. 80.

could be adopted by the most vigilant police, they considered it more for the advantage of the community, that a certain sacrifice should be made in order to secure the restitution of the remainder, than that the law, by taking on itself to protect the citizen, and discover the offender, should be the indirect cause of greater loss ; and that the Egyptians, like the Indians, and I may say the modern * inhabitants of the Nile, were very expert in the art of thieving, we have abundant testimony from ancient authors. †

It may be asked, what redress could be obtained, when goods were stolen by those who failed to enter their names on the books of the chief ; but, as it is evident that these private speculations would interfere with the interests of all the *profession*, the detection of such persons would inevitably follow, as the natural consequence of their avarice ; and thus all others were effectually prevented from robbing, save those of the privileged class.

The salary of the chief was not merely derived from his own demands upon the goods stolen, or from any voluntary contribution of the robbers themselves, but was probably a fixed remuneration

---

* The excellent police of Mohammed Ali has put a stop to this propensity of the Egyptian peasantry : few instances, therefore, now occur. Some of the robberies in the time of the Memlooks proved their great talent in this department; and the well known Indian feat of carrying off a horse in the open day, from the midst of a numerous party of English, was performed in nearly the same manner by an Egyptian from a Memlook camp.

† Conf. Theocrit. Idyl. xv. 48. : —

οὐδεὶς κακοεργος
Δαλειται τον ιοντα, παρερπων Αιγυπτιςι.

granted by the government, as one of the chiefs of the police; nor is it to be imagined that he was any other than a respectable citizen *, and a man of the greatest integrity and honour.

DEBT.

As in other countries, their laws respecting debt and usury underwent some changes, according as society advanced, and as pecuniary transactions became more complicated.

Bocchoris, who reigned in Egypt about the year 812 B. C., and who, from his learning, obtained the sirname of Wise, finding that in cases of debt many causes of dispute had arisen, and instances of great oppression were of frequent occurrence†, enacted‡, that no agreement should be binding unless it was acknowledged by a written contract §; and if any one took oath that the money had not been lent him, no debt should be recognised, and the claims of the suing party should immediately cease. This was done, that great regard might always be had for the name and nature of an oath ‖, at the same time that, by substituting the unquestionable proof of a written document, they avoided the necessity of having frequent recourse

---

* As the Shekh of the robbers in Cairo at the present day.
† The difficulty of legislating on the subject of debt and usury was not only felt by the Egyptians, Romans, and other ancient people, but is acknowledged at the present day.
‡ Diodor. i. 79.
§ The number of witnesses in Egyptian contracts is very remarkable. *Vide* Dr. Young on Hieroglyph. Lit. p. 71.; and *infrà*, p. 57.
‖ Plato, in his Republic, shows himself of a different opinion, and considers that it might open the way to perjury.   XII. leg.

to an oath, and its sanctity was not diminished by constant repetition.

Usury * was in all cases condemned by the Egyptian legislature; and when money was borrowed, even with a written agreement, it was forbidden to allow the interest to increase to more than double the original sum.† Nor could the creditors seize the debtor's person: their claims and right were confined to the goods in his possession, and such as were really his own ; which were comprehended under the produce of his labour, or what he had received from another individual to whom they lawfully belonged. For the person of every citizen was looked upon as the property of the state, and might be required for some public service, connected either with war or peace ; and, independent of the injustice of subjecting any one to the momentary caprice of his creditor, the safety of the country might be endangered through the avarice of a few interested individuals.

This law, which was borrowed by Solon from the Egyptian code, existed also at Athens; and was, as Diodorus observes, much more consistent with justice and common sense than that which allowed the creditor to seize the person, while it forbade him to take the ploughs and other implements of husbandry. For if, continues the historian, it is unjust thus to deprive men of the means of obtaining subsistence, and of providing for their families,

---

* As with the Moslems and the Jews, Psalm xv. 5.; Ezek. xviii. 8, 17.; and Levit. xxv. 36, 37.

† This was also a law at Rome.

how much more unreasonable must it be to im-
prison those by whom the implements were used?

To prevent the accumulation of debt, and to
protect the interests of the creditor, another remarkable law was enacted *, which, while it shows
how greatly they endeavoured to check the increasing evil, proves the high respect paid by the
Egyptians to the memory of their parents, and to
the sanctity of their religious ceremonies. By this
it was pronounced illegal for any one to borrow
money without giving in pledge the body of his
father, or of his nearest relative † ; and, if he failed
to redeem so sacred a deposit ‡, he was considered
infamous ; and, at his death, the celebration of the
accustomed funeral obsequies was denied him, and
he could not enjoy the right of burial either in the
tomb of his ancestors, or in any other place of
sepulture § ; nor could he inter his children, or
any of his family, as long as the debt was unpaid,
the creditor being put in actual possession of his
family tomb.

---

* Herodot. ii. 136. Diodor. i. 93. Herodotus says, by Asychis,
who must have lived about the same time as Bocchoris.

† Herodotus only says, his father. We must suppose that some
fathers did not die conveniently for their mummies to stand security for
their surviving sons. I have, therefore, suggested a relative.

‡ That is, if the debt was not paid within a certain time, the mummy
could be removed from the tomb. It is not to be supposed that this
alludes to mummies kept in the houses, which only remained there for
a certain time ; since it was honourable to be buried, and a disgrace
to be refused that right, as in the case of malefactors. We may conclude the body itself was seldom given up, since possession of the
tomb was sufficient, and much less inconvenient to the creditor than
to have a stranger's mummy in his sitting-room.

§ Herodot. ii. 136. Diod. i. 92, 93.

E 2

In the large cities of Egypt, a fondness for display, and the usual allurements of luxury, were rapidly introduced; and considerable sums were expended in furnishing houses, and in many artificial caprices. Rich jewels and costly works of art were in great request, as well among the inhabitants of the provincial capitals as at Thebes and Memphis: they delighted in splendid equipages, elegant and commodious boats, numerous attendants, horses, dogs, and other requisites for the chase; and, besides, their houses, their villas, and their gardens, were laid out with no ordinary expense. But while the funds arising from extensive farms, and the abundant produce of a fertile soil, enabled the rich to indulge extravagant habits, many of the less wealthy envied the enjoyment of those luxuries which fortune had denied to them; and, prompted by vanity, and a desire of imitation, so common in civilized communities, and so generally followed by fatal results, they pursued a career which speedily led to an accumulation of debt *, and demanded the interference of the legislature; and it is probable that a law so severe as this must have appeared to the Egyptians, was only adopted as a measure of absolute necessity, in order to put a check to the increasing evil.

The necessary expenses of the Egyptians were remarkably small, less indeed than of any people, and the food of the poorer classes was of the

---

* In the time of Sesostris, a very great number of persons were in prison for debt, for whose release he thought it necessary to interfere. Diod i. 54.

cheapest and most simple kind. Owing to the
warmth of the climate, they required few clothes,
and young children were in the habit of going
without shoes, and with little or no covering to
their bodies; and so trifling was the expense of
bringing up a child, that, as Diodorus affirms *, it
never need cost a parent more than 20 drachms
(13 shillings English), until arrived at man's estate.
It was, therefore, luxury, and the increasing wants
of an artificial kind, which corrupted the manners
of the Egyptians, and rendered such a law necessary for their restraint; and we may conclude, that
it was mainly directed against those who contracted
debts for the gratification of pleasure, or with the
premeditated intent of defrauding an unsuspecting
creditor.

DEEDS.

In the mode of executing deeds, conveyances,
and other civil contracts, the Egyptians were peculiarly circumstantial and minute; and the great
number of witnesses is a singular feature in those
documents. In the time of the Ptolemies, sales of
property commenced with a preamble, containing
the date of the king, in whose reign they were
executed; the name of the president of the court,
and of the clerk by whom they were written,
being also specified. The body of the contract
then followed. It stated the name of the individual who sold the land, the description of his

---

* Diod. i. 80.

E 3

person, an account of his parentage, profession, and place of abode, the extent and nature of the land, its situation and boundaries, and concluded with the name of the purchaser, whose parentage and description were also added, and the sum for which it was bought. The seller then vouched for his undisturbed possession of it; and, becoming security against any attempt to dispute his title, the name of the other party was inserted as having accepted it, and acknowledged the purchase. The names of witnesses were then affixed; and the president of the court, having added his signature, the deed was valid. Sometimes the seller formally recognised the sale in the following manner. — " All these things have I sold thee: they are thine, I have received their price from thee, and make no demand upon thee for them from this day; and if any person disturb thee in the possession of them, I will withstand the attempt; and, if I do not otherwise repel it, I will use compulsory means," or, " I will indemnify thee." * But, in order to give a more accurate notion of the form of these contracts, I shall introduce a copy of the whole of one of them, as given by Dr. Young †, and refer the reader to others occurring in the same work. " Translation of the enchorial papyrus of Paris, containing the original deed relating to the mummies: — ' This writing, dated in the year 36, Athyr 20, in the reign of our sovereigns Ptolemy and Cleopatra his sister, the children of Ptolemy

* Dr. Young on Hieroglyph. Literature, p. 70. 74.
† P. 72.

and Cleopatra the divine, the gods Illustrious : and
the priest of Alexander, and of the Saviour gods,
of the Brother gods, of the (Beneficent gods), of
the Father-loving gods, of the Illustrious gods,
of the Paternal god, and of the Mother-loving gods,
being (as by law appointed) : and the prize-bearer
of Berenice the Beneficent, and the basket-bearer
of Arsinoe the Brother-loving, and the priestess
of Arsinoe the Father-loving, being as appointed
in the metropolis (of Alexandria); and in (Ptole-
mais) the royal city of the Thebaïd ? the guardian
priest for the year ? of Ptolemy Soter, and the
priest of king Ptolemy the Father-loving, and the
priest of Ptolemy the Brother-loving, and the
priest of Ptolemy the Beneficent, and the priest of
Ptolemy the Mother-loving ; and the priestess of
queen Cleopatra, and the priestess of the princess
Cleopatra, and the priestess of Cleopatra, the
(queen) mother, deceased, the Illustrious ; and the
basket-bearer of Arsinoe the Brother-loving (being
as appointed) : declares : The Dresser ? in the
temple of the Goddess, Onnophris, the son of
Horus, and of Senpoeris, daughter of Spotus ?
(" aged about forty, lively,") tall, (" of a sallow
complexion, hollow-eyed, and bald"); in the temple
of the goddess to (Horus) his brother ? the son of
Horus and of Senpoeris, has sold, for a price in
money, half of one third of the collections for the
dead " priests of Osiris ? " lying in Thynabunun
... in the Libyan suburb of Thebes, in the Memnonia ... likewise half of one third of the liturgies :
their names being, Muthes, the son of Spotus, with

his children and his household; Chapocrates, the
son of Nechthmonthes, with his children and his
household; Arsiesis, the son of Nechthmonthes,
with his children and his household; Petemestus,
the son of Nechthmonthes; Arsiesis, the son of
Zminis, with his children and his household;
Osoroeris, the son of Horus, with his children and
his household; Spotus, the son of Chapochonsis,
surnamed? Zoglyphus (the sculptor), with his
children and his household: while there belonged
also to Asos, the son of Horus and of Senpoeris,
daughter of Spotus? in the same manner one half
of a third of the collections for the dead, and of
the fruits and so forth... he sold it on the 20th
of Athyr, in the reign of the King ever-living, to
(complete) the third part: likewise the half of one
third of the collections relating to Peteutemis,
with his household, and... likewise the half of one
third? of the collections and fruits for Petechonsis,
the bearer of milk, and of the... place on the Asian
side, called Phrecages, and... the dead bodies in it:
there having belonged to Asos the son of Horus
one half of the same: he has sold to him in the
month of... the half of one third of the collections
for the priests of Osiris? lying in Thynabunun,
with their children and their households: likewise
the half of one third of the collections for Peteutemis, and also for Petechonsis, the bearer of milk,
in the place Phrecages on the Asian side: I have
received for them their price in silver .... and
gold; and I make no further demand on thee for
them from the present day..... before the au-

thorities . . . . . (and if any one shall disturb thee in the possession of them, I will resist him, and, if I do not succeed, I will indemnify thee ?) . . . . Executed and confirmed. Written by Horus, the son of Phabis, clerk to the chief priests of Amonrasonther, and of the contemplar ? Gods, of the Beneficent gods, of the Father-loving gods, of the Paternal god, and of the Mother-loving gods. Amen.

" ' Names of the witnesses present : —

ERIEUS, the son of Phanres Erieus.
PETEARTRES, the son of Peteutemis.
PETEARPOCRATES, the son of Horus.
SNACHOMNEUS, the son of Peteuris.
SNACHOMES, the son of Psenchonsis.
TOTOES, the son of Phibis.
PORTIS, the son of Apollonius.
ZMINIS, the son of Petemestus.
PETEUTEMIS, the son of Arsiesis.
AMONORYTIUS, the son of Pacemis.
HORUS, the son of Chimnaraus.
ARMENIS, (rather Arbais,) the son of Zthenaetis.
MAESIS, the son of Mirsis.
ANTIMACHUS, the son of Antigenes.
PETOPHOIS, the son of Phibis.
PANAS, the son of Petosiris.' "

In this, as in many other documents, the testimony required is very remarkable, sixteen witnesses being thought necessary for the sale of a moiety of the sums collected on account of a few tombs, and for services performed to the dead, the total value of which was only 400 pieces of brass ; and the name of each person is introduced, in the true Oriental style, with that of his father. Nor is it unreasonable to suppose, that the same precautions and minute formulas were observed in similar transactions during the reigns of the Pharaonic kings ; however great may have been the change introduced by the Ptolemies * and Romans into the laws and local government of Egypt.

MARRIAGES.

Of the marriage contracts of the Egyptians we are entirely ignorant, nor do we even find the ceremony † represented in the paintings of their tombs.   We may, however, conclude that they were regulated by the customs usual among civilised nations ; and, if the authority of Diodorus can be credited, women were indulged with greater privileges in Egypt than in any other country.   He even affirms that part of the agreement entered into at the time of marriage was, that the wife should have control over her husband, and that no objection should be made to her *commands* whatever they might be ‡ ; but, though we have sufficient to convince us of the superior treatment of women among the Egyptians, as well from ancient authors as from the sculptures that remain, it may fairly be doubted if those indulgencies were carried to the extent mentioned by the historian, or that

* Diodorus (i. 95.) says, " Many laws which were thought to work well were changed by the Macedonian dynasty." *Vide infrà*, p. 78. and 80.
† With the Jews, it was frequently very simple. Job, vii. 13. The wedding feast continued seven days (Gen. xxix. 27. Judges, xiv. 12. Job, xi. 19), sometimes fourteen. Job, viii. 19.
‡ Diodor. i. 27.

command extended beyond the management of the house, and the regulation of domestic affairs.

It is, however, remarkable that the royal authority and supreme direction of affairs were entrusted without reserve to women, as in those states of modern Europe where the Salic law has not been introduced; and we, not only find examples in Egyptian history of queens succeeding to the throne, but Manetho informs us, that the law, according this important privilege to the other sex, dated as early as the reign of Binothris, the third monarch of the second dynasty.*

In primitive ages, the duties of women were very different from those of a later and more civilised period, and varied of course according to the habits of each people. Among pastoral tribes they drew water †, kept the sheep, and superintended the herds as well as flocks.‡ As with the Arabs of the present day, they prepared, both the furniture, and the woollen stuffs of which the tents themselves were made; and like the Greek women they were generally employed in weaving, spinning, and other sedentary occupations within doors. Needle-work and embroidery were a favourite amusement of the Grecian women; in which it is highly probable the Egyptian ladies also occupied much of their time; and we have positive evidence, from the sculptures, of numerous

* *Vide supra*, vol. i p. 26.
† Gen. xxiv. 15. Exod. ii. 16. As at the present day.
‡ Gen. xxiv. 20., and xxix. 6. 9. Rachel, and also Zipporah and her six sisters, kept their father's sheep. Andromache fed the horses of Hector. Il. θ. 187.

females being employed in weaving and in the use of the distaff. But Egyptian women were not

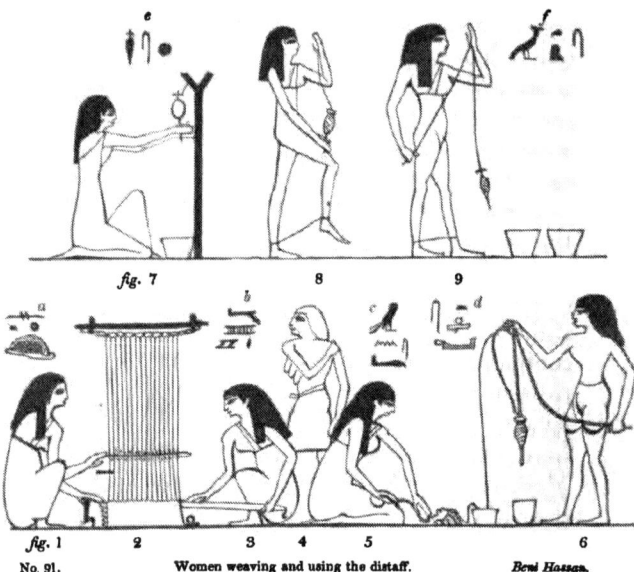

No. 91. Women weaving and using the distaff. *Beni Hassan.*

kept in the same secluded manner as those of ancient Greece; who, besides being confined * to certain parts of the house, called the γυναικωνίτης, or women's apartments, most remote from the hall of entrance, and generally in the uppermost part of the building, were not even allowed to go out of

---

* Often not allowed to pass from one part of the house to the other without leave: thus Antigone asked that of her mother, in Euripides' Phœniss. *v.* 88. This could not have been the case in Egypt, as we find from Potiphar's wife so constantly meeting Joseph; and from her having " called the men of her house." Gen. xxxix. 14. and 11.

doors without a veil *; as in many Oriental countries at the present day. Newly married women
were almost as strictly kept as virgins; and, by the
laws of Solon, no lady could go out at night without a lighted torch before her chariot, or leave
home with more than three garments. They were
guarded in the house and abroad by nurses, and
sometimes by old men and eunuchs; and the
secluded life they led was very similar to that
imposed upon females among the modern Moslems.
But the Egyptians treated their women very dif-
ferently, and in a manner much more worthy of a
civilised people; and, if the accounts of ancient
authors are sometimes unsatisfactory, and even
contradictory, on this head, the sculptures assist us
to form our conclusions, and to decide in their
favour. At some of the public festivals women
were expected to attend, — not alone, like the
Moslem women at a mosque, but in company with
their husbands or relations; and Josephus † states,
that on an occasion of this kind, " when it was the
custom for women to go to the public solemnity,
the wife of Potiphar, having pleaded ill health, in
order to be allowed to stay at home, was excused
from attending," and availed herself of the absence
of her husband to talk with Joseph.

---

* Their faces were covered, but the veil was thin enough to be seen
through. It was not, therefore, like the *boorko* of modern Egypt,
which has two holes exposing the eyes, but rather like that of the
Wahábees, which covers the whole head and face. The Jewish women also wore a veil; and in Solomon's Song one complains that her
veil had been taken from her. C. v. 7. Conf. Genes. xxiv. 65.

† Joseph. Ant. ii. 4. 3.

Diodorus informs us the Egyptians were not restricted to any number of wives, but that every one married as many as he chose, with the exception of the priesthood, who were by law confined to one consort.* It does not, however, appear that they generally took advantage of this privilege; and Herodotus† affirms that throughout Egypt it was customary to marry only one wife. It is easy to reconcile these statements, by supposing that Diodorus speaks of a law which permitted polygamy, and Herodotus of the usual custom of the people; and if the Egpytians were allowed to take more than one wife, we may conclude, from the numerous scenes illustrative of their domestic life, that it was an event of rare occurrence.

Polygamy is permitted to the Moslem, but it is neither reputable to have more than one wife, nor to divorce her without very cogent reasons; and though no objection can be made when there is no family, it is required, even in this case, that her wishes, and those of her parents, should be consulted; and many marriage contracts stipulate that the wife shall have no partner in the hareem. With much more reason, then, may we conclude that among the higher classes of Egyptians a similar custom prevailed, which will account for no instance of two consorts being given in the sculptures.

* The Jewish chief priest was allowed but one wife, and he could only marry a virgin. Levit. xxi. 13. Every Copt priest, at the present day, is forbidden to marry again on the demise of his wife. *Vide* Gibbon, ii. c. xv. p. 318., on the opinions of the early fathers respecting second nuptials.

† Herodot. ii. 92.

But a very objectionable law, which is not only noticed by Diodorus *, but is fully authenticated by the sculptures both of Upper and Lower Egypt, was in force among them from the earliest times, the origin and policy of which it is not easy to explain.   Diodorus supposes that the custom — the marriage of brother and sister — was owing to, and sanctioned by, that of Isis and Osiris; but as this was purely an allegorical fable†, and these ideal personages never lived on earth, his conjecture is of little weight; nor, indeed, would such a circumstance be sufficient to account for so strange a law.

In the time of the patriarchs, as in the case of Abraham and Sarah‡, and among the Athenians, an Egyptian colony, it was lawful to marry a sister by the father's side, not, however, if born of the same mother; but that this restriction was not observed in Egypt, we have sufficient evidence from the marriages of several of the Ptolemies.

Though the Egyptians generally confined themselves to one wife §, they, like the Jews and other Eastern nations, both of ancient and modern times, scrupled not to admit other inmates to their *hareem*,

---

* Diodor. i. 27.
† The same occurs in the Greek mythology. Jupiter and Juno were brother and sister.

> " . . . . Jovisque
> Et soror, et conjux."   Virg. Æn. i. 50.

Vide Hor. iii. Od. iii. 64., and Homer Il. xvi. 432.
‡ Gen. xx. 12. " She is my sister: she is the daughter of my father, but not the daughter of my mother, and she became my wife."
§ The Jews were generally contented with one wife, though a plurality was permitted also by their laws. 1 Kings, xi. 3. Like other Oriental people, the Egyptians buried their wives in the same tomb with their husbands. Job, iv. 4.

most of whom appear to have been foreigners,
either taken in war, or brought to Egypt to be sold
as slaves.   They became members of the family,
like those in a similar situation at the present day,
and not only ranked next to the wives and children
of their lord, but probably enjoyed a share of the
property at his demise.*   These women were white
or black slaves†, according to the countries from
which they were brought ; but, generally speaking,
the latter were employed merely as domestics, who
were required to wait upon their mistress and her
female friends.   The former, likewise, officiated as
servants, though they of course held a rank above
the black slaves ; and it is very probable that the
women represented at Medeenet Haboo, attending
upon Remeses, were of this class of persons, and,
at all events, not the wives of the monarch.

CHILDREN.

The same custom prevailed among the Egyptians
regarding children, as with the Moslems and other
Eastern people.: no distinction being made between their offspring by a wife or any other woman,
and all equally enjoying the rights of inheritance ;
for since they considered a child indebted to the
father for its existence‡, and the mother to be

---

* This Eastern custom I suppose also to have been adopted by the
ancient as well as the modern Egyptians. According to Moslem law,
the birth of a child gives the mother a claim, and, indeed, properly a
right, to enfranchisement.

† *Vide suprà*, p. 403, 404.

‡ " Τον πατερα μονον αιτιον ειναι της γενεσιως."   Diod. i. 80. Conf.
the Latin " genitor," a father.

" little more than a nurse*," it seemed unjust to deny equal rights to all their progeny. And, indeed, if Diodorus is correct†, they carried this principle so far, that, in diœcious plants, those which bore fruit were denominated males, as being the cause of production and of the continuation of the species.

PARENTS.

Of their laws respecting the duties of children, one only is recorded by Herodotus, which appears singular and unjust; that if a son was unwilling to maintain his parents, he was at liberty to refuse; but that a daughter, on the contrary, was compelled to assist them, and, on refusal, was amenable to law. We may, however, question the truth of this statement of the historian; and, drawing an inference from the marked severity‡ of filial duties among the Egyptians, some of which we find distinctly alluded to in the sculptures of Thebes, we may conclude, that in Egypt much more was expected from a son than in any civilised nation of the present day; and that this was not confined to the lower orders, but extended to those of the highest ranks of society. And if the office of fan-bearer was an honourable post, and the sons of the

---

* This does not agree with Diodorus's account of the superiority of the wife. *Vide* Diod. i. 80. and 27.

† This may be doubted.

‡ I have already observed, that among the modern Egyptians it is considered highly indecorous for a son to sit down in the presence of his father without permission, still less would he think of smoking before him; and an Arab of the desert deems it disrespectful to sit and talk in the company even of his father-in-law.

monarch were preferred to fulfil it, no ordinary
show of humility was required on their part; and
they walked on foot behind his chariot, bearing
certain insignia over their father *, during the
triumphal processions which took place in com-
memoration of his victories, and in the religious
ceremonies over which he presided.

It was equally a custom in the early times of
European history, that a son should pay a marked
deference to his parent; and no prince was allowed
to sit at table with his father, unless through his
valour, having been invested with arms by a
foreign sovereign, he had obtained that privilege,
as was the case with Alboin, before he succeeded
his father on the throne of the Lombards. The
European nations were not long in altering their
early habits, and this custom soon became disregarded; but a respect for ancient institutions, and
those ideas, so prevalent in the East, which reject
all love of change, prevented the Egyptians from
discarding the usages of their ancestors; and we
find this and many other primitive customs retained, even at the period when they were most
highly civilised.

In the education of youth they were particularly
strict; and " they knew," says Plato †, " that
children ought to be early accustomed to such
gestures, looks, and motions as are decent and
proper; and not to be suffered either to hear
or learn any verses and songs than those which

* *Vide suprà*, plate 1., and p.72.
† Plato, second book of laws.

are calculated to inspire them with virtue; and they consequently took care that every dance and ode introduced at their feasts or sacrifices should be subject to certain regulations." They particularly inculcated respect for old age; and the fact of this being required towards strangers, necessarily argues a great regard for the person of a parent; for we are informed * that, like the Lacedæmonians, they required every young man to give place to his superiors in years, and even, if seated, to rise on their approach † : and surely, if they were expected to reverence age alone, how much more must have been considered due to their parents, to whom they were so deeply indebted?

Nor were these honours limited to their lifetime: the memory of parents and ancestors was revered through succeeding generations : their tombs were maintained with the greatest respect, liturgies were performed by their children ‡, or by priests at their expense, and we have previously seen what advantage was taken of this feeling, in the laws concerning debt.

RESPECT TO THEIR MONARCHS.

Guided by the same principle, the Egyptians paid the most marked respect to their monarch, as the father of his people. He was obeyed with courteous submission, his will was tantamount to a

---

* Herodot. ii. 80.
† As the Jews, " thou shalt rise up before the hoary head, and honour the face of the old man." Levit. xix. 32.
‡ If they were priests.

law, and such implicit confidence did they place
in his judgment that he was thought incapable of
error.*   He was the representative of the Divinity
on earth : the Gods were supposed to communicate
through him their choicest benefits to man; and
they believed that the sovereign power had been
delegated to him by the will of the Deities themselves.†   They entertained a strong feeling of
gratitude for the services done by him to the
state ; and the memory of a monarch who had
benefited his subjects, was celebrated after death
with the most unbounded honours. " For of all
people," says Diodorus‡, " the Egyptians retain
the highest sense of a favour conferred upon them,
and deem it the greatest charm of life to make a
suitable return for benefits they have received."
Through this impulse, they were induced to so-
lemnise the funeral obsequies of their kings with
unparalleled magnificence ; and to this the historian also attributes the unexampled duration of
the Egyptian monarchy.§   Considering the high
estimation in which the feeling of gratitude was
held among them, we cannot deny that the Egyptians were fully capable of appreciating the advantages of civilised habits, and that they cherished
one of the noblest ornaments of social life : " and
honour ‖," adds the historian, " done to one who

* As in other countries where the ministers are responsible. But
the conduct of the king was also subject to animadversion ; and, at the
time of his death, that of the monarch, and of every Egyptian, underwent a severe scrutiny, and the usual funeral honours were sometimes
denied them.   Diod. i. 92, and 72.
† Diod. i. 90.   ‡ Loc. cit.
§ Diod. i. 71.   ‖ Diod. loc. cit.

cannot possibly know it, in return for a past benefit, carries along with it a testimony of sincerity so totally devoid of the least colour of dissimulation, that every one must admire the sentiments which dictate its performance."   Nor did it consist in mere outward show : the mourning continued for seventy-two days, during which time every one abstained from the comforts as well as the luxuries of life.   Meat, wheat bread, wine, and all delicacies were voluntarily renounced ; and they neither anointed themselves, nor indulged in the bath, nor in any kind of pleasure.

UNIFORMITY OF THEIR LAWS.

Another remarkable feature of the Egyptian laws was the sanctity with which old edicts were upheld.   They were closely interwoven with the religion of the country *, and said to be derived from the Gods themselves ; whence it was considered both useless and impious to alter such sacred institutions.   Few innovations were introduced by their monarchs, unless loudly called for by circumstances ; and we neither read of any attempts on the part of the people to alter or resist the laws, nor on that of their rulers to introduce a more arbitrary mode of government.†

* As the Jewish and Moslem laws.
† Herodotus' account of the tyranny of Cheops in building the pyramid cannot be received with any degree of credit.

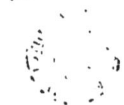

DIFFERENT LAWGIVERS.

As society advances, it must, however, necessarily happen that some alterations are requisite, either in the reformation of an existing code, or in the introduction of additional laws; and among the different legislators of the Egyptians, are particularly noticed the names of Mnevis, Sasyches, Sesostris, Bocchoris, Asychis, Amasis, and even the Persian Darius. The great merit of the first of these seems to have consisted in inducing the people to conform to those institutions, which he pretended to have received from Hermes, the Egyptian Mercury * ; " an idea," says Diodorus, " which has been adopted with success by many other ancient lawgivers, who have inculcated a respect for their institutions, through the awe that is naturally felt for the majesty of the Gods." The additions made by Sasyches chiefly related to matters of religious worship ; and Sesostris, in addition to numerous regulations of a military nature, is said to have introduced some changes into the agricultural system ; and having divided all the land of Egypt, with the exception of that which belonged to the priests and soldiers, into squares of equal areas †, he assigned to each peasant his peculiar

* Diod. i. 94.
† Herodot. ii. 109. *Vide suprà*, p. 73. and 104. In this instance, Sesostris could not be Remeses II.; and, indeed, the division of land is evidently of older date than the arrival of Joseph or the reign of Osirtasen I. Perhaps, as I have observed in p. 74. note 4., this refers to the crown lands.

portion *, or a certain number of these *arouras* †, for which he annually paid a fixed rent; and having instituted a yearly survey of the lands, any deficiency, resulting from a fall of the bank during the inundation, or other accidental causes, was stated in the returns, and deducted for in the government demands. Of the laws of Bocchoris and Asychis respecting debt, I have already spoken ‡; and the former is said to have introduced many others relating to the kings, as well as to civil contracts and commerce §, and to have established several important precedents in Egyptian jurisprudence.

Amasis was particularly eminent for his wisdom, and for the many salutary additions he made to the laws of his country. He remodelled the system of provincial government, and defined the duties of the monarchs with peculiar precision; and, though not of royal extraction ‖, his conduct in the management of affairs was so highly approved by the people, that their respect for him was scarcely inferior to that shown to his most glorious predecessors. Nor was Darius, though a Persian, and of a nation justly abhorred by the Egyptians, denied

* The land may still have belonged to the king.

† The aroura was a square of 100 cubits, containing, therefore, 10,000 cubits. The Egyptian " er," or " ert," " ploughing," or " tillage:" " aratrum," " a plough :" " arvum" " a field :" and the Arabic " hart," " ploughing," are related to it.

‡ *Vide supra*, p. 130. and 131.

§ Diod. i. 79.

‖ Herodotus says he was of plebeian origin; but Diodorus, while he allows him not to have been of royal extraction, affirms that he was a person of rank, which is much more consonant, as I have already observed, with the fact of his being of the military caste, and with the evidence of the hieroglyphics, in which he is stated to have married the daughter of a king. Herodot. ii. 172. Diod. i. 68.

those eulogiums which the mildness of his government, and the introduction of laws tending to benefit the country, claimed for him; and they even granted him the title of Divus, making him partaker of the same honours which were bestowed on their native princes.* But the Ptolemies in after times abrogated some of the favourite laws of the country; and though much was done by them, in repairing the temples, and in executing very grand and useful works, and though several of these sovereigns pretended to court the good will of the Egyptians, yet their name became odious, and Macrobius has stigmatised their sway with the title of tyranny.†

GOVERNORS OF PROVINCES.

After the king and council ‡, the judges or magistrates of the capital held the most distinguished post; and next to them may be considered the nomarchs, or governors, of districts.

The whole of Egypt was divided into nomes, or districts, the total of which, in the time of Sesostris §, amounted to thirty-six, but which afterwards was increased to the number, according to D'Anville, of fifty-three.

The limits of Egypt ‖ were the Mediterranean

---

* Diod. i. 95. This is confirmed by the mode of writing his name in hieroglyphics, which is preceded by the title Divus bonus, and is enclosed in two ovals, as that of the native Egyptian kings.
† Macrob. Sat. i. c. 4. *Vide suprà*, vol. ii. p. 58.
‡ Isaiah, xix. 11. Diod. i. 73.
§ Diod. i. 54.
‖ The oracle of Ammon pronounced all those who lived to the north of Elephantine, and drank the waters of the Nile, to be Egyptians. (Herodot. ii. 18.)

to the north, and Syene, or the Cataracts, to the south; and the cultivated land east and west of the Nile, contained within this space, or between latitude 31° 37′ and 24° 3′, was all that constituted the original territory of the Pharaohs : though the Mareotis, the Oases, and Nitriotis, were attached to their dominions, and were considered as part of the country. *

The main divisions of Egypt were " the Upper and Lower regions; " and this distinction, which had been maintained from the earliest times, was also indicated by a difference in the dialects of the language.† Thebes and Memphis enjoyed equal rank as capitals of Egypt; and every monarch at his coronation assumed the title of " lord of the two regions ‡," or " the two worlds." But a change afterwards took place in the division of the country, and the northern portion was subdivided into the two provinces of Heptanomis and Lower Egypt. The latter extended from the sea to the head of the Delta, and advancing to the natural boundary of the low lands, which is so strongly marked by the abrupt ridge of the modern Mokuttum, it included the city of Heliopolis within its limits.

Heptanomis, or Middle Egypt, extended thence

---

* Libya was probably attached to Egypt at one period of its history, as Ammianus Marcellinus (lib. xxii.) directly states, but without forming part of Egypt Proper.

† According to Herodotus, the people of Marea and Apis, on the Libyan side of the lake Mareotis, spoke a different language from the Egyptians. (ii. 18.)

‡ The similarity of this and the " rob el álemayn," " lord of the two worlds," in the Fát-ha of the Qorán, is singular.

to the Theban castle, which marked the frontier a few miles above Tanis, and which appears to have occupied the site of the present town of Dahroot*; and its name, Heptanomis, was derived from the seven nomes, or districts, it contained, which were those of Memphis, Aphroditopolis, Crocodilopolis, or Arsinoë, Heracleopolis, Oxyrinchus, Cynopolis, and Hermopolis.

The limits of the Thebaïd remained the same, and extended to the cataracts of Syene; but it appears that the Oases were all attached to the province of Heptanomis.† The chief towns of the three provinces were Thebes‡, Memphis, and Heliopolis; and from these three, as I have already observed, the bench of judges was elected.

According to Diodorus §, the celebrated Sesostris was the first who divided the country into nomes; but it is more reasonable to suppose, that long before his time, or at least before that of Remeses the Great, all necessary arrangements for

---

* Or Dahroot e'Shereéf, which stands near the mouth of the Bahr Yoósef. *Vide* my Egypt and Thebes, p. 386., where I have shown the probability of its being the Thebaïca Phylace (φυλακη).

† Ptolemy (lib. iv. c. 5.) says, the two Oases were attached to the Antinoïte nome, though it did not exist under this name in the time of the Pharaohs. The Oasis of Ammon was not, of course, in Egypt. By the "two Oases" he probably means those of El Khargeh and e'Dakhleh, the great and the western Oasis, rather than the former and the little Oasis.

‡ Thebes and the land around it composed two nomes, one on the east and the other on the west bank: the former called "Thebarum nomus," the latter "Pathyrites," which probably derived its name from Athyr, who is so frequently said in the sculptures to be the president of that side of the river.

§ This, as usual, involves the question concerning Remeses the Great; and it is difficult to decide, whether we ought to attribute the actions recorded of Sesostris to this monarch of the 18th, or to another of a previous dynasty. *Vide suprà*, vol. i. p. 74.

the organisation of the provinces had already been made, and that this was one of the first plans suggested for the government of the country.

The office of nomarch was at all times of the highest importance, and to his charge were committed the management of the lands, and all matters relating to the internal administration of the district.* He regulated the assessment and levying of the taxes, the surveying of the lands, the opening of the canals, and all other agricultural interests of the country, which were under the immediate superintendence of certain members of the priestly order; and, as his residence was in the chief town of the nome †, all causes respecting landed property, and other accidental disputes, were referred to him, and adjusted before his tribunal. The division of the country into thirty-six parts, or nomes, continued to be maintained till a late period, since in Strabo's time ‡ the number was still the same; ten, says the geographer, being assigned to the Thebaïd, ten to the Delta, and sixteen § to the intermediate province: though some changes were afterwards introduced both in the nomes and provinces of Egypt. The nomes, he adds, were

* The Turkish system of ruling Egypt was by twenty-four beys (beks) or governors of districts, under whom were the kashefs and qymaqams. The number of beys is now no longer twenty-four, as in the time of the Memlooks.

† This agrees with the definition of a nome given by St. Cyril of Alexandria: " A nome, according to the Egyptians, includes a city, its suburbs, and the villages within the district." Cellar. ii. lib. iv. 6, 7. We are not, however, to understand that the word *nome* is Egyptian.

‡ Strabo, lib. xvii.

§ These were the sixteen præfectures which, according to Pliny, assembled in the Labyrinth. Lib. 36.

subdivided into toparchiæ, or local governments,
and these again into minor jurisdictions; and we
may conclude, that the three offices of nomarchs,
toparchs, and the third or lowest grade, answered
to those of bey, kashef, and qýmaqám of the present day.   The distinctive appellation of each
nome, in later times at least, was derived from the
chief town, where the governor resided, and the
rank of each nomarch depended on the extent of
his jurisdiction.   But of the state of Egypt in the
early period of its history we have little or no information; owing to the uncivilised condition of
neighbouring states, to the indifference of those
Greeks who visited it, or to the loss of their writings, and above all to the jealousy of the Egyptians *
towards foreigners, to whom little or no information was imparted respecting the institutions and
state of the country.

Like the Chinese, they prevented all strangers
from penetrating into the interior; and if any
Greek was desirous of becoming acquainted with
the philosophy of their schools, he was tolerated,
rather than welcomed, in Egypt; and those who
traded with them were confined to the town of
Naucratis †, in the same manner that Europeans

* Strabo, lib. xvii.
† The Egyptians pretending to grant a *privilege* to this town,
obliged all Greek traders to repair to it. (Herodot. ii. 179.)   The Turks
confined European ambassadors in the Seven Towers for their *protection*.   The Ionian and Carian troops of Psamaticus had a place assigned
to them a little below Bubastis, called "the camp," and were afterwards removed by Amasis to Memphis.   Herodotus says they were the
first foreigners who were allowed to settle in the country.   Herodot.
ii. 154.

are now obliged to live in the Frank quarter of a Turkish, or a Chinese, city. And when, after the time of Amasis and the Persian conquest, foreigners became better acquainted with the country, its ancient institutions had begun to lose their interest, and the Egyptians mourned under a victorious and cruel despot. Herodotus, it is true, had ample opportunity of examining the state of Egypt during his visit to the country; but he has failed to give us much insight into its laws and institutions; and little can be gleaned from any author, except Diodorus, who, at least, deserves the credit of having collected, under far less favourable circumstances, much curious information upon this interesting subject.

Strabo mentions some of the offices which existed in Egypt in his time; but, though he asserts that many of them were the same as under the Ptolemies, we are by no means certain that they answer to those of an earlier period. " Under the eparch," says the geographer, " who holds the rank of a king, is the dicæodotes, that is, the lawgiver or chancellor, and another officer, who is called the privy-purse, or private accountant, whose business it is to take charge of every thing that is left without an owner *, and which falls of right to the emperor. These two are also attended by freedmen and stewards of Cæsar, who are entrusted with affairs of greater or less magnitude. . . . But of the natives who are employed in the government of the different cities, the principal

* The Bayt el mal, or " the property office," of the present day.

is the exagétes, or expounder, who is dressed in purple, and is honoured according to the usages of the country, and takes care of what is necessary for the welfare of the city : the register, or writer of commentaries : the archidicastes, or chief judge : and, fourthly, the captain of the night.* "

From all that can be collected on this subject, we may conclude, that in early times, after the king, the senate, and others connected with the court, the principal persons employed in the management of affairs were the judges of different grades, the rulers of provinces and districts, the government accountants, the chief of the police, and those officers immediately connected with the administration of justice, the levying of taxes, and other similar employments ; and that the principal part of them were chosen either from the sacerdotal or the military class.

During the reigns of the latter Ptolemies, considerable abuses crept into the administrative system ; intrigues, arising out of party spirit and conflicting interests, corrupted men's minds : integrity ceased to be esteemed : every patriotic feeling became extinguished : the interests of the community were sacrificed to the ambition of a successful candidate for a disputed throne : and the hope of present advantage blinded men to future consequences. New regulations were adopted to suppress the turbulent spirit of the times : the

---

* Strabo, lib. xvii. This officer answers to the Bash-agha of modern Egypt, who goes the rounds of the town at night, and is the chief of the police.

government, no longer content with the mild office of protector, assumed the character of chastiser of the people : and Egypt was ruled by a military force, rendered doubly odious, from being, in a great measure, composed of foreign mercenaries. The cast of soldiers had lost its consequence, its privileges were abolished, and the harmony once existing between that order and the people was entirely destroyed. Respect for the wisdom of the sacerdotal order, and the ancient institutions of Egypt, began to decline : and the influence once possessed by the priests over the public mind could only be traced in the superstitious reverence shown by fanatics to the rites of a religion, now much corrupted and degraded by fanciful doctrines ; and if they retained a portion of their former privileges, by having the education of youth intrusted to them, as well as the care of the national records, the superintendence of weights and measures, the surveying of the lands, and the equal distribution of the annual payments, they lost their most important offices — the tutelage and direction of the councils of government, and the right of presiding at the courts of justice.

The provincial divisions of Egypt varied at different times, particularly after the Roman conquest. The country, as already stated, consisted originally of two parts, Upper and Lower Egypt ; afterwards of three, the Thebaïd : Heptanomis, or Middle Egypt : and the Delta, or Lower Egypt : but Heptanomis, in the time of Arcadius, the son of Theodosius the Great, received the name of

Arcadia; and the eastern portion of the Delta, about the end of the fourth century, was formed into a separate province called Augustamnica *, itself divided into two parts. The Thebaïd was also made to consist of Upper and Lower, the line of separation passing between Panopolis and Ptolemaïs Hermii.†

Under the Romans ‡, Egypt was governed by a præfect, or Eparch, aided by three officers, who superintended the departments of justice, revenue, and police, throughout the country, the inferior charges being chiefly filled by natives. Over each of the provinces a military governor was appointed, who was "subordinate to the præfect in all civil affairs §, though frequently intruding on his jurisdiction, when it was necessary to use military coercion in the collection of the taxes. This charge, together with the superintendence of the tribunals, and the duty of denouncing unjust judges, (but more particularly the collection, and transmission to Constantinople, of that part of the taxes which was paid in grain,) were still vested in the præfect.

" Thus far it does not appear that there were any very serious defects in the organisation of the government of Egypt: but the same authority whence these facts are chiefly drawn (the Theodosian code,) furnishes us with still more ample de-

---

* It seems also to have encroached upon Heptanomis.
† *Vide* D'Anville's Mémoires sur l'Egypte, p. 32.
‡ *Vide suprà*, vol. ii. p. 72.
§ For the following observations I am indebted to Mr. Hamilton's valuable work Ægyptiaca, p. 231., to which I refer the reader.

tails on the nature of the subordinate institutions, both at Alexandria and in the rest of the country. And here the whole system seems to have been founded in error, and persevered in with a blind obstinacy, which preferred the accumulation of many bad and unjust laws to the repeal of a few which were imperfect.

" The decurions of Alexandria soon found that the honour bestowed upon them was to be paid for at the highest rate.   In return for their nominal and titular privileges, and in addition to the charge of supplying the inhabitants with provisions, of keeping the records, and preserving the police of the city, they were subjected to continual expenses for the public games and shows ; presents for honorary seats were arbitrarily demanded of them, and the office was converted from a benefit to a burden.   Some were reduced to poverty by these means : the expenses they were no longer able to bear were attached to the succeeding proprietor of their estates : others assumed dishonourable employments, or became the slaves of persons in power ; and laws were no sooner enacted to obviate these elusive steps, than all contrivances were invented on the part of the sufferers to facilitate them.

" In the public distress, private gifts and loans had been solicited by government ; these were soon converted into forced contributions ; and the charge of levying them added to the burdens of the decurions.   Immunities against such contributions were purchased at one time, and repealed by public orders when the money had been paid.

" That the municipal administrations of the different towns were not better protected against the abuses of a corrupt government, is evident from two laws preserved in the same code, one of which was enacted to recall the decurions who had quitted the duties of their office, and, among these, all who had taken refuge amongst the anchorites of the desert. By the other law, the right of reclaiming their property was denied to all who had abandoned it for the purpose of avoiding the duties to which it was liable.

" Throughout the villages, and the farms surrounding them, the triple division of the produce among the priests, the military, and the cultivators, had ceased with the Greek conquest. To this had succeeded a regular establishment of officers, who had severally the charge of collecting the tribute due from each proprietor, that of preserving the peace of the village, and that of superintending the maintenance of the dykes and canal, so important a part of the rural economy of Egypt. A fixed sum of money had been, from the first, set apart for this object; and a regular system had been long established, and strictly adhered to, for the mode in which repairs were to be made, the time or state of the inundation at which the principal embankments were to be opened, and for carrying into execution other precautionary measures of irrigating and of draining, which the physical organisation of the country had rendered necessary.

" In the edicts of Justinian are to be traced some

important alterations, introduced by that emperor into the civil government of the country. The province of Augustamnica appears to have been united to that of Egypt and Alexandria; and from this last, the two districts of Maræotis and Menelas were detached and added to Libya, for the avowed and singular reason, that, without them, this latter province would be unable to defray the expenses of its government.

" The civil and military powers were again united in the same person, both in Egypt and the Thebaïd, as they had been before the reign of Constantine; and the magistrates of the provinces or nomes, now called patrarchs, and those of the villages, or the pagarchs, were placed under their authority. The functions of these magistrates, when they were once named to the office, might be suspended by the præfects, but they could not be definitively removed without orders from Constantinople.

" The main, and almost the sole, object that appears to have dictated these edicts of Justinian, was the more punctual transmission of grain to the capital of the empire. Whether it was owing to the increasing poverty of the country, the connivance of the different agents employed in the service, or the corruptions of those in the higher offices of state, perpetual difficulties seem to have occurred. But what argues on the part of the Roman government a conviction of the necessity of cultivating, by a mild treatment, the native Egyptians, all the menaces held out against the

disobedience of the imperial orders are directed
against the præfects, who alone are held responsible,
in their persons and their effects, for the strict execution of them. In some instances a denunciation
is published against the higher orders of the
clergy, who, by unauthorised acts of protection,
shall have pretended to release any individuals
from the payments to which they were subject.

"The state of property in Egypt continued,
under the Romans, very similar to what it had been
in the earliest times. The proprietor of a district,
or of a certain part of it, had a kind of feudal claim
over his vassals, from whose gratuitous labour he
exacted all that was not absolutely necessary for
their existence. While Egypt retained its inde-
pendence it was fully sufficient to supply its own
wants; but, as a province, it suffered all the evils
of a corrupt and vicious administration; and it never
received any returns, in money or kind, for its
annual supply of grain to the capital. As this supply did not diminish, but rather increased in an
inverse proportion to the means which were to
furnish it, the proprietors, when obliged to add to
their demands upon the peasants, found them in
a situation to afford less. Industry was at a stand;
and the distressed serfs had no other method of
evading such claims, than either by abandoning
their farms for others more favourably situated, or
by seeking the protection of some powerful individual, whose patronage they purchased. This
abuse had been the natural consequence of the
system of honours established by Constantine; and

in Egypt it was productive of the most prejudicial
effects.   The evil grew rapidly : what was first
dictated by necessity was soon resorted to by
choice; and, when necessity could not be pleaded
in excuse, temptations were not wanting on the
part of the protectors, who soon found the means
of converting their powers of granting privileges
into a pecuniary speculation; and the next step
was that the proprietors, being abandoned by their
vassals, and, consequently, reduced to poverty, were
obliged to yield up their estates to those who had
succeeded in seducing them.   This iniquitous traf-
fic particularly prevailed among the military ;. and
for some years the new possessors were able to disguise from the government the truth of their situation, by paying no taxes from the estates they had
thus procured, and by returning as defaulters the
names of those whom they had ejected.

   " Various laws, from the time of Constantine to
Theodosius the Second and Justinian, were enacted
against these grievances ;   they successively increased in severity; and nothing but the extremest
rigour, and the attachment of responsibility on the
person of the præfects themselves, could succeed
in putting an end to them.   At first, the peasants
who remained behind were to make up for what
the fugitives ought to have paid.   Afterwards, an
ignominious punishment was denounced against
such fugitives, and the protectors sentenced to a
fine : — this fine was gradually augmented to a sum
equal to the whole fortune of the delinquent.
Theodosius the Second, finally established all such

usurpations of property as had taken place in this manner, prior to the consulate of Cæsarius and Atticus, and ordered the immediate restitution of all that had taken place since that period, subjecting, at the same time, the new proprietors to all the ancient charges and contributions attached to their estates, including those that would have fallen on the fugitive as well as the other vassals.

" The peculiar nature of the soil and locality of Egypt had fixed, at a very early period, the system of agriculture, the most congenial to them. No innovations appear to have been introduced on this head; and, as laws have only been made where changes were thought necessary, we are left without any other materials, whence we might form our judgment relative to the employment of the soil in ancient times, beyond those customs which have been handed down to the present age.

" Agriculture was always the principal object to which the government of Egypt was directed; and when the king, the priests, and the military, had each an equal share in the produce of the soil, the common interest would effectually prevent any abuses in the management of it. But, under a foreign yoke, these interests were too divided; and the defects of administration were to be supplied by the rigour of the laws. The destroyer of a dyke was, at one time, to be condemned to the public works and to the mines; at another, to be branded, and transported to the Oasis, — punishments more severe than are ever thought of even under the present Mahometan government.

" Some laws were made for the encouragement of the growth of timber trees in Egypt, but the same misguided policy, which had failed in so many other laws, preferred the menaces of a punishment for the sale or the use of the sycamore and napka*, rather than the offer of a reward for extending plantations of them. Here may be traced the same hand which, instead of ameliorating the situation of the oppressed peasantry, was contented with accumulating upon the fugitives useless punishments, or bringing them to their homes by an armed force.

" With respect to the amount of the public revenues of Egypt, Diodorus Siculus states them to have been, in his time, equal to six thousand talents, or about one million two hundred thousand pounds: and, notwithstanding the much higher amount stated by Strabo, we may conclude that in no future period they exceeded this sum. The disorders to which the people were subjected under its last kings would have tended rather to diminish its means of contribution; and, under the Roman government, its wealth and resources must have proceeded in an inverse ratio to the demands from the capital. Augustus, indeed, relieved Egypt from one cause of oppression, whereby Sicily and Sardinia had successively been ruined, — the presence and controlling authority of powerful Romans.

" The levying of the taxes, both in money and in

* Rhamnus Nabeca: in Arabic, nebq or sidr. *Vide* Egypt and Thebes, p. 211.

kind, appears to have been left to the immediate
care of the natives, whereof one or more presided
over each district and village; these, however,
were successively placed under the superintendence of the præfects of Egypt, the governors of the
Thebaïd, and the military force; and the responsibility, which at first rested with the superior
officers, was afterwards extended to the soldiers
themselves.

" The tributes, in whatever form they were paid,
were received at Alexandria by Roman agents com-
missioned for the purpose. After the time of
Constantine, it appears that the transport of the
grain was at the expense of a collective body of
the principal inhabitants of that city. This burden
was, at a later period, commuted for an annual
payment; but the object was still subject to many
delays, till the edict of Justinian directed the
charge to be borne by the chief custom-house
officer at Alexandria.

" Other expenses were also payable by individuals, in addition to the regular taxes of the country.
The freight of the corn vessels down the Nile, the
baking of the bread for the military, where they
happened to be quartered, and the clothing of the
troops, became so many occasions of extortion.

" It is difficult to fix the precise portion of the
entire taxes of Egypt which was paid, whether in
grain or in money, anterior to the reign of Justinian. When this emperor framed an edict expressly
for the purpose of regulating the transmission of
the grain to the capital, and of facilitating the levying of the rest of the taxes, the quantity of corn

then furnished by Egypt to Constantinople was eight hundred thousand artabæ, which, if calculated as equal to the ardeb of the present day *, amount to four hundred and fifty thousand quarters; and as, by the same law, a fine of three solidi for every three artabæ was to attach to all who, by neglect of their duty, should occasion any delay in the collection, the value of each artaba may be taken at one third of this sum, or about seven shillings; consequently, that of the corn annually sent to Constantinople would have been nearly three thousand pounds sterling; and, perhaps, a quantity not much inferior to this was detained in the country for the supply of the præfect's palace, the maintenance of the troops, and the gratuitous distributions of corn granted to Alexandria by Diocletian, and confirmed and augmented by other emperors.

" There would still, however, remain a large portion of the public revenues to be paid in money.

" One chief source of misunderstanding among the governors and the governed throughout Egypt, and of the occasional oppression of the latter, was, that the system of regulating the taxes of each province of the empire, once for each successive term of fifteen years, was unwisely extended to Egypt. This indiction, which was introduced by Constantine in lieu of the lustrum, or term of five years, however convenient it might be for other countries, was ill adapted to one wherein the produce of each year must so essentially depend on the extent of the inundation. One consequence of this was,

* In the year 1800.

that frequently the præfects were obliged to return different estates as totally deficient, which opened a door to endless acts of corruption and connivance.

" The obligations imposed on the præfect for the punctual supply of grain, were much more rigorous than those which related to the payments to be made in specie to the imperial treasury; so that he was enabled, from time to time, to desist from his pecuniary demands upon the people, the better to enable them to bring in the stated quantity of corn; but this pretext likewise led the way to infinite abuses. Although the payments in money ought to have equalled two thirds of that in kind, Justinian complains, in his edict, that they were frequently reduced to nothing, wholly absorbed in pretended expenses, and pillaged by the secret understanding of the Egyptian tax-gatherers and the public agents. It is scarcely possible to conceive the moral weakness of a government which knew not how to put a stop to evils of this nature, with all the military means of the empire at their disposal, and no ostensible resistance to their operations but the bare principle of corruption. These deductions from the tax demanded by the government, which nearly equalled their amount, appear the more extraordinary, as we find in the same edict of Justinian, that, throughout every village and district, the inhabitants were liable to other calls for the maintenance of the canals and dykes, public buildings, and the salaries of subaltern agents.

" The author * of the essay from which the greater

---

* Reynier, L'Egypte sous les Romains, 1807.

part of these observations are taken, is induced to suggest, whether the public accountants of those times may not have acted on the system now pursued under the Turkish establishment; who make an annual charge of near thirty thousand livres for the transport of the dirt and rubbish of Cairo to the seacoast, while it is notorious that not a single boat is employed upon this service.

" The duties of export and import in Egypt, which must have formed a considerable part of the revenue, particularly as long as it continued the emporium of goods between Europe and India, appear to have been farmed to Greeks and Romans, contrary to the system adopted with regard to the tax on land. These duties were payable on the coast of the Red Sea, at Canopus, and at Alexandria. At this latter place, the persons by whom they were farmed had so many opportunities of granting a temporary relief to the necessitous, in advancing money for them, that the vexations they could afterwards practise upon their debtors form the subject of one of the heads of Justinian's edict; and it was in consideration of the profits enjoyed by the same persons, that they were liable to the expenses of the transport of grain from their port to the capital.

" The corporation of Alexandria were released by the same emperor from the repairs of the canal which brought them water from the Nile; and they were allowed four hundred solidi out of a fund called *Dinummium Vectigal* which, by the explanation which follows, appears to refer to the duties levied upon the ships frequenting the harbour; and it was natural that those should pay a full portion of the expenses which procured them this necessary supply. Besides taxes upon the industry, the trades, and houses of its inhabitants, Alexandria was, from time to time, subjected to a contribution under the name of coronation money. This abuse had arisen out of the custom, once so laudable and useful, of presenting, in the name of the provinces, crowns of gold to proconsuls, or other commanders, who had acted honourably and liberally during their governments. This gradually became so general, that those who were not thus honoured considered themselves as insulted; and, under the emperors, it was soon converted from an honour into a means of raising money. And in addition to the amount demanded from each, grievous in itself to a suffering people, it became much more so by the irregularity and sudden manner in which it was imposed." *

* For many other interesting remarks on the state of Egypt about this period, *vide* Ægyptiaca, p. 243.

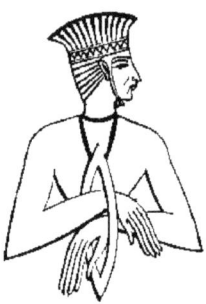

No. 92.   A Captive secured by a handcuff.   *Thebes.*

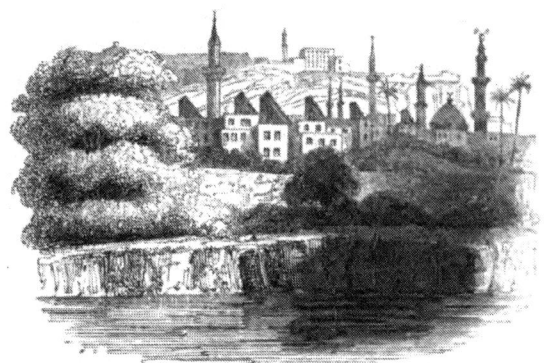

VIGNETTE E.   Part of Cairo, showing the *Mulguf* on the houses of modern Egypt.

CHAP. V.

Houses. — Brickmakers. — Villas. — Granaries. — Gardens. — Vineyards. — Wine-presses. — Wines. — Beer.

THOUGH the Egyptians are said* to have paid less attention to the splendour of their houses than to the decoration of their tombs, the plans of many that remain, and the extent of their villas represented in the sculptures, plainly show, that no precepts of philosophy can oblige man to renounce the luxuries of life. The priests may have taught them that their stay in this world was of short duration; that their present abodes were only inns at which they reposed during their earthly pilgrimage†; and that their tombs alone could be con-

---

* Diodor. i. 51.
† As Jacob said to Pharaoh, " The days of my pilgrimage are 130 years." Gen. xlvii. 9.

sidered as everlasting habitations*, which it was a
religious duty to adorn.   It was their interest to
inculcate similar notions: the persons employed
in making and decorating the tombs were of the
sacerdotal order; and the splendour of funeral obsequies tended to their emolument.   They induced
them to expend considerable sums on the celebration of those rites; and many, who had barely
sufficient to obtain the necessaries of life, were
anxious to save something for the expenses of their
death.   For besides the embalming process, which
sometimes cost a talent of silver †, or about two
hundred and fifty pounds English money, the tomb
itself was purchased at an immense sum; and
numerous demands were afterwards made upon
the estate of the deceased, for the celebration of
prayers, and other services for the soul.   We cannot, however, suppose, that temporary gratification
was denied to the rich of any class, or was deemed
unworthy the wisdom of the priesthood; and they
evidently enjoyed all the comforts and luxuries
which their means could so well provide.   Though
the priests may have kept up an external appearance
of self-denial, and avoided all unnecessary display
of wealth, it is natural that they should welcome
the blessings of this life, provided they did not
interfere with the practice of virtue.   And if they
taught others to avoid ostentation, if they themselves submitted, on some occasions, to severe

* Diodor. loc. cit.
† Diodor. i. 91. This was the most costly; the poor classes paid very
little; and every one in proportion to his means or inclination.

Pl. V.

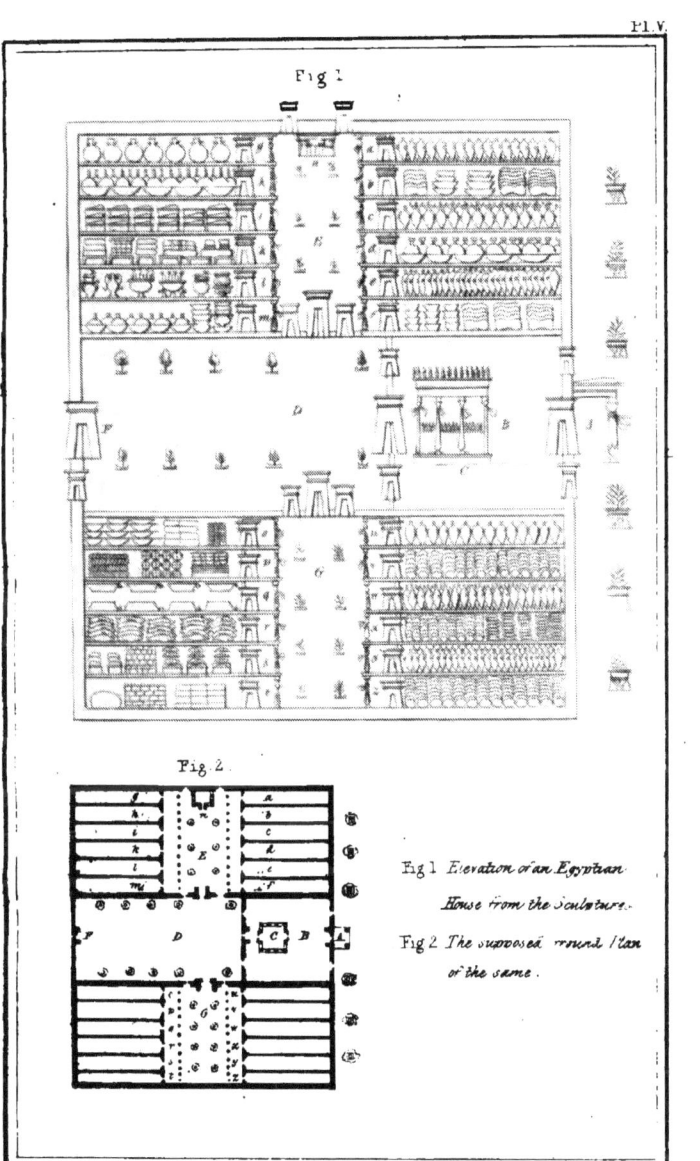

Fig 1

Fig 2.

Fig 1 Elevation of an Egyptian
House from the Sculpture.

Fig 2 The supposed ground Plan
of the same.

abstinence, and encouraged morality by their own
example, we must allow that they were deserving
of esteem; and little cause for censure can be
found, except in that exclusiveness which degraded the lower classes of their countrymen, and
in the disproportionate extent of their possessions,
compared with those of the other Egyptians.

HOUSES IN THE TOWNS.

 The houses in the towns varied of course in size
as well as plan; but, judging from the ruins that
remain, the streets were laid out very regularly;
nor does there appear to have been the constant
mixture of large houses and low hovels, so frequently met with in eastern towns.   As is usually
the case in hot climates, many of the streets were
narrow, and few, except the principal ones, were
large enough to allow the passage of a chariot.   In
Thebes, however, it is probable they were on a
somewhat larger scale, and proportionate with the
increased size of the houses, some of which, even
in the early age of its founder, are said to have
been four or five stories in height.*

In towns built at the mouths of mountain ravines,
the main street was, at the same time, the bed of
the torrent: several instances of which may be seen
in Spain and Italy; and, as storms of rain seldom
last long in the arid climate of Egypt, the communication by it was rarely impeded, or its surface

---

* Diodor. i. 45. The greater number I believe to have been confined to one or two stories. At Rome they had three. Augustus
confined the height of houses to 70 feet.

materially impaired. Indeed, if much rain had fallen in that country, it would have been necessary to construct houses of materials more capable of resisting its effects than mere crude brick; and, from the narrowness of some of the ravines, their foundations would have been in danger, as well as the lives of the inhabitants. But heavy rain was a rare phenomenon in Upper Egypt; and though much fell about the sea-coast of the Delta, and, during winter, in the interior of the eastern desert, a violent storm at Thebes was looked upon to presage an approaching calamity.*

The use of crude brick, baked in the sun, was universal in Upper and Lower Egypt, both for public and private buildings; and the brick-field gave abundant occupation to numerous labourers throughout the country. These simple materials were found to be peculiarly suited to the climate; and the ease, rapidity, and cheapness with which they were made, offered additional recommendations. Inclosures of gardens or granaries, sacred circuits encompassing the courts of temples, walls of fortifications and towns, dwelling-houses and tombs, in short, all but the temples† themselves, were of crude brick; and so great was the demand, that the Egyptian government, observing the pro-

---

* Herodotus says, " rain *never* falls at Thebes; but before the Persian invasion it rained violently." (lib. iii. 10.) The historian is not, however, borne out by fact, as we see from the appearance of the water-courses there, which were formed long before his time, and from the pains taken by the ancient Egyptians to protect their tombs and other monuments from rain. A continued storm of heavy rain during a whole day and night would be a rare occurrence; but showers fall about five or six times in the course of a year at Thebes. *Vide* my Egypt and Thebes, p. 75.

† Some small temples in the villages were of crude brick.

fit which would accrue to the revenue from a monopoly of them, undertook to supply the public at a moderate price, thus preventing all unauthorised persons from engaging in their manufacture. And, in order more effectually to obtain their end, the seal of the king, or of some privileged person, was stamped upon the bricks at the time they were made. This fact, though not positively mentioned by any ancient author, is inferred from finding bricks so marked, both in public and private buildings; some having the ovals of a king, and some the name and titles of a priest, or other influential person; and it is probable that those which bear no characters, belonged to individuals who had obtained a permission or license from government, to fabricate them for their own consumption.

The employment of numerous captives, who worked as slaves, enabled the government to sell the bricks at a lower price than those who had recourse solely to free labour; so that, without the necessity of a prohibition, they speedily became an exclusive manufacture; and we find that, independent of native labourers, a great many foreigners were constantly engaged in the brick-fields at Thebes, and other parts of Egypt. The Jews, of course, were not excluded from this drudgery; and, like the captives detained in the Thebaïd, they were condemned to the same labour in Lower Egypt. They erected granaries, treasure cities, and other public buildings for the Egyptian monarch: the materials used in their construction were the work of their hands; and the constant employment of brick-makers may be accounted for by the extensive supply required, and kept by the government for public sale.

To meet with Hebrews in the sculptures cannot reasonably be expected, since the remains in that part of Egypt where they lived have not been preserved; but it is curious to discover other foreign captives occupied in the same manner, overlooked by similar " taskmasters *," and performing the very same labours as the Israelites described in the Bible; and no one can look at the paintings of Thebes, representing brick-makers, without a feeling of the highest interest. That the scene in the accompanying wood-cut † is at the capital of Upper Egypt is shown by the hieroglyphics ‡, which expressly state, that the " bricks " (tôbi) are made for a " building at Thebes;" and this occurrence of the word implying bricks, similar both in modern Arabic § and ancient Coptic, gives an additional value to the picture.

It is scarcely fair to argue, in defiance of logic, that because the Jews made bricks, and the persons here introduced are so engaged, these must necessarily be Jews: since the Egyptians and their captives were constantly required to perform the same task; and the great quantity made at all times may be inferred from the number of buildings, which still remain, constructed of those materials: but it is worthy of remark, that more bricks bearing the

* *Figs.* 3 and 6 in the wood-cut, No. 93.
† *Vide* wood-cut, next page.
‡ At *e* in the wood-cut, over *fig.* 9.
§ " Tòb or toob," in Arabic, " a brick :" in Coptic " tôbi."

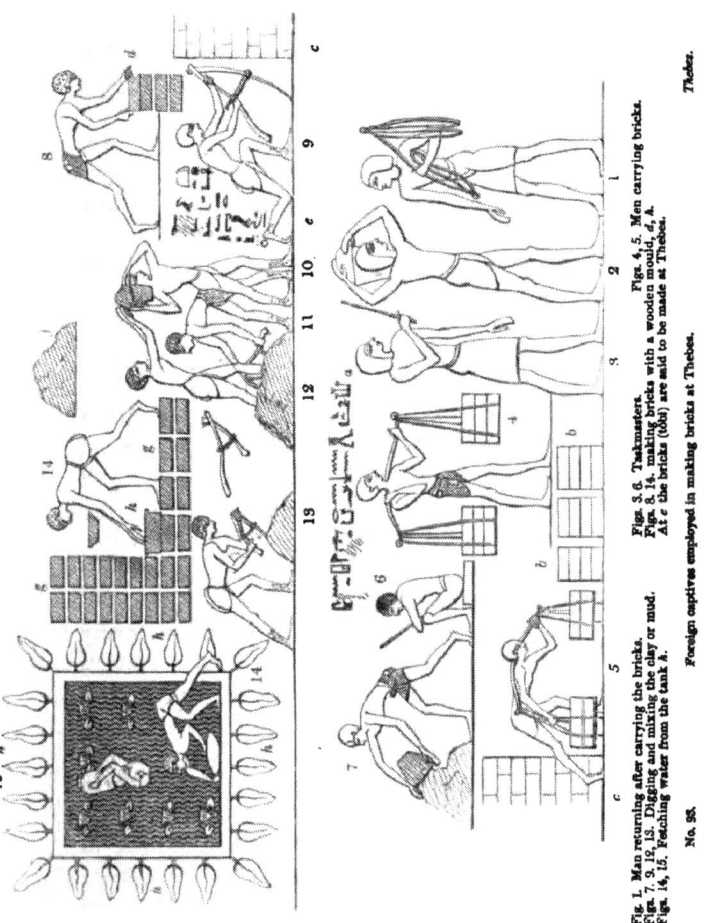

Fig. 1. Man returning after carrying the bricks.   Fig. 3. 6. Taskmasters.   Figs. 4, 5. Men carrying bricks.
Figs. 7. 9. 12. 13. Digging and mixing the clay or mud.   Figs. 8. 14. making bricks with a wooden mould, d, h.
Figs. 14, 15. Fetching water from the tank h.   At c the bricks (tôbi) are said to be made at Thebes.

No. 93.   Foreign captives employed in making bricks at Thebes.   Thebes.

name of Thothmes III. (whom I suppose to have
been king of Egypt at the time of the Exodus)

H 2

have been discovered, than of any other period: owing to the many prisoners of Asiatic nations employed by him, independent of his Hebrew captives.

With regard to the features of foreigners frequently resembling the Jews, it is only necessary to observe, that the Egyptians adopted the same character for all the inhabitants of Syria*, as may be seen in the sculptures of Karnak and other places, where those people occur, or in one of the sets of figures in Belzoni's tomb; and the brick-makers, far from having the very Jewish expression found in many of those figures, have not even the beard, so marked in the people of Syria and the prisoners of Sheshonk; and from the names of the captives throughout the tomb where they are found, it is evident they belong to a nation living far to the north of Judæa.

Houses of a small size were usually connected together, and formed the continuous sides of streets; they rarely exceeded two stories, and many of them consisted only of a ground floor, and an upper set of rooms. Nor, indeed, judging from the sculptures, do the Egyptians appear to have preferred lofty houses; and, as in modern Egyptian towns, the largest seldom had more than three stories. Those of the rich citizens frequently covered a considerable space†, and presented to

---

* Herodotus also calls the Jews Syrians, ii. 159.

† At Thebes, the largest houses seem to have been on the Libyan side and in that part of Diospolis between Karnak and Luqsor; but those in the immediate vicinity of the great temple stood in a more dense mass. Houses built in this manner present, of course, greater

the street either the sides of the house itself, or the walls of the court attached to it. Their plans were regular, the rooms being usually arranged round an open area *, or on either side of a long passage to which an entrance-court led from the street.† The court was an empty space, considerably larger than the Roman impluvium, probably paved with stone, or containing a few trees, a small tank‡, or a fountain, in its centre §; and sometimes, though rarely, a flight of steps led to the main entrance from without.‖ A court was frequently common

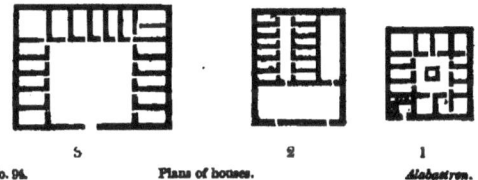

No. 94.   Plans of houses.   Alabastron.

to several houses; and again, some of the large mansions stood detached, and had the advantage of several doors of entrance, on two or three different sides. They had a portico, or porch, before the front door (Janua) supported on two columns, below whose capitals were attached ¶

mounds of ruins than the larger ones which had open courts, and which covered a greater space.
* *Vide* wood-cut, No. 94. *figs.* 1. and 3.
† *Vide* wood-cut, No. 94. *fig.* 2.
‡ Perhaps sometimes a well, as in modern Egyptian houses, and in the house mentioned in 2 Sam. 17. 18.
§ *Vide* wood-cut, No. 94. *fig.* 1.
‖ *Vide* wood-cut, No. 95. *fig.* 1.
¶ Probably, as at Rome, only on certain occasions. *Vide* wood-cut, No. 95. *fig.* 2.

ribands or banners: the name of the person who
lived there being occasionally painted within, on

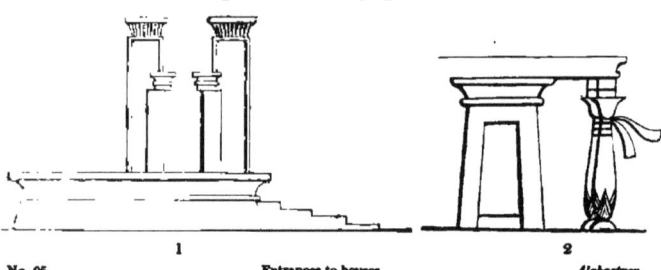

No. 95. Entrances to houses. *Alabastron.*

the lintel or imposts of the door* ; and sometimes
the portico consisted of a double row of columns,
between which stood colossal statues of the king.†

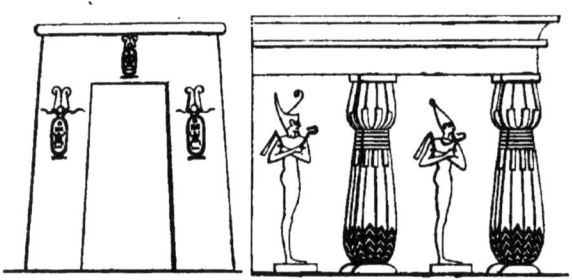

No. 96. Fig. 1. Doorway, with name upon it. Fig. 2. Porch. *Thebes and Alabastron.*

A line of trees ran parallel with the front of
the house; and, to prevent injuries from cattle
or from any accident, the stems were surrounded
by a low wall ‡, pierced with square holes to

* As in wood-cut, No. 96. *fig.* 1.
† Wood-cut, No. 96. *fig.* 2.
‡ *Vide* wood-cut, No. 97. *fig.* 2. at *c c.* between *a* and *b.*

admit the air. Nor were the Egyptians singular in the custom of planting trees about their town houses, as we find the same mentioned by Latin authors at Rome itself. *

The height of the portico was about twelve or fifteen feet, just exceeding that of the cornice of the door, which was only raised by its threshold above the level of the ground.† On either side of the main entrance was a smaller door, which stood at an equal distance between it and the side-wall, and was probably intended for the servants, and those who came on business. On entering ‡ by the porch, you passed into an open court (*aula*, or hall), containing a *mandara* §, or receiving room, for visitors. This building, supported by columns, decorated with banners, was closed only at the lower part by inter-columnar panels, over which a stream of cool air was admitted, and protection from the rays of the sun was secured by an awning that covered it. ‖ On the opposite side of the court was another door, the approach to the *mandara* from the interior; and the master of the house, on the announcement of a stranger, came in that way to receive him. ¶ Three doors led from this court to another of larger dimen-

* Hor. Epod. i. 10. 22.   Tibull. iii. 3. 15.
† *Vide* wood-cut, No. 95. *fig.* 2.; and plate 5. A.
‡ *Vide* the plan in plate 5. B.
§ I use the Arabic name for the same sort of room used for the same purpose. With the Romans, it seems to have been the place of the nuptial couch. Hor. Ep. i. 1. 87.   Plate 5. C.
‖ In the plans, we cannot, of course, see the awning, but we must give them credit for so simple an invention.
¶ This is the opinion I have formed from the different plans of their houses, the custom of the modern Egyptians, and the habits of the East in general.

sions*, which was ornamented with avenues of trees, and communicated on the right and left with the interior of the house; and this, like most of the large courts, had a back entrance (*posticum*) through a central † and lateral gateway. The arrangement of the interior was much the same on either side of the court: six or more chambers‡, whose doors faced those of the opposite set, opening on a corridor supported by columns on the right and left of an area, which was shaded by a double row of trees.

At the upper end of one of these areas was a sitting-room, which faced the door leading to the great court; and over this and the other chambers were the apartments of the upper story.§ Here were also two small gateways looking upon the street.

Another plan consisted of a court, with the usual avenue of trees, on one side of which were several sets of chambers opening on corridors or passages, but without any colonnade before the doors.‖ The receiving room (A) ¶ looked upon the court, and from it a row of columns led to the private sitting apartment, which stood isolated in one of the passages, near to a door communicating with the side chambers; and, in its position, with a corridor or porch in front, it bears a striking resemblance to the " summer parlour " of Eglon, king of

---

* *Vide* Plate 5.   † *Vide* Plate 5. F.
‡ *Vide* Plate 5. *a.* to *z.*
§ They could not be represented in the elevation plan, which is only intended to refer to the ground-floors.
‖ *Vide* wood-cut, No. 97. *fig.* 1.
¶ *Vide* wood-cut, No. 97. *fig.* 1.

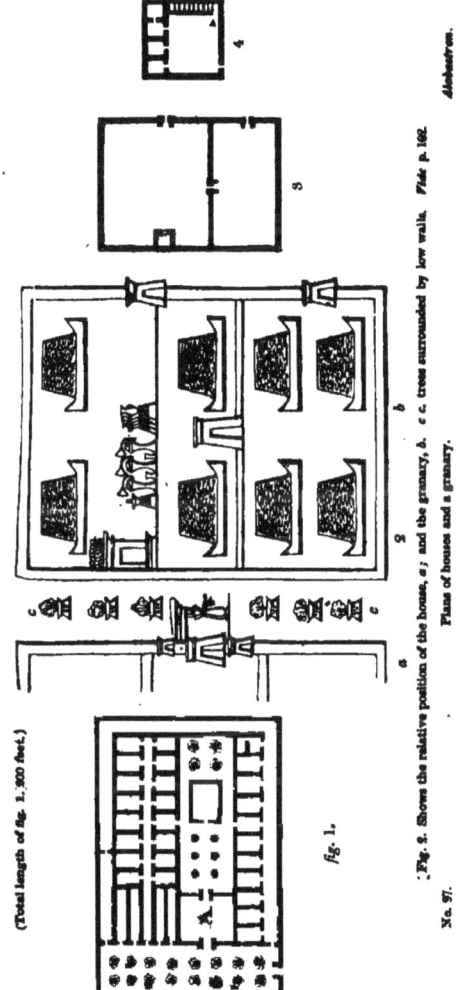

(Total length of fig. 1, 900 feet.)

fig. 1.

No. 97.

Fig. 1. Shows the relative position of the house, a; and the granary, b. c c, trees surrounded by low walk. *Vide* p. 162.

Plans of houses and a granary.

Alabastron.

... which was ...
trees, and communicat...
with the interior of the ...
of the large ... had ...
through a central ... ...
arrangement of the ...
on either side of the ...
whose doors faced the...
ing on a corridor ...
right and left of an ...
double row of trees.

At the upper end ...
sitting-room, which f...
great court; and over...
were the apartments...
were also two smal...
street.

Another plan con...
avenue of trees, on...
sets of chambers o...
but without any c...
receiving room (...
from it a row of ...
apartment, whic...
sages, near to a ...
chambers; an...
or porch in ...
to the "...

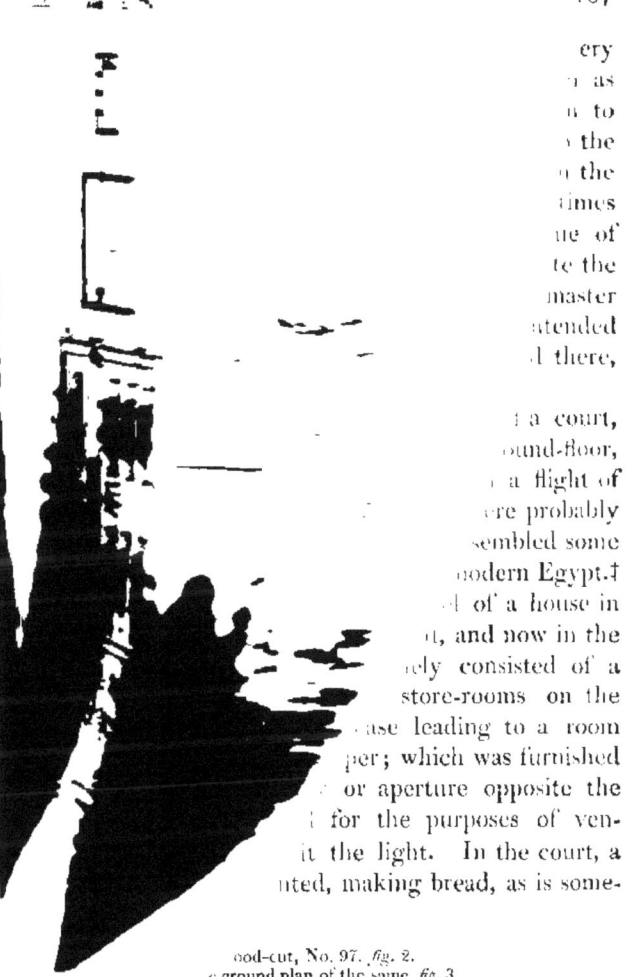

ery
as
to
the
the
times
ue of
te the
master
atended
there,

a court,
ound-floor,
a flight of
ere probably
sembled some
modern Egypt.†
of a house in
n, and now in the
ely consisted of a
store-rooms on the
ase leading to a room
per; which was furnished
or aperture opposite the
for the purposes of ven-
it the light. In the court, a
nted, making bread, as is some-

ood-cut, No. 97. *fig.* 2.
ground plan of the same, *fig.* 3.
Vide wood-cut, No. 97. *fig.* 4.
Vide wood-cut, No. 98.

Moab*, " which he had for himself alone," and
where he received Ehud the Israelite stranger.
And the flight of Ehud " through the porch,"
after he had shut and locked the door of the parlour, shows its situation to have been very similar
to some of these isolated apartments, in the houses
and villas of the ancient Egyptians.   The side
chambers were frequently arranged on either side
of a corridor, others faced towards the court, and
others were only separated from the outer wall
by a long passage.

In the distribution of the apartments, numerous
and different modes were adopted, according to circumstances; in general, however, the large mansions
seem to have consisted of a court and corridors, with
a set of rooms on either side, not unlike many of
those now built in oriental and tropical countries ;
but, in order to give a better notion of the general
arrangement of the houses and streets in an Egyptian town, I shall introduce the plan of an ancient
city near Tel el Amarna, which I believe to have
been Alabastron † : a place erroneously transferred
by geographers from the valley of the Nile to the
eastern desert.   The houses are in many places
quite destroyed, leaving few traces of their plans,
or even of their sites; and the position of the town
itself differs much from that of most Egyptian
cities, being of very inconsiderable breadth, and of
disproportionate length, extending upwards of two
miles and a quarter, though less than two thirds of
a mile broad.

* Judges, iii. 20.   † *Vide* plate 6.

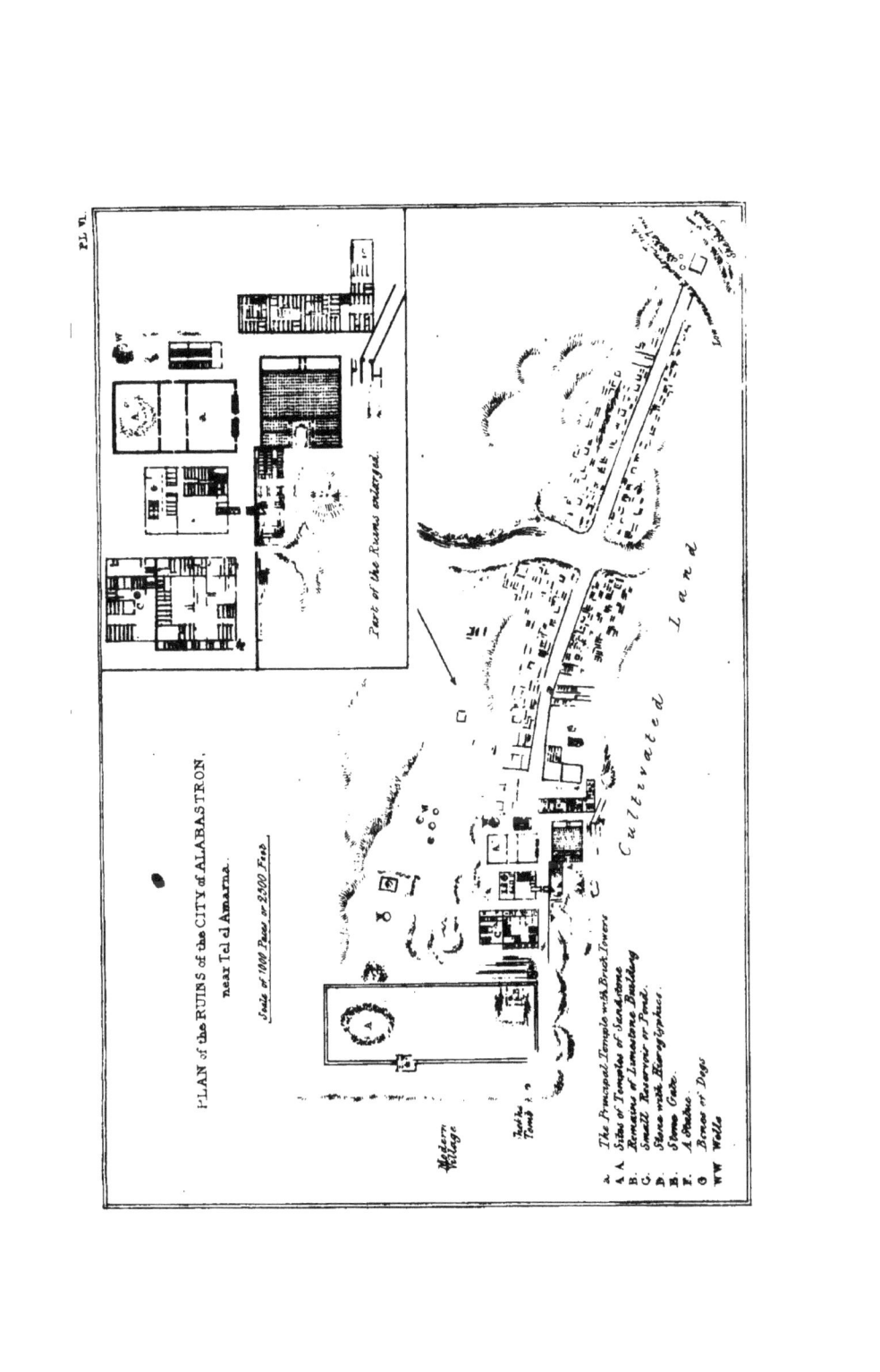

PL. VI.

PLAN of the RUINS of the CITY of ALABASTRON.
near Tel d Amarna.

Scale of 1000 Paces, or 2500 Feet.

Part of the Ruins enlarged.

Cultivated Land

Western Village

Part to Tomb a ⇒

a. The Principal Temple with Brick Towers.
A A. Sites of Temples of Sandstone.
B. Remains of Limestone Building.
C. Small Reservoir or Pond.
D. Stone with Hieroglyphics.
E. Stone Gate.
F. A Obelisk.
G. Bones of Dogs.
WW Wells.

Their granaries were also laid out in a very regular manner, and varied of course in plan as much as the houses, to which there is reason to believe they were frequently attached, even in the towns ; and judging from one represented in the sculptures of Alabastron, they were sometimes only separated from' the house by an avenue of trees.*   In this instance, the building opposite the upper doorway is a sitting-room for the master or the inspector of the granary, who superintended the arrangement of whatever was deposited there, and the whole is divided into two parts.†

Some small houses consisted merely of a court, and three or four store rooms on the ground-floor, with a single chamber above, to which a flight of steps led from the court ; but they were probably only met with in the country, and resembled some still found in the *fellāh* villages of modern Egypt.‡ Very similar to these was the model of a house in the possession of the late Mr. Salt, and now in the British Museum §, which, solely consisted of a court-yard and three small store-rooms on the ground-floor, with a staircase leading to a room belonging to the storekeeper; which was furnished with a narrow window or aperture opposite the door, rather intended for the purposes of ventilation than to admit the light.   In the court, a woman was represented, making bread, as is some-

* *Vide* wood-cut, No. 97. *fig.* 2.
† *Vide* ground plan of the same, *fig.* 3.
‡ *Vide* wood-cut, No. 97. *fig.* 4.
§ *Vide* wood-cut, No. 98.

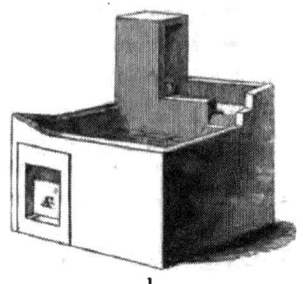
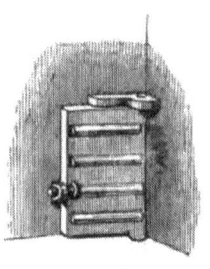

No. 98.   Fig. 1. Model of a small house in Mr. Salt's Collection.
Fig. 2. Shows how the door opened and was secured.

times done at the present day in Egypt, in the
open air; and the store-rooms were not only full of
grain when the model was found, but would still
have preserved their contents uninjured, had they
escaped the notice of a rat in the lazaretto of Leg-
horn, which in one night destroyed what ages had
respected. How readily would an Arab exclaim,
on learning the fate which awaited them, " Every
thing is written !"

The chamber on the top of the house appears,
from its dimensions, to be little calculated for comfort either in the heat of summer, or the cold of
winter; but it may only have been intended as a
shelter from the sun during the day, while the
inmate attended to the business of the servants,
or the peasants. It cannot, however, fail to call to
mind the memorable proverb, " It is better to
dwell in a corner of the house-top, than with a
brawling woman in a wide house * ;" though that

* Prov. xxi. 9.

character does not apply to the quiet and industrious female in the court below.

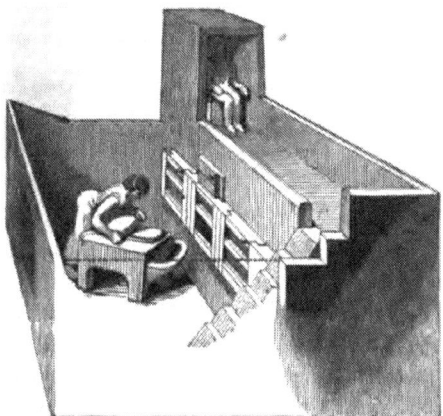

No. 99.   Showing the interior of the court, and upper chamber, in the same.

The chambers on the ground-floor of an Egyptian house were chiefly used for stores, furniture, and goods of different kinds; and amphoræ of wine and oil* were arranged as in the *apothecæ*† of a Roman mansion.   The rooms, and, indeed, all the parts of the house, were stuccoed within and without, and ornamented with various devices painted on the walls; and the doors were frequently stained to imitate foreign and rare woods.‡   They were

* The same custom of putting oil and honey and different comestibles into earthenware jars was common to the Romans as well as the ancient and modern Egyptians.   Some of these vases were not, properly speaking, amphoræ, having but one or no handle; but I use the name generally for *testæ,* or earthen casks (*cadi*).

† Vitruv. 6. c. 1.   " Apothecæ cæteraque quæ ad fructus servandos . . . . possunt esse."   *Vide* plate 5.

‡ This was even the case with their coffins.

either of one or two valves*, turning on pins of metal, and were secured within by a bar or bolts. Some of these bronze pins have been discovered in the tombs of Thebes, and the two given in the

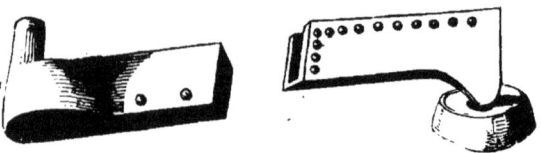

1   2

No. 100.   Fig. 1. The upper pin, on which the door turned.
        Fig. 2. Lower pin.   *Mr. Burton's Collection.*

wood-cut are in the possession of Mr. Burton, to whose kindness I am indebted for their insertion. They were fastened to the wood with nails of the same metal, whose round heads served also as an ornament, and the upper one had a projection at the back, in order to prevent the door striking against the wall.† We also find in the stone lintels

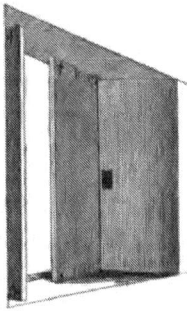

No. 101. A folding door.

. and floor, behind the thresholds of the tombs and temples, the holes in which they turned, as well as those of the bolts and bars, and the recess for receiving the opened valves. The folding doors had bolts in the centre, sometimes above as well as below : a bar was placed across from one wall to the other ; and in many instances wooden locks ‡ secured them by passing over the centre,

* *Vide* wood-cuts, Nos. 101 and 102. *fig.* 1.
† Wood-cut, No. 100. *fig.* 1. at *a.*
‡ *Vide* wood-cut, No. 102. *fig.* 2. I suppose wooden from their colour.

at the junction of the two folds. It is difficult
to say if these last were opened by a key, or merely

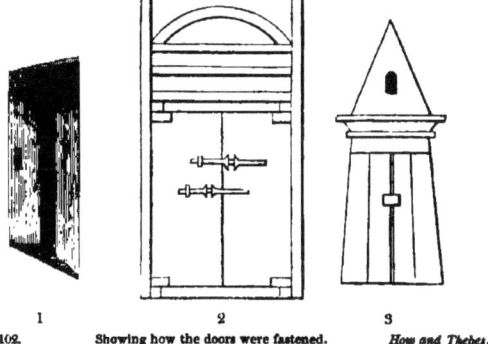

No. 102.   Showing how the doors were fastened.   *How and Thebes.*

slided backwards and forwards, like a bolt; but, if
they were really locks, it is probable they were
upon the principle of those now used in Egypt,
which are of wood, and are opened by a key
furnished with several fixed pins, answering to a
similar number that fall down into the hollow
moveable tongue, into which the key is introduced,
when they fasten or open the lock. For greater
security, they are occasionally sealed with a mass
of clay; and that this was also customary among
the ancient Egyptians we have satisfactory evidence, from some tombs found closed at Thebes,
as well as from the sculptures *, and the account given † by Herodotus of Rhampsinitus's

---

* *Vide* wood-cut, No. 102. *fig.* 3., where the door of the tomb is so
closed.

† Herodot. ii. 121. " The seals being entire and the door locked
(bolted)."

treasury. According to the scholiast of Aratus, " the keys of Egyptian temples bore the figure of a lion, from which chains were suspended having a heart attached to them ;" alluding, as he supposes, to the beneficial effects of the inundation, and the period of its commencement, when the sun was in the sign leo ; but not only were keys so ornamented, — the extremity of the stone spouts which conveyed the water from the roofs of the temples, projecting bosses upon the sides or handles of vases *, the prows of boats, funeral stands or biers, chairs, and numerous other objects of furniture were decorated with the same favourite emblem. Every deity, figure, and symbol, were formerly pronounced by the speculations of antiquaries to be connected with the sun ; and all capricorns, bulls, and scorpions were, with innocent simplicity, referred to their first parents in the zodiac ; but we may venture to believe the choice of the Egyptians was directed to an ornament common and popular in every country, and at all ages, without being under any obligation to the accidental form of a constellation.

At a later period, when iron came into general use, keys were made of that metal, and consisted of a long straight shank, about five inches in length,

No. 103.   Iron key, in my possession.

* I have a very elegant glass head of a lion in relief, probably from a vase.

and a bar at right angles with it, on which were three or more projecting teeth : and the ring at the upper extremity was intended for the same purpose as that of our modern keys; but we are ignorant of the exact time when they were brought into use, and the first invention of locks, distinct from bolts, is equally uncertain; nor do I know of any positive mention of a key, which, like our own, could be taken out of the lock, previous to the year 1336 before our era; and this is stated to have been used to fasten the door of the summer parlour of Eglon, the king of Moab.*

Egyptian doorways were generally surmounted by the usual cornice†, but many were decorated according to the taste of the person of the house.

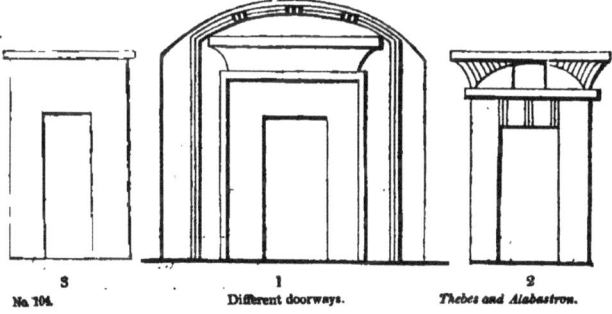

3   1   2
No. 104.   Different doorways.   Thebes and Alabastron.

* Judges, iii. 23. 25. "Ehud went forth through the porch, and shut the doors of the parlour upon him, and locked them" . . . . and "his servants . . . . took a key, and opened them."

† The niche at Persepolis, given in Sir R. Ker Porter's work, pl. li., calls to mind the Egyptian door. *Vide* wood-cut, No. 104. *fig.* 1.

In some the cornice was divided by a curved line*, others were simple†, and many of those in the tombs were charged with a profusion of ornament, and richly painted.‡   The doors opened inwards,

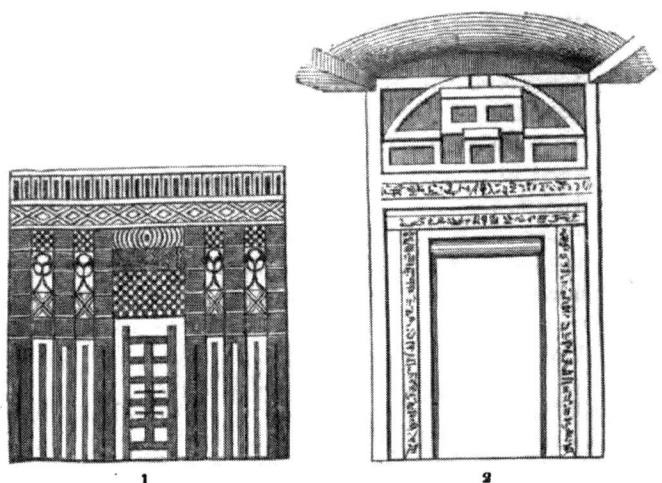

No. 105.   Ornamented doorways in the interior of tombs.   Thebes.

as well those of the rooms as the *janua* or street-door, contrary to the custom of the Greeks, who were consequently obliged to strike on the inside before they opened it, in order to warn persons passing by to keep at a distance.   The Romans resembled the Egyptians in this respect, and they

* *Vide* wood-cut, No. 104. *fig.* 2.
† *Vide* wood-cut, No. 104. *fig.* 3.
‡ *Vide* wood-cut, No. 105. *figs.* 1, 2.

were forbidden to open a street-door outwards without a special permission.*

Sometimes the door of an Egyptian house was in the centre, at others on the side of the court, or of the house itself; but I have found few instances of a flight of steps before the entrance, nor, indeed, is it usual in the towns of modern Egypt. The columns of the porch and corridors were coloured, and, when of wood, they were stained to represent stone; and this fondness for imitating more costly materials, as hard stone and rare woods, proves their love of show, and argues a great advancement in the arts of civilised life.

The floors were sometimes of stone, or a composition made of lime and other materials, and the roofs of the rooms were supported by rafters of the date tree, arranged close together†, or, more gene-

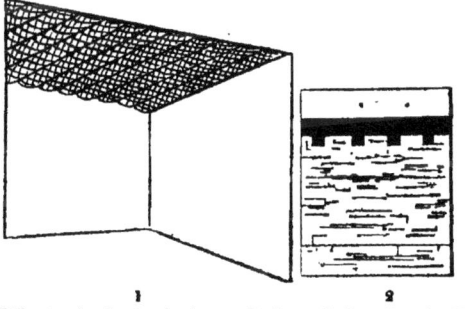

1   2

No. 106. Different modes of roofing chambers.   *Tombs near the Pyramids, and at Thebes.*

* As in the case of P. Valerius Poplicola and his brother. Plin. xxxvi. 15.

† I have only met with one representation of it, in a tomb behind the great pyramid. *Vide* wood-cut, No. 106. *fig.* 1.

rally, at intervals*, with transverse layers of palm
branches, or planks.   Many roofs were vaulted, and
built, like the rest of the house, of crude brick ; and
there is reason to believe that some of the chambers
in the pavilion of Remeses III., at Medeenet Haboo,
were arched with stone, since the devices on the
upper part of their walls show that the fallen roofs

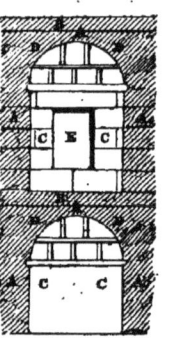

A. The part against which the other walls stood.
B. The level of the flooring of the rooms.
C. Inside walls of the rooms.
D. Indications of the rooms having been vaulted.
E. Window.

No. 107.   Traces of arched rooms.   Thebes.

had this form. †   At Saqqára, a stone arch still exists
of the time of the second Psamaticus, and, consequently, erected 600 years before our era ; nor can
any one, who sees the style of its construction, for
one moment doubt that the Egyptians had been long
accustomed to the erection of stone vaults.

It is highly probable that the small quantity of

---

* In the walls that remain, we sometimes find the places of the
beams, at others the signs of vaulted roofs.   *Vide* wood-cut, No. 106.
fig. 2.
   † *Vide* wood-cut, No. 107. at D D.

wood in Egypt, and the consequent expense of this
kind of roofing, led to the invention of the arch; it
was evidently used in their tombs as early as the
commencement of the eighteenth dynasty*, or
about the year 1540, B.C.; and, judging from some
of the drawings at Beni Hassan, it seems to have
been known in the time of the first Osirtasen, whom
I suppose to have been contemporary with Joseph.
So little timber, indeed, was there in the valley of
the Nile, that they were obliged to import cedar
and deal from Syria; and we therefore find those
woods, as well as sycamore, mimosa, and others of
native growth, in the tombs of Thebes. Rare woods
were also part of the tribute imposed on foreign
nations conquered by the Egyptians; and the sculptures inform us that they supplied them with
ebony, and various other kinds, which were required
for useful or ornamental purposes.

On the ground-floor of some houses, besides the
store-rooms, were receiving and sitting apartments;
and the upper part of the building contained those
for entertaining guests †, for sleeping, and, generally
speaking, the family chambers. Though in the
plans of their houses there is no indication of the
mill, it is reasonable to conclude it was either in
one of the rooms on the ground-floor, or in a court
connected with the house, as is usual at the present
day in Cairo and other towns of Egypt; and we

* In a tomb I found at Thebes, bearing the name of Amunoph I.
Vide my Egypt and Thebes, p. 81. and 126. Another has been discovered there of the time of Thothmes III.

† Conf. Mark, xiv. 15. " A large upper room furnished, there make
ready."

i 3

have authority for believing that, like the early
Romans*, their bread was made at home; the
wealthy having a baker† in the house, and women
performing that office in establishments of a smaller
scale, and among the poorer classes.   It was not in
Egypt alone that women were so employed: the
custom was prevalent also in Greece, in the days
of Homer‡, and even among the Romans, as it still
is in the valley of the Nile, and in other eastern
countries; and the Bible history distinctly states it
to have been the duty of a maid-servant to grind
corn, in the houses of the Egyptians.§

Their mills were of simple and rude construction.
They consisted of two circular stones, nearly flat,
the lower one fixed, while the other turned on a
pivot, or shaft, rising from the centre of that beneath
it; and the grain, descending through an aperture in
the upper stone, immediately above the pivot, gradually underwent the process of grinding as it
passed. It was turned by a woman, seated, and holding a handle, fixed perpendicularly near the edge;
and the hand-mill adopted by the modern Egyptian
peasants is probably borrowed from, and similar‖

---

* Pliny says, "There were no bakers at Rome..... till after the year
580 from the building of the city. The Romans made their bread at
home; and this was among the occupations of women, as it still is in
many countries." xviii. 11.

† Gen. xl. 2. 5. " The chief of the bakers;" " The baker of the
King of Egypt."

‡ Hom. Od. vii. 104. : —

" Πεντεκοντα δε οι δμωαι κατα δωμα γυναικες,
Αι μεν αλετρευουσι μυλης επι μηλοπα καρπον,
Αι δ' ιστους υφοωσι και ηλακατα στρωφωσιν,
Ημεναι."

§ Exod. xi. 5. " From the first-born of Pharaoh . . . . even unto
the first-born of the maid-servant that is behind the mill."

‖ I judge from fragments of the old stones which have been found.

to, that of their predecessors. They had also a large mill, on a very similar principle; but the stones were of far greater power and dimensions; and this could only have been turned by cattle or asses, like those of the ancient Romans, and of the modern Cairenes. The stone of which the hand-mills were made was usually a hard grit; and there is evidence, from an inspection of the site of He-liopolis, that the beds from which it is still taken, lying behind the mountains of the Mokuttum, near Cairo, were quarried by the inhabitants of that city for the same purpose; and many of the larger mill stones, which were usually of granite, have been found amidst the crumbled ruins of ancient towns.

On the top of the house was a terrace, which served as well for a place of repose as for exercise during the heat; since, being covered with a roof supported by columns, the sun was excluded, and a

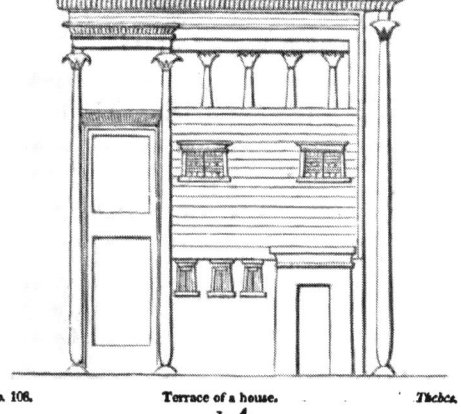

No. 108.   Terrace of a house.   Thebes.

1 4

refreshing stream of air passed through it. It was here, too, that they slept at night in the summer season, like the modern inhabitants of the country; and, according to Herodotus, they protected them-selves from the gnats by a (mosquito) net, or trusted to the current of wind passing over this elevated space, to prevent the visits of those troublesome insects.* The floors of the rooms were flat on the upper side, whether the roofs beneath were vaulted, or supported on rafters ; and instead of the covered

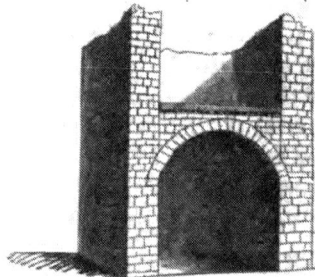

No. 109.   Flooring over an arched room.   *Thebes.*

terrace above mentioned, the upper chambers and passages were frequently surmounted by the wooden *mulquf*†, or wind conductor, still so common in eastern towns. It was open to the wind, and a con-stant stream passed down its slope; nor does there

---

* Herodotus says, that those who live in the low lands use the *same* net with which they fish in the day ; and the people of the upper part of the country sleep on a lofty tower, which the gnats are prevented by the wind from reaching. I have taken the liberty of suggesting a mos-quito net instead of the one he mentions, which would have been a poor protection from insects so cruelly resolute as to bite through the sleeper's clothes, as the historian affirms (ii. 95.).

† I use the Arabic name. *Vide* vignette E at the head of this chap-ter, which shows them on the houses of Cairo.

appear to have been any other difference in its
form from those of the present day, than that it
was double, and faced in two opposite directions,

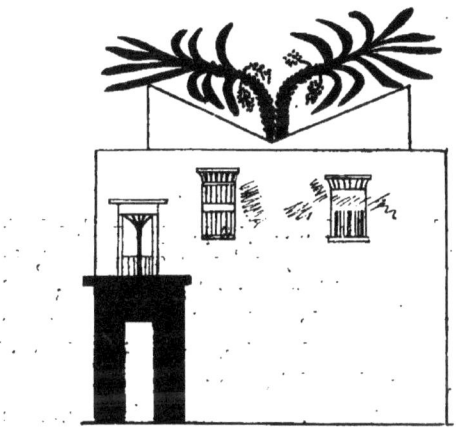

No. 110.   The mulquf for catching the wind.   *Thebes.*

the mulqufs of modern Egypt being directed only
towards the prevailing north-west wind. These last
consist of strong framework, to which several planks
of wood are nailed, according to the breadth and
length proposed; and if required of cheaper materials, the place of planks is supplied by reeds or
mats, covered with stucco, protected and supported
by wooden rafters : and it is probable that those
of former times were of a similar construction.

Sometimes a part of the house exceeded the
rest in height, and stood above the terrace like a
tower[*]; and this was ornamented with columns,

* *Vide* wood-cut, No. 111.

or with square panels, in the manner of false windows.

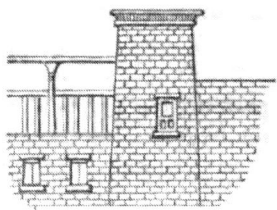

No. 111.   Tower rising above the terrace.   *Thebes.*

Other houses had merely a parapet wall, which surrounded the terrace, and was surmounted, in some instances, with a row of battlements; and though a similar style of building belonged more particularly to fortified castles, or to the palace of the king, they adopted it, like many Europeans of the present day, as an ornamental finish to a more peaceful habitation. The Egyptian battlements were an imitation of shields : which, doubtless, sug-

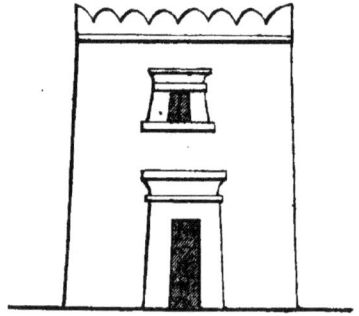

No. 112.   House with battlements.   *Thebes.*

gested the first idea of this mode of protecting the besieged, while they annoyed the assailants with missiles from the parapet; and the corners of the building always presenting a half shield, probably gave rise to that ornament so commonly used on Greek and Roman tombs; unless it was borrowed from a rude imitation of the body itself, like the lid of an Egyptian mummy-case, which was a representation of the person it contained.

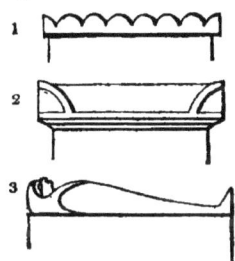

Fig. 1. Egyptian battlements.
    2. Top of a Greek or Roman sarcophagus.
    3. Top of a mummy case.

No. 113.

Besides the owner's name, they sometimes wrote a lucky sentence over the entrance of the house, for a favourable omen, as " the good abode," the

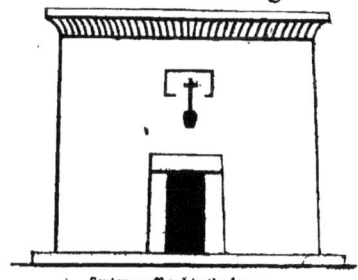

No. 114.   Sentence affixed to the house.   *Thebes.*

" *múnzel mobárak*" of the modern Arabs, or something similar; and the lintels and imposts of the doors, in the royal mansions *, were frequently covered with hieroglyphics, containing the ovals and titles of the monarch.

It was, perhaps, at the dedication of the house that these sentences were affixed †; and we may infer, from the early mention of this custom ‡ among the Jews, that it was derived from Egypt.; a conjecture greatly strengthened by the circumstance of our finding even the store-rooms, vineyards, and gardens of the Egyptians placed under the protection of a tutelary deity. §

Like the doors, the windows, or, properly speaking, the shutters, were closed with folding valves, secured in a similar manner with a bolt or bar, and ornamented with carved panels or coloured devices. The openings of the windows were small, upon the principle that where little light is admitted little heat penetrates ; and this custom has always been prevalent in the East, and even in the more temperate latitude of Italy. They were surmounted by cornices, resembling those of the doorways, and when on the passage or landing-place, over the street

---

* Besides their apartments in the temples, the kings, as well as the priests, had houses and villas.

† The modern Moslems write sentences from the Qorán, or commemorate the performance of the pilgrimage to Mekkeh by the owner of the house.

‡ Deut. xx. 5. " What man is there that hath built a new house, and hath not dedicated it ? Let him go and return to his house, lest he die in battle, and another man dedicate it."

§ It is worthy of remark, that this is retained by the modern Egyptians in the protecting genius supposed to preside over the different quarters of Cairo. *Vide* wood-cut, No. 142., and plate 10.

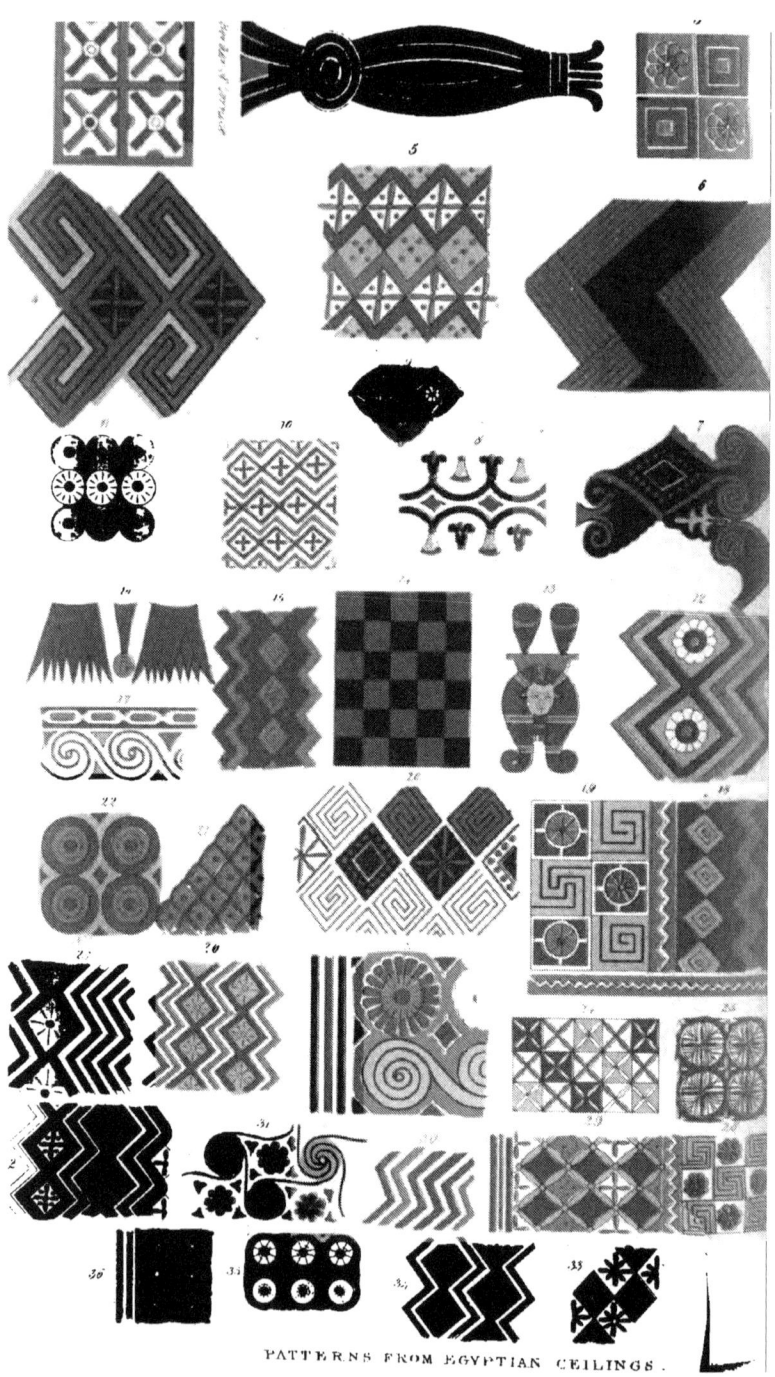

PATTERNS FROM EGYPTIAN CEILINGS.

door, they had occasionally a sort of balcony, or at least a row of bars*, with a column in the centre.

The walls and ceilings were richly painted†, and frequently with admirable taste; but of their effect we can only judge from those of the tombs, where they are preserved far more perfectly than in the houses, few of which retain any vestiges of the stucco, or of the coloured devices that once adorned them. The ceilings were laid out in compartments, each having a pattern with an appropriate border; in many instances reminding us so strongly of Greek taste, that we should feel surprised to find them on monuments of the early periods of the 18th and preceding dynasties, if there was not authority for believing that the Greeks borrowed numerous devices from Egypt; and we may ascribe to the same origin the scarab, the harpy, and several of the ornamental emblems on Greek and Etruscan vases. The favourite forms were the lotus, the square, the diamond, the circle, and above all, the succession of scrolls, and square within square, usually called the Tuscan border, both which are of ordinary occurrence, on Greek and Etruscan, as well as Egyptian vases; and those given in the accompanying plate‡, from a tomb at E' Sioot, painted upon a black or dark bronze ground, though of an age prior to the year 1600 before our era, are perhaps the most elegant, and, which is very remarkable,

---

* As in wood-cut, No. 110.

† Conf. Jer. xxii. 14. " I will build a large house . . . . ceiled with cedar, and painted with vermilion."

‡ Plate 7. *figs.* 4. 7. and 20.

bear the nearest resemblance to a Greek style.
Similar designs were adopted by the Romans,
some of which, having been found in the baths
of Titus, gave Raphael the idea of his celebrated
and *novel* arabesques; and the paintings of Pompeii make us acquainted with a still greater variety.

That the Greeks and Romans far surpassed the
Egyptians in taste, and in the numerous combinations they used to adorn their rooms, is evident;
a natural result of the encouragement given to invention, which Egypt, fettered by regulations and
prejudices, preventing the developement of taste,
and cramping the genius of her artists, never enjoyed; but however the *laqueata tecta* of the Romans surpassed in richness and beauty of effect the
ceilings of an Egyptian house, divided as they
were into numerous compartments, presenting cornices, mouldings, and embossed fretwork, painted,
gilt, and even inlaid with ivory*, still in the general
mode of decoration, they, like the stuccoed walls,
bore a striking analogy to those in the mansions of
Thebes, and other cities on the Nile.

SHOPS.

The form and character of the shops depended
on the will, or peculiar trade, of the person to whom
they belonged; and many, no doubt, sat and sold

---

* Plin. xxxiii. 3., and xxxv. 40. Virg. Æn. i. 726. The ceilings
of Turkish palaces, executed by Greek artists, are frequently very
handsome, and display great elegance and taste. Their painted walls,
adorned with columns and various designs, are an imitation of the ancient style: but very inferior.

in the streets, as at the present day. Poulterers suspended geese and other birds from a pole, in front of the shop, which at the same time supported an awning to shade them from the sun;

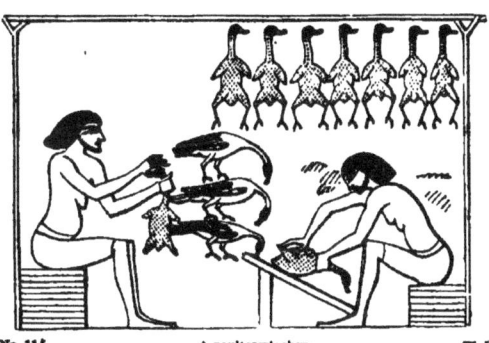

No. 114.   A poulterer's shop.   Thebes.

and many of the shops rather resembled our stalls, being open in front with the goods exposed on shelves, or hanging from the inner wall, as is still the custom in the bazars of eastern towns. But these belong more properly to a description of the trades.

VILLAS.

Besides the town houses, the Egyptians had extensive villas, which, with a very commodious mansion, contained spacious gardens, watered by canals communicating with the Nile. They had also tanks of water in different parts of the garden, which served for ornament, as well as for irrigation, when the Nile was low; and on these, the master of the house occasionally amused himself and friends, by an excursion in a pleasure-boat kept for the purpose. But, like the Orientals of the present day, or like people of the continent of Europe, who are incapable of understanding how the English can row for their amusement, the Egyptians were contented to sit, or stand in the boat, while their servants towed it round the lake; and, protected from the sun by a canopy, they felt additional pleasure in the contrast of their own ease with the labour of their menials.

They also amused themselves by angling, and spearing fish in the ponds within their grounds; and on these occasions they were generally accompanied by a friend, or one or more members of their family.

The mode of laying out the house and grounds varied according to circumstances. Some villas were of considerable extent, and, besides the arable land belonging to them, the gardens occupied a very large space, as did the offices and other buildings attached to the house.

Some large mansions appear to have been ornamented with propyla and obelisks, like the temples themselves; it is even possible that part of the building may have been consecrated to religious purposes, as the chapels of other countries, since we find a priest engaged in presenting offerings at the door of the inner chambers; and, indeed, but from the presence of women, the form of the garden, and the style of the porch, we should feel disposed to consider it a temple rather than a place of abode.*

* *Vide* wood-cut, No. 116.

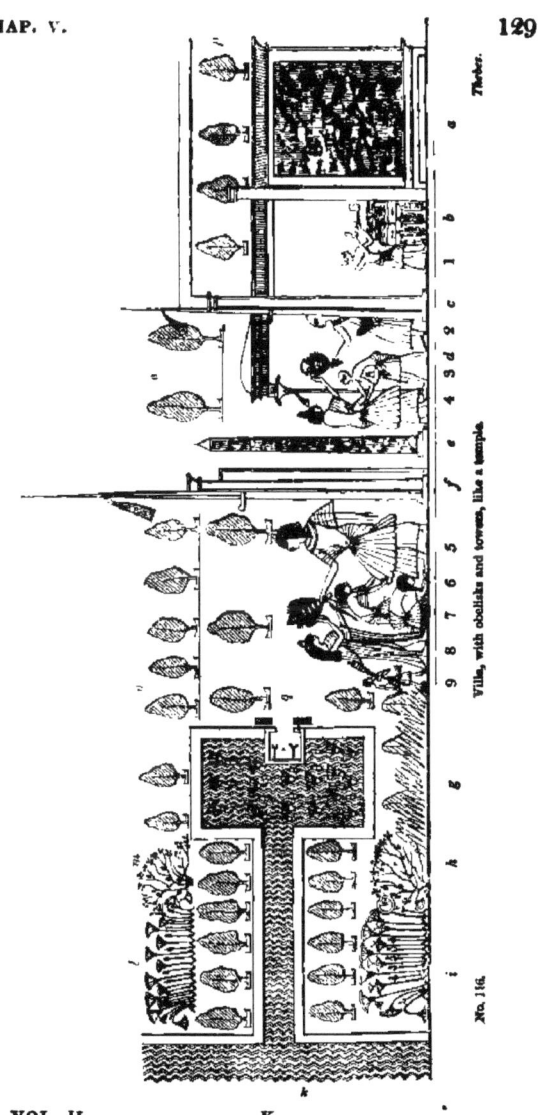

Villa, with obelisks and towers, like a temple.

No. 116.

Thebes.

The entrances of large villas were generally through folding gates, standing between lofty towers, as in the propylæa of temples*, with a small door at each side; and others had merely folding gates with imposts surmounted by a cornice.   A

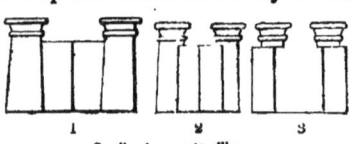

No. 117.   Small entrances to villas.   *Alabastron.*

wall of circuit extended round the premises; but the courts of the house, the garden, the offices, and all the other parts of the villa, had each their separate inclosure.   The walls were usually built of crude brick; and in damp places, or when within reach of the inundation, the lower part was strengthened by a basement of stone.   They were sometimes ornamented with panels and grooved lines †, generally stuccoed; and the summit was crowned either with Egyptian battlements, the usual cornice, a row of spikes in imitation of spear heads, or with some fancy ornament.

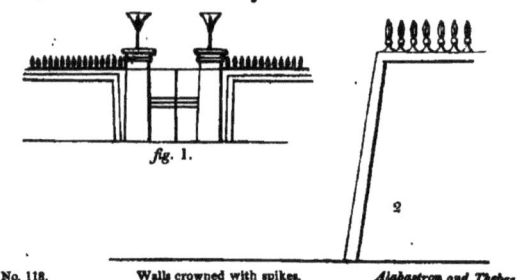

fig. 1.

2

No. 118.   Walls crowned with spikes.   *Alabastron and Thebes.*

* *Vide* elevation and plan of villa, plates 8. and 9.
† *Vide* wood-cut, No. 119.

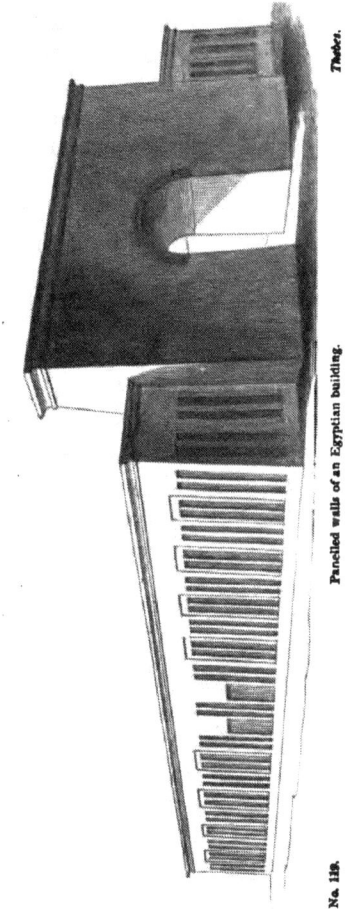

No. 113. Panelled walls of an Egyptian building. Thebes.

Those villas, or castles, belonging to the kings, which stood on the high road, where they were

K 2

accustomed to pass either in their hunting or military expeditions, were small and simple, being only
intended for their reception during the short stay
of a few days; but those erected in an enemy's
country may rather be looked upon as forts, than
as simple mansions.   Many, however, in provinces
at a distance from Egypt, were of very large dimensions, and had probably all the conveniences of
spacious villas; like those erected in later times by
the Ptolemies, on the confines of Abyssinia.

In order to give an idea of the extent of some of
their villas, it will be necessary to describe the plan
and arrangement of the different parts. *   About
the centre of the wall of circuit was the main entrance, and two side gates, leading to an open walk
shaded by rows of trees.   Here were spacious tanks
of water, which faced the door of the right and left
wing of the house, and between them an avenue led
from the main entrance to the stables, and to what
may be called the centre of the mansion.   After
passing the outer door of the right wing, you entered
an open court with trees, extending quite round a
nucleus of inner apartments, and having a back
entrance communicating with the garden.   On the
right and left of this court were six or more store-
rooms, a small receiving or waiting room at two
of the corners, and at the other end the staircases
which led to the upper story.   Both of the inner
façades were furnished with a corridor, supported
on columns, with similar towers and gateways.
The interior of this wing consisted of twelve rooms,
two outer and one centre court, communicating by

* *Vide* Plates 8. and 9.

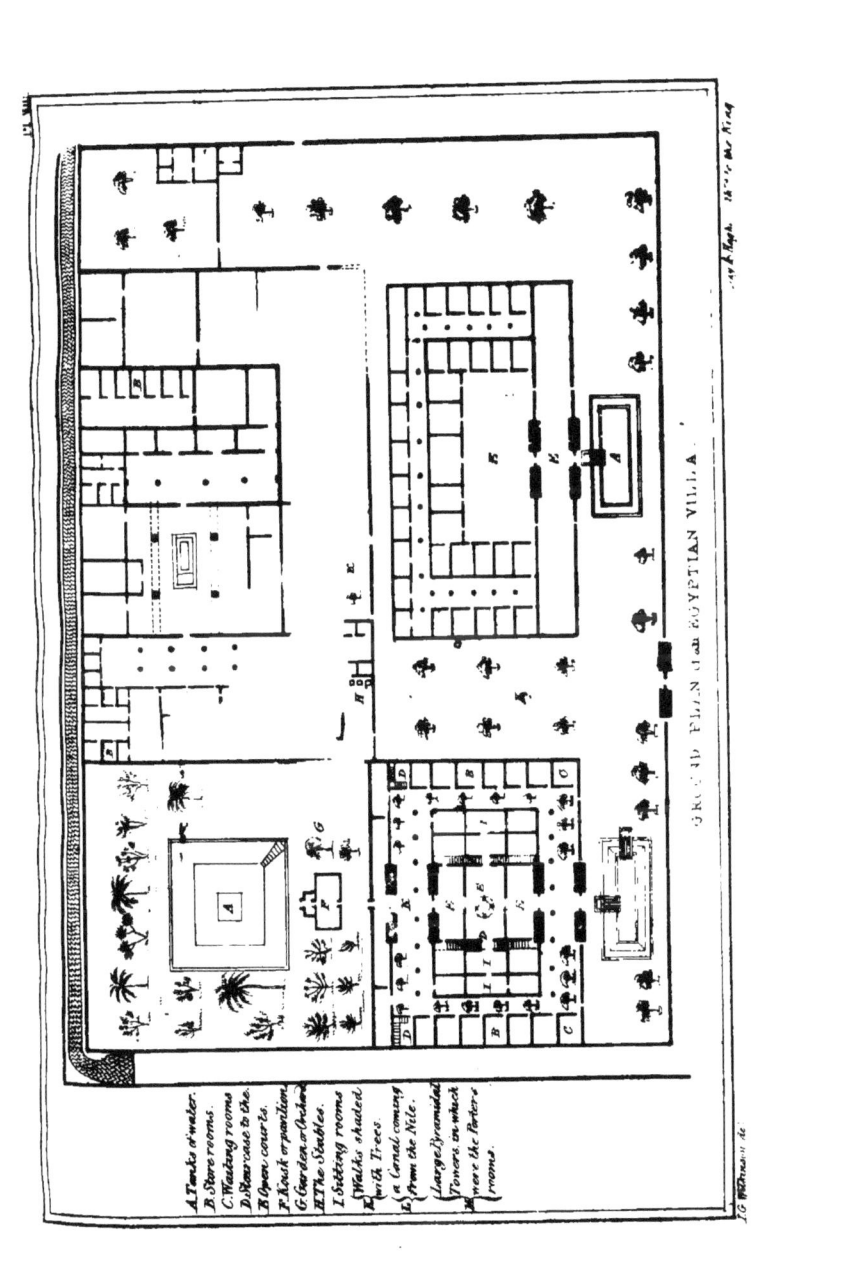

GROUND PLAN of an EGYPTIAN VILLA.

A. Tanks of water.
B. Store rooms.
C. Waiting rooms.
D. Stair-case to the.
E. Open courts.
F. Kiosk or pavilion.
G. Garden or Orchard.
H. The Stables.
I. Sitting rooms.
K. Walks shaded with Trees.
L. a Canal coming from the Nile.
(Large Pyramidal Towers on which were the Porters rooms.

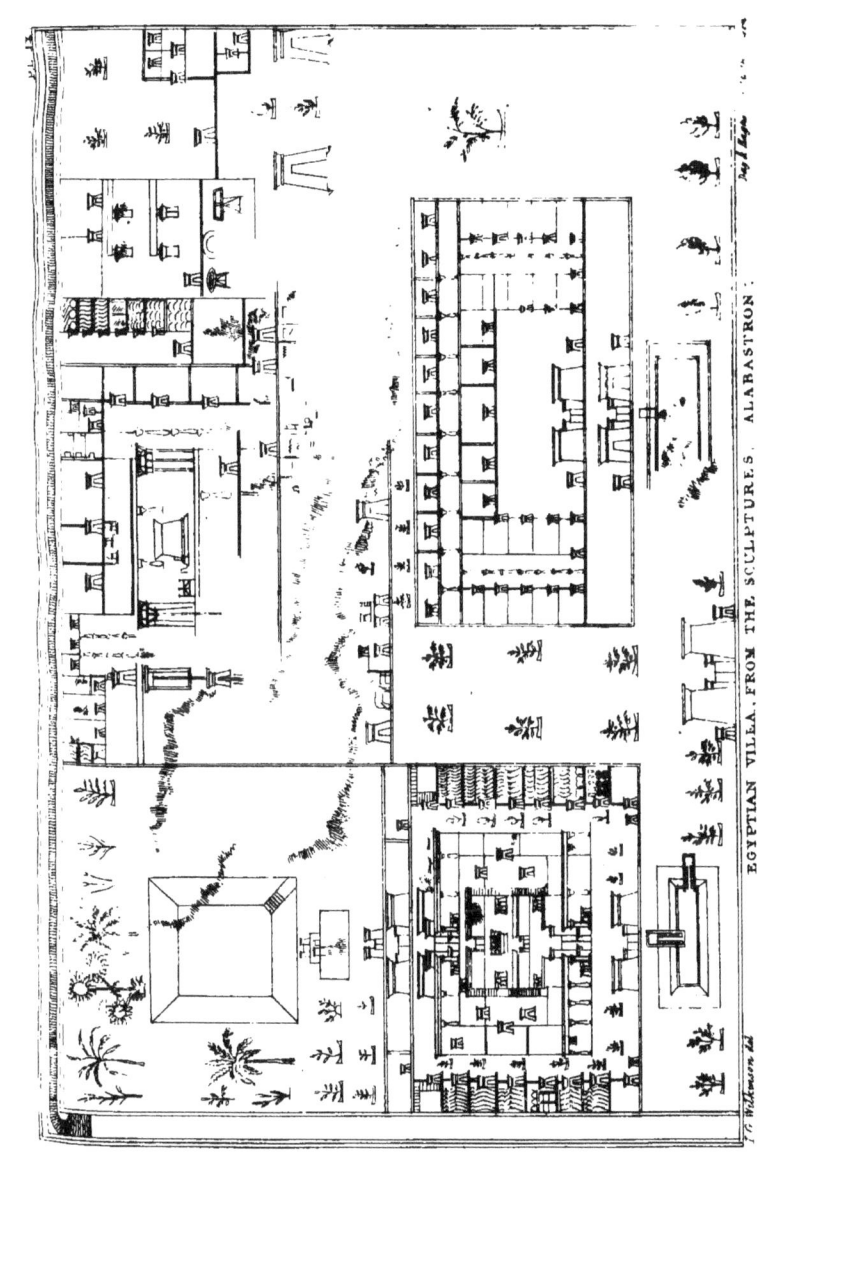

EGYPTIAN VILLA, FROM THE SCULPTURES, ALABASTRON.

folding gates ; and on either side of this last was the main entrance to the rooms on the ground-floor, and to the staircases leading to the upper story. At the back were three long rooms, and a gateway opening to the garden, which contained a variety of fruit trees, a small summer-house, and a tank of water.

The arrangement of the left wing was different. The front gate led to an open court, extending the whole breadth of the façade of the building, and backed by the wall of the inner part. Central and lateral doors thence communicated with another court, surrounded on three sides by a set of rooms, and behind it was a corridor, upon which several other chambers opened.

This wing had no back entrance, and, standing isolated, the outer court extended entirely round it; and a succession of doorways communicated from the court with different sections of the centre of the house, where the rooms, disposed, like those already described, around passages and corridors, served partly as sitting apartments, and partly as store-rooms.

FARM-YARD.

The stables for the horses, and the coach-houses for the travelling chariots* and *plaustra*, were in the centre, or inner part of the building†; but the

---

* "Joseph made ready his chariot." Gen. xlvi. 29. The difference between the plaustra and these chariots, or curricles, was that the latter were drawn by horses, the former by oxen.

† Vitruvius says, " The stable, especially in the villa, should be in the warmest place, and not with an aspect towards the fire, for if horses are stalled near a fire their coats soon become rough ; hence those stalls are excellent which are away from the kitchen, in the open space towards the east." Lib. vi. c. 9.

farm-yard where the cattle were kept stood at some distance from the house, and corresponded to the department known by the Romans under the name of *rustica*. Though enclosed separately, it was within the general wall of circuit, which surrounded the land attached to the villa; and a canal, bringing water from the river, skirted it, and extended along the back of the grounds. It consisted of two parts: the sheds for housing the cattle, which stood at the upper end, and the yard, where rows of rings were fixed, in order to tie them while feeding in the day-time: and men always attended, and frequently fed them with the hand.

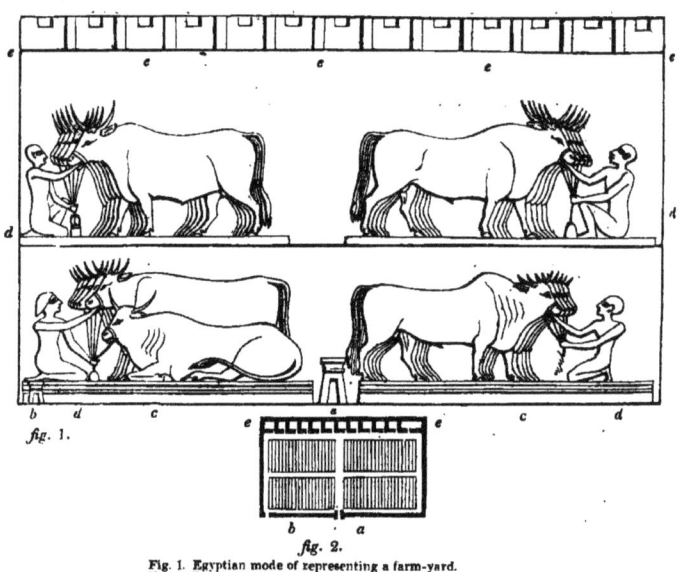

fig. 1.

fig. 2.

Fig. 1. Egyptian mode of representing a farm-yard.
Fig. 2. The supposed ground-plan of the same.

Alabastron.

GRANARIES.

The granaries* were also apart from the house, and were enclosed within a separate wall, like the *fructuaria* of the Romans; and some of the rooms in which they housed the grain appear, as I have already observed, to have had vaulted roofs. These

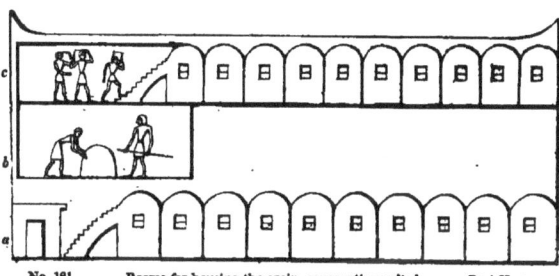

No. 121.   Rooms for housing the grain, apparently vaulted.   *Beni Hassan*.

were filled through an aperture near the top, to which the men ascended by steps, and the grain when wanted was taken out from a door at the base.†

STEWARDS.

The superintendence of the houses and grounds was intrusted to stewards‡, who regulated the tillage of the land, received whatever was derived from the sale of the produce, overlooked the returns

* Vitruvius, in like manner, recommends " the barn; bay room, meal room, and mill, to be without the boundaries of the villa, being thereby rendered more secure from fire." Lib. vi. 9.
† *Vide* wood-cut, No. 122.
‡ The villicus of the Romans.

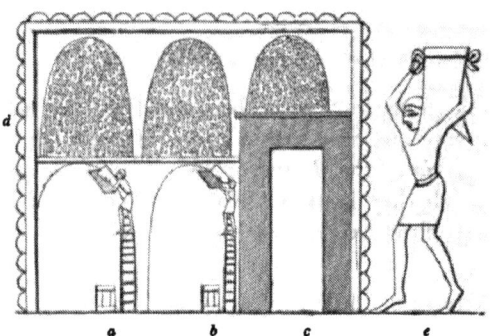

No. 122. — Granary, showing how the grain was put in, and that the doors *a b* were
intended for taking it out. *Thebes.*

of the quantity of cattle and stock upon the estate,
settled all the accounts, and condemned the delinquent peasants to the bastinado, or any punishment
they might deserve. To one were intrusted the
affairs of the house*, another overlooked the culture of the fields; and the extent of their duties, or
the number of those employed, depended on the
quantity of land, or the will of its owner.

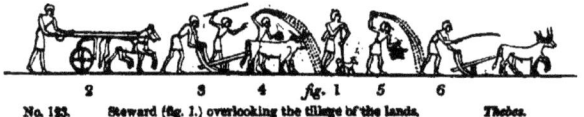

  2   3 4 *fig.* 1 5 6

No. 123. Steward (fig. 1.) overlooking the tillage of the lands. *Thebes.*

GARDENS.

The mode of laying out their gardens was as
varied as that of the houses; but in all cases they

* Gen. xliii. 16. "The ruler of his (Joseph's) house;" and xliii.
19., "They came near to the steward of Joseph's house;" xliv. 1.,
"Joseph commanded the steward of his house;" and xxxix. 5.,
"overseer of his house."

appear to have taken particular care to command a plentiful supply of water*, by means of reservoirs and canals. Indeed, in no country is artificial irrigation more required than in the valley of the Nile ; and, from the circumstance of the water of the inundation not being admitted into the gardens, they depend throughout the year on the supply obtained from wells and tanks, or the vicinity of a canal.

The mode of irrigation adopted by the ancient Egyptians was exceedingly simple, being merely the *shadóof*, or pole and bucket of the present day†; and, in many instances, men were employed to water the beds‡ with pails, suspended by a wooden yoke they bore upon their shoulders.

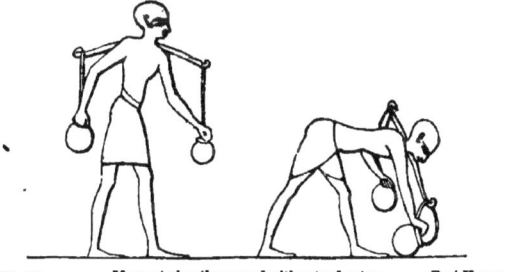

No. 194. Men watering the ground with pots of water. *Beni Hassan.*

The same yoke was employed for carrying other things, as boxes, baskets containing game and poultry, or whatever was taken to market; and

---

* Conf. Isaiah's comparison of " a garden that hath no water."
† *Vide* vignette D. and Vol. II., p. 4.
‡ " Egypt, where thou sowedst thy seed, and wateredst it with thy foot, as a garden of herbs." (Deut. xi. 10.) *Vide* Vol. II. p. 5.

every trade seems to have used it for this purpose, from the potter and the brick-maker*, to the carpenter and the shipwright.

One of them, which was found at Thebes, has been brought to England by Mr. Burton. The wooden bar or yoke is about three feet seven inches in length; and the straps, which are double, and fastened together at the lower as well as at the upper extremity, are of leather, and between fifteen and sixteen inches long. The small thong at the bottom not only served to connect the ends, but was probably intended to fasten a hook, or an additional strap, if required, to attach the burden: and though most of these yokes had two, some were furnished with four or eight straps; and the form, number, or arrangement of them varied according to the purposes for which they were intended.

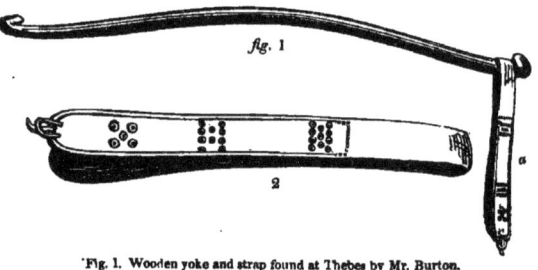

fig. 1

2

Fig. 1. Wooden yoke and strap found at Thebes by Mr. Burton.
Fig. 2. is the strap _a_, on a larger scale.
No. 125.

They do not appear to have used the water wheel, so universally employed in Egypt at the

* _Vide_ wood-cut, No. 93.

present day; and it is singular that they had devised no substitute for mere manual labour, if we except the hydraulic screw, which is said to have been a late introduction, and, according to Diodorus *, invented and first employed in Egypt by Archimedes. Indeed, if the foot machine mentioned by Philo was really a wheel turned by the foot, it cannot have been a very great relief to the labourer, and we must attach considerable blame to the priests for their indifference to the comforts of the people, when we contemplate the grandeur of their public buildings, and consider the great mechanical skill necessary for their erection.

The Egyptians were not singular in this neglect of useful improvements, or in their disregard for the waste of time and labour resulting from the use of such imperfect means : the same may be observed among the Greeks and Romans ; and those enlightened people, who bestowed the greatest attention upon ornamental objects, and who had arrived at a high degree of excellence in the manufacture of jewellery, and several articles of household furniture, were contented to remain on the level of barbarous communities in the imperfect style of many ordinary implements. To workmen who devised some novelty for adding to the splendour of a house, or the decoration of the person, great inducements were held out, by the certainty of immediate patronage; and their ingenuity, confident of reward, was naturally directed to such inventions. These

* Diod. i. 34., and lib. v., in treating of Spain. Strabo, xvii.

suited the caprices of a luxurious and wealthy
people, but they felt no disposition to repay the
laudable endeavours of an artist who suggested a
method for diminishing the toil of the lower classes;
and time and labour were deemed of far less value
than in modern days. All that was intended·for
external show, or was exposed to view*, was ex-
quisitely finished; but the keys and locks of that
door, whose panels, handles, and other external
parts, evinced no ordinary skill, were rude and imperfect: the latter, if they simply answered the purpose, satisfied; the former failed to ·please, unless
they promised to flatter the pride of their possessor,
by·commanding admiration.   The same remark
applies to the coarse and primitive construction of
the Roman mills; and these may justly be compared to the rude hydraulic mechanism of the ancient Egyptians.   Nor are these cases without a
parallel at the present day; and every one, who
visits the continent of Europe, must be struck with
a similar disregard to many improvements, which,
though long since known, and evidently tending to
comfort, and a decrease of labour, still continue to
be looked upon with indifference, while inventions
contributing to display and luxury are adopted on
their first appearance.

Water-skins were also used for irrigation by the
Egyptians, as well as for sprinkling the ground before the rooms or seats of the grandees†, and they

---

* This does not apply to Greek temples, where the parts concealed
from the spectator were wrought with the same care as the most exposed features.

† A common custom in the East.

were frequently kept ready filled at the tank for
that purpose.

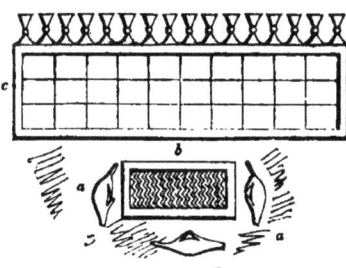

a a a Water-skins suspended close to the tank *b*.
  c Beds of a garden, laid out as at the present day in Egypt, very like our salt pans.
No. 196.   *Thebes.*

Part of the garden was laid out in walks shaded
with trees, usually planted in rows, and surrounded,
at the base of the stem, with a circular ridge of earth,
which, being lower at the centre than at the cir-
cumference, retained the water, and directed it
more immediately towards the roots.   It is difficult

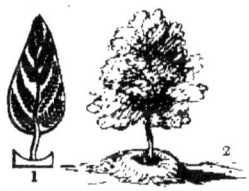

1. Tree with earth raised round the roots.
2. The same according to our mode of representing it.
No. 197.

to say if they were trimmed into any particular
shape, or if their formal appearance in the sculpture is merely owing to a conventional mode of
representing them; but, since the pomegranate,
and some other fruit trees, are drawn with spreading
and irregular branches, we might suppose that

sycamores, and others, which presented large masses
of foliage, were really trained in that formal manner; though from the hieroglyphic signifying
" *tree* " having the same shape, it may only be a
general character for all trees.

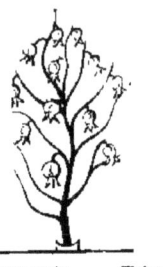

No. 128.   Pomegranate.   *Thebes.*   No. 129. Figurative hieroglyphic
                                                     signifying "tree."

Among the Romans, this mode of cutting trees
was confined to certain kinds, as the myrtle, laurel,
box, and others; and the office of trimming them
into different shapes was delegated to slaves, instructed in the art, or *opus topiarium**, from which
they received the name of *topiarii*.

The palms in the Egyptian sculptures are well
designed, and the *dôms* † may be easily recognised;
but most of the other trees and plants would per-
plex the most expert botanist, and few, except the
lotus, can be determined with certainty.

ORCHARD AND VINEYARD.

The large gardens were usually divided into
different parts; the principal sections being appro-

---

* *Vide* Plin. Nat. Hist. xv. 30., on the laurel.
† The Cucifera Thebaica, or Theban palm.

priated to the date and sycamore trees, and to the
vineyard. The former might be looked upon as
the orchard, but similar enclosures being also
allotted to other trees, they equally lay claim to this
name; we cannot therefore apply a fixed appellation to any part but the vineyard itself.

Gardens are frequently represented in the tombs
of Thebes and other parts of Egypt, many of which
are remarkable for their extent. The one, here introduced, is shown to have been surrounded by an

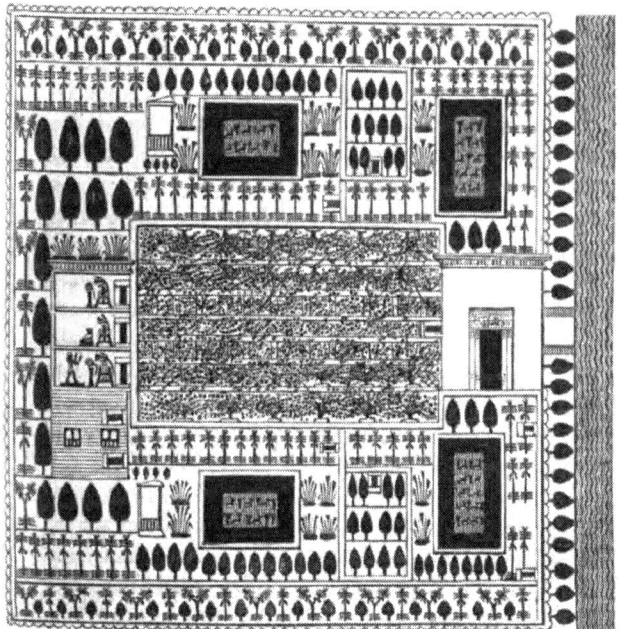

No. 150. — A large garden, with the vineyard and other separate enclosures, tanks of water, and a
small house.   From the Work of Prof. Rosellini.

embattled wall, with a canal of water passing in front
of it, connected with the river. Between the canal
and the wall, and parallel to them both, was a shady
avenue of various trees; and about the centre was
the entrance, through a lofty door, whose lintel and
imposts were decorated with hieroglyphic inscriptions, containing the name of the owner of the
grounds, who in this instance was the king himself.
In the gateway were rooms for the porter, and
other persons employed about the garden, and, probably, the receiving room for visitors, whose abrupt
admission might be unwelcome; and at the back,
a gate opened into the vineyard. The vines were
trained on a trellis-work, supported by transverse
rafters resting on pillars; and a wall, extending
round it, separated this part from the rest of the
garden. At the upper end were suites of rooms,
on three different stories, and the windows looking
upon green trees, and inviting a draught of air,
made it a pleasant retirement in the heat of summer. On the outside of the vineyard wall were
planted rows of palm trees, which occurred again
with the *dôms* along the whole length of the exterior
wall; four tanks of water, bordered by a grassplot,
where geese were kept, and the delicate flower of
the lotus was encouraged to grow, served for the
irrigation of the grounds; and small *kiosks* or summer houses, shaded with trees, stood near the water,
and overlooked beds of flowers. The spaces containing the tanks, and the adjoining portions of the
garden, were each enclosed by their respective
separate walls, and a small subdivision on either

side between the large and small tanks, seems to
have been reserved for the growth of particular
trees, which either required peculiar care, or bore
a fruit of superior quality.

In all cases, whether the orchard stood apart
from, or was united with, the rest of the garden,
it was supplied, like the other portions of it, with
abundance of water, preserved in spacious reservoirs, on either side of which stood a row of
palms, or an avenue of shady sycamores. Some-

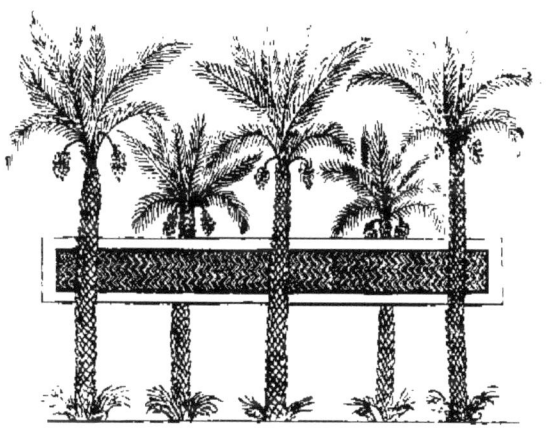

No. 131. — Egyptian mode of representing a tank of water with a row of palms on
either side.   *Thebes.*

times the orchard and vineyard were not separated
by any wall, and figs* and other trees were planted
within the same limits as the vines. But if not
connected with it, the vineyard was close to the

* Conf. Luke, xiii. 6. " A certain man had a fig-tree planted in his
vineyard," and 1 Kings, iv. 25. " Every man under his vine and under
his fig-tree."

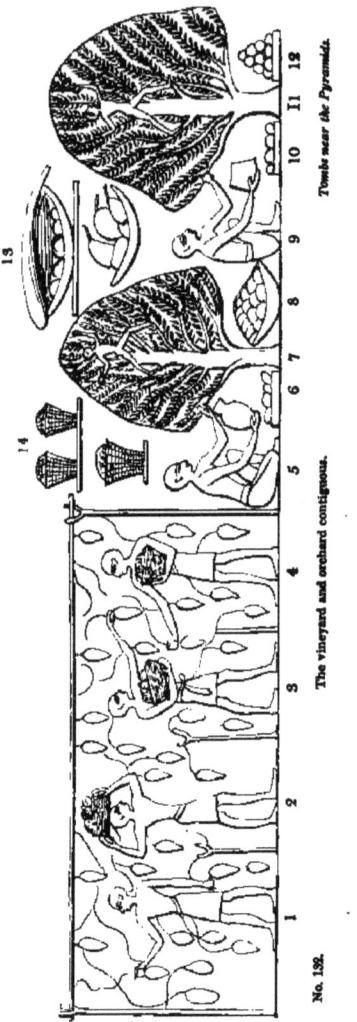

No. 132.

The vineyard and orchard contiguous.   Tombs near the Pyramids.

orchard*, and they displayed much taste in the mode of training the vines. Rows of columns, supporting wooden rafters, divided the vineyard into numerous avenues, which afforded great facility for communication from one end to the other, and retained a certain degree of moisture at the roots, by intercepting the rays of the sun.

The columns were frequently coloured, and were ornamental as well as useful ; but many were simple wooden pillars, supporting, with their forked summits, the poles that lay over them. Some vines were allowed to grow as standing bushes †, and, being kept low, did not require any support; others were formed into a series of bowers ; and from the form of the hieroglyphic, signifying vine-

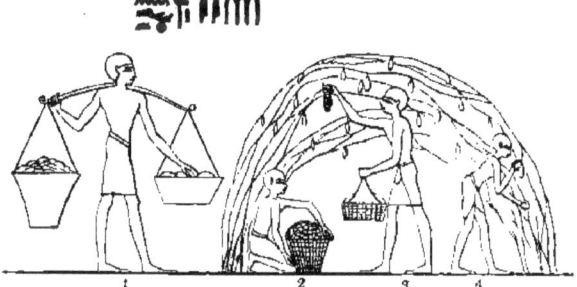

No. 133.   Plucking grapes in a vineyard : the vines trained in bowers.   *Thebes.*

yard, we may conclude that the most usual method of training them was in bowers, or in avenues formed by rafters and columns.‡   But they do not appear

---

* *Vide* wood-cut, No. 132.
† *Vide* wood-cut, No. 139., and plate 10. *fig.* 1.
‡ *Vide* wood-cut, No. 134.

to have attached them to other trees, like the Romans*, and the modern Italians†; nor have the

No. 134.   Figurative hieroglyphic signifying vineyard.

Egyptians of the present day adopted this European custom.

When the vineyard was enclosed within its own wall of circuit, it frequently had a reservoir of water attached to it, as well as the building which

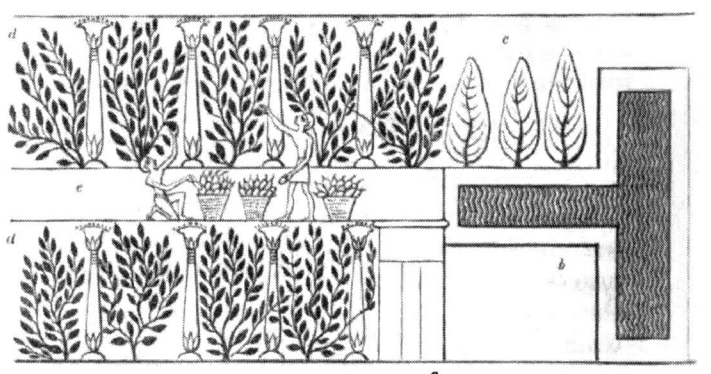

No. 135.   Vineyard, with a large tank of water, *b*.   *Thebes.*

* Hor. Epod. ii. 10. : —

"Adulta vitium propagine
Altas maritat populos."

Elms and poplars were generally used by the Romans : —

"Intexet vitibus ulmos." Virg. Georg. ii. 22.

The Romans also supported vines on reeds and poles. Plin. xvii. 22.
† They generally prefer the white mulberry tree.

contained the winepress* ; but the various modes
of arranging the vineyard, as well as the other
parts of the garden, depended, of course, on the
taste of each individual, or the nature of the
ground.   Great care was taken to preserve the
clusters from the intrusion of birds; and boys
were constantly employed, about the season of the
vintage, to frighten them with a sling and the sound
of the voice.†

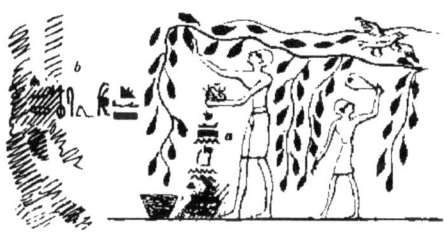

No. 136.   Frightening away the birds with a sling.   *Thebes.*

When the grapes were gathered, the bunches
were carefully put into deep wicker baskets‡, which
men carried, either on their head or shoulders, or
slung upon a yoke, to the winepress; but when intended for eating, they were put, like other fruits,
into flat open baskets, and generally covered with
leaves of the palm, vine, or other trees. §   These

---

* Conf. Isaiah, v. 1, 2., " And he fenced it (the vineyard), and
gathered out the stones thereof, and planted it with the choicest vine,
and built a tower in the midst of it, and also made a winepress therein,"
and Matthew, xxi. 33., " planted a vineyard . . . . and digged a winepress in it." *Vide* plate 10.

† Like the modern Egyptians, who strike large earthenware pots
instead of bells for the same purpose. They also use the sling.

‡ The " spisso vimine qualos " of the Romans. Virg. Georg. ii.
241.

§ *Vide* wood-cut, No. 137. and 132., *figs.* 8. and 13.

flat baskets were of wicker-work, and similar, no
doubt, to those of the present day, used at Cairo

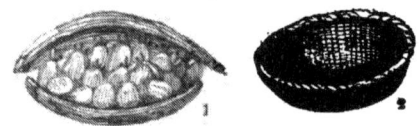

Fig. 1. Basket containing grapes covered with leaves, from the sculptures.
Fig. 2. Modern basket used for the same purpose.
No. 137.

for the same purpose, which are made of osiers or
common twigs. Monkies appear to have been
trained to assist in gathering the fruit, and the
Egyptians represent them in the sculptures handing

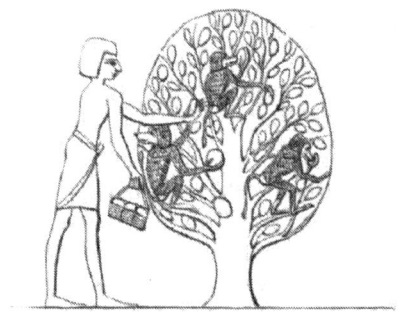

No. 138.   Monkies assisting in gathering fruit.   Beni-Hassan.

down figs from the sycamore trees to the gardeners
below : but, as might be expected, these animals
amply repaid themselves for the trouble imposed
upon them, and the artist has not failed to show
how much more they consulted their own wishes
than those of their employers.

Many animals were tamed in Egypt for various
purposes, as the lion, leopard, gazelle, baboon,

crocodile, and others; and in the Jimma country, which lies to the south of Abyssinia, monkies are still taught several useful accomplishments. Among them is that of officiating as torch-bearers at a supper party; and seated in a row, on a raised bench, they hold the lights until the departure of the guests, and patiently await their own repast as a reward for their services. Sometimes a refractory subject fails in his accustomed duty, and the harmony of the party is for a moment disturbed, particularly if an unruly monkey throws his lighted torch into the midst of the unsuspecting guests; but the stick, and privation of food, is the punishment of the offender; and it is by these persuasive arguments alone that they are prevailed upon to perform their duty in so delicate an office.

After the vintage was over, they allowed the kids * to browse upon the vines which grew as standing

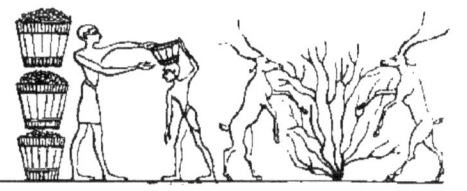

No. 139.   Kids allowed to browse upon the vines.   *Beni-Hassan.*

bushes; and the season of the year when the grapes ripened in Egypt was the month Epiphi †, to-

---

* The kids so fed were considered more delicate for the table. *Vide* Hor. ii. sat. iv. 43.: —

　　" Vinea summittit capreas non semper edules."

† Epiphi, or Epep, pronounced Ebib by the Copts. It began on the 25th of June.

wards the end of June, or the commencement of July. Some have pretended to doubt that the vine was commonly cultivated, or even grown, in Egypt; but the frequent notice of it, and of Egyptian wine, in the sculptures, and the authority of ancient writers*, sufficiently answer those objections; and the regrets of the Israelites on leaving the vines of Egypt prove them to have been very abundant, since even people in the condition of slaves could procure the fruit.†

WINEPRESS.

The winepress was of different kinds. The most simple consisted merely of a bag, in which the grapes were put, and squeezed, by means of two poles turning in contrary directions: a vase being placed below to receive the falling juice. The mode of representing it in Egyptian sculpture is not very intelligible, or in accordance with our notions of perspective; though we may easily understand that the man at the top of the picture‡ is in the act of pushing the poles apart, in order to stretch the bag§, as a *finale* to the process, the poles being at that time in a horizontal position, and opposite to each other. Another press, nearly on the same principle, consisted of a bag

---

* Athenæus, on the authority of Hellanicus, says, " The vine was first cultivated about Plinthine, a town of Egypt; to which circumstance Dion attributes the love of wine among the Egyptians," lib. i. 25. According to Strabo, it was grown in great abundance in the Mareotis and the Arsinoite nome. lib. 17.

† Numb. xx. 5.   Conf. also the butler of Pharaoh pressing the grapes into the king's cup. Gen. xl. 11.

‡ *Vide* plate 10., *fig.* 3.

§ It would be more reasonable to suppose that he pushed with his hands and one leg, while the other rested on the ground to support him.

Plate X.

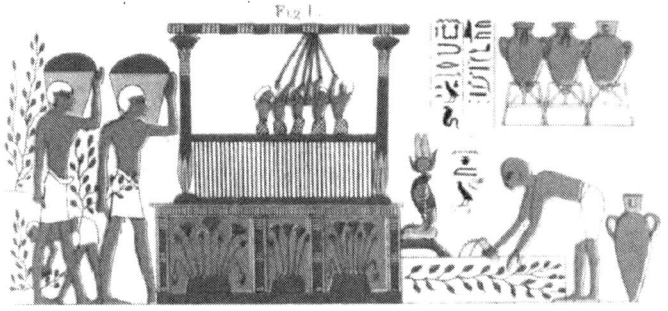

Fig. 1.

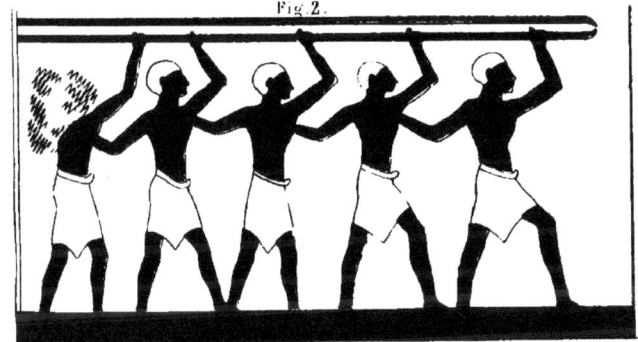

Fig. 2.

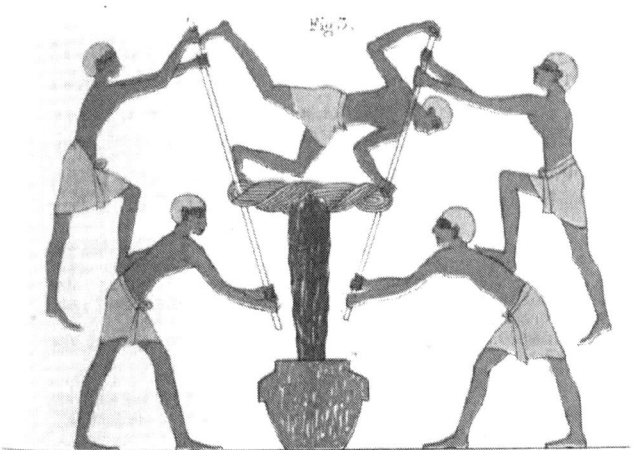

Fig. 3.

Printed in Colours by J & E Hughes.

WINE PRESSES.

such a mode of twisting or squeezing out the juice; but it appears that in this machine the grapes were crushed beneath a wooden beam (*prelum**), so that the process and principle were somewhat different; and we learn from Vitruvius that the Roman torcular was of two kinds, one turned by a screw, and the other by levers.

The two Egyptian handpresses were used in all parts of the country, but principally in Lower Egypt, the grapes in the Thebaïd being generally pressed by the feet. The footpress was also used in the lower country; and we even find the two methods of pressing the grapes represented in the same sculptures; it is not, therefore impossible† that, after having been subjected to the foot, they may have undergone a second pressure in the twisted bag. This does not appear to have been the case in the Thebaïd, where the footpress ‡ is always represented alone; and the juice was allowed to run off by a pipe directly to an open tank.

Some of the large presses were highly ornamented §, and consisted of at least two distinct parts: the lower portion or vat (*lacus*): and the

---

* Virg. Georg. ii. 242. Hor. Od. i. 9.: —

" prælo domitam caleno
tu bibes uvam."

† *Vide* plate 10., *fig.* 2. and 3. Or one of these may represent the pressing of grapes, the other of some other fruits.

‡ This sort of press was also used by the Jews. " I have *trodden* the winepress alone." Is. lxiii. 3. " In those days saw I in Judah some *treading* winepresses on the Sabbath." Nehem. xiii. 15., Judges, ix. 27. Virgil also notices the same custom, Georg. ii. 7.: —

. . . . . " nudataque musto
Tinge novo mecum direptis crura cothurnis."

§ *Vide* wood-cut, No. 141.

trough, where the men, with naked feet, trod the
fruit, supporting themselves by ropes suspended

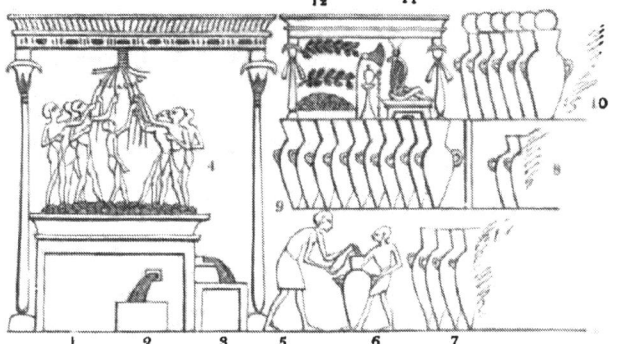

No. 141.— Large footpress; the amphora; and the protecting deity of the store-room, fig. 11.
Thebes.

from the roof; though, from their great height,
some might be supposed to have an intermediate
reservoir, which received the juice in its passage
to the pipe, answering to the strainer, or *colum,*
of the Romans.

A comparison of ancient customs is always a subject of great interest, particularly when the same
scenes are treated in the paintings of an early age;
I shall therefore introduce the representation of a
Roman winepress, from the mosaics of a supposed
Temple of Bacchus *, at Rome, which not only
serves to illustrate the description of Latin authors,
but to show its resemblance to the footpress of the
ancient Egyptians. †

* By some supposed to be of the time of Constantia. *Vide* a re-
mark on the adoption of the vine by the early Christians, in Hope's
Architecture, p. 180.
† *Vide* wood-cut, No. 142.

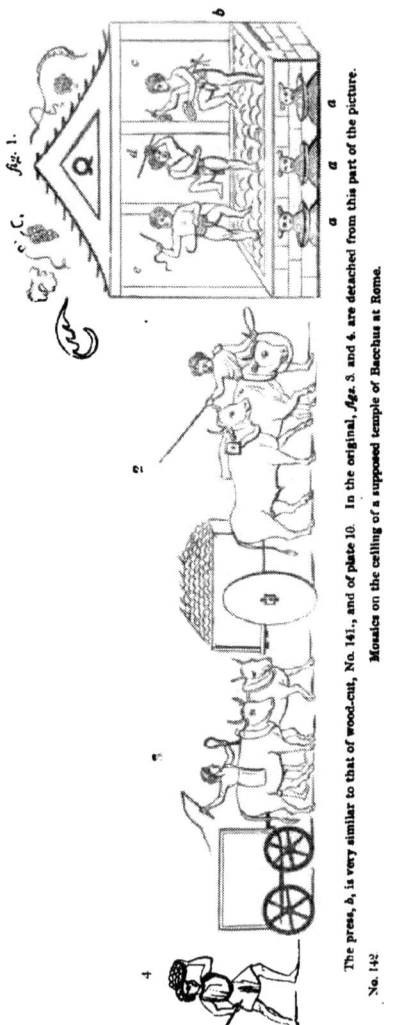

The press, b, is very similar to that of wood-cut, No. 141., and of plate 10.   In the original, figs. 3. and 4. are detached from this part of the picture.

Mosaics on the ceiling of a supposed temple of Bacchus at Rome.

No. 142.

After the fermentation was over, the juice was taken out in small vases, with a long spout, and poured into earthenware jars, which corresponded to the cadi, or amphoræ, of the Romans * : but

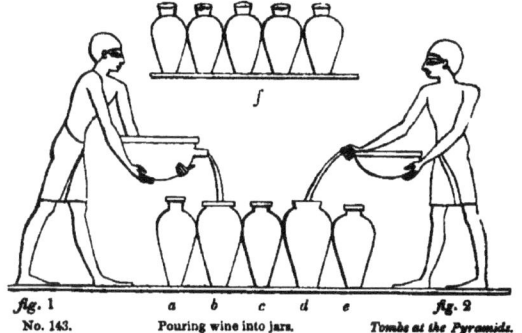

fig. 1   *a*   *b*   *c*   *d*   *e*   *fig.* 2
No. 143.   Pouring wine into jars.   *Tombs at the Pyramids.*

whether any thing was added to it after or previous to the fermentation, it is difficult to determine; though, from our finding men represented in the sculptures pouring some liquid from a small cup into the lower reservoir, we may conclude that this was sometimes the case.† When the *must* was considered in a proper state, the amphoræ were

* Amphoræ had properly two handles : they were very common in Egypt with and without them. Being of earthenware, the Romans also called them testæ. Conf. Hor. Od. i. 17. 2. : —

       " Græcâ quod ego ipse testâ
       Conditum levi."

The name amphora was likewise, and very properly, applied to a two-handled vase in which the wine was brought to table. Petron. Satyric. c. xxxiv. " Adlatæ sunt amphoræ vitreæ diligenter gypsatæ, quarum in cervicibus pittacia (labels) erant adfixa, cum hoc titulo, Falernum, Opimianum, annorum centum."

   † The Greeks put water into their wines. Plin. xiv. 19. " Græca (vina) quoniam aquam habeant." And even sea-water. Plin. xiv. 20. *Vide* pl. 10., *fig.* 1.

closed with a lid, resembling an inverted saucer,
covered with liquid clay, pitch, gypsum, mortar,

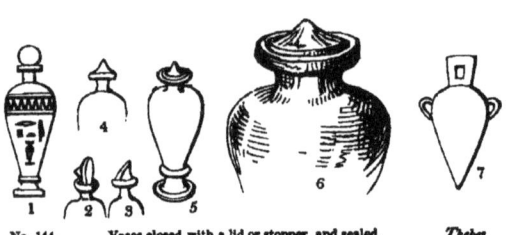

No. 144. Vases closed with a lid or stopper, and sealed. *Thebes.*

or other composition, which was stamped with a
seal : they were then removed from the winehouse,
and placed upright in the cellar.

WINES.

They generally put a certain quantity of resin or of
bitumen at the bottom of the amphora, previous to
pouring in the wine, which was intended to preserve
it, and was even supposed to improve its flavour ;
a notion, or rather an acquired taste, owing, probably, to their having at first used skins* instead of
jars : and the flavour imparted by the resin, which
was necessary to preserve the skins, having become,
from long habit, a favourite peculiarity of the wine,
it was afterwards added from choice, after they had
adopted the use of earthenware. And this custom,
formerly so general in Egypt, Italy, and Greece, is
still preserved throughout the islands of the Archi-

---

* According to Herodotus, wine was also carried in skins in the time
of Rhampsinitus, lib. ii. 121.

pelago. In Egypt, a resinous, or a bituminous substance is always found at the bottom of amphoræ which have served for holding wine; the Romans, according to Pliny*, employed the Brutian pitch, or resin of the picea pine, in preference to all others, for this purpose: and if, "in Spain, they used that of the pinaster, it was little esteemed, on account of its bitterness, and oppressive smell." In the East, the terebinthus was considered to afford the best resin, superior even to the mastic of the lentiscus; and the resins of Judæa and Syria only yielded in quality to that of Cyprus. This resinous coating for the interior of amphoræ was very generally used by the Romans, and was one of the numerous means† they had for preserving and improving the flavour ‡ of wine; and, besides smoking it, they sometimes boiled down a certain portion, which gave it a greater body, and insured its keeping.

The mode of arranging amphoræ in an Egyptian cellar was similar to that adopted by the Greeks and Romans. They stood upright in successive rows, the innermost set resting against the wall §; some-

---

* Plin. xiv. c. 20.

† Honey was also used. Pliny (xiv. 4.) mentions some wine nearly 200 years old.

‡ Plin. *loc. cit.* " Ut odor vino contingat, et saporis quædam acumina."

§ Homer Odyss. ii. 340. : —

> " εν δε πιθοι οινοιο παλαιου ηδοποτοιο
> εστασαν . . . .
> εξειης ποτι τοιχον αρηροτες . . . . "

The innermost row, being the last used, was the oldest wine; and this accounts for the expression of Horace, " interiore notâ Falerni." Hor. Od. ii. 3. 8. Each amphora being marked with the date of its wine. Hor. passim. *Vide* pl. 5. *figs. w, y.*

times each jar was secured by means ot a stone ring,
fitting round its pointed base, or was raised on a

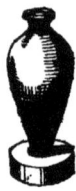

wooden stand ; and, from the position they are occasionally shown to have occupied *, we may conclude that many were placed in upper rooms, as the
amphoræ in a Roman *apotheca*.†

· The Egyptians had several different kinds of
wine, some of which have been commended by
ancient authors for their excellent qualities.   That
of Mareotis was the most esteemed ‡, and in the
greatest quantity.§   Its superiority over other
Egyptian wines may readily be accounted for, when
we consider the nature of the soil in that district ;
being principally composed of gravel, which, lying
beyond the reach of the alluvial deposit, was free
from the rich and tenacious mud usually met with
in the valley of the Nile, so little suited for the

* *Vide* wood-cut, No. 141.
† It was thought to ripen the wine; and hence Horace tells his amphora to come down : —
    " descende . . . . promere languidiora vina."   Od. iii. 15. 7.
    ‡ Plin. xiv. 3.   Hor. i. Od. xxxi. 14.   Athenæus says that of An-
thylla.
    § Strabo, lib. xvii.   " In this part (about the lake Mareia) is the
greatest abundance of wine."   Athen. Deipnosoph. i, 25. " πολλη δε η
περι την γην ταυτην αμπελος."

culture of delicate vines; and from the extensive
remains of vineyards still found on the western
borders of the Arsinoïte nome *, or Fyoóm, we
may conclude that the ancient Egyptians were
fully aware of the advantages of land situated
beyond the limits of the inundation, and that they
generally preferred similar localities, for planting
the vine. According to Athenæus, " the Mareotic
grape was remarkable for its sweetness," and the
wine is thus described by him : " Its colour is
white†, its quality excellent, and it is sweet and light
with a fragrant *bouquet;* it is by no means astringent, nor does it affect the head."   But it was not
for its flavour alone that this wine was esteemed,
and Strabo ascribes to it the additional merit of
keeping to a great age.‡   " Still, however," says
Athenæus, " it is inferior to the Teniotic, a wine
which receives its name from a place called Tenia,
where it is produced.   Its colour is pale and white,
and there is such a degree of richness in it, that
when mixed with water it seems gradually to be
diluted, much in the same way as Attic honey
when a liquid is poured into it : and besides the
agreeable flavour of the wine, its fragrance is so
delightful as to render it perfectly aromatic, and
it has the property of being slightly astringent.
There are many other vineyards in the valley of
the Nile, whose wines are in great repute, and these

---

* Near the Qaar Kharóon. Strabo mentions the abundance of vines
in this province, lib. xvii.
† Conf. Virg. Georg. ii. 91. :—
        " Sunt Thasiæ vites; sunt et Mareotides *albæ.*"
‡ Strabo, xvii. " ωστε διαχεισθαι προς παλαιωσιν τον Μαρειωτιν οινον."

differ both in colour and taste: but that which is produced about Anthylla is preferred to all the rest;" and Anthylla, as it is reasonable to suppose, was situated near the edge of the stony desert.[*] Some of the wine made in the Thebaïd was particularly light, especially about Coptos, and " so wholesome," says the same author, " that invalids might take it without inconvenience, even during a fever." The Sebennytic[†] was likewise one of the choice Egyptian wines; but, from the position of that town and nome, we may infer that it differed greatly in quality from those just mentioned, and that it was inferior in body as well as flavour. Pliny, however, cites it among the best of foreign wines, and says it was made of three different grapes, a sort of Thasian, the *œthalos*, and *peuce*. The Thasian grape he afterwards describes[‡] as excelling all others in Egypt in sweetness, and as being remarkable for its medicinal effects.

Another singular wine, called by Pliny *ecbolada* [§] (εκϐολας), was also the produce of Egypt; but, from its peculiar powers, we may suppose that men alone drank it, or at least that it was forbidden to newly married brides. And, considering how prevalent the custom was amongst the ancients of altering [||] the qualities of wines, by drugs and divers

---

* Herodotus says, that on going to Naucratis by the plain, in order to avoid the inundation, you pass by Anthylla (ii. 97.). According to Athenæus, the revenues derived from that city were bestowed on the queens of Egypt, both under the Persians and the native princes. lib. i. 25.
† Plin. xiv. 7.   ‡ Plin. xiv. 18.   § Plin. ibid.
|| Condiendi, medicandi, concinnandi vini. Plin. xiv. 20. It was also mixed or perfumed with myrrh and other ingredients. Plin. xiv. 13.

processes, we may readily conceive the possibility of the effects ascribed to them ; and thus it happened that opposite properties were frequently attributed to the same kind.

Wines were much used by them for medicinal purposes, and many were held in such repute as to be considered specifics in certain complaints. But the medical men of the day were prudent in their mode of prescribing them ; and as imagination has on many occasions effected the cure, and given celebrity to a medicine, those least known were wisely preferred, and each extolled the virtues of some foreign wine. In the earliest times, Egypt was renowned for drugs *, and foreigners had recourse to that country for wines as well as herbs ; yet Apollodorus, the physician, in a treatise on wines, addressed to Ptolemy, king of Egypt, recommended those of Pontus as more beneficial than any of his own country, and particularly praised the Peparethian †, produced in an island of the Ægean Sea ; but he was disposed to consider it less valuable as a medicine, when its good qualities could not be discovered in six years.

The wines of Alexandria and Coptos are also

Mark, xv. 23.　Diodor. iii. 61.　Hor. i. Sat. iv, 24.　J. Poll. Onom. vi. 2., and Martial, Epig.

"Si calidum potas, ardenti myrrha Falerno
　Convenit, et melior sit sapor inde mero." xiv. 113.

* Hom. Od. Δ. 229.　Jerem. xlvi. 11.

† Plin. xiv. 7. " Quod cunctis prætulit Peparethium." Some read Præparentium. Peparethos was one of the Cyclades, famous for its vines and olives. " Nitidæque ferax Peparethos olivæ." Ovid. Met. vii. 470. Athenæus, Deipnos. i. 52., quotes it from Aristophanes. Jul. Pollux. Onom. vi. 2.

cited among the best of Egyptian growth ; and the latter was so light as not to affect even those in delicate health.

In offerings to the Egyptian deities wine frequently occurs, and several different kinds are noticed in the sacred sculptures ; but it is probable that many of the Egyptian wines are not introduced in those subjects, and that, as with the Romans[*] and other people, all were not admitted at their sacrifices. It was in the temple of Heliopolis[†] alone that wine was totally forbidden in libations[‡], and when used by the priests in other places for this purpose, says Plutarch, " they poured it on the altars of the gods, as the blood of those enemies who had formerly fought against them." According to Herodotus[§] their sacrifices commenced with this ceremony[||], and some was also sprinkled on the ground where the victim lay : yet at Heliopolis, if Plutarch may be credited, it was forbidden to take it into the temple[¶], and the priests of the god worshipped in that city were required to abstain from its use. " Those of other deities," adds the same author, " were less scrupulous in these mat-

---

[*] Plin. xiv. 12. 19.

[†] Herodotus (ii. 63.) says, " those who go to Heliopolis and Buto only offer sacrifices."

[‡] Plut. de Is. s. 6. Romulus performed libations with milk. Plin. xiv. 12.

[§] Herodot. ii. 39.

[||] Conf. the Jewish custom "with the one lamb . . . flour mingled with . . . . oil and . . . . wine for a drink offering." Exod. xxix. 40.

[¶] I am inclined to believe that they did perform libations in the temple of Heliopolis as in other parts of Egypt ; and Herodotus says the custom was common *throughout* the country (ii. 39.). It may be supposed that Plutarch intends to say the priests of Heliopolis were forbidden to drink it *in the temple*, " it being indecent to do so under the eyes of their lord and king." *loc. cit.*

ters," but still they used wine very sparingly, and the quantity allowed them for their daily consumption was regulated by law; nor could they indulge in it at all times, and the use of it was strictly prohibited during their more solemn purifications, and in times of abstinence. The same writer also affirms, on the authority of Eudoxus, that it was wholly forbidden to the kings of Egypt, previous to the reign of Psamaticus; and, though we may feel disposed to question the truth of this assertion *, there is every probability that they were on the same footing in this respect as the priests, and that a certain quantity was allowed them, in accordance, as Hecatæus states, with the regulations of the sacred books.† The number of wines, mentioned in the lists of offerings presented to the deities in the tombs or temples, varies in different places. Each appears with its peculiar name attached to it; but they seldom exceed three or four kinds, and among them I have observed, at Thebes, that of the " northern country ‡," which was, perhaps, from Mareotis, Anthylla, or the nome of Sebennytus.

Private individuals were under no particular restrictions with regard to its use, and women were not forbidden it, whether married or single. In this they differed widely from the Romans: for in

* *Vide* Vol. I. p. 253., and Herod. ii. 133. The six last years of king Mycerinus's life.
† In spite of these regulations, the kings probably committed excesses on some occasions, like Mycerinus and Amasis. Herod. ii. 133. 173.
‡ Not a foreign production. Wine prepared by an unclean Greek would of course be excluded by the prejudices of an Egyptian from the altars of the gods, if not from the table.

early times no female at Rome enjoyed the privilege, and it was unlawful for women, or, indeed, for young men below the age of thirty, to drink wine, except at sacrifices.* And so scrupulous were they on this point, in the time of Romulus †, that Egnatius Mecennius caused his wife to be put to death for infringing this law, as if guilty of a crime. Such was the custom at the earliest periods of Roman history; and even at a later time prejudice pronounced it disgraceful for a woman to drink wine; and they sometimes saluted a female relation ‡, whom they suspected, in order to discover if she had secretly indulged in its use. It was afterwards allowed them on the plea of health, and no better method could have been devised for removing the restriction.

The Egyptian women, as I have already observed, appear to have enjoyed greater privileges, and to have been treated with more courtesy on all occasions, than in other ancient communities: and if they sometimes sat apart from the men, on another side of the same room, equal attentions were shown to them as to the other guests. That they were not restricted in the use of wine §, and in the enjoyment of other luxuries, is evident from the frescoes which represent their feasts; and the painters, in illustrating this fact, have sometimes sacrificed their gallantry to a love of caricature. Some call the servants to support them as they

* Plin. xiv. 13.   † Ibid. *loc. cit.*   ‡ Ibid.
§ The Moslems include all wine under the same name, khumr (fermented drink), and thereby forbid whatever has undergone the process of fermentation. It is prohibited to both sexes in the Qorán.

sit, others with difficulty prevent themselves from falling on those behind them; a basin is brought

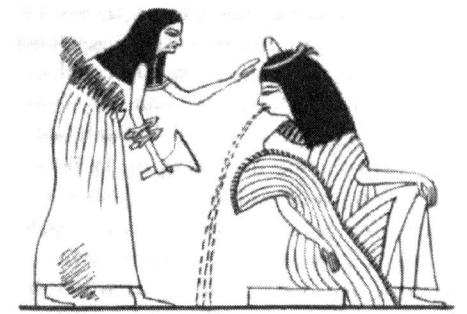

No. 146.   A servant called to support her mistress.   Thebes.

too late by a reluctant servant, and the faded flower, which is ready to drop from their heated hands, is intended to be characteristic of their own sensations.

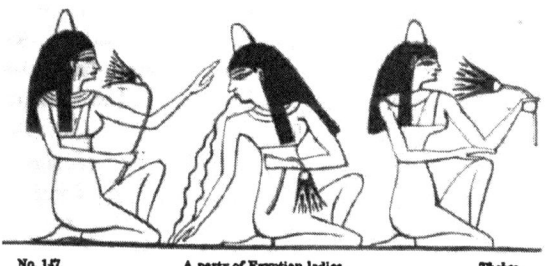

No. 147.   A party of Egyptian ladies.   Thebes.

In Greece, women enjoyed the same privileges regarding wine, as in Egypt; and thus we find[*] Nausicaë and her companions scrupled not to in-

* Homer. Od. Z. v. 77. and 99.

M 4

dulge in it; but the Greek custom of allowing virgins, as well as matrons, so much freedom in its use was looked upon by many as highly indecorous.[*]

That the consumption of wine in Egypt was very great is evident from the sculptures, and from the accounts of ancient authors, some of whom have censured the Egyptians for an immoderate love of excess ; and so much did the quantity used exceed that made in the country, that, in the time of Herodotus, twice every year a large importation was received from Phœnicia and Greece.   It was brought in earthen jars, and these, when emptied, were applied to another and very different purpose, being collected and sent to Memphis from every part of Egypt, and forwarded, full of water, to the confines of Syria.[†]

Notwithstanding all the injunctions or exhortations of the priests in favour of temperance, the Egyptians of both sexes appear from the sculptures to have committed occasional excesses, and men were sometimes unable to walk from a feast, and were carried home by servants.[‡]   These scenes,

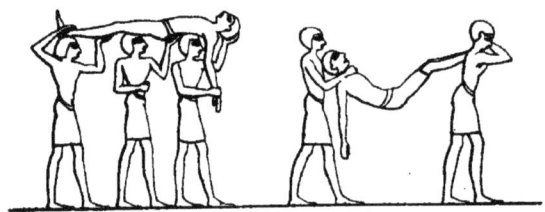

No. 148.   Men carried home from a drinking party.   *Beni Hassan.*

[*] Athenæus. Deipn. lib. x.   [†] Herodot. lib. iii. 6.
[‡] Juvenal, Sat. xv. 45., speaking of the Ombites, says, —
————— " sed luxuriâ . . . .
Barbara famoso non cedit turba Canopo.

however, do not appear to refer to members of the higher, but of the lower classes, some of whom indulged in extravagant buffoonery, dancing in a ludicrous manner, standing on their heads, and

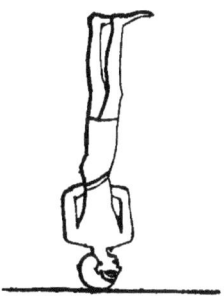

No. 149.   Man standing on his head.   *Beni Hassan.*

frequently in amusements which terminated in serious disputes.

At the tables of the rich, stimulants* were sometimes introduced, to excite the palate before drinking, and Athenæus mentions cabbages as one of the vegetables used by the Egyptians for this purpose; from which, and from the authority of Dion, he concludes they were a people systematically addicted to intemperance.†

The Romans frequently mulled their wines‡,

Adde quod et facilis victoria de madidis et
Blæsis, atque mero titubantibus.   Inde virorum
Saltatus nigro tibicine, qualiacumque
Unguenta et flores, multæque in fronte coronæ."

* The Romans, like the modern Italians, used stimulants to excite the appetite before dinner (Hor. ii. Sat. ii. 44.), as well as before wine.
† Athenæus, i. c. 25.   Josephus says they were a people addicted to pleasures.   Antiq. ii. 9.
‡ The Greeks and Romans mixed water with their wine. Hom. Od. A. cx. 209.   Athen. ii. 2.   Jul. Pollux. vi. 2.

and some were mixed with spice and various aromatics; but it is difficult to say if these compounds were in use among the Egyptians, though highly probable, from being so much esteemed by the Jews*, who adopted numerous customs from that people.

Throughout the upper and lower country, wine was the favourite beverage of the wealthy: they had also very excellent beer, called *zythus*, which Diodorus†, though wholly unaccustomed to it, and a native of a wine country, affirms was scarcely inferior to the juice of the grape. And that it was superior to the beer made in other countries may be readily inferred, from the eulogiums passed upon it by the historian, contrasted with the contempt in which this beverage was held by the Greeks.‡ Strabo and other ancient authors have likewise mentioned it under the name of zythus; and though Herodotus pretends that it was merely used as a substitute for wine in the lowlands, where corn was principally cultivated §, it is more reasonable to conclude it was drunk by the peasants‖ in all parts of Egypt, though less in those districts where vines were abundant. Indeed, he would lead us to sup-

---

* "I would cause thee to drink of spiced wine." Solomon's Song, viii. 2. "Mixed wine" is frequently mentioned.

† Diodor. i. 34.

‡ Conf. Æschyl. in the Suppliants, v. 960. : —

　　" Αλλ' αρσενας τοι τησδε γης οικητορας,
　　Ευρησετε ου πινοντας εκ κριθου μεθυ."

　　" You shall be met by men whose lively blood
　　Dull draughts of barley-wine have never clogg'd."

§ He means in the extensive level tract of the Delta. Corn was cultivated throughout Upper and Lower Egypt.

‖ As in some parts of France.

pose[*] that in the corn country, as he terms it, the use of wine was totally unknown, because the vine was not grown there; but, as wealth can always procure a luxury of this kind, we may be allowed to confine his remark to the poorer classes, and to conclude that the rich throughout Egypt supplied themselves with it, whether the growth of their own neighbourhood, or brought from another part of the country. The historian would, probably, have made a similar observation, if he had travelled in these days in England; but it is generally allowed that, though the English excel in the quality of their beer, the annual consumption of wine is not inconsiderable, and that there is no difficulty in procuring it from a far greater distance. In Egypt, native wines of a choice kind, whether made in the vicinity or brought from another province, were confined to the rich; and we learn from Strabo [†] that this was the case even at Alexandria, where wine could be obtained in greater quantity than in any other part of Egypt, owing to the proximity of the Mareotic district [‡], and the common people were there content with beer and the poor wine of the coast of Libya.

BEER.

The Egyptian beer was made from barley [§]; but, as hops were unknown, they were obliged to have recourse to other plants, in order to give it a grate-

---

[*] Herodot. ii. 77.   [†] Strabo, lib. xvii.
[‡] " Mareotic wine, which they also call Alexandrian, from the lake near that city." Athenæus, Deipnosoph. i. c. 25.
[§] Herod. ii. 77. Diodor. i. 34. Strabo, xvii. Plin. xxii. 25.

ful flavour ; and the lupin, the skirret*, and the
root of an Assyrian plant, were used by them for
that purpose. †

The vicinity of Pelusium appears to have been
the most noted for its beer, and the Pelusiac zythus
is mentioned by more than one author.   The account given by Athenæus of Egyptian beer is that
it was very strong, and had so exhilarating an
effect that they danced, and sang, and committed
the same excesses, as those who were intoxicated
with the strongest wines : an observation confirmed
by the authority of Aristotle, whose opinion on
the subject has at least the merit of being amusing.
For we must smile at the philosopher's method of
distinguishing persons suffering under the influence
of wine and beer, however disposed he would
have been to accuse us of ignorance, in not having
yet discovered · how invariably the former in that
state " lie upon their face, and the latter on their
backs." ‡

Though beer was common to many countries,
that of Egypt was of a peculiar kind, and, as Strabo §
observes, different methods of preparing it were
adopted by different people.   Nor can we doubt
that it varied as much in quality as at the present
day ; in the same manner that English and Dutch

---

* Siser ; the Sium sisarum of Linn. " Quod zythum Ægyptus ap-
pellat." Theoph. de caus. Plant. vi. 10.

†   " Jam siser, Assyrioque venit quæ semine radix,
   Sectaque præbetur madido satiata lupino,
   Ut Pelusiaci proritet pocula zythi." Columella, l. x. 114.

‡ Athen. *loc. cit.* quoting Aristotle.
§ Strabo, xvii. " ιδιως σκευαζεται παρ' αυτοις."

beer is a very different beverage from that of France, or from the *booza* of modern Egypt. In this last, indeed, it is impossible to recognise any resemblance, and no attempt is made to give it the flavour common to beer, or to obtain for it any other recommendation than its intoxicating properties. The secret of preparing it from barley has remained from old times, but indolence having banished the trouble of adding other ingredients, they are contented with the results of simple fermentation ; and bread, and all similar substances, which are found to undergo that process, are now employed by the Egyptians, almost indifferently, for making booza.

Besides beer, the Egyptians had what Pliny calls factitious, or artificial, wine *, extracted from various fruits, each sort, no doubt, known by some peculiar name, which pointed out its nature and quality. The Greeks and Latins comprehended every kind of beverage made by the process of fermentation under the same general name, and beer was designated as barley-*wine ;* but, by the use of the name zythos, they show that the Egyptians distinguished it by a totally different appellation. It is equally probable that those made from other fruits were, in like manner, known by their respective

---

* Plin. xiv. 16. " de vinis factitiis." If no wine was made from grapes (as Herodotus states) in the " corn country," these might have been there styled " home-made wines," a name applied to similar mixtures in other vineless districts. But it is not likely that they were included by the Egyptians under the head of wines. Conf. Theophr. de causis Plant. vi. 10. " Alios succos exprimimus " . . . . " nonnulli fructus à naturâ suâ alienant atque aliquatenus putrefacientes in succos potabiles convertunt."

denominations, as distinctly specified, as the perry and cider of the present day; and, indeed, we may expect to find them mentioned in the hieroglyphic legends accompanying the offerings in the tombs and temples of Egypt, where the contents of each vase are evidently indicated, and where, as I have already observed, several wines of the country are distinctly pointed out. Palm wine, says Pliny, was common throughout the east, and one sort is noticed by Herodotus as having been used by the Egyptians in the process of embalming [*] ; but it is uncertain whether this last was made in the manner described by Pliny [†], which required a *modius*, or peck and a half, of the ripe fruit to be macerated and squeezed into three *congii*, or about twenty-two pints, of water.

The palm wine made at the present day is simply from an incision in the heart of the tree [‡], immediately below the base of the upper branches, and a jar is attached to the part to catch the juice which exudes from it. But a palm thus tapped is rendered perfectly useless as a fruit-bearing tree, and generally dies in consequence [§] ; and it is reasonable to suppose that so great a sacrifice is seldom made except when date trees are to be felled, or when they grow in great abundance, as in the Oases

---

[*] Herodot. ii. 86.   [†] Plin. xiv. 16.

[‡] Called by Pliny the " medulla," or " cerebrum," and in Arabic qulb, " the heart," or jummár. It is sold at Cairo, and considered as a delicacy; in taste, it resembles a sweet turnip.

[§] Hence Pliny observes of one species, " dulcis medulla earum in cacumine quod cerebrum appellant, exempta que vivunt, quod non aliæ." Conf. Athen. Deip. lib. ii. *ad fin.*, and Xenoph. Exped. Cyr. ii. " ὁ δε φοινιξ, ὁθεν εξαιρεθειη ὁ εγκεφαλος, ὁλος αυαινετο."

and some other districts.   The modern name of this beverage in Egypt is *lowbgeh* : in flavour it resembles a very new light wine, and may be drunk in great quantity when taken from the tree ; but, as soon as the fermentation has commenced, its intoxicating qualities have a powerful and speedy effect.   It is not confined to Egypt and the Oases : the inhabitants of other parts of Africa* and many palm-bearing countries are in the habit of making it in the same manner ; nor do scruples of religion prevent the Moslems from indulging in its use.   In Nubia a wine is extracted from the dates themselves ; but this is now less common than the more potent brandy which they distil from the same fruit, and which is a great favourite in the valley of the Nile.

In former times, figs, pomegranates, *myxas* †, and other fruits were also used in Egypt for making artificial wines, and herbs of different kinds were applied to the same purpose ; many of which, it may be presumed, were selected for their medicinal properties.‡

FRUIT TREES.

Among the various fruit-trees cultivated by the ancient Egyptians, palms, of course, held the first

---

* The blacks are particularly fond of intoxicating drinks.   In the valley of the Nile the propensity may be said to augment in proportion to the intensity of colour, and the Nubians surpass the Egyptians in their love of booza and other fermented liquors in about the same ratio as the increased darkness of their hue.

† Plin. xiii. 5. " Ex myxis in Ægypto et vina fiunt."   The Cordia myxa of Linnæus, Arabice Mokhayt.

‡ Rue, hellebore, absinthium, and numerous others.   Wines were also imbued or flavoured with the juice of those herbs.   Plin. xiv. 16.

rank, as well from their abundance as from their great utility. The fruit constituted a principal part of their food, both in the month of August, when it was gathered fresh from the trees, and at other seasons of the year, when it was used in a preserved state. They had two different modes of keeping the dates; one was by the simple process of drying them, the other was by making them into a conserve, like the *agweh* * of the present day; and of this, which was eaten either cooked or as a simple sweetmeat, I have found some cakes †, as well as the dried dates, in the sepulchres of Thebes. For though Pliny affirms that the dates of Egypt, Ethiopia, and Arabia were, from the heat and dryness of the soil ‡, incapable of being preserved, modern experience, and the knowledge we have of the ancient customs of Egypt, prove the reverse of what is stated by that author. Yet he § speaks of dates of the Thebaïd kept in vases, which he supposes to be necessary for their preservation; and it would appear that he alluded to the *agweh*, did he not also suggest the necessity of drying them in an oven.

The same author makes a just remark respecting the localities where the palm prospers, and the

---

* Agweh, or adjweh, is a mass of dates pressed and preserved in baskets, which is commonly sold in all the markets of modern Egypt.

† One of these is in the British Museum.

‡ Plin. Nat. Hist. xiii. 4. " Servantur hi demum qui nascuntur in salsis atque sabulosis, ut in Judæa et Cyrenaica Africa: non item in Ægypto, Cypro, Syria, et Seleucia Assyriæ."

§ Plin. xiii. 4. " Thebaïdis fructus extemplo in cados conditur, . . ni ita fiat, celeriter expirat."

constant irrigation it requires *; and though every one in the East acknowleges this fact, and knows that the tree will not grow, except where water is abundant, we still read of "palm trees of the desert," as though it delighted in, or was peculiar to, an arid district.   Wherever it is found, it is a sure indication of water: there are therefore no palms in the desert, except at the Oases, and those spots where springs lie near the surface; and if it may be said to flourish in a sandy soil, this is only in situations where its roots can obtain a certain quantity of moisture. The cultivated tree is reared from offsets, those grown from the stone producing an inferior fruit; and the offsets, which are taken at about seven years' growth, bear dates in other five or six years, the tree living sixty or seventy, and even upwards †, according to circumstances connected with the soil or the mode of its culture.

Dates were also given to camels and other animals ‡, as is still the custom in the East; and this alone would suffice to prove their great abundance §, and the utility of the palm as a valuable and productive fruit-tree. ‖   But the numerous

* "Gignitur levi, sabulosaque terra, majore in parte et nitrosa. Gaudet et riguis, totoque anno bibere cum amet, anno sitienti."
† Conf. Plin. xiii. 4. "In Ægypto quadrimæ aliæ, aliæ quinquennes . . . . ferunt." Strabo says, the palm either bore no fruit, or a bad kind, in Lower Egypt, but the dates of the Thebaïd were excellent. Lib. xvii. p. 563.
‡ Plin. xiii. 4. "Etiam quadrupedum cibus." In going to the Oasis, my camels were always fed with them when beans failed.
§ For the different kinds of dates now known in Egypt, vide my Egypt and Thebes, p. 266.
‖ A tree can produce as much as four qantars of dates, or 440 lbs. troy, on about eight bunches, but generally it bears much less. I found the bunch of a wild tree at the water of Wadee el Enned, in the

purposes to which its branches, and other parts, might be applied, tended still more to render its cultivation a matter of primary importance : for no portion of this tree is without its peculiar use. The trunk serves for beams, either entire or split in half ; of the *geréet*, or branches, are made wicker baskets, bedsteads, coops, and ceilings of rooms, answering every purpose for which laths or any thin wood-work are required ; the leaves are converted into mats, brooms, and baskets ; of the fibrous tegument, at the base of the branches, strong ropes are made ; and even the bases of the *geréet* are beaten flat and formed into brooms. Nor are the stalks of the bunches without their use ; and their fibres, separated by the mallet, serve for making ropes, and for the *leef* which is so serviceable in the bath. Besides the brandy, the *lowbgeh*, and the date wine, a vinegar is also extracted from the fruit : and the large proportion of saccharine matter contained in dates might, if required, be applied to useful purposes.

In Upper Egypt, another tree, which has been called the Theban palm *, was also much cultivated ; and its wood, more solid and compact than the date tree, is found to answer as well for rafts and other purposes connected with water, as for

eastern desert, which was composed of 125 fruit-stalks, each containing from 30 to 60 dates, so that, on an average of 45, the bunch bore 6625 dates ; and every tree had from 5 to 15 bunches, and one of them as many as 22. The above-mentioned bunch was of unusual size, which made me count the dates, but the fruit was small and bad, as of all the wild trees, and, probably, some of the dates did not come to maturity. In the valley of the Nile, a feddan (1¼ acre) is sometimes planted with 400 trees.

* The Cucifera Thebaica. *Vide* Plin. xiii. 4. and 9.

beams and rafters. The general character of its growth differs essentially from that of the date tree, having always bifurcated limbs*, and this peculiarity enables us to recognise it when represented in the sculptures. The fruit is a large rounded nut, with a fibrous exterior envelope, which has a sweet flavour, very similar to our gingerbread. The nut itself, when gathered unripe, is also eaten, and then presents a substance resembling cartilage or horn; but so soon as it is ripe it becomes exceedingly hard, and is not unlike, though much smaller than, the cocoa-nut. It was employed by the Egyptians for the hollow socket of their drills; and being found peculiarly adapted for this purpose, from its great durability, it still continues to be used by carpenters and cabinet-makers in Egypt. That the mode of applying it among the ancients was precisely similar to that adopted at the present day, we have ample testimony from the sculptures of Thebes, where it occurs apart from, and affixed to †, the instrument itself in the hands of the workmen.‡ But it was not exclusively used, and we find they frequently substituted some hard wood; a specimen of which § may be seen in the highly interesting collection of tools found at Thebes by Mr. Burton, and now in the British Museum; this, with the drills, and

---

* About five feet, sometimes more, sometimes less, from the ground, it divides into two branches, each of which again separates into two others, and these again into two other pairs, always by twos, the uppermost sets being crowned by the leaves and fruit.
† *Vide* wood-cut, No. 150. *figs.* 1, and 3.
‡ *Vide* wood-cut, No. 150.
§ *Vide* wood-cut, No. 151. *fig.* 6.

their bow, chisels, a saw, mallet, and a bag of skin,
perhaps for holding nails, having been put into

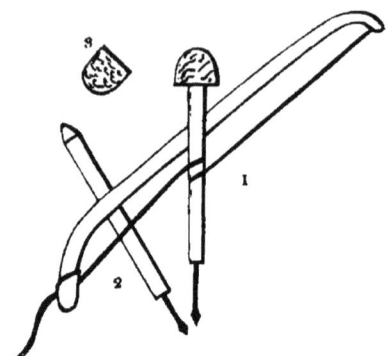

Fig. 1. Drill and the bow for turning it.
2. The drill alone.
3. The socket, of the dôm-nut, in which it turned.
No. 150.   *Thebes.*

a basket, together with a horn of oil and the hone
for sharpening the chisels, and buried in the tomb
of a deceased workman. *

Of the dôm-nut were made beads, which, from
their hardness, were capable of taking a high
polish, as we observe in those now used in Egypt
for the *sibhas,* or rosaries, of the Moslems † ; and
both the manufactured parts of the nut and many
specimens of the fruit have been found, perfectly
preserved, in the sepulchres of Thebes.

The leaves of the tree served for baskets, sacks,
mats, and other similar interlaced works‡, or, in-

* *Vide* wood-cut, No. 151.
† These sibhas are sold in the bazars of all the country towns.
‡ Strabo, lib. xvii.   Objects of these materials are found in the
tombs.

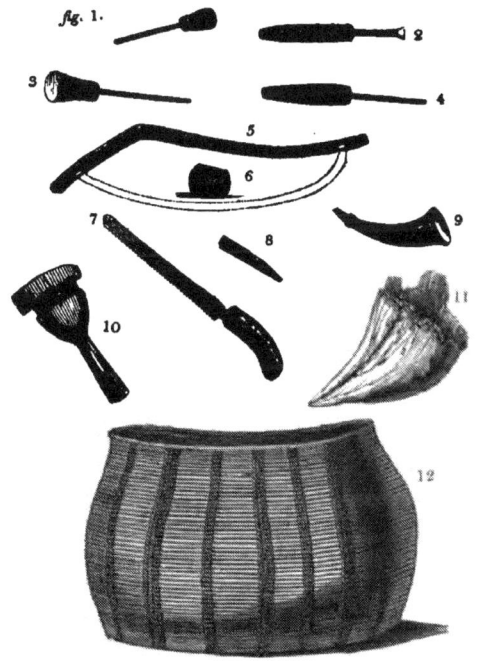

Carpenters' tools.

Figs. 1, 2, 3, 4. Chisels and drills.
   6. Nut of wood belonging to it.
   9. Horn of oil.
  11. Bag for nails.
No. 151.

Fig. 5. Part of drill.
  7, 8. Saws.
 10. Mallet.
 12. Basket which held them.

Mr. Burton's Collection.

deed, for all the purposes to which those of the date tree were applied; and among these we may mention fans, fly-flaps, brushes, and sometimes parts of sandals.

Besides the date and dôm trees were the sycamore[1], fig, pomegranate, olive, peach[2], almond[3], persea, *nebq* or *sidr*[4], *mokhayt* or *myxa*[5], *kharoob*[6] or locust tree, and some others; and among those which bore no fruit the most remarkable were the tamarisk[7], and *áthul*[8], cassia fistula, and senna, the palma christi, or castor-berry tree[9], myrtle[10], the *sont,* or acanthus[11], the *sayal*[12], *fitneh*[13], *tulh*[14], *lebbekh*[15], and several other mimosas, besides many trees now only known in the desert, or in the more southerly region of Ethiopia. But I confine myself for the present to the produce of the garden, in connection with their festivities and domestic wants.

So fond were the Egyptians of trees and flowers, and of gracing their gardens with all the profusion and variety which cultivation could obtain, that they even exacted a contribution of rare productions from the nations which were tributary to them, and foreigners from distant countries are re-

---

[1] Plin. xiii. 7.

[2] Plin. xv. 13. He denies the improbable story of the Persians having introduced it into Egypt as a poisonous fruit.

[3] Plin. xv. 28. " Amygdalæ quam in Ægypto gigni diximus." The cherry, he says, could never be reared in Egypt. xv. 25. It is not now grown there.

[4] Rhamnus nabeca, Forsk.

[5] Cordia myxa, Linn.

[6] Ceratonia siliqua, Linn. Ceraunia siliqua of Pliny, xiii. 8., which he says did not grow in Egypt.

[7] Tamarix gallica, Linn. Arabic, Tárfah.

[8] Tamarix orientalis, Forsk. Perhaps the africana of Desf.

[9] Plin. xv. 7.

[10] Pliny says, " Myrtus odoratissima est in Ægypto." xv. 29., and xxi. 11. It is not now a native of Egypt.

[11] Mimosa, or acacia nilotica. Spina Ægypti, Plin. xiii. 9. Athen. xv. 7. &c.

[12] Acacia seyal.

[13] Acacia farnesiana.

[14] Acacia gummifera.

[15] Acacia lebbeck. Mimosa lebbeck, Linn.

presented bringing plants, among the presents to
the Egyptian king. They carried this love for
them still farther, and not only painted the lotus
and other favourite flowers among the fancy devices of their walls, and on the furniture of their
houses, on their dresses, chairs, and boxes, on
their boats, and, in short, whatever they wished to
ornament, but they appear from Pliny * to have
composed artificial flowers, which received the
name "Ægyptiæ ;" if indeed we may be allowed
to consider these similar to the "hybernæ" he
afterwards describes.   And it is not improbable
that they, like the Romans, in their town houses,
had representations of gardens, or the rich blossoms
of favourite flowers, painted on the stuccoed walls.
Wreaths and chaplets were likewise in common use
among the Egyptians at a very early period; and
though the lotus was principally preferred for
these purposes, many other flowers and leaves were
employed; as of the chrysanthemum †, acinon ‡,
acacia §, strychnus, persoluta, anemone, convol-
vulus, olive, amaricus ||, xeranthemum, baytree ¶,
and others; and Plutarch tells us **, that when
Agesilaus visited Egypt he was so delighted with

---

* Plin. xxi. 2.   This is confirmed by discoveries in the tombs, noticed
infrà, p. 218.
† Plin. xxi. 25.   ‡ Ibid. c. xxvii.
§ Plin. xiii. 9. " Flos et coronis jucundus."   Athen. Deipn. xv. 7.
|| Athen. xv. 6.
¶ I have already observed (p. 401.), that some of those found in the
tombs appear to be of bay-leaves; and though not an indigenous pro-
duction of Egypt, the plant may have been cultivated there.   That called
Alexandrian was probably a Greek introduction.   Plin. xv. 30. and
xxiii. 8.
** *Vide* also Athen. xv. 6.

the chaplets of papyrus sent him by the king, that he took some home when he returned to Sparta.

GOD OF GARDENS.

The deity whom they considered more immediately to preside over the garden was Khem, the generative principle, who was supposed to answer to the Grecian Pan. It was also under the special protection of Ranno, a goddess frequently represented in the form of an asp, or with a human body and the head of that serpent; and thus we find the emblematic figure of an asp* attached to the sculptured representations of a winepress, a vineyard, or other parts of a villa †; and the same deity appears in the capacity of protecting genius to a king, or the nurse of a young prince. Indeed the connection between the goddess Ranno, or the asp, and royalty is very remarkable; and the name *uræus*, which was applied to that snake ‡, has, with good reason, been derived by the ingenious Champollion from ouro, the Coptic word signifying "king," as its appellation of basilisk originated in the *basiliscos* § of the Greeks.

Khem, or Pan, from his character as god of generation, was naturally looked upon as the deity to

---

* I formerly supposed this protecting genius to be the god Hat, who has the same emblematic serpent.

† *Vide* plate 10. *fig.* 1., and wood-cut, No. 141.

‡ It resembles the cobra di capello, the coluber naja of Linnæus, in every thing except the spectacles on the head, which are wanting. It has now received the name of naja haye, which is certainly a misnomer, haye being the Arabic name for the cerastes (vipera cerastes), or horned snake.

§ βασιλισκος, " royal."

whose influence every thing was indebted for its procreation, and for the continuation of its species; and we therefore frequently find, in the sacred sculptures of Egyptian temples, the emblematic representation of a king breaking up the soil with a hoe, in the presence of this god, as if to prepare it for his beneficent influence.* And this allegorical mode of worship was offered him, as well in his character of Khem, as when under the name of Amunra Generator, which was one of the forms of the Theban Jupiter. On the altar or table, carried behind his statue in sacred processions, or placed

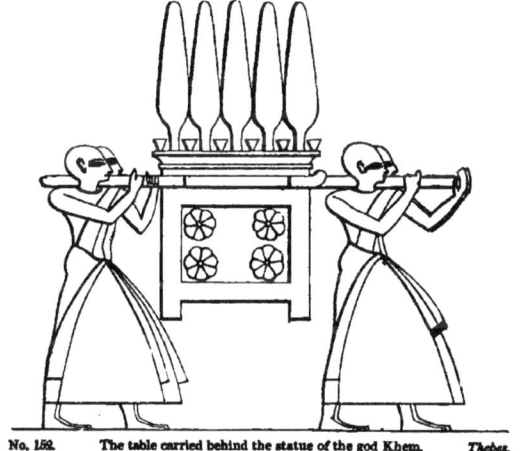

No. 152.   The table carried behind the statue of the god Khem.   *Thebes.*

near it in his sanctuary, were two or more trees, together with his peculiar emblems†; and the hieroglyphics implying "Egypt," which occur on the

---

* *Vide* my Materia Hieroglyphica, plate 6. of the Pantheon.
† *Vide* wood-cuts, Nos. 153, 154.

Rosetta stone, as well as on other Egyptian monuments, and have been supposed to read "the land

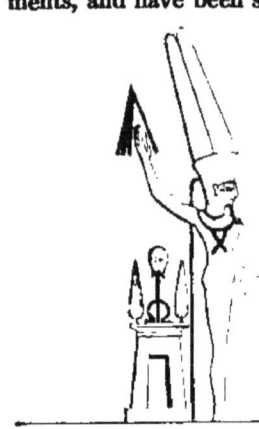

No. 153.   Emblems of the god Khem.

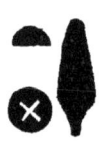

No. 154. Hieroglyphical group, containing
a tree and the sign of land, meaning
"Egypt."   *Rosetta Stone.*

of trees," bear an evident relation to the deity,
whose name Khem* is so similar to the word
Chemi, by which Egypt was known in Coptic, and
in the ancient language of the country.   In the
form of the god of generation originated, no doubt,
the Greek and Roman custom of placing their gardens under the protection of Priapus†, though,
instead of an abstract notion ‡ of the generative in-

* Panopolis was also called Chemmis, from the Egyptian name,
which can still be traced in its modern appellation, E'Khmim.
  † Hor. i. 8. 8. 1. : —

"Olim truncus eram ficulnus, inutile lignum,
  Cum faber incertus scamnum faceret ne Priapum
  Maluit esse Deum.   Deus inde ego furum, aviumque
  Maxima formido, nam fures dextra coercet."

  ‡ It is remarkable that the Greeks and Romans continually took abstract and metaphysical notions literally, and that the Egyptians, on
the other hand, converted the physical into metaphysical.

fluence, they, as in many other instances, merely attached to it an idea according with the grossness of their imaginations.

It is reasonable to suppose that the Egyptians spent much time in the cool and shady retirement of their gardens, where, like the Romans, they entertained their friends during the summer season ; and from the size of some of the *kiosks*, which occur in the paintings of the tombs, we may conclude they were rather intended for this purpose, than for the sole use of the master of the villa. That the gardens were originally laid out with a view to utility, and were chiefly stocked with vegetables for the consumption of the family, is more than probable ; but as riches and luxury increased, to the simple beds of herbs were added avenues of shady trees, and the usual variety of aromatic plants and ornamental flowers. It then became divided into different parts, distinguished by a peculiar name, according to the purpose for which they were intended ; and the vineyard, orchard, kitchen and flower garden, had each its own fixed limits, whose dimensions depended on the means or the caprice of its owner. Some of the richer individuals extended still farther the range of their villas ; and a park ($\pi\alpha\rho\alpha\delta\epsilon\iota\sigma\sigma$*) was added, which, independent of its fish-ponds† and preserves for game, contained many different sections, as the gallinarium for keeping hens, the cheno-

---

* Conf. Rosetta stone. " $\alpha\pi\sigma$ $\tau\epsilon$ $\tau\eta\varsigma$ $\alpha\mu\pi\epsilon\lambda\iota\tau\iota\delta\sigma\varsigma$ $\gamma\eta\varsigma$ $\kappa\alpha\iota$ $\tau\omega\nu$ $\pi\alpha\rho\alpha$-$\delta\iota\sigma\omega\nu$." line 15.

† " All that make ponds or sluices for fish." Isaiah, xix. 10.

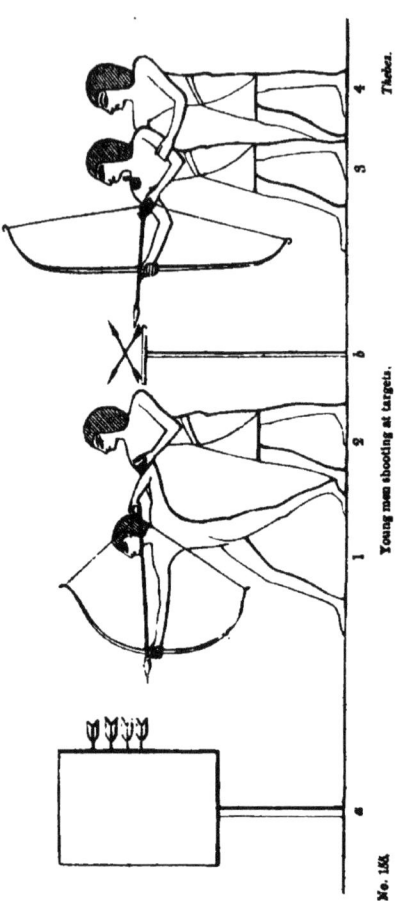

No. 155.   Young men shooting at targets.   Thebes.

boscium for geese, the stalls for fattening cattle, and for keeping the wild goats and other animals originally from the desert, whose meat was reckoned among the dainties of the table. It was in these extensive preserves that the rich amused themselves with the pleasures of the chase; and they also enclosed a considerable space in the desert with net fences, into which the animals were driven for the purpose of being hunted, though the usual custom in those districts was to course in view over the open plains.

Many, as I have already observed, occupied their leisure hours in fowling and fishing on their own grounds; and there many a youth, and sometimes even a damsel, was wont to practise the bow by shooting at a target.*

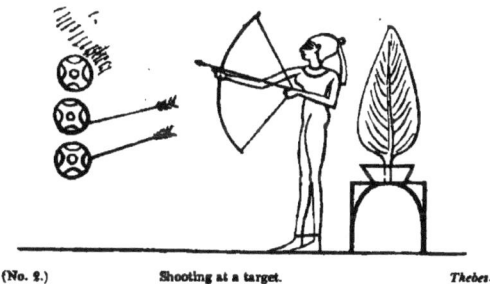

(No. 2.) Shooting at a target. *Thebes.*

* *Vide* wood-cut, No. 155.

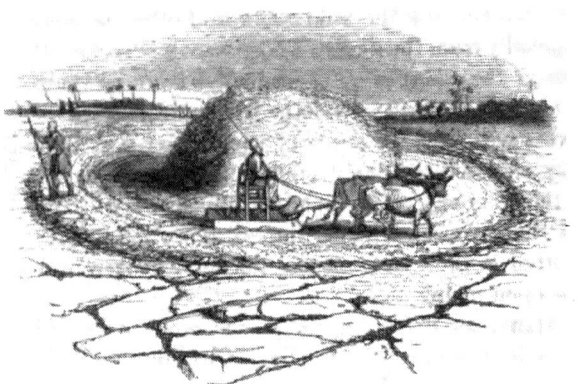

VIGNETTE F.   The Nôreg, a machine used by the modern Egyptians for threshing corn.

CHAP. VI.

Furniture of their Rooms. — Chairs, Stools, Ottomans, Mats, Couches, Tables. — Mode of sitting. — Headstools. — Bedsteads. — Palanquins. — Washing and anointing. — Bouquets. — Bands of Music. — Cymbals, Trumpets, Drums, Harps, Guitars, Lyres, Flutes, Pipes, Sistra, Sacred Instruments. — Dancing. — The Pirouette and Figure Dances.

THE apartments appropriated to the reception of their friends were sometimes on the ground floor, at others on the first story; and the party usually sat on handsome chairs and fauteuils, each, like the Ͽρονος of the Greeks, containing one person.* They occasionally used stools and low seats, raised very little above the ground, and some sat cross-legged, or on one knee, upon mats or carpets; but

* *Vide* wood-cut, No. 165. *fig.* 1.

men and women were generally apart, though apparently in the same room.   While conversing, they did not recline upon *diwáns*, like eastern people at the present day, nor did they, like the Romans, lie in a recumbent position, supported by the left elbow *, on a triclinium, or couch, during meals; though couches and ottomans formed part of the furniture of an Egyptian saloon.

Besides the *thronus*, or single chair, was what the Greeks termed the διφρος †, from its holding two persons; which was sometimes kept as a family seat, and occupied by the master and mistress of the house.‡   This kind of chair was not, however,

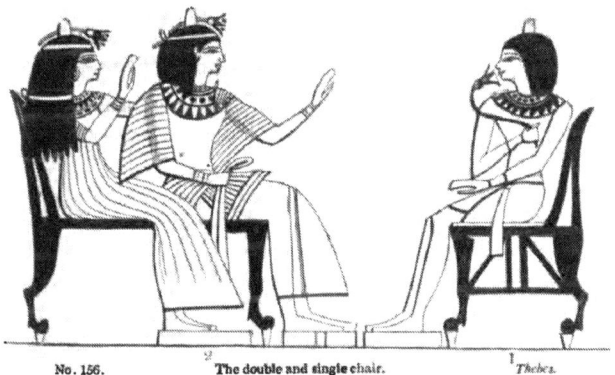

No. 156.   The double and single chair.   *Thebes.*

always reserved exclusively for them, nor did custom require them to occupy the same seat, since we

---

* Conf. Hor. i. Od. xxii. 8. : —
  " Et cubito remanete presso."
† Διφρος was also applied to a single chair, as in Theocr. Id. xv. 2. : —
  " Ορη διφον Ευνοα αυτᾳ."
‡ *Vide fig.* 2.

frequently find that they sat, like the guests, on separate chairs; and a *diphros* was occasionally offered to visiters, both men and women.

Many of the fauteuils were of the most elegant form, and were made of ebony and other rare

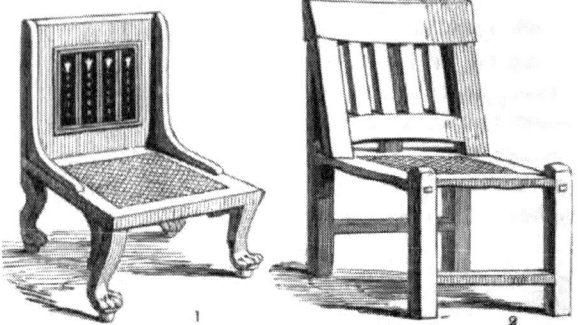

Chairs of an ordinary description.
The seat of fig. 1. is 8 inches high, and the back 1 foot 4 inches. That of fig. 2. is 14 inches,
and total height 2 feet 6 inches.

No. 157.   *Mr. Salt's Collection.*

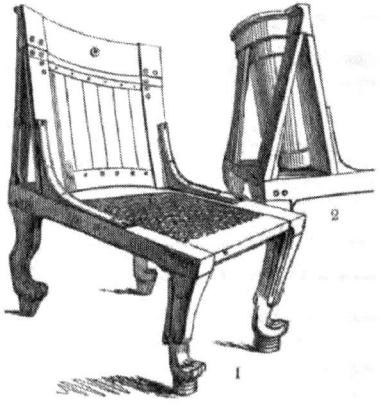

No. 158.   Chair in the Leyden Museum, the seat 13 inches high, and the back 17 inches.

woods, inlaid with ivory, covered with rich stuffs, and very similar to some now used in Europe*, to which, indeed, they have frequently served as models. None of these have yet been found in the tombs of Thebes; but chairs of more ordinary quality are occasionally met with, some of which are in the British Museum, and in the Leyden Collection. They are much smaller than the fauteuils of the sculptures, the seat being only from eight to fourteen inches high, and are deficient both in elegance of form and in the general style of their construction: in some the seat is of wood, in others of interlaced string or leathern thongs, in appearance, as well as in rank, not very unlike our own rush-bottomed chairs; and they probably belonged to persons of inferior station, or to those rooms which were set apart for casual visitors.

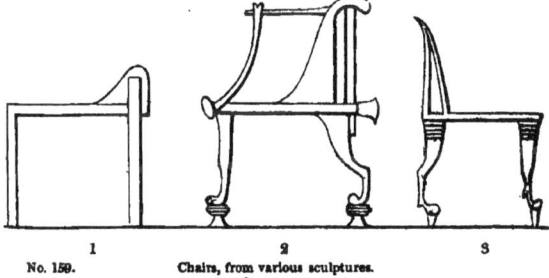

1　　　　　　2　　　　　　3

No. 159.　　　Chairs, from various sculptures.

Various are the forms of chairs which occur in the sculptures, representing † scenes of domestic life, and sacred subjects. Some were on the prin-

* *Vide* plate 11.
† The Chinese have chairs of similar form.

ciple of our camp stools, furnished with a cushion, or covered with the skin of a leopard or other animal*, which could be easily removed when the chair was folded up; and it was not unusual to make

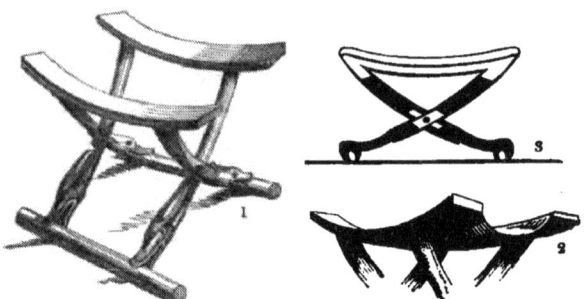

Fig. 1. A stool in Mr. Salt's collection, on the principle of our camp stools.
2. Shows the manner in which the leather seat was fastened.
3. A similar one from the sculptures, with its cushion.

No. 160.

other seats, and wooden head-stools or pillows, in the same manner; one of which was found by me at Thebes, and is now in the British Museum.† They were adorned in various ways: being bound with metal plates, or inlaid with ivory and foreign woods; and, even in some ordinary chairs, sycamore, or other native wood, was painted to imitate that of a more rare and valuable quality.

The seat was frequently of leather, painted with flowers or fancy devices; and the figure of a captive, or a conquered foe, was frequently represented at the side, or among the ornaments, of the chair. Sometimes the seat was formed of interlaced work of string, carefully and neatly arranged, which, like our

* *Vide* pl. 11. *fig.* 11.
† *Vide* wood-cut, No.172. *fig.* 2.

Indian cane chairs, appears to have been particularly adapted for a hot climate; but over this even they occasionally placed a leather cushion *, painted in the manner already mentioned.

Most of the chairs and stools were about the ordinary height of those now used in Europe, the seat nearly in a line with the bend of the knee; but some were very low, and others offered that variety of position which we seek in the kangaroo chairs †
of our own drawing room.   The ordinary fashion

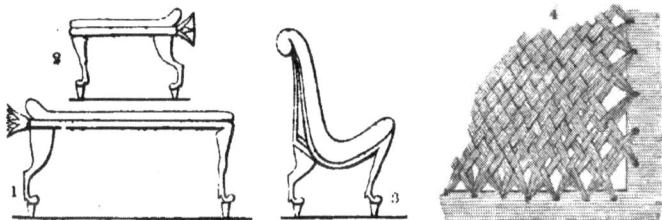

Fig. 1. A δίφρος or double chair, without a back.
　2. A single chair, of similar construction.
　3. A kangaroo chair.
　4. The seat, formed of interlaced string.
No. 161.　　　　　　　　　　　　　　*Thebes, Alabastron, and Mr. Salt's Collection.*

of the legs was in imitation of those of some wild animal, as the lion, or the goat, but more usually the former, the foot raised and supported on a short pin; and, what is remarkable, the skill of their cabinet-makers, even in the early era of Joseph, had already done away with the necessity of uniting the legs with bars.   Stools, however, and, more rarely, chairs, were occasionally made with these

* Conf. Theocrit. Idyl. xv. lib. iii.: —

　　" Oρη διφρον, Εννοα, αυτα
　　　Εμβαλε και ποτικρανον."

† *Vide* wood-cut, No. 161. *fig.* 3.

o 2

strengthening members, as is still the case in our own country; but the form of the drawing-room fauteuil and of the couch was not degraded by so unseemly and so unskilful a support. The back of the chair was equally light and strong. It was occasionally concave, like some Roman chairs *, or the throne of Solomon †, and in many of the large fauteuils a lion ‡ formed an arm at either side; but the back usually consisted of a single set of upright and cross bars, or of a frame, receding gradually, and terminating at its summit in a graceful curve, supported from without by perpendicular bars §; and over this was thrown a handsome pillow of coloured cotton, painted leather, or gold and silver tissue, like the beds at the feast of Ahasuerus, mentioned in Esther‖; or like the feather cushions covered with stuffs, and embroidered with silk threads of gold, in the palace of Scaurus.

The stools used in the saloon were of the same

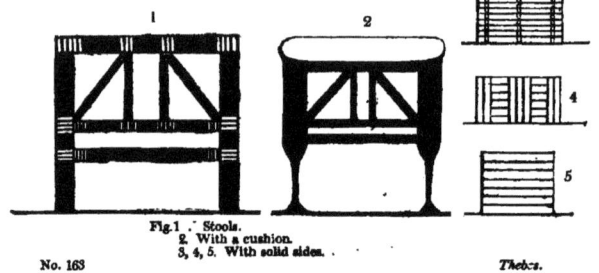

Fig. 1 .   Stools.
2. With a cushion.
3, 4, 5. With solid sides. .

No. 163   Thebes.

* *Vide* wood-cut, No. 158.
† 1 Kings, x. 19. " The top of the throne was round behind; and there were stays on either side on the place of the seat, and two lions stood beside the stays."
‡ As the throne of Solomon.   *Vide* plate 11.
§ *Vide* wood-cut, No. 165.   ‖ Esther, i. 6.

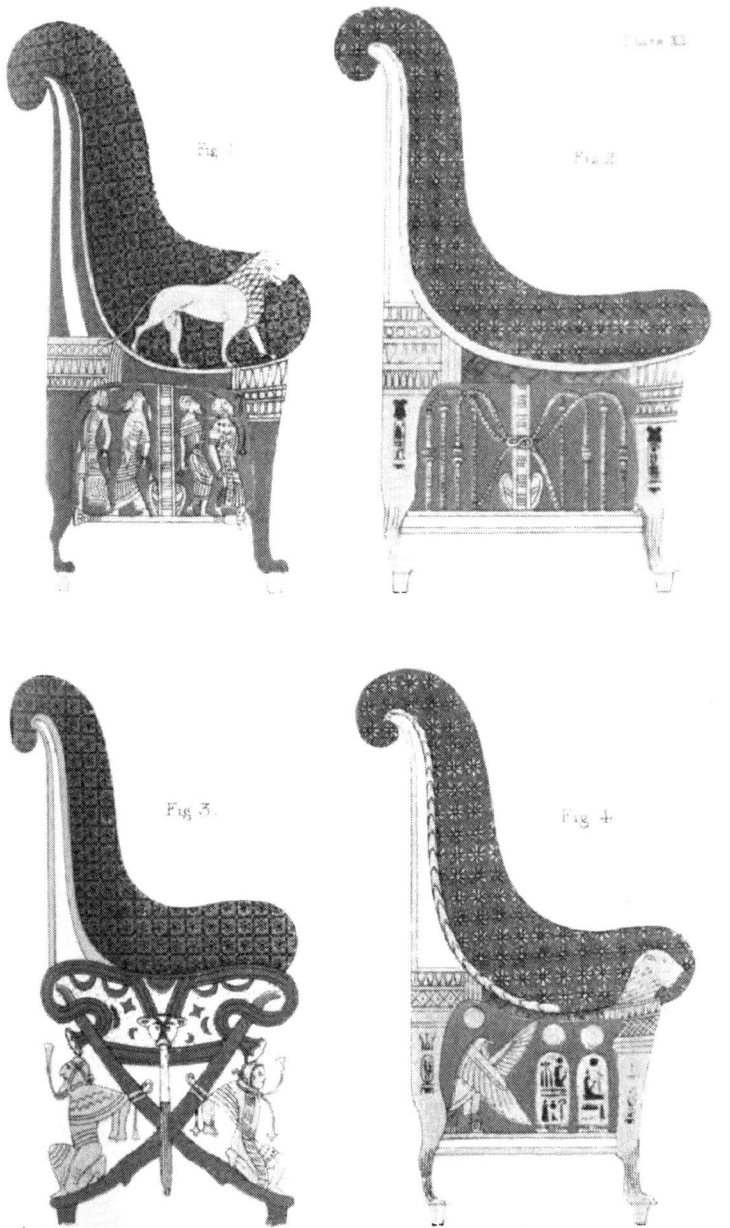

Plate XI

Fig. 1. Fig. 2.

Fig. 3. Fig. 4.

Wilkinson del. Day & Haghe Lith.

FAUTEUILS, from the Tombs of the Kings.—Thebes

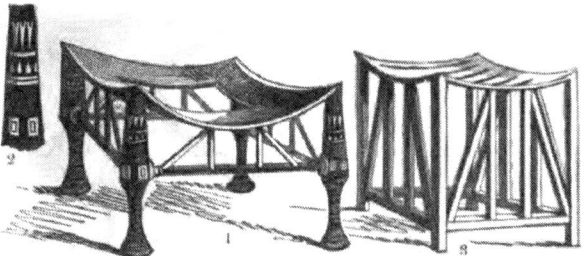

Fig. 1. Stool in Mr. Salt's Collection, of ebony inlaid with ivory.
 2. Shows the inlaid parts of the legs.
 3. Of ordinary construction, in the same collection.

No. 164.

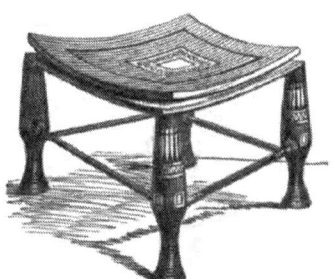

No. 164 a. A stool with leather cushion, in Mr. Salt's Collection.

style and elegance as the chairs, and frequently only differed from them in the absence of a back; those of more delicate workmanship were made of ebony, and inlaid, as I have already stated, with ivory or rare woods; and many, as already observed, folded up, on the principle of our camp stools.* Some of an ordinary kind had solid sides, and were generally very low; and others, with three legs, not unlike those used by the peasants of England, belonged to persons of inferior rank.

* _Vide_ wood-cut, No. 160.

o 3

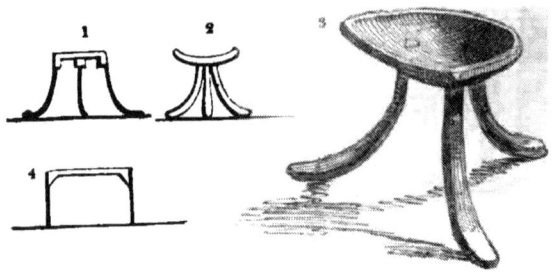

Figs. 1, 2. Three-legged stools, from the Sculptures.
3. Wooden stool, in Mr. Salt's Collection.
4. and 1. are probably of metal.

No. 165.

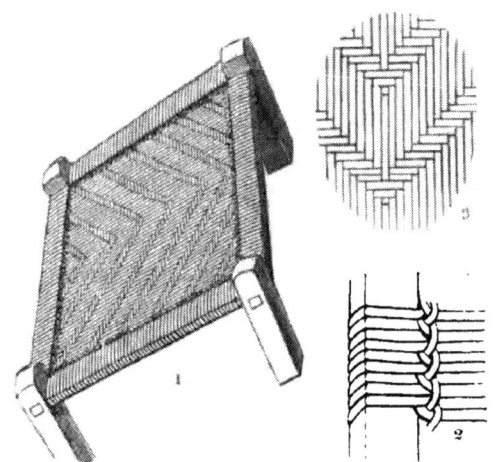

Fig. 1. Low stool, in the Berlin Museum.
2, 3. Mode of fastening, and the pattern of the seat.

No. 166.

The ottomans were simple square sofas, without backs, raised from the ground nearly to the same level as the chairs. The upper part was of

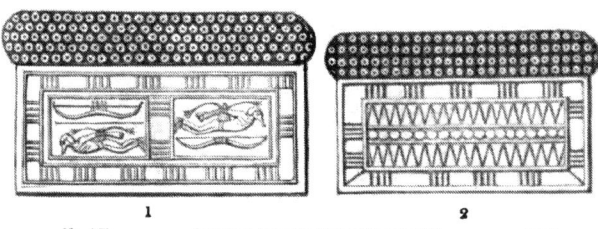

No. 167.   Ottomans, from the tomb of Remeses III.   *Thebes.*

leather, or a cotton stuff, richly coloured, like the
cushions of the fauteuils; and the base was of wood,
painted with various devices, and ornamented with
the figures of captives, who were supposed to be
degraded by holding so humiliating a position.
And the same idea gave them a place on the soles
of sandals, on the footstools of a royal throne, and
on the walls of the palace at Medeenet Haboo, in
Thebes, where their heads support some of the ornamental details of the building.

Footstools * also constituted part of the furniture
of the sitting room; they were made with solid or
open sides, covered at the top with leather or interlaced string, and varied in height according to
circumstances, some being of the usual size now
adopted by us, others of inconsiderable thickness,
and rather resembling a small rug.   These last, indeed, and some of the low seats above alluded to,
might be supposed to represent carpets, which
have been mentioned by Homer † and Diodo-

* Answering to the 3ρηνυς and scabellum of the Greeks and Romans.
† Hom. Odyss. iv. 124. : —

" Αλκιππη δε ταπητα φερεν μαλακου εριοιο."

o 4

rus* as a very early invention, since we find instances of several persons sitting upon them;

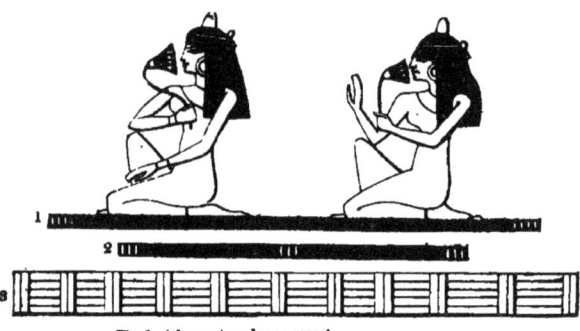

Fig. 1. A low seat, perhaps a carpet.
    2. Either similar to fig. 1., or of wood.
    3. A mat.

No. 168.

though we may, with equal reason, imagine, from
the mode of representing them, that some were of
wood, and that they closed or folded in the centre.†
Mats were commonly used in their sitting rooms,
as at the present day; and we not only see them
represented in the sculptures‡, but remnants of
them have been found in the Theban tombs.

Their couches evinced no less taste than the
fauteuils. They were of wood, with one end
raised, and receding in a graceful curve; and the
feet, as in many of the chairs already described,
were fashioned to resemble those of some wild ani-

---

* The στρωμνας πολυτελεστατας, mentioned by Diodorus, as spread
for the sacred animals of Egypt, are supposed to have been carpets.
Lib. i. 34.
† As in wood-cut, No. 168. *fig.* 2.
‡ *Vide* wood-cut, No. 168. *fig.* 3.

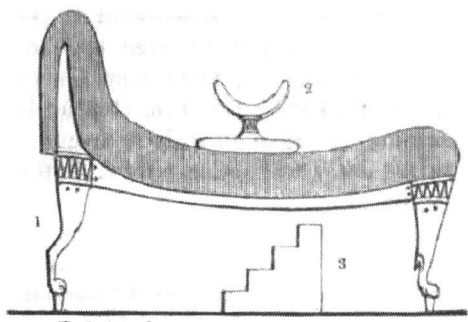

Fig. 1. A couch.
2. Pillow or head stool.
3. Steps for ascending a lofty couch.

No. 169. (*Tomb of Remeses III.*) *Thebes.*

mal.* But, though the Egyptians had couches, they do not appear to have reclined upon them more frequently than modern Europeans, in whose houses they are equally common; and, indeed, we have authority, both from the sculptures and from sacred history, for believing that the Egyptians, like the *early* Greeks and Romans †, were accustomed to sit at meals; for, as Philo justly observes, when Joseph entertained his brethren, he ordered them to *sit* according to their ages, the custom of reclining at meals not having yet been introduced. ‡

The couches appear, also, to have been intended as bedsteads; and it is not impossible that they were used to sleep upon at night, and, in the day-

---

* The Greeks ornamented the legs of their tables and other furniture in the same manner.

† The custom of reclining is said to have been introduced from Carthage, after the Punic wars.

‡ Philo. lib. de Joseph. p. 555. ed. Francf.

time, a rich covering being substituted for the bedding, they were readily transformed into an ornamental piece of furniture; and the presence of the head pillow placed upon it, and the steps at the side for ascending it, argue strongly in favour of this supposition: nor is the custom unusual in the East at the present day.

The Egyptian tables were round, square, or oblong; the former were generally used during their repasts, and consisted of a circular flat summit, supported, like the *monopodium* of the Romans, on a single shaft, or leg, in the centre, or by the figure of a man, intended to represent a captive.[*]   Large tables had usually three or four legs, but some were made with solid sides; and though generally of wood, many were of metal or stone; and they varied in size, according to the purposes for which they were intended.[†]

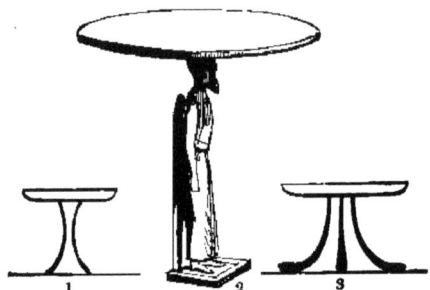

Fig. 1. Table, probably of stone or wood, from the sculptures.
2. Stone table supported by the figure of a captive.
3. Probably of metal, from the sculptures.

No. 169. *a.*

[*] *Vide* wood-cut, No. 169. *a, fig.* 2.
[†] *Vide* wood-cuts, No. 169. *a, b, c.*

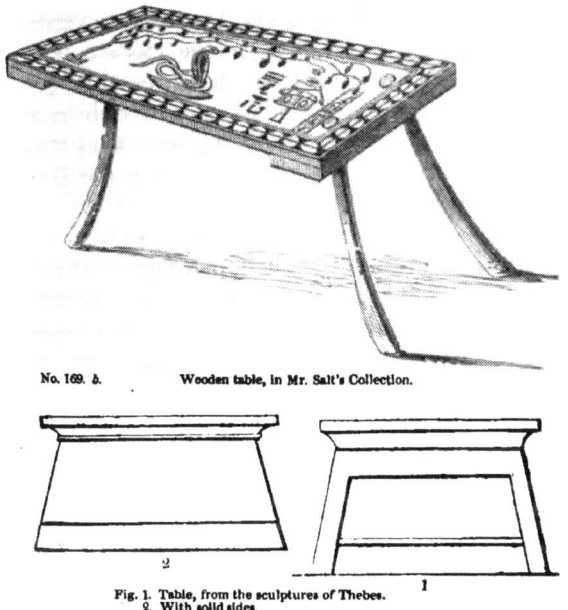

No. 169. *b.*   Wooden table, in Mr. Salt's Collection.

Fig. 1. Table, from the sculptures of Thebes.
2. With solid sides.
No. 169. *c.*

Common people either sat cross-legged, as the modern Asiatics, or crouched, on the ground; in

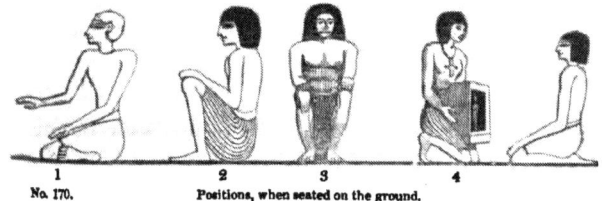

No. 170.   Positions, when seated on the ground.

which last position many Egyptian statues and painted figures are represented; and no one, who

has seen the peasants of Egypt, can fail to recognise
a position equally common to the modern inhabitants of the country, as to other oriental people.
When bearing sacred emblems before the shrine of
a deity, or desirous of showing respect to a superior,
they generally sat upon their heels *; and it is remarkable that this attitude continues to be adopted
by persons of inferior rank in Moslem society.

Of the furniture of their bed-rooms we know little
or nothing : but that they universally employed
the wooden pillow above alluded to is evident,
though Porphyry would lead us to suppose its use
was confined to the priests, when, in noticing
their mode of life, he mentions a half cylinder of
well polished wood sufficing to support their
head†, as an instance of their simplicity and self-
denial.‡ For the rich, they were made of oriental
alabaster, with an elegant grooved or fluted shaft,
ornamented with hieroglyphics, carved in intaglio,

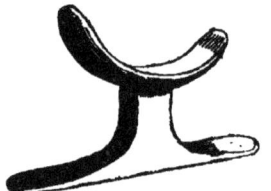

No. 171.   Wooden pillow or head-stool, found at Thebes.

and painted of a blue colour§ ; others were of rare
wood ; and those of a more ordinary kind were

* As *figs.* 4, 5. in wood-cut, No. 170.
† Porph. de Abstin. lib. iv. s. 7.
‡ *Vide* wood-cut, No. 171, 172.; and Vol. I. p. 281.
§ *Vide suprà*, Vol. I. p. 214. Wood-cut, No. 6.

of sycamore, tamarisk, and other woods of the country; the poorer classes being contented with a cheaper sort, of pottery or stone.   Porphyry

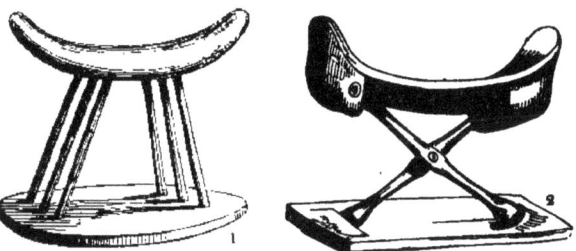

Fig. 1. Wooden pillow of unusual form.
   2. Another found by me at Thebes, and now in the British Museum.   The base was lost.
No. 172.

mentions a kind of wicker bedstead of palm branches called *baïs* *, which, he says, was used by the priests; but it is reasonable to conclude they were also met with in the houses of other individuals, at least among the middle and lower classes; and it is remarkable that the same species of framework is still employed by the modern Egyptians, as a support to the *diwans* of sitting rooms, and to their beds.   In size they vary according to the dimensions of the room and other circumstances; but they are invariably made of the *geréet*, or sticks of the palm branch, and are known by the general name of *kaffass*. †   Each side consists of a number of upright bars, which pass through three rods at right angles with them, the upper

* Baï is the Coptic for palm branch.
† Hencoops, and all other wicker-work made of the geréet, have the same name.

and lower one forming the edge of the framework. The summit, on which the bed is placed, is constructed in the same manner with transverse *geréets*, and in the centre is a small mass of them in closer order, intended more for ornament than for use; and the usual dimensions of these bedsteads are about seven feet, by three and a half, and from one foot to two feet in height. Wooden, and,

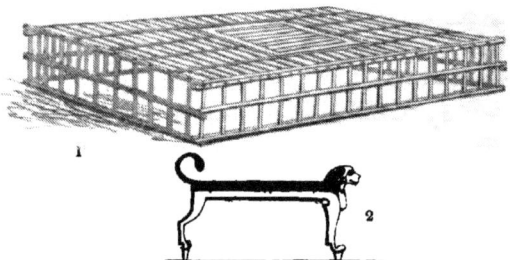

Fig. 1. Kaffass bedstead of palm sticks used by the modern Egyptians.
2. Ancient bier on which the bodies were placed after death.

No. 173.

perhaps, also bronze bedsteads *, may have been used by the wealthier classes of the ancient Egyptians; and it is at least probable that the couches they slept upon were as elegant as those on which their bodies reposed after death; and the more so, as these last, in their general style, are very similar to the furniture of the sitting room.†

* We read of a bedstead of *iron* belonging to Og, King of Bashan. Deut. iii. 11.
† *Fig.* 2. of wood-cut, No. 173.

GUESTS AND ENTERTAINMENTS.

In their entertainments they appear to have omitted nothing which could promote festivity and the amusement of the guests. Music *, songs, dancing †, buffoonery, feats of agility, or games of chance, were generally introduced, and they welcomed them with all the luxuries which the cellar and the table could afford. The party, when invited to dinner, met about midday ‡, and they arrived successively in their chariots, in palanquins § borne by their servants, or on foot. Sometimes their attendants carried a sort of parasol to shade them from the sun, as represented in the accompanying wood-cut, which in the present instance appears to have been of leather, stretched over a light frame ‖ ; but those which were borne behind, and belonged exclusively to, the king, were composed of feathers, and were not very unlike the flabella carried on state occasions behind the Pope, in modern Rome. The same custom prevailed in Persia, and other eastern countries; and in the sculptures of Persepolis, we have a satisfactory in-

---

* Conf. Isaiah, v. 12. " The harp and the viol, the tabret and pipe, and wine, are at their feasts."

† Conf. the feast given on the arrival of the prodigal son : " Bring hither the fatted calf, and kill it ; and let us eat and be merry :" and his brother, when he drew nigh to the house, " heard music and dancing." Luke, xv. 23. 25.

‡ Joseph said, " These men shall dine with me at noon," Gen. xliii. 16.

§ Vide wood-cut, No. 174.

‖ From the man having a battleaxe in the other hand, I was inclined to suppose it a shield; but from his being in the act of raising it aloft, we may conclude it was for the purpose of a parasol.

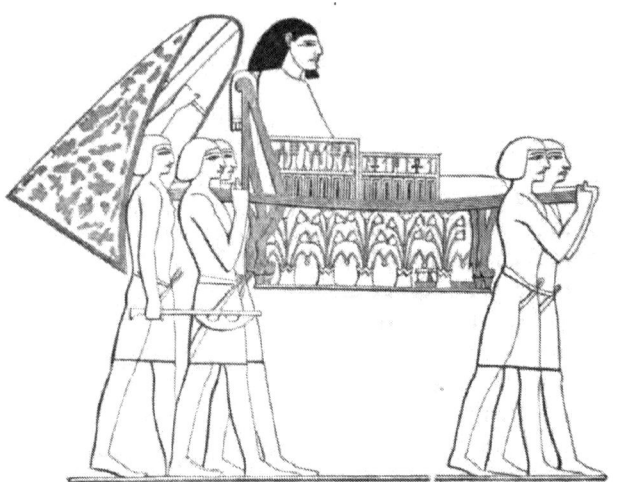

No. 174. — Military chief carried in a sort of palanquin, an attendant bearing a parasol behind him.   *Beni Hassan.*

stance of the use of a parasol, or umbrella, which bears a greater resemblance to those of the present day *, and conveys a better idea of its form, than an Egyptian artist would have given; though, from their general character, presenting so strong an analogy to those of Egypt, we may suppose many of these sculptures executed by captives taken from Thebes at the Persian conquest.

When a visitor came in his car, he was attended by a number of servants, some of whom carried a stool, to enable him to alight, and others his writing tablet, or whatever he might want during his stay

* *Vide* wood-cut, No. 175.

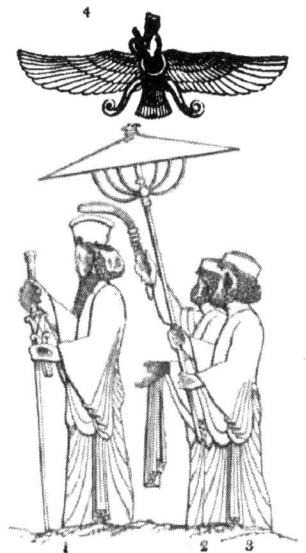

No. 175.   Persian sculptures.

Figs. 1, 2, 3. Attendants bearing a parasol and flyflap over a Persian chief, in some sculptures of Persepolis, which have a very Egyptian character.
Fig. 4. Is evidently borrowed from the winged globe.

at the house.   In the accompanying wood-cut*
the guests are assembled in a sitting room within,
and are entertained with music during the me-
lancholy interval preceding the announcement of
dinner; for, like the Greeks, they considered it a
want of good breeding to sit down to table immediately on arriving, and, perhaps, as Bdelycleon, in
Aristophanes †, recommended his father Philocleon

* *Vide* wood-cut, No. 176.
† Aristoph. Vesp. line 1209. : —

      " Επειτ' επαινεσον τι των χαλκωματων·
      Οροφην θεασαι, κρεκαδι' αυλης θαυμασον."

Noticed by Athenæus, lib. iv. c. 27.

to do, they admired the beauty of the rooms, and commended the furniture, taking care to bestow unqualified praise on those objects which were intended for their approbation.   As usual in all countries, some of the party arrived earlier than others; and the consequence, or affectation of fashion, in the person who now drives up in his curricle, is shown by his coming some time after the rest of the company; one of his footmen runs forward to knock at the door, others, close behind the chariot, are ready to take the reins, and to perform their accustomed duties; and the one holding his sandals in his hand, that he may run with greater ease, illustrates a custom, still common in Egypt, among the Arabs and peasants of the country; who find the power of the foot greater when freed from the encumbrance of a shoe.

To those who arrived from a journey, or who desired it, water was brought * for their feet, previous to entering the festive chamber; and it was either now, or immediately before dinner, that the guests washed their hands †, the water being brought in the same manner as at the present day; and ewers not unlike those used by the modern Egyptians are represented with the

---

* Joseph ordered his servants to fetch water for his brethren, that they might wash their feet before they ate. Gen. xliii. 24.   Conf. also xviii. 4. and xxiv. 32. 1 Sam. xxv. 46.   It was always a custom of the East, as with the Greeks and Romans; and they considered it a great want of hospitality to neglect to offer water for this purpose.   Conf. Luke, vii. 44. 46.

† Conf. Petron. Satyric. " Tandem discubuimus pueris Alexandrinis aquam in manus nivatam infundentibus, aliisque insequentibus ad pedes, ac paronychia cum ingenti subtilitate tollentibus.   Ac ne in hoc . . . tacebant officio, sed obiter cantabant." c. xxxi.

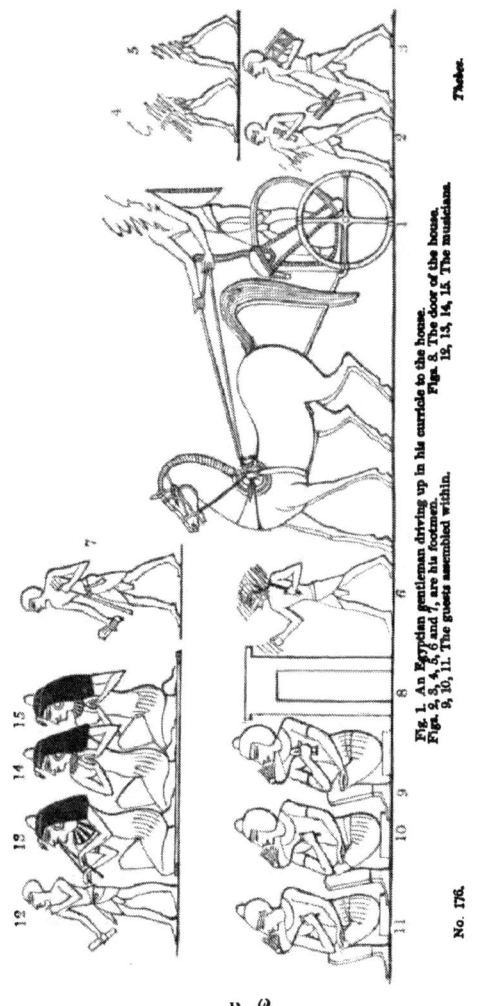

Fig. 1. An Egyptian gentleman driving up in his curricle to the house.
Fig. 2, 3, 4, 5, 6 and 7, are his footmen.   Fig. 8. The door of the house.
Fig. 9, 10, 11. The guests assembled within.   12, 13, 14, 15. The musicians.

No. 176.

P 2

basins belonging to them, in the paintings of a Theban tomb. It is certain that basins were kept

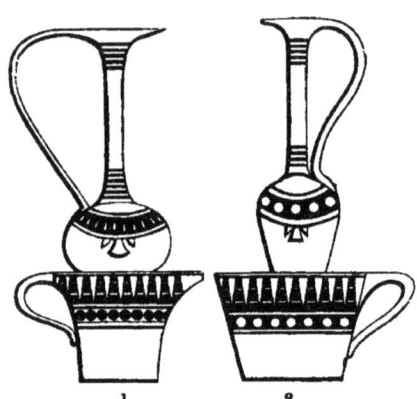

No. 177.   Golden ewers and basins in the tomb of Remeses III.   *Thebes.*

for the purpose of washing the hands and feet of the guests, and that in the houses of the rich they were of gold*, or other costly materials; but those who lived near their host were probably expected to perform their ablutions before they left home; and hence, I conceive, we may account for not finding any representation of this preliminary cere- mony in the paintings at Thebes. Athenæus† seems to apply the same remark to the Greeks; and "it was deemed indecent," says that author, "for any one to go to a feast without having previously cleansed himself;" though persons

---

* Herodotus mentions a gold basin (ποδανιπτηρ), belonging to Amasis, which he and the guests who dined with him used for washing their feet.

† Athen. lib. iv. c. 27.

arriving from a journey not only washed, but
were even clothed, at the mansion of their
host.*   However, with the Greeks, as well as
other people of antiquity, the usual custom was to
· bring water to the guests, numerous instances of
which we find in Homer; as when Telemachus
and the son of Nestor were received at the house
of Menelaus†, and when Asphalion poured it upon
the hands of his master and the same guests on
another occasion ‡; and Virgil describes the servants bringing water for this purpose, when Æneas
was entertained by Dido. §   Nor was the ceremony
thought superfluous, and declined, even though
they had previously bathed and been anointed
with oil. ‖

It is also probable that, like the Greeks, the
Egyptians anointed themselves before they left
home; but still it was customary for a servant to
attend every guest, as he seated himself, and to
anoint his head ¶; and this was one of the principal

* Homer, Odyss. iv. 50.
† Hom. Od. xv. 135. : —

    " Χερνιβα δ' αμφιπολος προχοψ επεχευε φερουσα
     Καλη, χρυσειψ, υπερ αργυρεοιο λεβητος
     Νιψασθαι."

‡ Hom. Od. iv. 216. : —

     " Ασφαλιων δ'αρ υδωρ επι χειρας εχευεν
     Οτρηρος Θεραπων Μενελαου κυδαλιμοιο."

§ Virg. Æn. i. 705. " Dant famuli manibus lymphas."
‖ Hom. Od. iv. 49. and 53.   This is the case with the Moslems of the
present day, who also require the water to be *poured upon* the hands.
Conf. 2 Kings, iii. 11.   Elisha, " who poured water on the hands of
Elijah."
¶ The Egyptians were shaved, and wore wigs. Vide Herodot. ii. 36.
and the sculptures.   The Greeks, Jews, and other ancient people,
were very fond of ointment and perfume. Prov. xxvii. 9.   " Ointment
and perfume rejoice the heart." Psalm xxiii. 5.; and Horace says,
" Nardi parvus onyx eliciet cadum." Od. xii. 4.

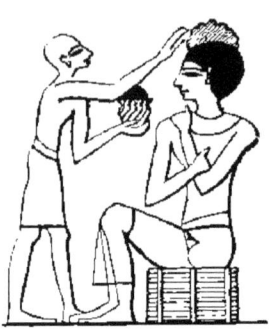

No. 178.   A servant anointing a guest.   *Thebes.*

tokens of welcome.*   The ointment was sweet-scented, and, unlike the Lacedæmonians, who banished those who sold perfumed ointments from their country, the Egyptians were particularly partial to this species of luxury.   It was contained, sometimes, in an alabaster†, sometimes in an elegant porcelain vase; and so strong was the odour, and so perfectly were the different component substances amalgamated, that it has been known to retain its scent for several hundred years.‡   Servants took the sandals of the guests as they arrived, and either put them by in a convenient place in the house, or held them on their arm while they waited upon them.§

After the ceremony of anointing was over, and,

* *Vide* Athenæus, xv. 13.

† Mary, when she washed Jesus' feet, brought an alabaster box of ointment.   Luke, vii. 37.   Matt. xxvi. 7.

‡ One of the alabaster vases in the museum at Alnwick Castle contains some of this ancient ointment, between two and three thousand years old, and yet its odour remains.

§ *Vide suprà,* wood-cut, No. 146.

in some cases, at the time of entering the saloon, a lotus flower was presented to each guest, who held it in his hand during the entertainment.* Servants then brought necklaces† of flowers, composed

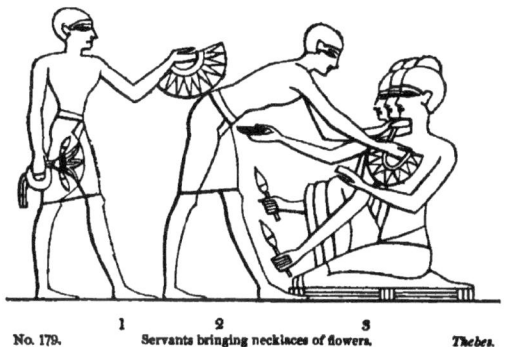

No. 179.　　　Servants bringing necklaces of flowers.　　　*Thebes.*

chiefly of the lotus; a garland was also put round the head, and a single lotus bud, or a full-blown flower, was so attached as to hang over the forehead.‡ Many of them, made up into wreaths and other devices, were suspended upon stands placed in the room to be in readiness for immediate use, and servants were constantly employed to bring other fresh flowers from the garden§, in order to supply the guests as their bouquets faded; and, to prevent

* *Vide* pl. 12.; and wood-cut, No. 168.

† To put on a ring or a necklace was a token of respect and welcome. Gen. xli. 42. " Pharaoh took off his ring from his hand, and put it upon Joseph's hand . . . . and put a gold chain upon his neck." The ring was generally a seal, as it is at the present day in the East, whence it is called, in Arabic, *khátom.* Necklaces were also put upon the figures of the gods and kings of Egypt.

‡ *Vide* plate 12. *Vide* Athen. Deipn. xv. cc. 4, 5. 9, 10.

§ Ibid.

their withering, they were generally put close to
jars of water, into which the stalks were probably
immersed.

The stands that served for holding the flowers,
and garlands, were similar to those of the amphoræ
and vases *, some of which have been found
in the tombs of Thebes; and the same kind of
stand was introduced into a lady's dressing-room,
or the bath, for the purpose of holding clothes and
other articles of the toilet. They varied in size
according to circumstances, some being low and
broad at the top, others higher, with a small summit,
merely large enough to contain a single cup, or a

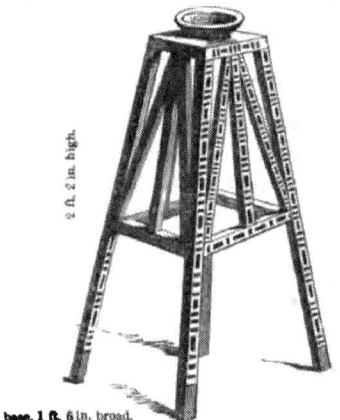

base, 1 ft. 6 in. broad.

No. 180.   Wooden stand, eight inches square at the summit, holding a small cup.
Mr. Salt's Collection.

small bottle, one of which, from Mr. Salt's collection, may be seen in the British Museum; but
those of a larger size were more generally used,

* *Vide* plate 12.

and were more convenient for ordinary purposes. Others, though much smaller than the common stands, were broader in proportion to their height, and answered as small tables, or as the supports of cases containing bottles; and one of these last, preserved in the Berlin Museum, is supposed to have belonged to a medical man, or to the toilet of a Theban lady.

Diodorus * informs us that when the Egyptians

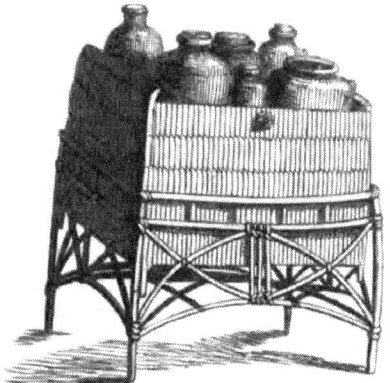

No. 181.   A case containing bottles, supported on a stand.   *Berlin Museum.*

approached the place of divine worship, they held the flower of the *agrostis* in their hand, intimating that man proceeded from a well-watered or marshy land, and that he required a moist rather than a dry aliment; and it is not improbable that the reason of the great preference given to the lotus, on these occasions, was derived from the same notion.   This

* Diod. i. 43.

did not, however, prevent their using many other kinds of flowers in the composition of bouquets, garlands, and chaplets; and artificial represent- ations of them were employed by the Egyptians for the same purpose, as we may infer from an expression of Pliny * already noticed, and from the imitation of flowers and leaves in painted linen discovered in the tombs of Thebes.   The Greeks and Romans had the same custom, and their guests were, in like manner, decked with flowers or gar- lands; which were brought in, according to Athen- æus, at the beginning of their entertainments, or, according to some, before the second course; and in all cases they were provided by the master of the house.   They not only adorned their *heads* †, *necks* ‡, and *breasts* §, like the Egyptians, but often bestrewed the couches on which they lay, and all parts of the room, with flowers; though the head was chiefly regarded, as appears from Horace ||, Anacreon ¶, Ovid **, and other ancient authors. And this ceremony, like that of anointing the head with sweet-scented ointment ††, was probably de- rived by the Greeks from Egypt, or, as some suppose, through the Ionians, from Asia.   They also

---

* Plin. xxi. 2. *Vide suprà*, p. 183.
† Hor. Od. lib. ii. 7. vii. : —

    " Coronatus nitentes
      Malobathro Syrio capillos." . . . .

And, Athen. xv. cc. 4. and 9.
‡ Athen. xv. 5.   § Ibid.
|| Hor. Od. lib. i. 26. and 38. lib. iv. 11, &c.
¶ Anacreon, Od. iv.
** Ovid, Fast. lib. v.
†† Hor. Od. lib. ii. 7. 22 :—" Funde capacibus unguenta de conchis.'

perfumed the apartment with myrrh, frankincense, and other choice odours, which they obtained from Syria * ; and if the sculptures do not give any direct representation of this practice among the Egyptians, we know it to have been adopted and deemed indispensable among them ; and a striking instance is recorded by Plutarch, at the reception of Agesilaus by Tachos.† A sumptuous dinner was prepared for the Spartan prince, consisting, as usual, of beef, goose, and other Egyptian dishes : he was crowned with garlands of papyrus, and received with every token of welcome ; but when he refused "the sweetmeats, confections, and perfumes," the Egyptians held him in great contempt, as a person unaccustomed to, and unworthy of, the manners of civilised society.

The Greeks, and other ancient people, usually put on a particular garment at festive meetings‡, generally of a white colour § ; but it does not appear to have been customary with the Egyptians to make any great alteration in their attire, though probability, as well as the sculptures, lead us to conclude that they abstained from dresses of a gloomy hue.

The guests being seated, and having received these tokens of welcome, wine was offered them by the servants. To the ladies it was generally brought in a small vase ‖, which, when emptied

---

* Athen. iii. 22.   † Plut. in Agesil.
‡ Conf. Matt. xxii. 11.
§ Whence Cicero, " Quis unquam cænavit atratus ? " in Vatinium.
‖ Wine was not only indispensable at an Egyptian, but also at a
Greek feast ; where " wine, bread, meat, couches, and tables were considered absolutely necessary." Plut. Sympos. ii.

into the drinking cup, was handed to an under
servant, or slave, who followed; but to the men it
was frequently presented in a one-handled goblet,
without being poured into any cup, and sometimes in a large or small vase of gold, silver, or
other materials.   Nor does it appear to have been

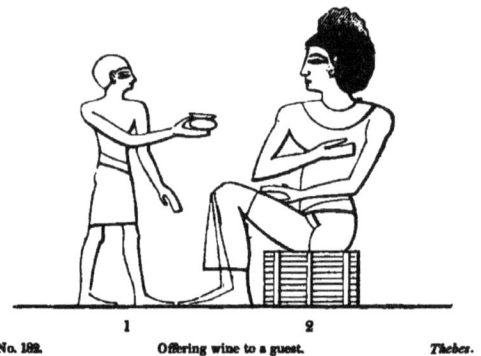

No. 182.   Offering wine to a guest.   Thebes.

the custom of the Egyptians to provide each
guest with his own cup, as among the ancient
Greeks*, though we have evidence of its having
been the case in some instances, and one was kept
exclusively for the use of the master of the house.†

Herodotus and Hellanicus both say that they
drank wine out of brass or bronze goblets; and, indeed, the former affirms that this was the only kind
of drinking cup known to the Egyptians‡; but he is

* Homer, Il. iv. 262. " Σον δε δεπας."
† Conf. Gen. xliv. 5. " Is not this it (the cup) in which my lord
drinketh ? "
‡ Herodot. ii. 37. " They drink out of brass cups, which they take
care to cleanse every day ; nor is this custom confined to certain indi-

not supported by fact, since we find that Joseph[*]
had one of silver, and the sculptures represent
them of glass and porcelain[†], as well as bronze
and the metals above mentioned.   That those who
could not afford the more costly kind should be
satisfied with a cheaper quality, is highly probable,
and many were doubtless contented with cups of
common earthenware : and though it may be said
that the modern Egyptians have the custom of
drinking water from earthen bottles, yet many
of the richer classes have brass[‡] or, occasionally,
porcelain and silver cups; and if these are used by
a far less civilised and opulent people, for so simple
a beverage as water, how much more likely were
they to have been adopted by the ancient Egyptians, a people who were possessed of great riches,
fond of luxury and show, and known to have employed vases of glass, porcelain, and the precious
metals, for numerous purposes, both in their houses
and in the temples of the gods.

The practice of introducing wine at the commencement[§] of an entertainment, or before dinner
had been served up, was not peculiar to this people;
and the Chinese, to the present day, offer it at

---

viduals, but is universally adopted by every one." " Ουχ ο μεν, ο δ' ου,
αλλα παντες."

[*] Gen. xliv. 2. 5. " My cup, the silver cup."

[†] The pocula murrina of the Romans.   Plin. xxxiii. 1., and
xxxvii. 2.

[‡] These are also used by the *subbalin*, who sell water in the streets
of Cairo.

[§] The same was usual at banquets in Judæa and other parts of Syria.
" That drink wine in bowls, and anoint themselves with the chief ointments." Amos, vi. 6.

their parties, to all the guests, as they arrive, in the same manner as the ancient Egyptians. We also find that they drank wine during the repast * ; perhaps, also, to the health of one another, or of an absent friend, like the Romans † ; and if they had no *rex convivii* ‡, or president, to encourage hilarity, or to check excess, we may conclude that the master of the house recommended a choice wine, and pledged them to the cup.§   They sometimes crowned the bowl with wreaths of flowers ‖, a custom prevalent also among the Greeks and Romans ¶, and a vase filled with blossoms of the lotus was frequently placed on a stand before the master of the house, or presented to him by a servant.

MUSIC.

While dinner was preparing **, the party was enlivened by the sound of music; and a band, consist-

* Gen. xliii. 34. " They drank wine, and were merry with him." The Hebrew is ישכרו, which is to be merry from strong drink. Sikr, שכר, implies the same in Hebrew and Arabic.

† Pers. v. 1. 20. Hor. Od. i. 27. 9. Ovid. Fast. iii. 531.

‡ Arbiter bibendi, or συμποσιαρχος, chosen by lot. Hor. Od. lib. i. 4.

§ Gen. xliii. 34. Thus Trimalchio to his guests, " Ergo vivamus dum licet esse bene." Conf. Isaiah, xxii. 13. Luke, xii. 19., and Wisdom of Solomon, ii. 6. " Let us enjoy the good things that are present, ... let us fill ourselves with costly wine and ointments ; and let no flower of the spring pass by us : let us crown ourselves with rose-buds before they be withered ;" and 1 Cor. xv. 32. " Let us eat and drink, for to-morrow we die ; " which were borrowed from the sayings of the day.

‖ *Vide* plate 12.

¶ Virg. Æn. i. 747. and iii. 525. : —

     " Tum pater Anchises magnum cratera corona
     Induit, implevitque mero " . . . .

** In early times, as with the modern Arabs, the master of the house killed the sheep, or whatever was to be brought to table ; as Achilles, at the reception of Priam. Il. Ω. 621.   At the feast of the Eed, among the Moslems, the same custom continues, even in the cities.

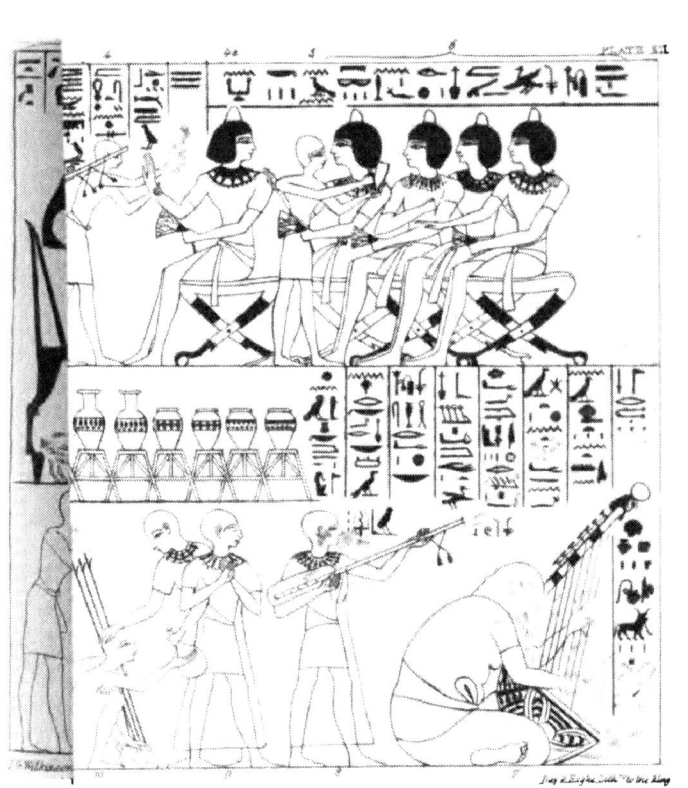

ing of the harp, lyre, *guitar*, tambourine, double
and single pipe, flute, and other instruments, played
the favourite airs and songs of the country.   Nor
was it deemed unbecoming the gravity and dignity
of a priest to admit musicians into his house, or to
take pleasure in witnessing the dance ; and, seated
with their wives and family in the midst of their
friends, the highest functionaries of the sacerdotal
order enjoyed the lively scene.   In the same manner, at a Greek entertainment, diversions of all
kinds were introduced ; and Xenophon and Plato
inform us that Socrates, the wisest of men, amused
his friends with music, jugglers, mimics, buffoons,
and whatever could be desired for exciting cheer-
fulness and mirth.

   Though impossible for us now to form any
notion of the character or style of Egyptian music,
we may be allowed to conjecture that it was studied
on scientific principles ; and, from the great attention paid to it by Pythagoras, many years of whose
life were spent in learning " the wisdom of the
Egyptians," there is every reason to believe that
whatever defects existed in the skill of ordinary
performers, who gained their livelihood by playing
in public, or for the entertainment of a private
party, music was looked upon as an important
science, and diligently studied by the priests themselves. According to Diodorus it was not customary
to make music part of their education, being
deemed useless and even injurious, as tending to
render the minds of men effeminate ; but this remark can only apply to the custom of studying it

as an amusement, which might lead to luxurious
and dissolute habits : and Plato, who was well acquainted with the usages of the Egyptians, distinctly says that they considered music of the
greatest consequence, from its beneficial effects
upon the mind of youth.   This is confirmed by
the following assertion of Strabo, that the children
of the Egyptians were taught letters, the songs
appointed by law, and a certain kind of music,
established by government, to the exclusion of
every other ; and Diodorus himself not only allows
the invention of music to have been ascribed by
the Egyptians to divine origin, but shows that
the poets and musicians of Greece visited Egypt
for the purpose of improvement.*

The authority of Plato, who had spent thirteen
years in the country, and had paid particular attention to the institutions of the Egyptians, is of the
greatest weight on this question ; and the whole
passage connected with it is of so much interest,
that I cannot refrain from introducing the dialogue
in which it occurs. †

" *Athen. Guest.*   The plan we have been laying
down for the education of youth was known long
ago to the Egyptians, that nothing but beautiful
forms and fine music should be permitted to enter
into the assemblies of young people.   Having
settled what those forms and what that music
should be, they exhibited them in their temples ;

---

* Diod. i. 96.
† Plato, 2d book of Laws.

nor was it allowable for painters, or other imitative artists, to innovate or invent any forms different from what were established; nor lawful, either in painting, statuary, or any branches of music, to make any alteration : upon examination, therefore, you will find that the pictures and statues made ten thousand years ago are in no one particular better or worse than what they now make.

Clin. What you say is wonderful.

Athen. Yes, it is in the true spirit of legislation and policy : other things, practised among that people, may, perhaps, be of a trifling nature ; but what they ordained about music is right, and it deserves consideration, that they were able to make laws about things of this kind, firmly establishing such melody as was fitted to rectify the perverseness of nature. This must have been the work of the Deity, or of some divine man ; as in fact they say in Egypt, that the music which has been so long preserved was composed by Isis, and the poetry likewise ; so that, as I said, if any one is able to apprehend the rectitude of them, he ought to have the courage to reduce them to law and order. For the search of pleasure and pain, which is always directed to the use of new music, perhaps possesses no great power of corrupting the consecrated choir by an accusation of its antiquity. It appears, therefore, that the choir of the Egyptians was by no means capable of being corrupted, but that the contrary was entirely the case."

That the Egyptians were particularly fond of

music, is abundantly proved by the paintings in
their tombs of the earliest times; and we even
find they introduced figures performing on the
favourite instruments of the country, among the
devices with which they adorned fancy boxes or
trinkets; and the representation of a woman playing
the guitar, which forms part of an ornamental de-
sign on a wooden box, in the Berlin Museum, will
serve to illustrate this fact, and to show how much
grace is sometimes evinced in Egyptian designs.
Of this I shall have occasion to speak hereafter.*

That they paid great attention to the study of
music, and had arrived at a very accurate knowledge of the art, is evident, when we consider the
nature of the instruments they used, and the perfect acquaintance they must have had with the
principles of harmony; and not only do the sculptures prove the fondness, and, I may add, the skill
of the Egyptians, in the use of musical instruments,
but the fact is confirmed by a statement of Athenæus †, who expressly tells us that both the Greeks
and barbarians were taught by refugees from Egypt,
and that the Alexandrians were the most scientific
and skilful players on pipes and other instruments.

In the infancy of music, as Dr. Burney has justly
observed, " no other instruments were known than
those of percussion, and it was, therefore, little

* In Vol. III., beginning of Chap. VII.
† Athen. iv. 25. He quotes Menecles of Barca and Andron (in his
annals of Alexandria); and these migrations appear to have been most
numerous at the period when the 7th Ptolemy, called Cacergetes, per-
secuted men of art and science.

more than metrical." Pipes of various kinds, and the flute, were afterwards invented; at first very rude, and made of reeds, which grew in the rivers and lakes. The flute*, says Horace †, was originally small and simple, with a few holes, and if it was introduced at the chorus of a play, its sound had only sufficient power to suit a theatre of a very limited size. But in process of time it was made larger, with more notes and a louder tone, and, bound with brass, it rivalled the tone of the trumpet. To discover, we can scarcely say to invent, such simple instruments, required a very slight effort, which observation afterwards improved; and music must have undergone a regular progression, through the early stages of infancy and youth, till it attained the age of maturity. But, ere it reached this stage of perfection, the powers of the human mind had been called forth to exalt its character; improvement followed improvement, and music became a noble and valuable science. To the alterations made in the simple instruments of early times, succeeded the invention of others of a far more complicated kind; and the many-

---

* Tibia was the flute; but it also signified a pipe, and the name tibia dextra et sinistra was applied to the double pipe. Tibia obliqua, πλαγιαυλος, was properly the flute.

†   " Tibia non ut nunc orichalco vincta, tubæque
       Æmula, sed tenuis simplexque, foramine pauco
       Adspirare et adesse choris erat utilis, atque
       Nondum spissa nimis implere sedilia flatu:
       Postquam . . . . .
       Accessit numerisque modisque licentia major . . . .
       Sic priscæ motumque et luxuriem addidit arti."
                               Hor. de Art. Poët. 202.

stringed harp, lyre, and other instruments, added
to the power and variety of musical sounds.

To contrive a method of obtaining perfect melody from a smaller number of strings, by shortening them on a neck during the performance, like
our modern violin, was, unquestionably, a more
difficult task than could be accomplished in the
infancy of music, and great advances must have
been already made in the science before this could
be attained, or before the idea would suggest itself
to the mind. With this principle, however, the
Egyptians were well acquainted, and the sculptures
unquestionably prove it, in the frequent use of the
three-stringed guitar.

A harp or lyre, having a number of strings,
imitating various sounds, and disposed in the order
of notes, might be invented even in an early stage
of the art; but a people who had not attentively
studied the nature of musical sounds would necessarily remain ignorant of the method of procuring
the same tones from a limited number of strings;
nor are our means simplified till they become perfectly understood. It is, then, evident, not only
from the great fondness for music evinced by the
early Egyptians, but from the nature of the very
instruments they used, that the art was studied
with great attention, and that they extended the
same minute and serious investigation to this as
to other sciences. And though Diodorus * thinks

* Diod. i. 1.

that the Egyptians did not consider music a necessary part of an accomplished education, yet he
attributes * the invention of it to the same deity
who gave them laws and letters, who regulated the
affairs of religion, and who taught them astronomy,
and all useful and ornamental arts.

. This fabulous account of its origin evidently
shows music to have been sanctioned, and even
cultivated, by the priests themselves, who invariably pretended to have derived from the gods the
knowledge of the sciences they encouraged, of
which their body was the sole repository and
source. Hermes or Mercury was, therefore, reputed to be the first discoverer of the harmony and
principle of voices or sounds, and the inventor of
the lyre.†

From his limiting the number of its chords to
three, the historian evidently confounds the lyre
with the Egyptian guitar; yet this traditional
story, which he learnt during his visit to the country, serves to attest the remote antiquity of stringed
instruments, and proves the great respect paid to
music by the Egyptian priests, who thought it not
unworthy of a deity to be its patron and inventor.
In Greece, too, where music was particularly encouraged, its invention was attributed to the gods.
Wind instruments were said to owe their origin to

* Diod. i. 16.
† The same fable passed into Greece; but Apollo was said to have
been the first who accompanied the lyre with his voice, and this was
supposed to have given him a decided superiority over the flute of
Marsyas.

Q 3 .

Minerva, as the lyre to Mercury, and Apollo was the patron of the science.

In noticing the harps of a tomb at Thebes[*], Bruce makes the following remark, that they " overturn all the accounts hitherto given of the earliest state of music and musical instruments in the East; and are, altogether, in their form, ornaments, and compass, an incontestable proof, stronger than a thousand Greek quotations, that geometry, drawing, mechanics, and music were at the greatest perfection when this instrument was made, and that the period from which we date the invention of these arts was only the beginning of the era of their restoration." [†] But if his remark applies to the harp, with much greater force does it to the three-stringed guitar above mentioned; and though we cannot fix the precise era of the invention of this, or of any other Egyptian instrument, sufficient is known from the sculptures to prove that they were in common use[‡] at the earliest periods of their known history.[§]   The tomb in which the harps described by Bruce are painted, is one of those called Bibán el Moloók, where the kings of Egypt were interred; the description of which I

[*] Of the time of Remeses III. b. c. 1235 ; consequently far from being the oldest harps represented in Egyptian sculpture.   *Vide* plate 13.

[†] Bruce's Travels, book i. c. 6.

[‡] The harp, or a sort of lyre, was a common instrument in Syria in the time of Jacob. Gen. xxxi. 27.; and this and the " organ " ? *kinoor* and *aogab*, were said to have been invented by Jubal, the sixth descendant of Cain. Gen. iv. 21.

[§] Those at the pyramids are apparently of a date long previous to Osrtasen, or the arrival of Joseph.

have given in a previous work *, under the title of
" Bruce's, or the Harper's, tomb."

The name of Bruce ought not to be passed by
without a tribute to the injured memory of one
whose zeal was rewarded with reproach and disbe-
lief. †   How easy is the part of a sceptic!   What a
slight effort, yet what an air of superiority, and appearance of learning, attend the expression of a
doubt!   Bruce had been *provokingly* enterprising.
Many of his readers were incredulous, because he
had done what they, in the plenitude of their wisdom, conceived impossible ;   and many of those
most violent in their censures had neither sufficient
experience or knowledge of the subject to hazard
an opinion.   Envy prompted some, and fashion
more, to speak of Bruce's narrative as a tale of wonder, or a pure invention ‡ ;   and those who had never
read his work fearlessly pronounced a censure to
which others were known to assent.   But it is gratifying to find that the more mature investigations
of the present day have vindicated the character
of this distinguished traveller ;   and it is to be

---

* Egypt and Thebes, p. 109.

† This was particularly striking with regard to his visit to the emerald
mines. Bruce, book i. c. 11.

‡ In the Walpoliana are this remark and anecdote. " Bruce's over-
bearing manner has raised enmity and prejudices; and he did wrong in
retailing the most wonderful parts of his book in companies. A story
may be credible, when attended with circumstances, which seems false
if detached. I was present in a large company at dinner, where Bruce
was talking away. Some one asked, ' What musical instruments are
used in Abysinnia ? ' Bruce hesitated, not being prepared for the question, and at last said, ' I think I saw one *lyre* there.' George Selwyn
whispered his next man, ' Yes ; and there is one less since he left the
country.' "

hoped that his name will henceforward continue to be attached to the interesting monument above alluded to, as a memorial of his diligence under the most unfavourable circumstances, and as a token of his veracity. And so shall the name of Bruce be honoured *in his tomb*.

It is sufficiently evident, from the sculptures of the ancient Egyptians, that their hired musicians were acquainted with the triple symphony ; the harmony of instruments ; of voices ; and of voices and

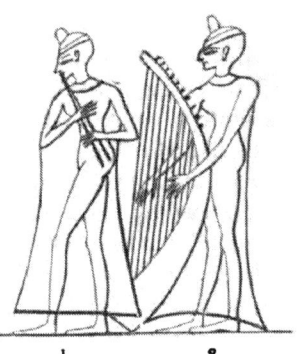

No. 183.   1   2   *Thebes.*
The harp and double pipe.

instruments.* Their band was variously composed, consisting either of two harps, with the single pipe † and flute; of the harp and double pipe, frequently with the addition of the guitar; of a fourteen-stringed harp, a guitar, lyre, double pipe,

* *Vide* wood-cut, No. 184. etc.
† It was played by the Greeks and Romans, to accompany the lyre and other instruments. Whence Horace : —
" Cur pendet tacita fistula cum lyra." Od. lib. iii. 19. 19.

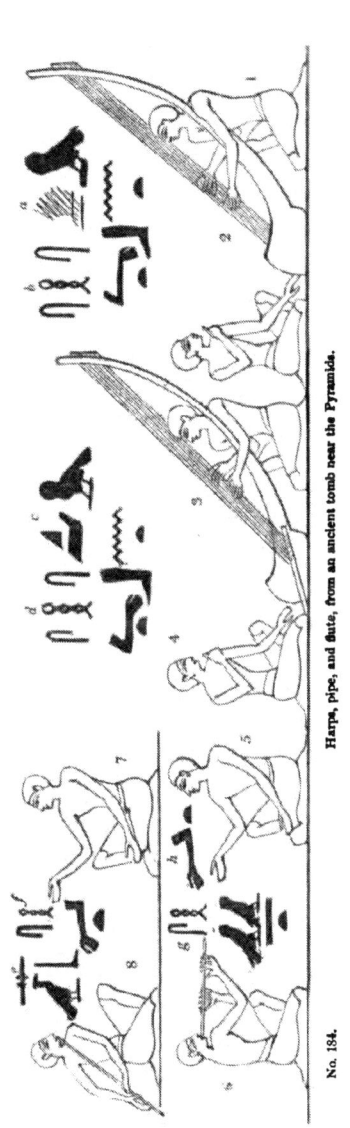

No. 184.

Harp, pipe, and flute, from an ancient tomb near the Pyramids.

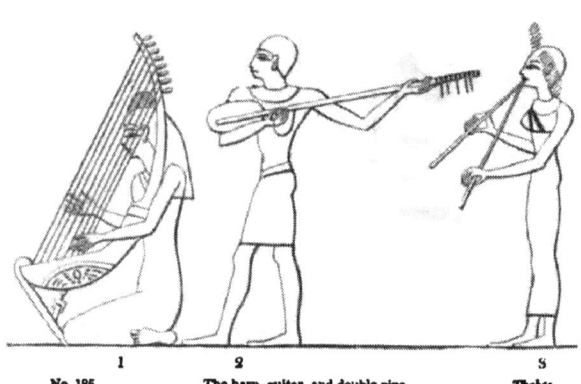

No. 185.   The harp, guitar, and double pipe.   *Thebes.*

and tambourine; of two harps, sometimes of different sizes, one of seven, the other of four, strings;
of two harps of eight chords, and a seven-stringed

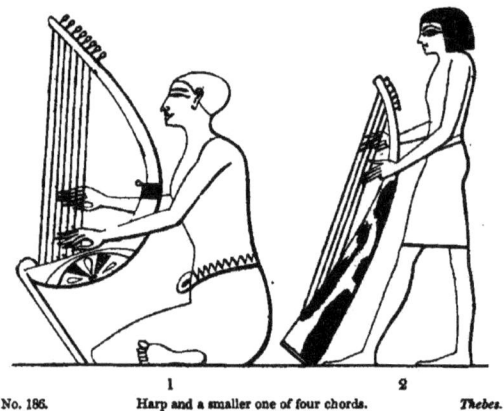

No. 186.   Harp and a smaller one of four chords.   *Thebes.*

lyre; of the guitar, and the square or oblong tambourine; of the lyre, harp, guitar, double pipe, and

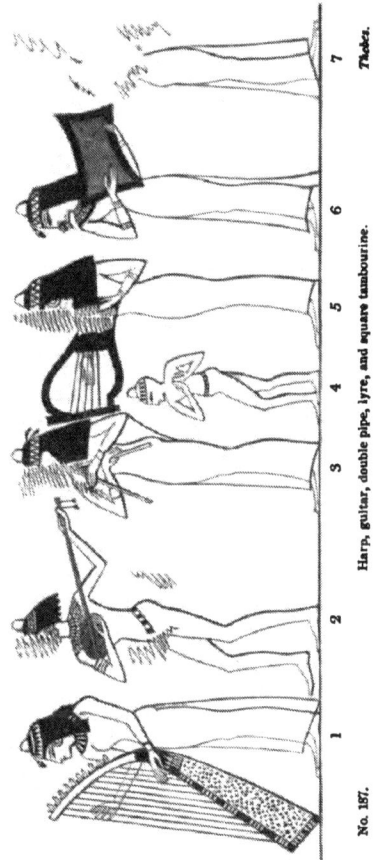

No. 187.   Harp, guitar, double pipe, lyre, and square tambourine.   Thebes.

a sort of harp with four strings, which was held upon the shoulder *; of the harp, guitar, double pipe,

* *Vide* wood-cut, No. 209.

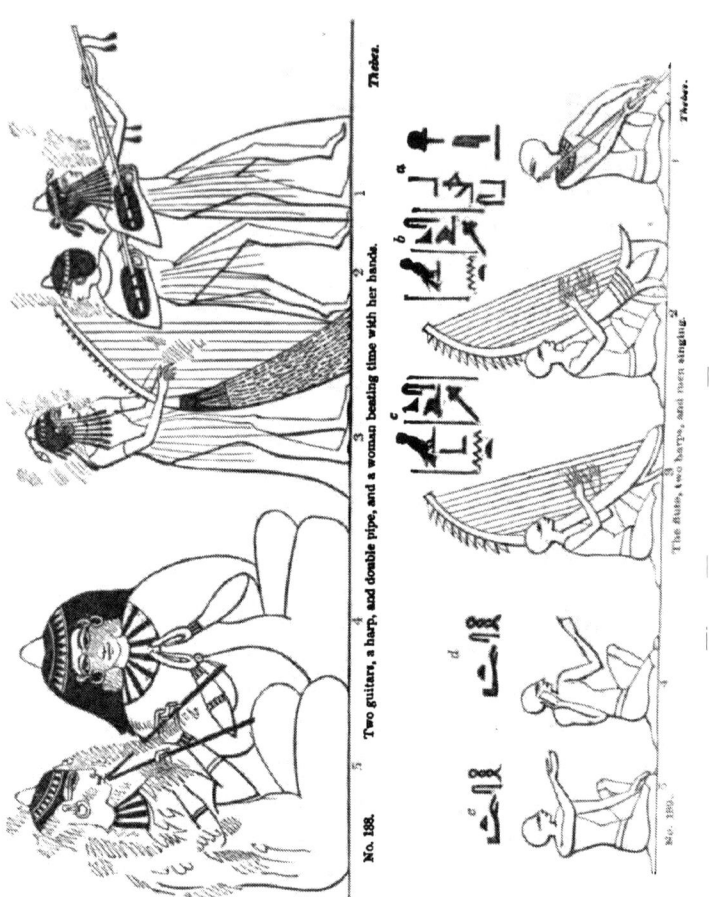

lyre, and square tambourine *; of the harp, two
guitars, and the double pipe †; of the harp, two
flutes, and a guitar ‡; of two harps and a flute; of

* *Vide* wood-cut, No. 187.   † *Vide* wood-cut, No. 188.
‡ *Vide* sacred music, wood-cut, No. 229.

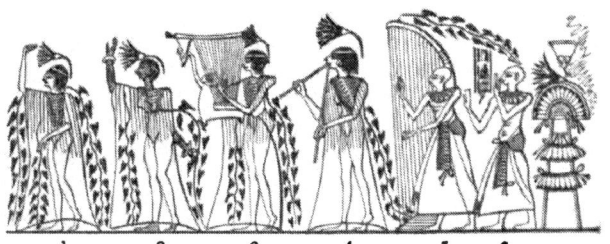

No. 190.   Men and women singing to the harp, lyre, and double pipe.   *Thebes.*

a seventeen-stringed lyre, the double pipe, and a harp of fourteen chords; of the harp and two guitars; or of two seven-stringed harps and an instrument held in the hand, not unlike an eastern

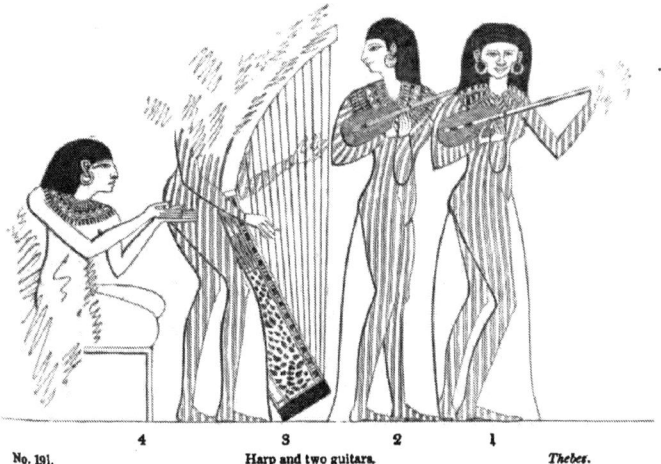

No. 191.   Harp and two guitars.   *Thebes.*

fan *, to which were probably attached small bells, or pieces of metal that emitted a jingling sound

* *Vide* wood-cut, No. 192. *fig.* 3.

when shaken, like the crescent-crowned *bells* of our modern bands; besides many other combinations

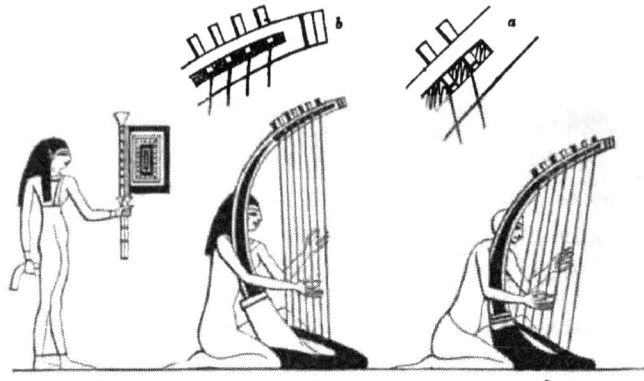

No. 192.—Two harps, and another instrument which perhaps emitted a jingling sound.
a and *b* show how the strings were wound round the pegs.   *Beni Hassan.*

of these various instruments; and in the Bacchic festival of Ptolemy Philadelphus, described by Athenæus, more than 600 musicians were employed in the chorus, among whom were 300 performers on the *cithara.*[*]

Sometimes the harp was played alone, or as an accompaniment to the voice; and a band of seven or more choristers frequently sang to it a favourite air, beating time with their hands between each stanza.   They also sang to other instruments [†], as the lyre, guitar, or double pipe, or to several of them played together, as the flute and one or more harps, or to these last with a lyre, or a

---

[*] Athen. lib. v.
[†] *Vide* wood-cuts, Nos. 188, 189, 190, and 191.

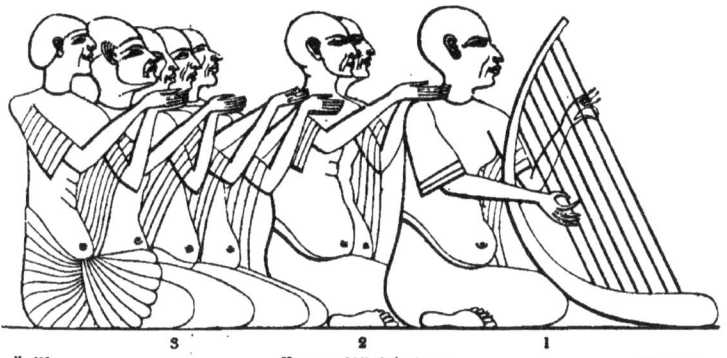

No. 193.   3 .   Harper and blind choristers.   2   1   *Alabastron.*

guitar. It was not unusual for one man or one woman to perform a solo; and a chorus of many persons occasionally sang at a private assembly without any instrument, two or three beating time at intervals with the hand. Sometimes the band of

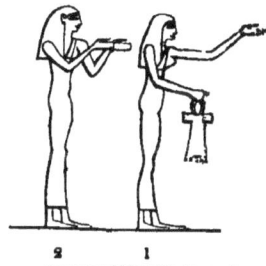

No. 194.   An unusual kind of instrument.   2   1   *Thebes.*

choristers consisted of more than twenty persons, only two of whom responded by clapping their hands *; and in one instance I have seen a female

* *Vide* Herodot. ii. 60., where they are said to play the flute and cymbals, and to clap their hands; and the sculptures *passim.*

represented holding what is, perhaps, a species of instrument, whose use and sound may have been similar to the one above mentioned.*

The custom of beating time by clapping the hands between the stanzas, is still usual in Egypt, though I conceive it to be no longer done in the same manner by the modern as by the ancient Egyptians, whose notions of music, as of every other subject, must have been very different from those of their uncivilised successors.

On some occasions women beat the tambourine and *darabooka* drum†, without the addition of any

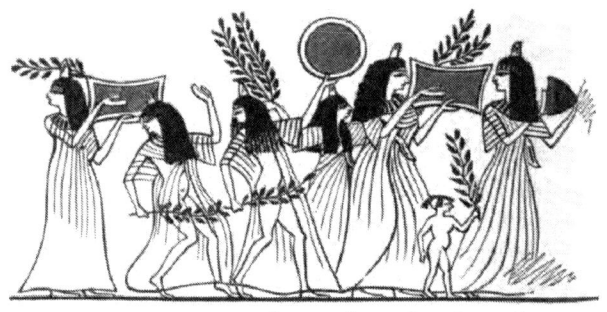

| 7 | 6 | 5 | 4 | 3 | 2 | 1 |

No. 195.   Women beating tambourines, and the *darabooka* drum (fig. 1.).   *Thebes*

other instrument, dancing or singing to the sound; and, bearing palm branches, or green twigs in their hands, they proceeded to the tomb of a deceased friend, accompanied by this species of music: and the same custom may still be traced in the Friday visit to the cemetery, and in some other funeral

* In p. 237.   *Vide* wood-cut, No. 194. *fig.* 1.
† The darabooka is a sort of drum still used in Egypt, where it bears this name.   *Vide* wood-cut, No. 195.

ceremonies among the Moslem peasants of modern Egypt.

If it was not customary for the higher classes of Egyptians to learn music for the purpose of playing in society, and if few amateur performers could be found among persons of rank, still some general knowledge of the art must have been acquired by a people so alive to its charms ; and the attention paid to it by the priests regulated the taste, and prevented the introduction of a vitiated style.   Those who played at the houses of the rich, as well as the ambulant musicians of the streets, were of the lower classes, and made this employment the means of obtaining their livelihood ; and in many instances both the minstrels and the choristers were blind.*

From what has been said, it appears, first, that music was studied by the Egyptian priests with other views than that of affording pleasure and entertainment, the same science being borrowed by Pythagoras from Egypt.   Secondly, that it was universally used at their private parties, where professional people were hired to perform.   Thirdly, that we are to understand from the remark of Diodorus, of its not being customary for the Egyptians to learn music, that the higher orders did not study it as an amusement; and though the twelfth Ptolemy obtained the surname of Auletes from his skill in playing the flute, we cannot infer a general custom from the caprice of a Greek.   Strabo, in-

* *Vide* wood-cut, No. 193.

deed, censures his taste ; but this was rather owing
to the feelings of a Roman*, than to the conviction
that the conduct of the monarch was at variance
with the customs of his people : for the Greeks†
had not the same prejudices against music and the
dance as many of the Romans; and, so far from
deeming it unworthy a person of rank to excel in
them, no one was thought to have received a proper education who possessed not those accomplishments. Cicero observes ‡, that "they considered
the arts of singing and playing upon musical instruments a very principal part of learning;
whence it is related of Epaminondas, who, in my
judgment, was the first of all the Greeks, that he
played very well upon the flute. And, some time
before, Themistocles, upon refusing the harp at an
entertainment, passed for an uninstructed and ill-
bred person. Hence Greece became celebrated
for skilful musicians ; and as all persons there
learned music, those who attained to no profi-
ciency in it were thought uneducated and unac-
complished." Cornelius Nepos, again, mentioning
Epaminondas, observes that "he played the harp
and flute, and perfectly understood the art of
dancing, with other liberal sciences;" "though,"
he adds, "in the opinion of the Romans, these
are trivial things, and not worthy of notice, yet in

* Strabo was born at Amasia, in Pontus, on the borders of Cappadocia, and had studied in Greece, but was educated as a Roman.
† Polybius, lib. iv. 20, 21., commends the Arcadians for their love of
music and the dance. *Vide* Plato's Crito. s. xii. ; Phædo. s. iv.; Al-
cibiad. A. s. vi. ; and Olympiodorus' Life of Plato.
‡ Cic. Tusc. Quæst. lib. i.

Greece they were reckoned highly commend-able."

Nor was it regarded with any other feeling by the Israelites; and they not only considered it becoming to delight in music and the dance, but persons of rank deemed them a necessary part of their education. Like the Egyptians, with whom they had so long resided, and many of whose customs they adopted, the Jews carefully distinguished sacred from profane music. They introduced it at public and private rejoicings, at funerals, and in religious services: but the character of the airs, like the words of their songs, varied according to the occasion; and they had canticles of mirth, of praise, of thanksgiving, and of lamentation. Some were *epithalamia*, or songs composed to celebrate marriages; others to com-memorate a victory, or the accession of a prince; to return thanks to the Deity, or to celebrate his praises; to lament a general calamity, or a private affliction; and others, again, were peculiar to their festive meetings. On these occasions they introduced the harp, lute, tabret *, and various in-struments, together with songs and dancing, and the guests were entertained nearly in the same manner as at an Egyptian feast. In the temple, and in the religious ceremonies, the Jews had female as well as male performers, who were gene-

* Conf. Luke, xv. 25. " He heard music and dancing;" and Gen. xxxi. 27., where Laban complains that Jacob did not allow him to ce-lebrate his departure with a festive meeting, " with mirth and with songs, with tabret and with harp." This last, however, in the Hebrew, is kinoor, כנור, which is rather a lyre. It was known in the days of Seth, Gen. iv. 21., and of Job, xxi. 12.

rally daughters of the Levites, as the Pallaces * of
Thebes were either of the royal family, or the
daughters of priests; and these musicians were attached exclusively to the service of religion, as I
believe them also to have been in Egypt, whether
men or women.   David was not only remarkable
for his taste and skill in music, but took a delight
in introducing it on every occasion.   " And seeing
that the Levites were numerous, and no longer
employed as formerly in carrying the boards, veils,
and vessels of the tabernacle, its abode being fixed
at Jerusalem, he appointed a great part of them to
sing and play on instruments, at the religious festivals."   Solomon, again, at the dedication of the
temple, employed " 120 priests, to sound with
trumpets † ; " and Josephus pretends that no less
than 200,000 musicians were present at that ceremony, besides the same number of singers, who
were Levites.‡

It has always been doubted whether the Jews
studied music with the same systematic views as
the Egyptians and Greeks; and as all airs, previous
to the invention of notation, must have been traditional, and in some degree dependent on the taste
and memory of the performers, many have questioned the possibility of their being either numerous
or faithfully preserved.

* *Vide suprà*, Vol. I. p. 258., on the orders of the Egyptian priesthood.

† 2 Chron. v. 12.

‡ Joseph. Antiq. lib. viii. 3. " Solomon made 200,000 trumpets, according to the command of Moses, and 200,000 garments of fine linen
for the singers, who were Levites . . . . . and instruments for singing
hymns, nablæ and cinyr, made of the finest brass, 40,000."

The early Greeks and Egyptians may not have had the means of handing down their compositions with the same fidelity as modern nations, yet this objection does not apply to the study of the science itself; their object being rather to touch the feeling than to delight the ear. It is impossible for us to determine whether the Egyptian priests, in later times, devised any method of preserving their melodies, or trusted entirely to oral tradition, as this secret would have been concealed by them with the same jealous care as the mysteries themselves; judging, however, from that adopted in Greece *, which was by disposing the letters of the alphabet in different ways, we may conclude that if the Egyptians really had any, it was equally cumbrous and imperfect.

Respecting the origin of this invention among the Greeks there is a diversity of opinion; it is generally attributed to Terpander, a celebrated poet and musician†, who flourished about 670 years before our era; but the complication of sixteen hundred and twenty different notes must at all times have presented a considerable difficulty in reading and recollecting them. '

To inquire into the notions of Pythagoras, Plato ‡, and other Greek sages, who spent much

* In one of the paintings from Herculaneum, a woman is seen playing on a lyre of eleven strings, and another sings from a paper which she holds in her hand, and which has either the notes, or the words of the song, written upon it.

† Plutarch, de Musicâ.

‡ Plato and Eudoxus were thirteen years in Egypt, according to Strabo (lib. xvii.). In one of the tombs of the kings at Thebes is an inscription, written by a *daduchus* or torchbearer of the Eleusynian

time in Egypt, must be highly interesting, as it is almost the only means of obtaining any information respecting the character of Egyptian music, and their notions on the subject; and we have the authority of Plutarch and other authors for believing that Plato* and Pythagoras paid the greatest attention to this science. The latter considered one of the noblest purposes to which it could be applied was to soothe and calm the mind†, and deemed it the duty of a philosopher to look upon it as an intellectual study, rather than an amusement; for the gravity of Pythagoras censured the custom of judging music by the senses, and required that it should be submitted to the acumen of the mind, and examined by the rules of harmonic proportion.‡ It was the idea of this philosopher " that air was the vehicle of sound, and that the agitation of that element, occasioned by a similar action in the parts of the sounding body, was its cause. The vibrations of a string, or other sonorous body, being communicated to the air, affected the auditory nerves with the sensation of sound; and this sound," he argued, " was acute or grave in proportion as the vibrations were quick or slow." Others were of a different opinion; and "Aristoxenus held the ear to be the sole standard of musical proportions. He esteemed that

---

mysteries, who says he examined those monuments many years " after the divine Plato."

* Plut. de Musicâ.

† Plut. de Virtute morali.   Strabo, lib. i. p. 11., ed. Cas.   Jamblich. de Vita Pythag. &c.

‡ Plut. de Musicâ.

sense sufficiently accurate for musical, though not for mathematical, purposes; and it was, in his opinion, absurd to aim at an artificial accuracy in gratifying the ear, beyond its own power of distinction.   He, therefore, rejected the velocities, vibrations, and proportions of Pythagoras, as foreign to the subject, in so far as they substituted abstract causes in the room of experience, and made music the object of intellect, rather than of sense." *   Modern investigations, however, have confirmed the statements of Pythagoras, and absolute demonstration has placed them beyond the possibility of doubt.

An interesting question now suggests itself: Whence did Pythagoras derive his notions respecting the theory of sound? Did he arrive at these conclusions from his own experience? Or is it not more probable that he was indebted to those under whom he studied for this insight into a subject they had so long been examining? But the fact of Pythagoras being the sole teacher of this doctrine, goes far to prove that it did not originate in Greece, and that his opinions were founded on Egyptian data.   For what that philosopher asserted respecting sound, emitted by a long and short string of the same quality and thickness, " that the shorter made the quicker vibrations and uttered the acuter sound," had been already shown by the Egyptians; and we may fairly conclude that he derived his knowledge of this

* *Vide* Encyclop. Brit. art. Music.

R 4

subject from the same source * as that of the solar
system, which remained unknown in Europe from
his time to the days of Copernicus, and with
which Pythagoras, of all the Greeks, was alone
acquainted. †

On the sacred music of Egypt I shall make a
few remarks in another part of this work: I
now return to their customs at private entertainments.   When hired to attend at a party, the musicians either stood in the centre or at one side
of the festive chamber, and some sat cross-legged
on the ground ‡, like the Turks and other Eastern
people of the present day.   They were usually.
accompanied on these occasions by dancers, either
men or women, sometimes both ; whose art consisted in assuming all the graceful or ludicrous
gestures, which could obtain the applause, or tend
to the amusement, of the assembled guests.

Music § and dancing are also mentioned as having

---

* Jamblichus informs us that Pythagoras derived his information
upon different sciences from Egypt, and taught them to his disciples
(Jambl. de Vita Pythag. lib. i. c. 29.); that he learnt philosophy from
the Egyptian priests (Jambl. i. c. 28.); and that he employed music
for curing diseases both of body and mind. (Jambl. i. cc. 25. 29. and 31.)
" Ὑπελαμβανε δε και την Μουσικην μεγαλα συμβαλλεσθαι προς ὑγιειαν . . . . .
πολυωφελεστατην κατεστησατο Πυθαγορας την δια Μουσικης των αν-
θρωπινων ηθων τε και βιων επανορθωσιν." He maintained that music
greatly conduced to health . . . . and that to temper and direct the
morals and lives of men by means of music was most beneficial." i. 25.

† Cicero, quoting Theophrastus, says that Icetas of Syracuse was
of opinion that the heavens, the sun, moon, stars, and all bodies above
us stood still, and that the earth alone moved, having the same effect
when turned on its axis as if all the others were in motion.   Acad.
Qu. 54. 39.

‡ Vide wood-cut, No. 170. fig. 1. No. 185. and 192. and pl. 12.

§ The Nabathæans of Arabia Petræa always introduced music at
their entertainments (Strabo, xvii.); and the custom appears to have
been very general among the ancients.

been considered essential at entertainments, among the Greeks, from the earliest times; and are pronounced by Homer * to be diversions requisite at a feast; " an opinion," says Plutarch †, " confirmed by Aristoxenus, who observes, that music is recommended in order to counteract the effect of inebriety; for as wine discomposes the body and mind, so music has the power of soothing them, and of restoring their previous calmness and tranquillity."   Such, indeed, may have been the light in which the philosophic mind of Plutarch regarded ‡ the introduction of those diversions, and such he attributed to the observation of the poet; but it may be questioned whether they always tended to the sobriety either of the Greeks or of the lively Egyptians.

Of the style and nature of Egyptian music we can glean but little from Herodotus, or any other writer who has mentioned the subject. The remark of the father of history, that some of their songs bore a plaintive character, is probably just; yet we cannot imagine it applicable to the generality of those introduced at the festive meetings of a cheerful people. That called Maneros, he sup-

---

* Homer, Od. i. 152. : —

    " Μολπη τ' ορχηστυς τε, τα γαρ τ' αναθηματα δαιτος,"
quoted by Plutarch, de Musicâ.

† Plut. *loc. cit.*

‡ The ancients had very high notions of the effects of music; some founded on fact, others on fable and imagination. Of these last were the building of the walls of Thebes by the sound of Amphion's lyre, to which Pausanias gravely refuses to lend his authority (lib. ix.); and some of the stories related by Ælian of its effects upon wild animals, Nat. Hist. xii. 46. &c.

poses to be the same as the Linus of the Greeks,
" which was known in Phœnicia, Cyprus, and other
places * : " and he expresses his surprise that the
same song should be met with on the banks of the
Nile.   " I have been struck," says the historian,
" with many things during my inquiries in Egypt,
but with none more than this song, and I cannot
conceive from whence it was borrowed ; indeed,
they seem to have had it from time immemorial,
and to have known it by the name Maneros † : for
they assured me it was so called from the son of
their first monarch, who, being carried off by a pre-
mature death, was honoured by the Egyptians with
a funeral dirge.   And this was the first and only
song they used at that early period of their history."

Though this account is highly improbable, yet
we learn from it that one of the many songs of the
Egyptians was similar to the Linus of Greece,
which was of a plaintive character, peculiarly
adapted to mournful occasions ; but whether it was
of Egyptian or of Phœnician origin, it is of little
moment to inquire.   Plutarch, on the other hand,
asserts, that it was suited to festivities‡ and the pleasures of the table §, and that, "amidst the diversions of a sociable party, the Egyptians made the
room resound with the song of Maneros."   In

* Herodot. ii. 79.
† Pausanias (Græc. lib. ix.) says, " The Egyptians call the song of
Linus in their language Manerôs ; " and mentions two persons named
Linus. *Vide* also Hor. Od. lib. i. 12. 7. xxiv. 13., and Od. lib. iii.
11. 2.
‡ I have sometimes doubted, whether there may not have been also
a musical instrument of this name.
§ Plut. de Is. s. 17.

order, therefore, to reconcile these conflicting state-ments, we are naturally led to the conclusion, that the Egyptians had two songs, bearing a name re-sembling Maneros, which have been confounded together by Greek writers; and that one of these bore a lugubrious, the other a lively, character.

Many conjectures have been offered respecting the nature and origin of the song of Maneros, and some doubt its having derived this name from a son of the first Egyptian monarch *, contending that it was so called from the person to whom music owed its invention †; both which opinions are noticed by Plutarch; who in another work‡ states, on the authority of Heraclides, that Linus § was a native of Euboea. And from his adding, that Linus was famed for making lugubrious poems, it is evident that the song mentioned under this name by Herodotus, and considered to be the Maneros of Egypt, had a similar origin with the fabulous Linus himself.

If, however, conjecture is permitted, we may presume the song of Maneros did not derive its

* Herodotus, *loc. cit.* Plutarch says Maneros was the child who watched Isis as she mourned over the body of Osiris. *Vide* Athenæus, lib. xiv. Plut. de Is. s. 17.

† Plut. de Is. xvii. J. Pollux calls him the inventor of agriculture, and says the song Maneros was sung by husbandmen. Onom. iv. 7.

‡ Plut. de Musicâ.

§ But he does not confound the songs of Linus and Maneros, as Herodotus has done. Pausanias says Linus, the inventor of songs, was a son of Apollo (de Græc. lib. ii.); but refers to another part of his work (lib. ix.), where he mentions one Linus, the son of Amphimarus (the son of Neptune) and Urania, killed by Apollo; the other a son of Ismenius, killed by Hercules. Some suppose there were three of this name; but authors are not agreed upon the subject. Pausanias asserts " positively, that neither of the two just mentioned composed any poems; or, at least, any that came down to posterity." lib. ix.

name from any individual; * and if this and the Greek Linus resembled each other, it was probably merely in their general character.   The former idea is partly confirmed by another observation of Plutarch †, " that others say Maneros is not a name, but a complimentary manner of greeting made use of by the Egyptians to one another, at their solemn feasts and banquets, implying a wish 'that what they were then engaged in might prove fortunate and successful;' for such is the true import of the word." It is, indeed, reasonable to suppose, that their songs were made to suit the occasions, either of rejoicing and festivity, of solemnity, or of lamentation; and all their agricultural and other occupations had, undoubtedly, as at the present day, their appropriate songs.

At the religious ceremonies and processions, where music was introduced, there is reason to believe the attendance of ordinary performers was not permitted, but that musicians attached to the priestly order, and organised for this special purpose, were alone employed; who were considered to belong exclusively to the service of the temple, as each military band of their army to its respective corps.

When an individual died, it was usual for the women to issue forth from the house, and throwing dust and mud upon their heads ‡, to utter cries of lamentation as they wandered through the streets

* I think that this expression occurs in a hieroglyphic legend: " Menre, the maker of hymns:" perhaps applied to Re, the Sun.
† Plut. de Is. 17.
‡ Herodot. ii. 85.   Diod. ii. 91. as in 2 Sam. i. 2.

of the town, or amidst the cottages of the village. They sang a doleful dirge in token of their grief; they by turns expressed their regret for the loss of their relative or friend, and their praises of his virtues; and this was frequently done to the time and measure of a plaintive, though not inharmonious, air.* Sometimes the tambourine was introduced, and the "mournful song" was accompanied by its monotonous sound. On these occasions, the services of hired performers were uncalled for; though during the period of seventy days, while the body was in the hands of the embalmers, mourners† were employed, who sang the same plaintive dirge to the memory of the deceased; a custom prevalent also among the Jews, when preparing for a funeral. ‡

At their musical *soirées*, men or women played the harp, lyre, *guitar*, and the single or double pipe, but the flute appears to have been confined to men; and the tambourine and *darabooka* drum were generally appropriated to the other sex.

THE DARABOOKA DRUM.

The *darabooka* is rarely met with in the paintings of Thebes, and it is probable that it was only used on certain occasions, and chiefly, as at the present day, by the peasant women, and the boatmen of the

---

* Diod. ii. 72. 91.

† "Conducti ut plorant," hired to mourn, as with the Romans, and others. The Egyptians mourned for Jacob seventy days. Exod. l. 3. Herod. ii. 86.

‡ Matt. ix. 23. "And saw the minstrels and people making a noise." Jer. xvi. 5. 7.

Nile. From the representation given of it, I conclude it to be the same as that of the present day,

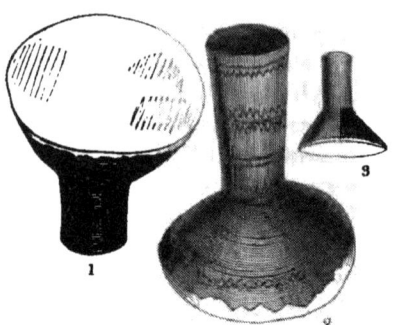

No. 196.   The darabooka of modern Egypt.

which is made of parchment, strained and glued
over a funnel-shaped case of pottery, which is a
hollow cylinder, with a truncated cone attached to
it. It is beaten with the hand, and if relaxed, they
brace the parchment by exposing it a few moments
to the sun, or the warmth of a fire. It is generally supported by a band round the neck of the
performer, who, with the fingers of the right hand,
plays the air, and with the left grasps the lower
edge of the head, in order to beat the bass, as in the
tambourine; which we find from the sculptures
was played in the same manner by the ancient
Egyptians.*

CYMBALS.

Besides these instruments, they had cymbals†,

* *Vide* wood-cut, No. 195.
† They have been found in the tombs of Thebes. *Vide infrà*, Sacred
Music.

and cylindrical maces, two of which were struck together, and probably emitted a sharp metallic sound.   The cymbals were of mixed metal, apparently brass, or a compound of brass and silver, and of a form exactly resembling those of modern times, though smaller, being only seven, or five inches and a half, in diameter.   The handle I believe to have been also of brass, bound with leather, string, or any similar substance, and being inserted in a small hole at the summit, was secured by bending back the two ends.   The same kind of instrument is used by the modern inhabitants of the country;

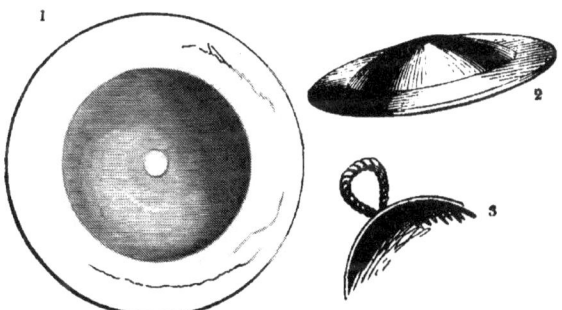

No. 197.   Egyptian cymbals five inches and a half in diameter.   *Salt's Collection.*

and from them have been borrowed those very small cymbals played with the finger and thumb *, which supply the place of castanets in the *almeh* dance.   Indeed, there can be no doubt that these

---

* The same manner of holding them is represented in the paintings of Herculaneum.

were the origin of the Spanish castanet, having been
introduced into that country by the Moors, and
afterwards altered in form, and made of chestnut
(castaña) and other wood, instead of metal.

The cymbals of modern Egypt are chiefly used
by the attendants of sheikhs' tombs, who travel
through the country at certain periods of the year,
to collect the charitable donations of the credulous,
or the devout, among the Moslems, who thus, indi-
rectly and unconsciously, encourage the idleness
of these pretenders, in the hopes of obtaining some
blessing from the indulgent saint. Drums and some
other noisy instruments, which are used at marriages and on other occasions, accompany the cymbals, but these last are more peculiarly appropriated
to the service of the sheikhs, and the external ceremonies of religion : and this is the more remarkable, as we find no instances in the paintings of
Thebes of their having been used at the festive
meetings of the ancient Egyptians ; and a female,
whose coffin contained a pair of cymbals, was
described in the hieroglyphics of the exterior as
the minstrel of a deity.   We may, therefore,
conclude, that this instrument belonged, as with
the modern Egyptians, to the service of religion,
though probably not so exclusively* as the sacred
sistrum.

---

* I am not certain that the two figures represented in the wood-cut
No. 201. are not playing cymbals, though from the injury done to
those sculptures we are unable to discover what they hold in their
hands. To judge, however, from their position, we may conclude
they are playing this instrument. " Sic geminant Corybantes æra."
Hor. Od. lib. i. 16. 8.

The cylindrical maces were also admitted among the instruments used on solemn occasions ; though they more properly formed part of the military band, or regulated the dance.   They varied slightly in form, but consisted generally of a straight handle,

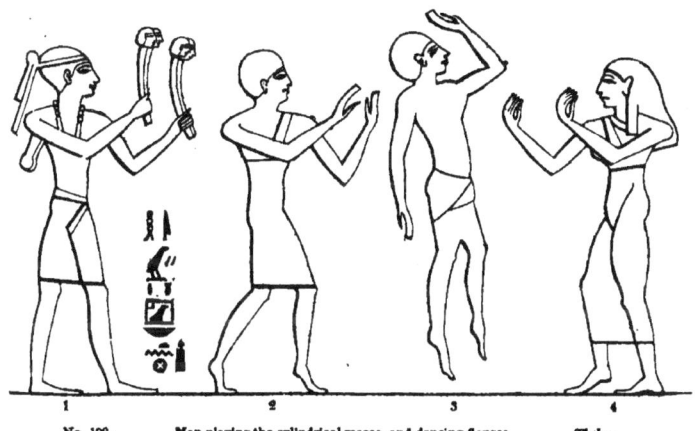

No. 198.   Man playing the cylindrical maces, and dancing figures.   *Thebes.*

or cylinder, surmounted by a head, or some orna-mental device, the whole being probably of brass, or other sonorous metal.   Sometimes the handle was slightly curved, and double, with two heads at the upper extremity; but in all cases, the performer held one in each hand; and the nature of the sound depended greatly on the force with which he struck them together.   It is not improbable, that their hollow head contained a loose metallic ball, which gave a jingling noise when shaken : and we find that the clang of such instruments was thought as essential for martial music three thousand years ago, as at the present day.

Similar to these maces* appear to have been the round-headed pegs, resembling large nails, seen in the hands of some dancing figures in the paintings of Herculaneum, and supposed to have been struck together, as an accompaniment to the lyre, which is played by another person, in the same picture : but I am not aware of their having been mentioned by any Greek or Latin writer.

We may conclude the Egyptians were not guilty of the same extravagance in music and other amusements, as the Greeks and Romans, extraordinary instances of which are mentioned by ancient authors. The flute of Ismenias, a celebrated Theban musician, cost at Corinth three talents, or 581l. 5s. of our money ; and if, says Xenophon, a bad flute-player would pass for a good one, he must, like those whose reputation is established, expend considerable sums on rich furniture, and appear in public with a large retinue of servants. Amœbæus, again, an Athenian harper of great repute, received an Attic talent, or 193l. 15s. a day for his performance : and the actors of the Roman stage were not only paid immense sums, Roscius making 500 sestertia, or 4036l. 9s. 2d. per annum ; but in later times they became such favourites, that they established parties in the city, and had sufficient influence to induce the people to espouse their quarrels.

* Similar instruments of wood are used in the same manner by the Japanese.

Though the Egyptians were fond of buffoonery and gesticulation, they do not seem to have had any public show which can be said to resemble a theatre; nor were their pantomimic exhibitions, which consisted chiefly in dancing and gesture *, accompanied with any scenic representation. The stage is, indeed, allowed to have been purely a Greek invention; and to dramatic entertainments, which were originally of two kinds, comedy and tragedy, were added the Roman pantomime. Music formed a principal part of the old comedy; and a chorus was present, as in tragedy, to sing between the acts.† And indeed when we consider the license of ancient comedy, and the frequent decrees which it was found necessary to make, in order to suppress it, and sometimes even to prohibit dramatic performances, or the erection of a theatre, we may be assured that similar representations would not have been tolerated by the severity of an Egyptian priesthood, whether the idea had originated in the country, or had been accidentally introduced at a later period from the Greeks.‡

MILITARY MUSIC.

Some instruments of the military band differed from those of ordinary musicians; but it may be

* At Rome, after the time of Augustus, the mimi, or pantomimi, were confined to these, and did not speak.

† Our orchestra performs this office of the chorus. — The duties of the Greek chorus varied at different times.

‡ There was a theatre at Antinoë, a city of central Egypt, founded by Adrian, and at Alexandria; but these were Greek or Roman towns, and no building of the kind is met with in any of ancient Egyptian date.

questioned whether the sculptures have recorded
all the various kinds used in the Egyptian army.
The principal ones appear to have been the trumpet and drum : the former used to marshal the
troops, summon them to the charge, and direct
them in their evolutions * ; the latter to regulate
and enliven their march.

THE TRUMPET ($\sigma\alpha\lambda\pi\iota\gamma\xi$).

The trumpet, like that of the Israelites, was
about one foot and a half long, of very simple form,
apparently of brass ; and when sounded, it was
held with both hands, and either used singly, or
as part of the military band, with the drum and
other instruments.   The musicians were not dis-

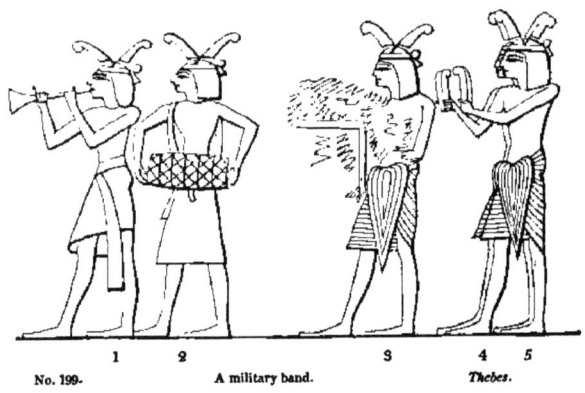

No. 199.   A military band.   *Thebes.*

tinguished by any particular dress from the rest of
the soldiers : whole regiments are represented at-

* In the battle scenes at Medéenet Háboo, in Thebes.

tired in the same costume as their trumpeters; and
if any difference can be perceived, it consists in
their being without arms, either offensive or defen-
sive.   It is true, that the other figures given in the
last wood-cut are clad in different dresses, which
might be supposed to indicate a peculiar garb for
the trumpeters; but some corps of archers are re-

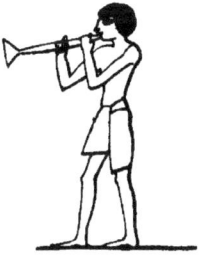

No. 200.   The trumpeter.   *Thebes.*

presented in another part of the picture wearing
both these costumes : and that all the privates of the
same regiment had a similar uniform is still more
satisfactorily shown, in a procession of soldiers
at Thebes, marching to celebrate a sacrifice, a small
portion of which is given in a previous part of this
work.*   Though the drummers, trumpeters, and
other musicians of the Egyptian army are represented in the sculptures without arms, we cannot
suppose this really to have been the case; and when
equipped for war, and marching to the attack of
an enemy, they were probably armed like the rest

* *Vide* p. 291.   Wood-cut, No. 13.

s 3

of the troops, at least, with a sword and shield, or other requisite means of defence.

The trumpet was particularly, though not exclusively, appropriated to martial purposes. It was straight, like the Roman tuba, or our common trumpet; but it is uncertain whether that used in the Egyptian cavalry was of another form, as in the Roman army; where the lituus, or clarion, bent a little at the end like an augur's staff, supplied the place of the tuba of the infantry.

In Greece, various instruments were adopted for summoning troops to battle. The Lacedæmonians and Cretans advanced to the sound of flutes (αυλοι — *pipes?*)*, others to that of lutes; and many preferred the lyre, which, according to Plutarch †, was long employed by the Cretans for this purpose. The trumpet, indeed, does not appear to have been in very early use among the Greeks, and it is rarely mentioned by Homer at the siege of Troy, where the chief instruments were the flute, lyre, and pipe, or συριγξ. The trumpet or σαλπιγξ was, however, known in Greece before that event: it was reputed to have been the invention of Minerva, or of Tyrrhenus ‡, a son of Hercules; and in later times it was generally adopted §, both as a martial instrument, and by the ambulant musicians of the streets.‖ In some parts of Egypt a prejudice existed

---

* Polyb. l. iv. 20., and Plut. de Musicâ, et in Lycurgo.
† Plut. de Mus.
‡ According to Athenæus (iv. 25.), the *Tyrrhenians* invented trumpets and horns (σαλπιγγες και κερατα).
§ Plut. de Mus.
‖ Plut. de Solertia Animalium, where he relates a curious anecdote of a magpie imitating the performances of a band of trumpeters.

against the trumpet, and the people of Busiris and Lycopolis abstained entirely from its use, conceiving, says Plutarch *, from the sound of this instrument resembling the braying of an ass, that it was Typhonian; or, at least, that it reminded them too forcibly of an animal emblematic of the evil genius.

The Israelites had trumpets for warlike † as well as sacred purposes ‡, for festivals and rejoicings § ; and the office of sounding them was not only honourable, but was committed solely to the priests.‖ They were of different kinds. Some of silver ¶, which were suited to all occasions, as I have already stated; others appear to have been of horns, like the original *cornu* of the Romans; and these are distinctly stated to have been employed at the siege of Jericho. ** The Greeks had six species of trumpets; the Romans four, in their army—the tuba, cornuus, buccina, and lituus; and in ancient times the *concha,* so called from having been originally made of a shell. They were the only instruments employed by them for military purposes, and in this they differed from the Greeks and Egyptians.

The sculptures of Thebes fail to inform us if the long and short drum were both comprehended in

* Plut. de Iside. et Osir. s. 30.
† Numb. x. 2. 5. 9, 10.
‡ Exod. xix. 13., Levit. xxiii. 24., and Numb. x. 10.
§ 2 Chron. xv. 14., and Numb. x. 10.
‖ Numb. x. 8., Josh. vi. 4.
¶ Josephus says, they were nearly a cubit, or 1½ ft. long, with a tube of the thickness of a flute.
** These were the *sóferóth,* cornets; the silver ones were the *khetztzróth* or *khetzotzróth,* trumpets. From the name, I should think the former had a shrill tone. Josh. vi. 4. " Trumpets of rams' horns."

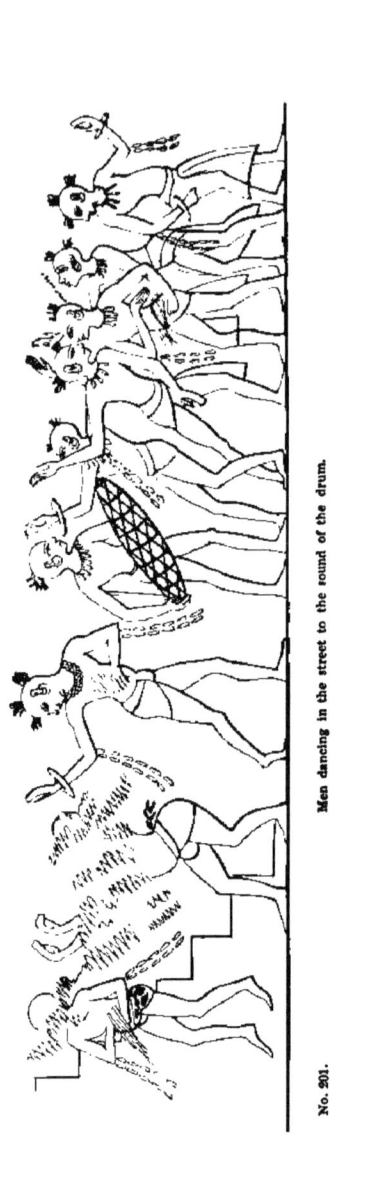

Men dancing in the street to the round of the drum.

No. 201.

Egypt under the head of martial music: it is, however, evident that the former was not only used in
their army, but by the buffoons who danced to its
sound.*

MUSIC TAUGHT TO SLAVES.

The buffoons were sometimes foreigners; and
in the accompanying picture they appear to be
blacks, who amused the spectators with their own
national dance, or one which they had learned from
the Egyptians.   Among many ancient people it
was customary to teach slaves to dance and sing,
in order that they might divert their master, or
entertain a party of guests; and the Romans even
employed them in various trades and manufactures.
Those, too, who gave proofs of ability and genius,
were frequently instructed in literature and the
liberal arts, and the masters profited by their industry, or sold them at a great price in consequence
of their accomplishments.   The Egyptians, indeed,
pursued this system to a certain extent; slaves
were employed in public works †, and in domestic
occupations ‡; and there is evidence from the
sculptures that many of the musicians and dancers,
both men and women, were slaves, who had been
taken captive in war from their Ethiopian and
Asiatic enemies.   Yet it is not probable they were
instructed in the same manner as those above mentioned at Rome; though the very kind treatment

* *Vide* wood-cut, No. 201.
† Exod. i. 11. 14.   Herodot. ii. 108.
‡ Sculptures frequently.

of Joseph, the mode of his liberation, and his subsequent marriage* with the daughter of a free-
born Egyptian, a high functionary of the sacerdotal
order †, are striking proofs of the humanity of the
Egyptians‡, and of their indulgent conduct towards
manumitted slaves.

THE DRUM (TYMPANUM).

The only drum represented in the sculptures is
a long drum, very similar to one of the *tomtoms* of
India. It was about two feet, or two feet and a
half in length, and was beaten with the hand, like
the Roman tympanum. §   The case was of wood

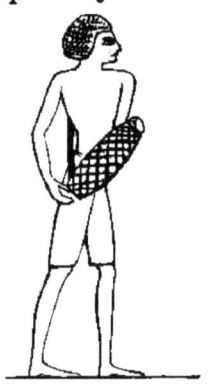

No. 202.   The drum.   *Thebes.*

* Gen. xli. 45. The case of Joseph was, no doubt, of an extraordinary nature.
    † " Asenath, the daughter of Potipherah, (in Hebrew, Poti-Phra;
in Egyptian, Pet-Phre or Pet-re, Heliodotus,) priest of On," the City
of the Sun, or Heliopolis.
    ‡ As was the lenient punishment of Joseph, when with his master
Potiphar. Gen. xxxix. 19, 20.
    § Lucretius says, " Tympana tenta tonant palmis." Horace calls
them " sæva tympana."

or copper, covered at either end with parchment
or leather, braced by cords, extending diagonally
over the exterior of the cylinder, which in this respect differed from our modern drums; and when
played, it was slung by a band round the neck of
the drummer, who during the march carried it in a
vertical position at his back.   Like the trumpet, it

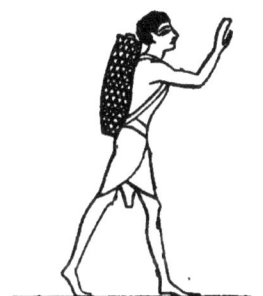

No. 203.   Mode of slinging the drum behind them, when on a march.

was chiefly employed in the army; and the evidence of the sculptures is confirmed by the authority of Clement of Alexandria, who states that
the drum was used by the Egyptians in going to
war.* Both these instruments are found to have
been common at the earliest period, of which we
have any account from the sculptures of Thebes, or
about the sixteenth century before our era; and
there is no reason to suppose them to have been
then a recent invention.

When a body of troops marched to the beat of

* Clemens Alex. Stromat. ii. 164.

drum, the drummer was often stationed in the centre, or the rear, and sometimes immediately behind the standard bearers; the trumpeter's post being generally at the head of the regiment, except when summoning them to form or advance to the charge[*]; but the drummers were not always alone, or confined to the rear and centre; and when forming part of the band, they marched in the van, or, with the other musicians, were drawn up on one side while the troops defiled, as in our European armies.

Besides the long drum, the Egyptians had another, not very unlike our own, both in form and size, which was much broader in proportion to its length than the *tomtom* just mentioned, being two feet and a half high, and two feet broad. It was beaten with two wooden sticks; but as there is no representation of the mode of using it, we are unable to decide whether it was suspended horizontally and struck at both ends, as is usual with a drum of the same kind still used at Cairo, or at one end only, like our own; though, from the curve of the sticks, I am inclined to think it was slung and beaten as the *tamboor* of modern Egypt. Sometimes the sticks were straight, and consisted of two parts, the handle and a thin round rod, at whose end a small knob projected, for the purpose of fastening the leather pad with which the drum was struck: they were about a foot in length, and, judging from the form of the handle of one in the

---

[*] Conf. Joshua, vi. 9. " And the armed men went before the priests that blew the trumpets, and the rereward came after the ark."

Berlin Museum*, we may conclude they belonged, like those above mentioned, to a drum beaten at both ends. Each extremity of the drum was covered with red leather, braced with catgut strings passing through small holes in its broad margin, and extending in direct lines over the copper body, which, from its convexity, was similar in shape to a cask. †

In order to tighten the strings, and thereby to brace the drum, a piece of catgut extended round each end, near the edge of the leather; and crossing the strings at right angles, and being twisted round each separately, braced them all in proportion as it was drawn tight: but this was only done when the leather and the strings had become relaxed by constant use; and as this piece of catgut was applied to either end, they had the means of doubling the power of tension on every string. It is true that this kind of drum does not occur in any sculptures hitherto discovered; yet it is not less certain that it was among the instruments of the country, one of them having been found in the excavations made at Thebes, by S. Janni D'Athanasi, during Mr. Madox's stay at that place in 1823; to whom I am indebted for the original sketch of the accompanying wood-cut. ‡

THE HARP.

Besides the ordinary forms of Egyptian instruments, several were constructed according to a

* Given in wood-cut, No. 34 a. p. 314. Vol. I.
† I believe it to be the same which is now in the Museum at Paris.
‡ *Vide* wood-cut, No. 204.

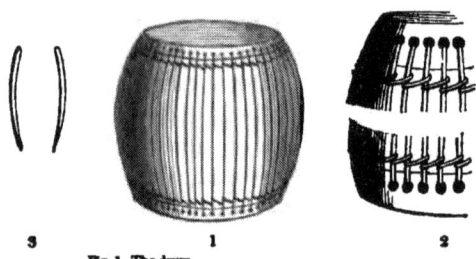

3   1   2

Fig. 1. The drum.
    2. Shows how the strings were braced.
    3. The sticks.

No. 204.   *Found at Thebes.*

particular taste or accidental caprice. Some were
of the most simple kind, others of very costly
materials, and many were richly ornamented with
brilliant colours and fancy figures; particularly the

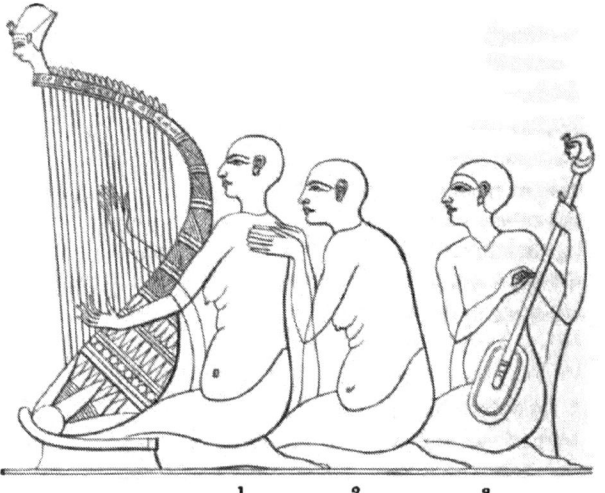

1   2   3

No. 205.   A richly painted harp on a stand, a man beating time with his hands, and a
                player on the guitar.

harps and lyres. The harps varied greatly in form, size, and the number of their strings : they are re-presented in the ancient paintings with four, six, seven, eight, nine, ten, eleven, twelve, fourteen, seventeen, twenty, twenty-one, and twenty-two chords : that in the Paris collection appears also to have had twenty-two; and the head of another, found by me at Thebes, was made for seventeen strings, as is shown by the number of its pegs. They were frequently very large, even exceeding

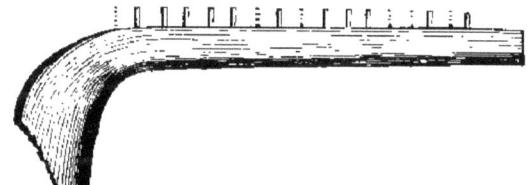

No. 206.   Head of a harp brought by me from Thebes, and now in the British Museum.

the height of a man, tastefully painted with the lotus and other flowers, or with fancy devices ; and those of the royal* minstrels were fitted up in the most splendid manner, adorned with the head or bust of the monarch himself.   The oldest harps found in the sculptures are in a tomb, near the pyramids of Geezeh, between three and four thousand years old.   They are more rude in shape than those usually represented ; and though it is impossible to ascertain the precise number of their chords†, they do not appear to have exceeded seven or eight,

* *Conf.* the royal minstrels of David and Solomon.   Asaph was chief master of music to David. 1 Chron. xvi. 7. and xxv. 6.   *Vide* plate 13.
† *Vide* wood-cut, No. 183.

and are fastened in a different manner from ordinary Egyptian harps.

I have already noticed the great antiquity of the harp, and its early use in some Eastern or Asiatic countries*, which is fully confirmed by the oldest Egyptian sculptures. It does not appear to have been known to the Greeks, but many stringed instruments, as the cithara (κιθάρα) went from Asia to Greece: and this last, according to Plutarch, was originally styled Asiatic†, having been introduced from Lesbos‡, where music was long cultivated with success. The same author observes that the cithara was employed upon sacred and festive occasions §, and Heraclides of Lesbos supposed it to have been invented by Amphion‖; but a diversity of opinion always existed upon the subject of its introduction into Greece.

Terpander¶, who lived about two hundred years after Homer, was one of the first to attain any celebrity in its use, and he is reputed to have instituted laws for this instrument some time before they were arranged for the flute or pipe. Cepion, his disciple, who followed the Lesbian model, esta-

* Egypt was included in Asia by some ancient writers. *Vide* also Herodot. ii. 15, 16.
† Plut. de Musicâ.
‡ The Lesbians were famed for the lyre and other instruments. Conf. Horace, Od. lib. i. 21. 11.: —
      . . . . . " Hunc fidibus novis,
         Hunc Lesbio sacrare plectro."
And Od. i. l. 34. : —
       " Lesboum . . . tendere barbiton."
§ Plut. Sympos. lib. vii.   ‖ Plut. de Musicâ.
¶ He was a native of Lesbos, or of Antissa; and was said to have added three strings to the lyre, which had until then only four. Plutarch says it had seven strings till his time, and that he added many more tones.

blished its form ; and few changes were introduced
into it till Timotheus of Miletus[*], who flourished
about the year 400 B. c., added four to the previous
seven chords.

How far, then, do we find the Egyptians surpassed the Greeks, at this early period, in the
science of music ! Indeed, long before the lyre
was known in Greece, the Egyptians had attained
the highest degree of perfection in the form of
their stringed instruments ; on which no improvement was found necessary, even at a time when
their skill was so great that Greek sages visited
Egypt to study music, among the other sciences, for
which it was renowned.   And harps of fourteen,
and lyres of seventeen strings, are found to have
been used by the ordinary Egyptian musicians, at
the remote period of the reign of Amosis, the first
king of the 18th dynasty, who lived about 1570
B. c.[†], nine hundred years before the time of Terpander.

The strings of the Egyptian harp were of catgut ;
and some of those discovered at Thebes, in 1823,
were so well preserved, that they emitted a sound
on being touched, as I shall presently have occasion
to observe.   Some harps stood upon the ground,
having an even broad base ; others were placed
upon a stool [‡], or raised upon a stand or limb
attached to the lower part [§] ; and from the ap-

---

[*] Pausan. Græc. lib. iii.

[†] Some harps of the time of Osirtasen I., B. c. 1700, have seven
chords.

[‡] Instances of this are also found at Herculaneum. *Vide* wood-cut,
No. 208.

[§] *Vide* wood-cut, No. 207.

pearance of that given in the wood-cut, we may suppose they intended to show that the harp, like many Greek lyres, was occasionally made of tortoise-shell. In many instances the minstrel stood to the instrument[*]; and it was customary for the harps they used in this manner to be flat at the base, like those in Bruce's tomb, represented in the accompanying plate[†]: but many which were squared for this purpose were inclined towards the performer, who supported the harp as she played[‡]; for this kind of instrument seems to have been more generally appropriated to women than

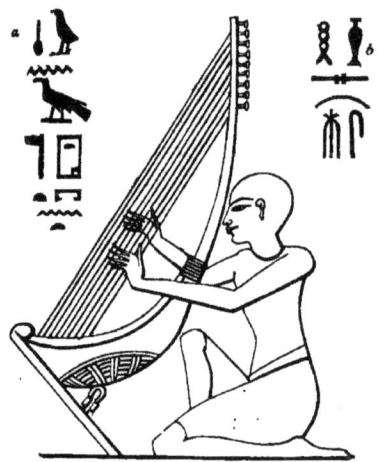

No. 207.   Harp raised on a stand, or support.   *Thebes.*

* *Vide* wood-cut, No. 208.
† *Vide* plate 13.
‡ *Vide* wood-cut, No. 191.; but not always.

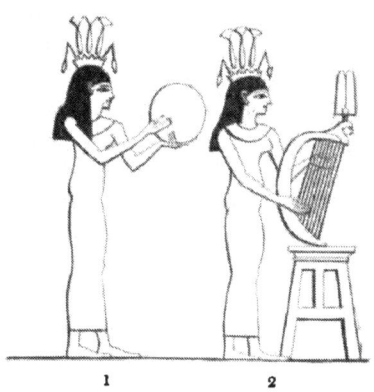

No. 208.   Minstrel standing, while playing the harp.   *Dendera.*

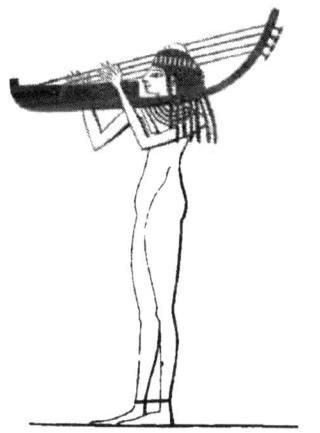

No. 209.   A light kind of instrument borne on the shoulder.   *Thebes.*

to men. Minstrels indeed were of both sexes;
but we more frequently meet with representations

T 2

of men seated to the harp, though instances occur of their kneeling and standing, and of women sitting, as they struck the chords.

A light species of four-stringed instrument, which I shall presently have occasion to mention, was supported upon the shoulder, and played with both hands; but this manner of holding it, and perhaps its use, may have been confined to women.* There was also a small four-stringed harp usually played by men, which stood upon the ground † like others of more ordinary form, and served as an accompaniment to one of larger dimensions. Many of the harps were covered with bulls' hides‡, or with leather, which was sometimes of a green § or of a red‖ colour, frequently painted with various devices, vestiges of which may be traced in that of the Paris collection.¶

It may be questioned whether the four-stringed instrument above mentioned ought to bear the name of harp; for certainly the difference in its form from that used as an accompaniment to the large harp** suffices to show that these two are not the same, and this is further confirmed by the appearance of two of the very same portable instruments in the Paris and British Museums.†† It may also be observed, that though the small harp has only four strings, it has six pegs, which would in-

---

* *Vide* wood-cut, No. 209.
† *Vide* wood-cut, No. 186.
‡ As that of wood-cut, No. 186.
§ One found at Thebes by Mr. Salt.
‖ One seen by Mr. Madox at Thebes.
¶ *Vide* wood-cut, No. 213.
** In wood-cut, No. 186.
†† *Vide* wood-cut, No. 215. *figs.* 2. and 2 *a.*

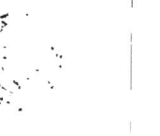

dicate the occasional use of two more chords; and it is not impossible that the absence of those strings may be attributed to some neglect of the artist.* The representation of the other instrument agrees exactly with those of the London and Paris collections, having four pegs, and the same number of chords, fastened at the lower end to a bar extending down the centre of its concave body, which was covered with leather, strained over it, and perforated here and there with small holes to allow the sound to escape. It was always played with the hands, and never, like the guitar and some lyres, with a plectrum. Another of very similar form, and with the same number of chords, was found at Thebes; and from the copy I have seen of it, made by Mr. Madox, it appears to have been furnished with a peg at the lower end, whose use it is not easy to determine, but which probably served to secure the strings.

It does not appear that the Egyptians had any mode of shortening the strings during the performance, either in this instrument or the harp, or had invented any substitute for our modern pedals; nor is there any instance of a double set of chords, as in the old Welsh harp. They could, therefore, only play in one key, until they tuned it afresh, which was done by turning the pegs.

There is, however, reason to believe that the want of pedals was partially supplied by the intro-

* I have seen a harp with six strings and nine pegs, probably an oversight of the draughtsman; unless those additional pegs were used for some purpose. One of the lyres of Herculaneum has eleven strings and seven pegs.

duction of a second row of pegs, since we find that these are frequently double, or two to each string* ; and a contrivance of this kind might have the effect of giving an additional half note.

In playing the harp, some minstrels sat cross-legged on the ground, like Asiatics of the present day, or upon one knee†, whether men or women‡ ; others preferred a low stool; and many stood, even while performing on ordinary occasions in the houses of private individuals.

Before the images of the gods, and in religious ceremonies, it is natural to suppose that the sacred minstrels adopted this posture, out of respect to the deity in whose service they were engaged ; and we have abundant evidence from the harpers in Bruce's tomb, who are officiating before Ao§, and from several other instances, that this instrument was employed in their form of worship, and to celebrate the praises of the gods. So suitable, indeed, was the harp considered for this purpose, that they represented it in the hands of the deities themselves, as well as the tambourine and the sacred sistrum. It was held in the same consideration by the Jews ; and there is reason to believe that in this respect they followed the example of the Egyptians, from whom many of their customs were derived. Harps and psalteries appear from the Scriptures‖ to have obtained the

---

* In the harp given in wood-cut, No. 188. are eight strings and sixteen pegs.
† *Vide* wood-cut, No. 207.
‡ *Vide* wood-cuts, Nos. 185. and 193., and plate 12.
§ One of the Egyptian deities.
‖ 1 Chron. xvi. 5.

first rank; and cymbals, trumpets, and cornets [*] were also designated as part of the sacred band, as in some of the religious ceremonies of Egypt.

The Jewish psaltery I am inclined to suppose the same as, or similar to, the four-stringed instrument above described, though Josephus gives it "twelve musical notes." [†] In Hebrew, it was called psanterin[‡], and probably sometimes nabl, a name from which was borrowed the ναϐλα of the Greeks; and this last is mentioned in Strabo as one of many instruments known by barbarous appellations.[§]

Athenæus considers the nablum, pandurum, sambuca, magadis, and trigon, not to be new instruments; but yet they may have been brought originally from foreign countries: and he afterwards states, on the authority of Aristoxenus, that the " Phœnicica, pêctis, magadis, trigon, clepsiangus,

---

[*] 1 Chron. xv. 28, &c.

[†] Josephus, Antiq. vii. 12. 3., says, "The viol was of ten strings, played with the bow (perhaps plectrum): the psaltery had twelve musical notes, and was played with the fingers; . . . the cymbals were broad and large instruments of brass." Some of the instruments mentioned in Dan. iii. 15. "cornet, flute, harp, sackbut, psaltery, and dulcimer," are very uncertain; in the Hebrew, they are korna, mushrookítha, kítharus, sabka, psanterín, and sumphonéeh; the third and last of which are evidently Greek names: the Syriac version gives the karno, mushrookítho, kíthoro, kinoro, and tziphunio, the fourth being omitted: the Arabic has البوق والناي والكيثارة والونج والمزمار والصفارة, "trumpet, flute, harp, lyre, psaltery, and pipe;" and the Septuagint " σαλπιγγος, συριγγος, κιθαρας, σαμϐυκης, ψαλτηριου, συμφωνιας." The trumpet was called in Hebrew שופר, sófer. Job, xxxix. 24. Numb. vii. 20. In Arabic siffer is "to whistle."

[‡] The initial letter p looks like the Egyptian article.

[§] " Και ο μεν τις φησιν κιθαραν Ασιατιν ρασσων, ο δε τους αυλους βρεκυντικους καλει, η φρυγιους . . . των οργανων ενια βαρϐαρως ωνομασται, ναϐλα, δε σαμϐυκη, η και βαρϐιτος, και μαγαδες, και αλλα πλειω." Strabo, lib. 10.

scindapsus, and enneachordon (of nine strings) were foreign instruments." *

Some light might be thrown on the names of the various harps, lyres, and other musical instruments of Egypt, if those mentioned in the Bible were more accurately defined ; but much confusion exists between the cithara or kitarus, the áshúr†, the sambuc, the nabl, and the kinoor: nor can the various kinds of drums, cymbals, or wind instruments of the Jews be more satisfactorily ascertained.   The difficulty of identifying them is not

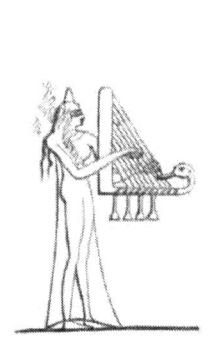
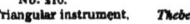
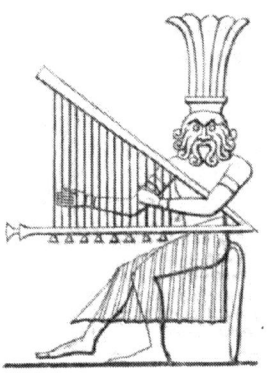

No. 210.   No. 211.
Triangular instrument.   *Thebes.*   Another, held under the arm.   *Dakkeh.*

* Athen. iv. c. 25. The pandurum (πανδευρον) he supposes to have been made from the laurel which grows in the Red Sea ; probably Strabo's olive of that coast, the *shorai*, or shora maritima of the present day.   J. Pollux calls it pandoura, and says it was a three-stringed instrument, invented by the Assyrians. Lib. iv. 9. The magadis of Anacreon he supposes to be the same as the psithyra, or ascarum, a stringed instrument of quadrangular form, apparently played like the Arab qanóon, but not resembling it in sound.

† So called from having *ten* strings.

surprising, when we observe how many names * the Greeks had for their stringed instruments, and how the harps and lyres represented in the Egyptian sculptures approach each other in principle and form; and we sometimes hesitate whether to ascribe to them a place among the former or the latter.   One of these, with nine strings, was carried by the musician, and sometimes held by pressing it between the side and elbow, perhaps supported at the same time by a belt over the shoulder † : and another, which stood upon the ground, had eight strings, and was also played by the hand, the minstrel standing.‡   The tassels on the lower limb of the former appear to be merely ornamental; though it is posssible that, since

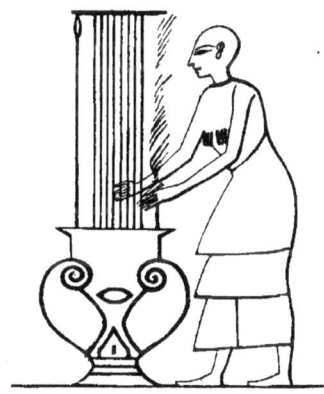

No. 212.   An unusual kind of instrument.   *Alabastron.*

---

* Witness those given by J. Pollux, iv. 9. " Των μεν ουν κρουομενων, ειη αν λυρα, κιθαρα, βαρβιτον, το δ' αυτο, και βαρυμιτον, χελυς, ψαλτηριον, τριγωνα, σαμβυκαι, πηκτιδες, φορμιγγες, φοινιξ, σπαδιξ, λυροφοινικιον, κλεψιαμβος, παριαμβος, ιαμβυκη σκινδαψος, επιγονειου, και τα λοιπα."

† Wood-cuts, Nos. 210, 211.   ‡ At Alabastron.

there are no pegs, they were intended for tightening
the chords, in order to alter the key; and in some instances, each chord of a large harp is accompanied
by one of these tassels, which terminates a long
string, wound round the upper limb of the instrument, as may be seen on that of the Paris Museum. *
This harp is of moderate dimensions, and had either
twenty-one or twenty-two strings.   It is highly
interesting, as well from its preservation as from
the insight it gives us into the form and principle of
these instruments; and if it is far from being the
first quality of harp, either in elegance of shape or
in the richness of its materials, yet, from the number of its strings, it must have been one of the high-

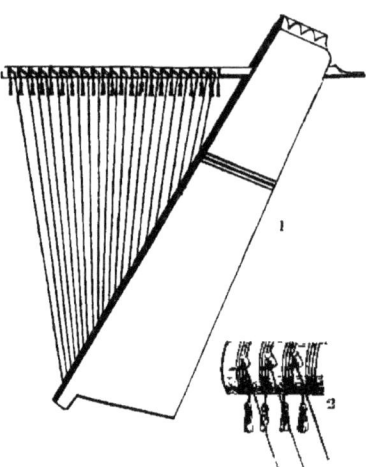

No. 213.   The harp of the Paris collection.
                Fig. 2. shows how the chords were fastened.

* Wood-cut, No. 213.

est power in use among the Egyptians, since they are seldom represented in the sculptures with more than two octaves.

All the Egyptian harps have a peculiarity, for which it is not easy to account—the absence of a pole, and, consequently, of a support to the bar, or upper limb, in which the pegs were fixed; and it is difficult to conceive how, without it, the chords could have been properly tightened, or the bar sufficiently strong to resist the effect of their tension, particularly in those of a triangular form.

Another instrument, of nearly the same capacity as the Paris harp, was found at Thebes in 1823, where it was seen by Mr. Madox, to whom I am indebted for the sketch I have given of it, in a succeeding wood-cut.* It had twenty chords of cat-gut, so well preserved that, as I have already observed, they still retained their sound, after having been buried in the tomb probably three thousand years; a length of time which would appear incredible, if we had not repeated instances of the perfect preservation of numerous perishable objects, even of an older date, in the sepulchres of Thebes. It is to the excessive dryness of the soil, and of the rock in which the pits are hewn, frequently to the depth of fifteen, thirty, and even seventy feet, and to the total exclusion of air, that this is to be attributed; and grains of corn and other seeds have been found, which have remained entire, without undergoing any

* *Vide fig.* 3. in wood-cut, No. 215.

change, and without making any effort to strike root in the sand, or the vase in which they were deposited.

Experiments are said to have been tried with some grains of corn thus preserved, which sprouted when sown*; and though I cannot speak of this as a fact, yet I am inclined to believe that if seed thus discovered were immediately put into the earth, the results would be as stated; since experience shows that seeds buried at certain depths are unable to germinate, till removed nearer the surface of the earth; and I have known them to remain for years on the plains of the Egyptian desert, awaiting that rain which has at length enabled them to take root in the previously parched soil.

The instrument just mentioned was of a form which might require it to hold an intermediate rank between the lyre and the harp, like the two previously noticed: nor would the number of twenty strings be any objection, since we meet with Egyptian lyres of nearly the same power, having eighteen chords. The frame was of wood, covered with red leather, on which could be traced a few hieroglyphics. The strings were fastened to the upper limb, and wound round a rod inserted into the lower part, which was probably turned in order to tighten them, and may be considered similar in principle to that on the summit of many ancient lyres, or of the *kistrka* used in modern

* Several are now in the different collections of Europe. The experiments are said to have been made in France.

Ethiopia. In the former, the rod itself was turned; in the latter, each string is fastened over a ring of some adhesive material, intervening between it and the rod, and the turn of this ring regulates the tension of the chord.   Neither this nor the two above alluded to were provided with pegs, a peculiarity which may be considered a distinctive mark between this class of instruments and the harp.

There are still two others, which appear unconnected either with the harp or lyre, and yet differ from the two already described, having pegs to brace the strings.   Of these, one has a flat broad body, covered with a sounding board, in the centre of which is a rod securing the chords; and perpendicular to it is another rod at the upper end of the instrument, into which the pegs are inserted that supported and tightened its ten strings.*

The other, which bears still less analogy to the Egyptian harp†, appears to have had five strings, each secured by a peg, and passing over a hollow circular body, covered probably with a thin piece of wood or leather.   It was seven inches in length, the neck about one foot three inches, and the five pegs were fixed in the lower side, in a direct line, one behind the other.   At the opposite end of the circular part were two holes, for fastening the rod that secured the strings, as in the preceding instrument; which may be seen in one of the two found at Thebes, some years since, by Mr. Salt, and now in the British Museum.   They

* Given in wood-cut, No. 215., *fig.* 5., from Prof. Rosellini's work.
† *Vide* wood-cut, No. 215., *fig.* 1., and wood-cut, No. 214.

are not of the best quality, nor very perfectly preserved, and the one I have described has lost two
of its rude pegs. The other has only four, and
the lower part is much injured. They are both
of sycamore wood, and exactly like that in the
Berlin collection, which has the five pegs entire,
and has the body composed of three pieces of wood.

At first sight this instrument appears to resemble
the Egyptian guitar, both in its form and the
position of the strings; on restoring it, however,
and introducing them, we find that the principle
was totally different, and that the neck was not

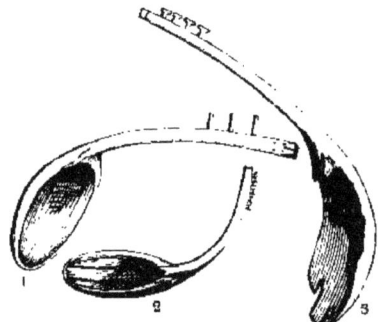

No. 214.   Figs. 1, 3. Instruments in Mr. Salt's collection.
                Fig. 2. In the Berlin Museum.

intended, as in the guitar, for shortening the
chords, and consequently the instrument was of a
very inferior kind, and of an exceedingly limited
power.

In addition, then, to the guitar, harp, and lyre,
we may enumerate at least five, independent of the

four-stringed harp previously mentioned*, which
do not come under the denomination of any of the
three; nor do I include in the five that represented in the sculptured tombs of Alabastron†,
which may deserve the name of standing lyre; nor
one occurring in the same tomb, and played as an

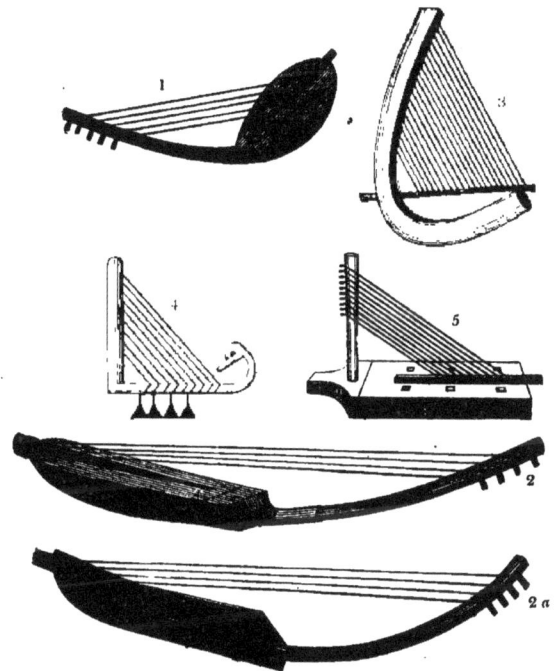

No 215.   Five instruments differing from the harp, lyre, and guitar.

* In p. 276. *vide* wood-cut, No. 186.
† Wood-cut, No. 212.

accompaniment to the lyre. Unfortunately it is much damaged, and the appearance of several bars or chords can alone be traced, which the performer strikes with a stick.*

It is true that, of the five instruments here represented, *figs.* 1. and 2. are very similar in principle, as are 3. and 4., however different their tones and powers may have been; but still they must be considered distinct from the harp, lyre, and guitar : and they may, perhaps, bear some analogy to the nabl †, the sambuc, and the ten-stringed *āshúr* of the Jews; though these were generally played with a sort of plectrum, and the former always with the hand.

Of the instrument, *fig.* 2. the most curious and perfect specimen I have seen was brought by Mr. Burton from Thebes, and is now in the British Museum. It only wants the four strings ; the exact form, the pegs, the bridge or rod to which the chords were attached, and even the parchment, covering its wooden body, and serving instead of a sounding board, still remain ; and from its lightness as well as size, we may judge how portable it was, and how conveniently it might be used in the manner described in the sculptures, upon the shoulder of the performer. ‡

THE LYRE — λυρα.

The Egyptian lyre was not less varied in its form

* Wood-cut, No. 216.
† " That chant to the sound of the (nabl) viol." Amos, vi. 5. The nabl may have been a sort of guitar.
‡ Wood-cut, No. 209.

and the number of its chords than the harp; and they ornamented it with the numerous fancy devices their taste suggested.   Diodorus limits the number of its chords to three; however, as his description does not apply to the Egyptian lyre, but to the guitar, it is unnecessary to introduce it till I mention that instrument.

A singular story of its supposed invention* is related by Apollodorus.   "The Nile," says the Athenian mythologist, "after having overflowed the whole country of Egypt, when it returned within its natural bounds, left on the shore a great number of animals of various kinds, and among the rest a tortoise†, the flesh of which being dried and wasted by the sun, nothing remained within the shell but nerves and cartilages, and these being braced and contracted by the drying heat became sonorous.   Mercury, walking along the banks of the river, happened to strike his foot against this shell, and was so pleased with the sound produced, that the idea of a lyre presented itself to his imagination.   He therefore constructed the instrument in the form of a tortoise‡, and strung it with the dried sinews of dead animals."

* The invention of the Greek lyre is also attributed to Mercury. Pausanias states that Mercury having found a tortoise-shell on a mountain of Arcadia, called Chelydorea, near Mount Cyllene, formed it into a lyre. Paus. Græc. lib. viii. Arcad.   And he mentions a statue of Mercury, in the temple of Apollo at Argos, " holding a tortoise-shell, of which he proposes to make a lyre." lib. ii.

   " Curvæque lyræ parentem." —Hor. Od. lib. i. 10. 6.

† Pausanias says the tortoise of Mount Parthenius, in Arcadia, was particularly suited for making lyres, as well as that·of the Soron oak forest, which, for this purpose, rivalled the Indian species. Lib. viii.

‡ From having been made of a tortoise-shell, the lyre received the name testudo. Hor. Od. lib. iii. 11. 3.

Many of the lyres were of considerable power, having five, seven, ten, and eighteen strings. They were usually supported between the elbow and the side, and the mode of playing them was generally with the hand, and not, as in Greece and Rome, with a plectrum. This custom, however, was also adopted by the Egyptians; and as it occurs in sculptures of the earliest periods, it is evident they did not borrow it from Greece; nor

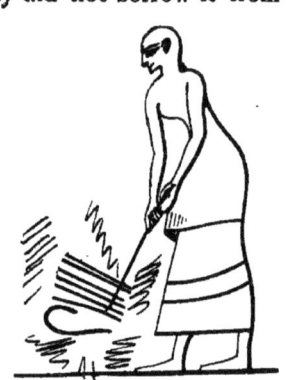

No. 216.   An instrument played as an accompaniment to the lyre.   *Alabastron.*

was it unusual for the Greeks to play the lyre with the hand without a plectrum; and many instances of both methods occur in the paintings of Herculaneum. Sometimes the Egyptians touched the chords with the left hand, while they struck them with the plectrum; and the same appears in the frescos of Herculaneum, where I have observed lyres of three, six, nine, and eleven strings, played with the plectrum: of four, five, six, seven, and ten, with the hands: and of nine and eleven with the plectrum and fingers at the same time.

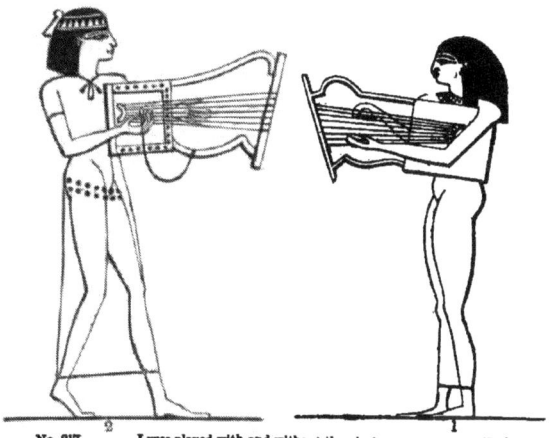

No. 217.   Lyres played with and without the plectrum.   *Thebes.*

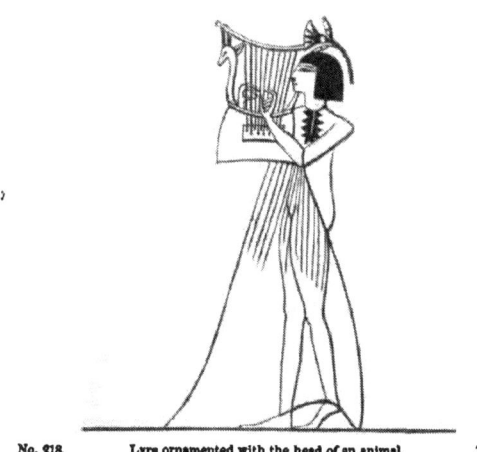

No. 218.   Lyre ornamented with the head of an animal.   *Thebes.*

Some lyres were ornamented with the head of a favourite animal carved in wood, as the horse, ibex, or gazelle; and others were of more simple shape.* The strings were fastened at the upper end to a cross bar connecting the two sides, and at the lower end they were attached to a raised ledge or hollow sounding-board, about the centre of the body, which was of wood, like the rest of the instrument. The Berlin and Leyden Museums possess lyres of this kind, which, with the exception of the strings, are perfectly preserved. That in the former collection is ornamented with horses' heads, and in form, principle, and the alternating length of its chords, resembles the one given in the pre-ceding wood-cut; though the board to which the strings are fastened is nearer the bottom of the in-strument, and the number of strings is thirteen instead of ten; and thus we have an opportunity of comparing real Egyptian lyres with the represent-ations of them drawn by Theban artists, in the reign of Amunoph I., and other early monarchs, more than 3000 years ago.

The body of the Berlin lyre is about ten inches high, and fourteen and a half broad, and the total height of the instrument is two feet.† That of Leyden‡ is smaller, and less ornamented, but it is

* As in the preceding wood-cut, No. 218.
† *Vide* wood-cut, No. 219.
‡ In mentioning these harps, I feel it a pleasing duty to acknowledge the obliging assistance and free access I met with at both those mu-seums, particularly at that of Leyden; and I take this opportunity of expressing my obligations to Baron A. von Humboldt, Signor Passal-acqua, Dr. Liemans, and M. Jansen. The two museums where the greatest facilities are given to strangers for copying the monuments they contain, appear to me to be the British Museum and the Museum of Leyden.

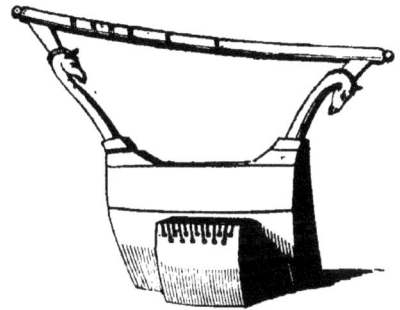

No. 219.   Lyre in the Berlin Collection.

equally well preserved, and highly interesting from a hieratic inscription written in ink upon the front. It had no extra sounding-board : its hollow body sufficiently answered this purpose; and the strings probably passed over a movable bridge, and were secured at the bottom by a small metal ring, or staple. Both these lyres were entirely of wood, and one of the sides, as of many represented in the sculptures *, was longer than the opposite one ; so that they tuned the instrument by sliding the chords upwards, along the bar.

Similar to these were many of the Greek lyres, sometimes imitating the shape and position of the horns of a gazelle, and other elegant forms, and the number of their strings was as varied as those of the Egyptians. In Greece, the instrument had at first only four chords, till an additional three were introduced by Amphion†; who, as Pausanias

* *Vide* wood-cuts, Nos. 217. and 218.
† Pausan. lib. ix.

U 3

seems to hint, borrowed his knowledge of music
from Lydia, and was reputed to have been taught
the use of the lyre by Mercury; a fable which

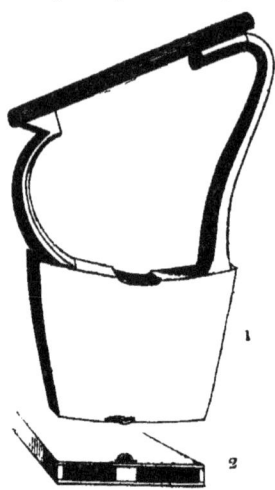

No. 220.   Lyre of the Leyden Collection.
                  Fig. 2. shows the lower end.

may be solved in the same manner as the legend
respecting the invention of that instrument and of
the Egyptian guitar, which I shall presently notice.

Seven continued to be the number of its strings,
until the time of Terpander[*], a poet and musician
of Antissa near Lesbos (670 b. c.), who added
several other notes[†]: but many were still made
with a limited number; and though lyres of great

---

[*] Plutarch, de Musicâ.
[†] Pliny's account differs from Plutarch, and he attributes the addition
of the eighth string to Simonides, the ninth to Timothe. Lib. vii. 56.,
where he mentions the inventors of different instruments.

power had long been known, and were constantly used by them, still many Greeks and Romans * con-tented themselves with, and perhaps preferred, those of a smaller compass. The lyres in the paint-ings of Herculaneum vary in the number of their strings, as much as those in the Egyptian frescos ; and we there find them with three, four, five, six, seven, eight, nine, ten, and eleven chords.

There is no instance of a harp in those paintings ; but a triangular instrument† of eight strings, car-ried under the arm and played with both hands, bears some analogy to that previously described from Thebes, which, as I have observed‡, we doubt whether to class among the harps or lyres: and another of seven chords is played with the two hands in the manner of a harp, by a woman re-clining on the ground. It is difficult to say whe-ther any one of these comes under the denomination of *magadis*, which, according to Athenæus, " was furnished with strings§, like the cithara, lyra, and barbiton;" but though little can be ascertained respecting the form of the numerous instruments alluded to by ancient authors‖, the triangular lyre

* Conf. Hor. *loc. cit.* : — " Resonare septem callida nervis."
† The two limbs supporting the strings form the two opposite sides, as the outer string the third, or base of the isósceles triangle.
‡ In p. 281. *Vide* wood-cut, No. 210.
§ The name magadis was also applied to a kind of pipe. Athen. iv. 25.
‖ Aristotle (Repub. lib. viii. c. 6., de Musicâ) says, " Many ancient instruments, as *pectides* and *barbiti*, and those which tend to delight the ear by their sound; *heptagona* (septangles), *trigona* (triangles), *sambucæ*, and all that depend upon skilful execution in fingering the chords." We cease to wonder at the difficulty of ascertaining the nature of ancient instruments, when we read Chambers's description of the " modern *cymbal* . . . . . of steel wire in a *triangular* form," &c. *Vide* Dict.

above mentioned cannot fail, from its shape, to call
to mind the *trigon**, or the sambuca, which is also
described as being of a triangular form. †

The Jewish lyre, or *kinôor*, had sometimes six,
sometimes nine strings, and was played with the
hand, or with a plectrum ; and if, when we become
better acquainted with the interpretation of hieroglyphics, the " strangers" at Beni Hassan should
prove to be the arrival of Jacob's family in Egypt,
we may examine the Jewish lyre drawn by an
Egyptian artist.   That this event took place about
the period when the inmate of the tomb lived, is
highly probable ; at least, if I am correct in considering Osirtasen I. to be the Pharaoh the patron
of Joseph ; and it remains for us to decide whether
the disagreement in the number of persons here introduced, thirty-seven being written over them in
hieroglyphics, is a sufficient objection‡ to their
identity.

It will not be foreign to the present subject to
introduce those figures, which are curious, if only
considered as illustrative of ancient customs at that
early epoch, and which will be looked upon with

---

* Athen. *loc. cit.*

† Suidas gives this account of the σαμβυκη, " οργανον μουσικον
τριγωνον." It was said to be made of strings of unequal length and
thickness, answering to the appearance of the one above alluded to at
Herculaneum.   There is another of triangular form at Herculaneum,
with ten strings, which is held over the shoulder while played with
the two hands.

‡ In my Egypt and Thebes, p. 26., I have expressed a fear that in
consequence of this number, and of the expression " captives," we can
only rank them among the ordinary prisoners taken by the Egyptians
during their wars in Asia; but the contemptuous expressions common
to the Egyptians in speaking of foreigners might account for the use of
this word.   Those presented by Joseph to Pharaoh were only five ; and
the person seated here is not the king.   Ex. xlvii. 2.

PLATE XLV

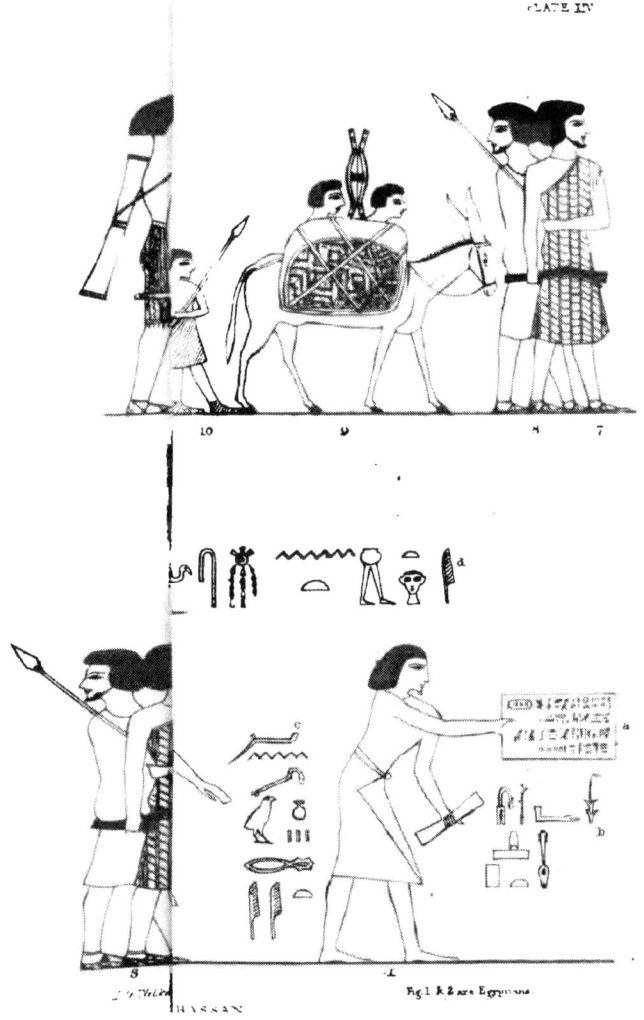

10   9   8   7

8

BASSAN

Fig. 1 & 2 are Egyptians.

unbounded interest should they ever be found to refer to the Jews.* The first figure is an Egyptian scribe, who presents an account of their arrival to a person seated, the owner of the tomb, and one of the principal officers of the reigning Pharaoh. The next, also an Egyptian, ushers them into his presence; and two advance, bringing presents, the wild goat or ibex, and the gazelle, the productions of their country. Four men, carrying bows and clubs, follow, leading an ass on which two children are placed in panniers, accompanied by a boy and four women; and last of all, another ass laden, and two men, one holding a bow and club, the other a lyre, which he plays with the plectrum. All the men have beards, contrary to the custom of the Egyptians, but very general in the East at that period, and noticed as a peculiarity of foreign uncivilised nations throughout their sculptures. The men have sandals, the women a sort of boot reaching to the anclet†, both which were worn by many Asiatic people. The lyre is rude, and differs a little in form from those generally used in Egypt; but its presence here, and in others of the oldest sculptures, amply testifies its great antiquity, and claims for it a rank among the earliest stringed instruments.

THE GUITAR.

The Egyptian guitar has only three chords; and to it I believe Diodorus alludes, when he applies

* Plate 14.
† Similar high shoes, or boots, were also worn by Greek and Etruscan, and even by Egyptian women, being found in the tombs of Thebes.

that number to the lyre, which he says corresponded to the three seasons of the year. Its invention he attributes to Hermes or Mercury *, who taught men letters, astronomy, and the rites of religion, and who gave the instrument three tones, — the treble, bass, and tenor ; the first to accord with summer, the second with winter, and the third with spring.

That the Egyptian year was divided into three parts, is abundantly proved by numerous hieroglyphic inscriptions, as well as by the authority of Greek writers ; and each season consisted of four months of thirty days each, making a total of three hundred and sixty days in the year. To these were added five more at the end of the twelfth month ; and every fourth, or leap year, another intercalary day increased this number to six, and thereby regulated the calendar, in the same manner as at the present day. †

That Diodorus confounds the guitar with the lyre, is probable, from his attributing its origin to Mercury, who was always the supposed inventor of the latter ; though there is reason to believe that the same fable was told him by the Egyptians, in connection with the other three-stringed instrument, and that it led to his mistake respecting the lyre.

It was no doubt from a conviction of the great talent required for the invention of an instrument

* Diod. i. 16.

† *Vide* the appendix of my Materia Hieroglyphica ; and Diodorus, i. 50., who mentions this quarter day, and who " visited Egypt in the reign of Ptolemy Neus Dionysus." i. 44.

having only three chords, and yet equalling the
power of one with numerous strings, that the Egyptians were induced to consider it worthy of the
deity who was the patron of the arts ; and the
fable * of his intervention, on this and similar occasions, is merely an allegorical mode of expressing
the intellectual gifts communicated from the Divinity, through his intermediate *agency.*

The Egyptian guitar consisted of two parts,—a
long flat neck or handle, and a hollow oval body,
either wholly of wood or covered with leather,
whose upper surface was perforated with several
holes, to allow the sound to escape. Over this

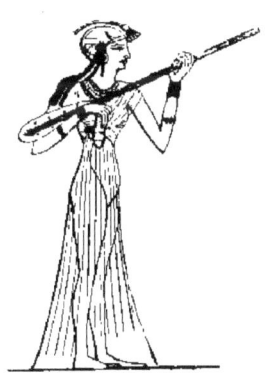

No. 221.   Female playing the guitar.   *Thebes.*

body, and the whole length of the handle, extended
three strings, no doubt, as usual, of catgut, secured

---

* Of a similar nature is that mentioned by Diodorus concerning
Osiris, who was reputed to have been the first to plant the vine, and
to teach man the use of the grape.   Diod. i. 15.

at the upper extremity, either by the same number of pegs, or by some other means peculiar to the instrument. It does not appear to have had any bridge; but the chords were fastened at the lower end to a triangular piece of wood or ivory, which raised them to a sufficient height; and in some of those represented in the sculptures, we find they were elevated at the upper extremity of the handle, by means of a small cross-bar, immediately below each of the apertures where the strings were tightened. This answered the same purpose as the depressed end of our modern guitar; and, indeed, since the neck was straight, some contrivance of the kind was absolutely necessary.

It is true that the paintings do not indicate the existence of pegs in this instrument for securing and bracing the strings, but their common use in the harps and psalteries strongly argues their adoption in the guitar; and it is more probable that the artist may have omitted them, than that the two or four tassels attached to that part of the handle should be the substitute for a more perfect method well known to them, and adopted in other instruments. In one instance, however, the strings appear to have been each passed through a separate aperture in the handle, and then bound round it and tied in a knot.*

The length of the handle was sometimes twice, sometimes thrice, that of the body; and I suppose the whole instrument to have measured about four

* *Vide* wood-cut, No. 185.

feet, the breadth of the body being equal to half its length.   It was struck with the plectrum, which was attached by a string to the neck, close to its junction with the body ; and the performers usually stood as they played.   Both men and women * used the guitar.   Some danced whilst they touched its

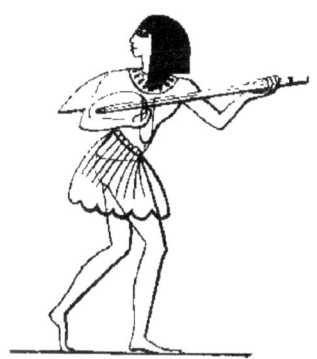

No. 222.   Dancing while playing the guitar.   *Thebes.*

strings, supporting it on the right arm; and I have met with one instance of it slung by a band round the neck, like the modern Spanish guitar. †

It is, indeed, from an ancient instrument of this kind, sometimes called cithára (κιθάρα), that the modern name guitar has been derived; though the cithara of the Greeks and Romans, in early times at least, was always a lyre.‡   The Egyptian guitar

* *Vide* also pl. 12, and wood-cut, No. 191.
† *Vide* wood-cut, No. 223.
‡ Pausan. Græc. lib. iii.   *Vide suprà.*

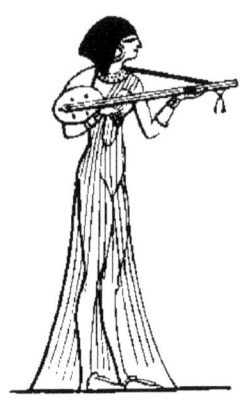

No. 223.   Guitar slung by a belt.   *Thebes.*

may be called a lute; but I cannot suppose it to
have been at all similar to the barbiton*, so frequently mentioned by Horace and other authors;
though this last is believed by some to have had only
three strings.† Athenæus ‡, on the contrary, describes it with many chords, and attributes its invention to Anacreon; and Theocritus also applies to
it the epithet πολυχορδον. It was particularly consecrated to Polyhymnia; and, like the cithara §, appears to have been derived from Lesbos. ‖

---

* The barbitos of Strabo, who mentions it as an instrument of
foreign origin. Its name was not derived from βαρβαρος.

† The Greeks had a lyre of three strings, which might have been the
barbiton, if this really had only three chords; but it is generally supposed to have been a large instrument,

‡ " Βαρβιτον οργανον εντατον και πολυχορδον." Athen. 4.

§ The eyes upon a cithara in pl. 192. of Mr. Hope's Costumes recall
an Egyptian ornament.

‖ Conf. Hor. Od. lib. i. 1. 33. : —

. . . . . " nec Polyhymnia
Lesboum refugit tendere barbiton."

An instrument of an oval form, with a circular or cylindrical handle, was found at Thebes, not altogether unlike the guitar; but, owing to the imperfect state of its preservation, nothing could be ascertained respecting the pegs, or the mode of tightening the chords. The wooden body was faced with leather, the handle extending down it to the lower end, and part of the string remained which attached the plectrum. Three small holes indicated the place where the chords were secured, and two others, a short distance above, appear to have been intended for fastening some kind of bridge; but this is merely conjecture, as I had not an opportunity of examining it, and am indebted to Mr. Madox for the accompanying sketch.

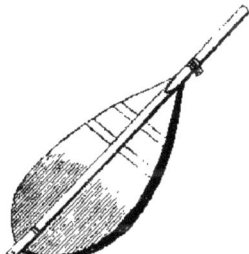

No. 224.   An instrument like the guitar found at Thebes.

Wire strings were not used by the Egyptians in any of their instruments, nor, as far as we can learn from ancient authors, were they of any other quality than catgut; and the employment of this last in the warlike bow is supposed to have led to its adoption in the peaceful lyre, owing to the accidental discovery of its musical sound. We are not, therefore, surprised to find that the Arabs, a nation of hunters, should have been the inventors of the *monochordium* *, an instrument of the most imperfect kind (especially when the skill of a Paganini is not employed to command its tones): but it is a remarkable fact, that the same people still possess the instrument; and poor singers in the streets of Cairo accompany the voice with a one-stringed *raháb*.

This circumstance may also be adduced as a proof of its antiquity; for, being used by the reciters of poems†, it has evidently been the instrument of their early bards, who are the first musicians in every country. There is no instance of it in the sculptures of the ancient Egyptians, nor is it probable that, even if known to them, it would have been admitted in their musical entertainments; unless, indeed, it were used, as at present, for an accompaniment in recitative.

THE FLUTE (ϗ λαγιαυλος, *or* OBLIQUA TIBIA).

The flute was at first very simple, and, as Horace observes, "with a few holes;" the number being limited to four, until Diodorus, of Thebes in Bœotia, added others; improving the instrument, at the same time, by making a lateral opening for the mouth.‡ It was originally of reed; but in

* J. Pollux. iv. 9.: — " μονοχορδον δε Αραβων το ευρημα."
† Hence called raháb e sháor, " the poet's viol." Mr. Lane has given a drawing and description of it in his accurate and minute work on the Modern Egyptian Customs, vol. ii. p. 74.
‡ J. Poll. Onom. iv. 10.

process of time it increased in size, and in the number of its notes, and was made of better and more sonorous materials.   It is impossible to say whether the Egyptians had one or several kinds of flutes, adapted, as with the Greeks *, to different pur-poses — some to mournful, others to festive occasions; but it is evident that they employed the flute both at banquets and in religious processions.

Most of those used by the Greeks were borrowed, like their names, from Asia; as the Lydian, Phrygian, Carian, and Mysian flutes; and Olympus, the disciple of Marsyas, introduced the instrument from Phrygia† into Greece, and was reputed by some‡ to have brought the lyre from the same country.   Clonas, who lived many years after Terpander, was said to have been the first to invent laws and suitable airs for the flute, though these were supposed to have been borrowed from the Mysians §; and Pausanias ascribes ‖ the construction of the flute to Ardalus, the son of Vulcan.¶

Aristotle, in mentioning Minerva as its inventor, merely alludes to one of the many allegorical fables connected with that goddess, Apollo, and Mercury; and the story of Minerva's throwing aside the flute, offended at the deformed appearance of her mouth

* Pausanias mentions three, as being different, the Doric, Lydian, and Phrygian.   Lib. ix.
† Plut. de Musicâ.
‡ Alexander on Phrygia, quoted by Plutarch, *loc. cit.*
§ Plut. de Musicâ.
‖ Paus. Corinth. lib. ii.
¶ Athenæus considers Marsyas the inventor of the αυλος; the καλαμος, or reed, having been used before his time.   The μονοκα λαμος, according to Euphorion, was a reputed invention of Mercury. Athen. iv. 25.

during the performance, is supposed by him to refer to the disrepute into which it fell, when its acquirement appeared to interfere with mental reflection. " For," he adds, " the flute is not suited to improve morals, but is rather a bacchanalian instrument, and very properly'forbidden to be used by young people and freemen. Nor was it till after the Persian war that the Greeks, inflated by the pride of victory, laid aside their previous discrimination, and introduced all kinds of instruction, without consulting propriety or the maintenance of morality ; forgetting that music is good, if it tends to guide and correct the mind of youth, but highly prejudicial, when indulged in merely as a pleasure."

To Pronomus, of Thebes in Bœotia*, they were indebted for an improvement in the instrument, by uniting the powers of three, the Doric, Lydian, and Phrygian, into one : but this may perhaps refer to the double pipe ; and, as we have already observed in the harp and lyre, all the improvements, and the reputed invention of the instrument, date long subsequently to that era when it had been already perfected among the Egyptians.

Indeed, in the earliest sculptures, which are those in the tomb of an individual behind the Great Pyramid, between three and four thousand years old, is a concert † of vocal and instrumental music, consisting of two harps, a pipe, *a flute*, and several voices ; and during the reigns of the Pharaohs of

* Paus. lib. ix.   † *Vide* wood-cut, No. 189. 4.

the 18th dynasty many other combinations frequently occur.

The performers either stood, knelt *, or sat upon the ground : in every instance I have met with, they are men; and, what renders the introduction of the instrument more interesting, is the presence of the word Sèbi in the hieroglyphics †, which is the Coptic name of the flute.   It was held with both hands, was sometimes of extraordinary length, and the holes were placed so low that, when playing, the musician was obliged to extend his arms.

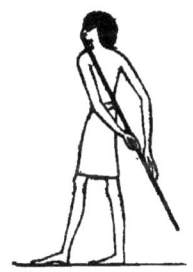

No. 225.   Flute player. The flute is of great length.   Thebes.

THE SINGLE PIPE (συριγξ, OR μοναυλος).

The pipe seems also to have belonged principally, if not exclusively, to male performers ; but as it is very rarely introduced in the sculptures, I con-

---

* *Vide* wood-cut, No. 189.

† This name is very remarkable, and goes far to prove that flutes were made, as in Bœotia, and in some countries of the present day, of the leg-bones of animals.   It has the same meaning as the Latin *tibia*, " a flute," or " thigh-bone : " thus, CHBI-N-PAT is the " *tibia cruris*," or " thigh-bone."

x 2

clude it was not held in great estimation. The
same remark applies to it in many other countries,-
where it was considered rather a pastoral instrument * ; and in Greece it was at first peculiar to
Arcadia. In form, the Egyptian pipe may have
differed slightly from the Greek μοναυλος and the
Roman fistula †, though the μοναυλος, or single
pipe of Greece, is allowed to have been introduced
from Egypt.‡ It was a straight tube, without any
increase at the mouth ; and, when played, was held
with both hands. It was of moderate length, apparently not exceeding a foot and a half, and
many have been found much smaller ; but these
may have belonged to the peasants, without merit-
ing a place among the instruments of the Egyptian
band : indeed, I have seen one measuring only nine
inches in length §, and those in the museum of
Leyden vary from seven to fifteen inches.

Some have three, others four holes, as is the
case with fourteen of those at Leyden, which are
made of common reeds ; and some‖ were furnished
with a small mouth-piece of the same humble
materials, or of a thick straw, inserted into the
hollow of the pipe, the upper end so compressed

---

* Athenæus says (iv. 25.), some pipes were made of reeds, and
called tityrine by the Dorians of Italy. The name καλαμαυλης was
also applied to this sort of pipe, as well as μονοκαλαμος.
† Hor. Od. iii. 1ꝟ. 19.
‡ " Μοναυλος ευρημα μεν εστιν Αιγυπτιων." J. Poll. Onom. iv. 10.
Athenæus says the same, and ascribes the invention of it and the
photinx to Osiris. Deipnos. 4.
§ It had probably been broken at the joint of the centre of the
reed.
‖ One of these is in the British Museum. Vide wood-cut, No. 226.
fig. 1. a and b.

as to leave a very small aperture for the admission of the breath.

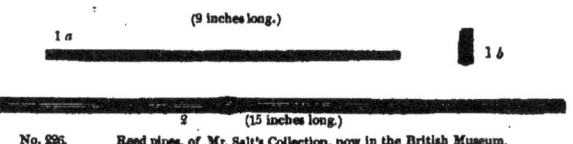

(9 inches long.)

1 a

1 b

2   (15 inches long.)

No. 296.   Reed pipes, of Mr. Salt's Collection, now in the British Museum.

J. Pollux seems to attribute to this simple pipe a much more varied power than we should imagine, giving it, as he does, the title of " many-toned." " It was made," he adds, " of the straw of barley, and was the reputed invention of Osiris * ; " but we are at a loss to know to what instrument he alludes, when he speaks of " the giglarus, a small sort of pipe used by the Egyptians †," unless it be one of the reed pipes above mentioned.

Another kind, which is given in Professor Rosellini's admirable work on Egyptian Antiquities, appears to have been made of separate pieces, like our flutes, unless those divisions represent the joints of the reed ; and the form of the upper end seems more complicated, though the number of holes is limited to five.

THE DOUBLE PIPE.

This instrument consisted of two pipes, perhaps occasionally united together by a common mouth-

* J. Poll. *loc. cit.*
† J. Poll. *loc. cit.* " Γιγλαρος μικρος   τυλισκος, Αιγυπτιος, μοναυλιᾳ προσφορος."

piece, and played each with the corresponding hand. It was common to the Greeks * and other people, and, from the mode of holding it, received the name of right and left pipe, the *tibia dextra* and *sinistra* of the Romans. † The latter had but few holes, and, emitting a deep sound, served as a bass. The other had more holes, and gave a sharp tone ‡; and for this purpose they preferred the upper part of the reed (when made of that material) for the right-hand pipe, and the lower part, near the root, for the left tube. § To them, also, the name of αυλοι was applied by the Greeks, as was that of μοναυλος to the single pipe.

In the paintings of Herculaneum, some of the double pipes are furnished with pegs, fixed into the upper side of each tube, towards the lower extremity; but it is difficult to ascertain the purpose for which they were intended. Some have two in each; others five in the left, and seven in the right hand pipe; and others again five in the right, and none in the other, which is of much smaller dimensions, both in length and thickness. ‖

Nothing of the kind has yet been met with in

* The double pipe of the Greeks had sometimes two pegs at the lower end, or five on one and seven on the other pipe. *Vide* wood-cut, No. 227.

† " The pipe called magadis and palæomagadis emits a deep and an acute sound, as Alexander says, ' Μαγαδιν λαλησω μικρον αμα σοι και μεγαν.' " Athen. iv. 25.

‡ " Biforem dat tibia cantum." Virg. Æn. ix. 618.

§ Plin. xvi. 36. The reed of Orchomenus was called auletic, from being suited to the flute; another was named syringia, being more proper for making pipes.

‖ This does not agree with the above statement of the tibia dextra emitting the sharper sound; but it is possible that they varied according to the pleasure of the performer, being separate. *Vide* wood-cut, No. 227. *fig.* 1.

the sculptures of the Egyptians ; but as they may
have had pipes of similar construction, and these
tend to throw some light on the general appearance

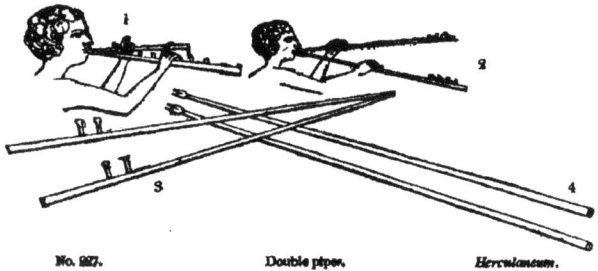

No. 227.   Double pipes.   Herculaneum.

and use of the instrument, I have introduced them
in the accompanying wood-cut.

The double, like the single pipe, was at first of
reed, and afterwards of box *, lotus thorn †, and
other sonorous wood; or of horn, ivory, bone ‡,
iron, or silver.   It was not only used on solemn
occasions, but very generally at festive banquets §,
both among the Greeks and Egyptians.   Men,
but more frequently women, performed upon it ||,
occasionally dancing as they played ; and from its

* Plin. *loc. cit.*   Boxwood for the pipes used on solemn occasions,
the lotus-thorn for the lively-toned instruments.   " Nunc sacrificæ
Thuscorum è buxo, ludicræ verò loto, ossibusque asininis, et argento
fiunt." *Vide* J. Poll. Onom. iv. 9.

† Athenæus tells us, the pipes made of the lotus-wood of Africa were
called by the Alexandrians *photinges.*

‡ Some were made at Thebes, in Bœotia, of the thigh-bone of the
fawn. Athen.; and J. Poll. iv. 10. The latter writer mentions the bones
of vultures and eagles used by the Scythians.

§ According to the same author, the name of boys' pipe, or hemi-
opus, was applied to one of those used at feasts.

|| *Vide* wood-cut, No. 228. 176., etc.

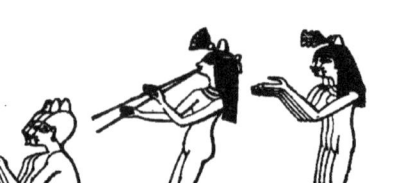

No. 298.   Woman dancing, while playing the double pipe.   Thebes.

repeated occurrence in the sculptures of Thebes, we may suppose the Egyptians preferred it to the single pipe. Of its tone no very accurate notion can be formed; but it is easy to conceive the general effect of an instrument emitting a tenor and bass at the same time. The modern Egyptians have imitated it in their *zummára,* or double reed; but not, I imagine, with very great success, since it is both harsh and inharmonious, and of the rudest construction. Nor is it admitted, like the ancient double pipe, at festivals, where other instruments are introduced; nor allowed to hold a rank in their bands of music, humble and imperfect as they now are; and its piping harshness and monotonous drone are chiefly used for the out-of-doors entertainment of the peasants, or as a congenial accompaniment to the tedious camel's pace.

Many of the instruments of the ancients, whether Greeks, Romans, or Jews, bore a noisy and inharmonious character; and Lucian relates an anecdote of a young flute-player named Harmo-

nides, who, thinking to astonish and delight his
audience, at the Olympic games, blew with such
violence into the instrument, on which he was
performing a solo, that, having completely ex-
hausted himself, he died with the effort *, and may
be said to have breathed his last into the flute.
But that it was really a flute, seems highly improbable; and on this, and many other occasions,
ancient writers appear to have confounded the
instrument with a species of clarionet, or bell-
mouthed pipe, which, being different from the
straight fistula, was comprehended under the more
general name of αυλος, or *tibia.* Of the clarionet
we have no instance in the sculptures of Egypt;
and the modern inhabitants have probably derived
their clamorous and harsh-toned instrument from
some model introduced by the Romans, or other
foreigners; who, after the reign of Amasis, visited
or took possession of the country.

Nor do we meet with that combination of long
and short reeds, now known by the name of pan-
pipes †, in any of the musical scenes portrayed in
the tombs; which, from its having been used by
the Jews, we might expect to find in Egypt. It
was called in Hebrew *āogab*‡, and is one of the
oldest instruments mentioned in sacred history,

* No doubt from the bursting of a blood-vessel. J. Pollux mentions
a player on the trumpet, one Herodorus of Megara, whose instrument
stunned every one. Onom. iv. 11.
† Some of those at Herculaneum have all the reeds of the same
length, in others they decrease towards one end; as described by
J. Pollux. iv. 9., who says they were bound together with waxed
string.
‡ Job, xxi. 12. and Gen. iv. 21., translated " organ."

its invention being said to date *before* the age of Noah.

THE TAMBOURINE.

The tambourine was a favourite instrument both on sacred and festive occasions. It was of three kinds, differing, no doubt, in sound as well as form. One was circular, another square or oblong, and the third consisted of two squares separated by a bar.* They were all beaten by the hand, and used as an accompaniment to the harp and other instruments.

Men and women played the tambourine; but it was more generally appropriated to the latter, as with the Jews†; and they frequently danced to its sound, without the addition of any other music. It was of very early use in Egypt, and seems to have been known to the Jews‡ previous to their leaving Syria: being among the instruments mentioned by Laban, under its Hebrew name *taph*, the *tar* of the modern Arabs.

From the imperfect representations of those in the tombs of Thebes, it is difficult to say whether the Egyptian tambourine had the same moveable pieces of metal, let into its wooden frame, as in

* *Vide* wood-cut, No. 236.
† Exod. xv. 20. " And Miriam took a timbrel in her hand, and all the women went out after her with timbrels and with dances." Judg. xi. 34. Jephthah's daughter, and xxi. 21. 1 Sam. xviii. 6.
‡ As was the harp, which I before mentioned. Gen. xxxi. 27. " With tabret and with harp; " " be taph oo be kinoor." The harp, tabret, and *aogab* were known in the days of Job. Job, xxi. 12.

that of the present day; but their mode of playing it was similar, and from their holding it up after it had been struck, we may venture to conclude the adoption of the metal rings, for the free emission of whose sound that position was particularly suited. It is evident, from the paintings at Herculaneum, that the Greek tambourine was furnished with balls of metal, pendent from the front part, or from the centre, of its circular rim, to which each appears to have been attached by a short thong; and this instrument was mostly confined to women, as with the Egyptians, and chiefly used by the Greeks in festivals of Bacchus and Cybele.

With the name of tambourine that of Anacharsis will always be connected; and, however improbable the story, it has been very generally believed that he fell a sacrifice to the indignation of his countrymen, in consequence of having introduced the instrument into Scythia, when he returned from Greece. Some, with more reason, suppose that an attempt to reform the laws of his country, after the Athenian model, was the cause of his death.

SACRED MUSIC.

Among the instruments of sacred music * may be reckoned the harp, lyre, flute, double pipe, tambourine, cymbals, and even the guitar; but neither the trumpet, drum, nor *mace*, were ex-

* *Vide* wood-cut, No. 229.

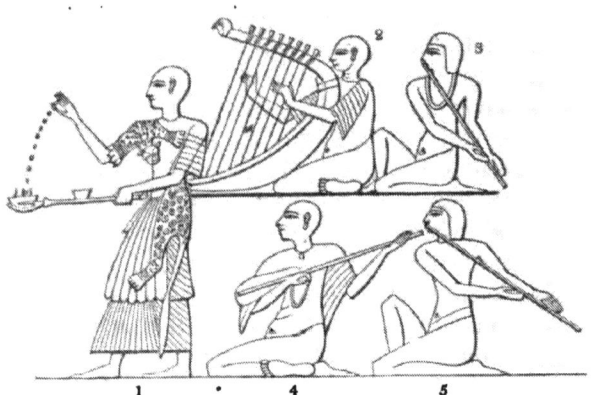

No. 229.   Sacred musicians, and a priest offering incense.   *Leyden Museum.*

cluded from the religious processions, in which the
military were engaged. They do not, however,
appear to have been admitted, like the former,
among those, whose introduction into the courts
of the temple was sanctioned on ordinary occasions; and perhaps the peculiar title of "the holy
instrument" ought to be confined to the sistrum.

The harp, lyre, and tambourine were often
admitted during the religious services of the
temple *; and in a procession in honour of Athor,
represented on the frieze at Dendera†, two god-
desses are observed to play the harp and tam-

---

* With the Jews, the harp, lute, and ten-stringed *ashur*, were employed in the praise of the Deity, as well as trumpets, cymbals, and
other instruments. Psalm xxxiii. 2., and again in Psalm lxxxi. 2. " The
tabret (timbrel), the merry harp, with the lute (psaltery)," and " the
trumpet." 1 Chron. xxv. 1. Asaph even played the cymbals, 1 Chron.
xvi. 5.

† Formerly Tentyris, in Upper Egypt.

bourine*; and this last again occurs in the hand of
another deity at Hermonthis.   The priests, bearing
various sacred emblems, frequently advanced to
the sound of the flute†, and entered the temple to
celebrate their most important festivals; and with
the exception of those of Osiris at Abydus‡, the
sacred rites of an Egyptian deity did not forbid the
introduction of the harp, the flute, or the voice of
singers.

At the fête of Diana, or Pasht, at Bubastis,
music was permitted as on other similar occasions §; and Herodotus ‖ mentions the flute and
the *crotala*, which were played by the votaries of
the goddess, on their way down the Nile to the
town where her far-famed temple stood.   In the
processions during the festival of Bacchus, the same
author ¶ says the flute-player goes first, and is
followed by the choristers, who chant the praises
of the deity; and we find the flute represented in
the sculptures in the hands of a sacred musician
attached to the service of A'mun, who is in attendance, while the ceremonies are performed, in

---

* In a painting at Herculaneum, representing a sacrifice in the
Temple of Isis, the tambourine is introduced, and a man blowing what
appears to be the *cornu* or horn.

† The flute is mentioned by Apuleius, in speaking of the mysteries
of Isis:— " Ibant et dicati magno Serapidi tibicines, qui per *obliquum
calamum* ad aurem porrectum dextram, familiarem templi deique mo-
dulum frequentabant, et plerique qui facilem sacris viam dari prædi-
carent." Metamorph. lib. xi. *Vide* Herodot. ii. 48.

‡ Strabo, lib. xvii.

§ J. Pollux. Onom. iv. 11. " The trumpet was used in some processions, and religious services, by the Egyptians, Greeks, Tyrrheni, and
Romans."

‖ Herodot. ii. 60.

¶ Herodot. ii. 48.

honour of the god. And that cymbals were appropriated to the same purpose, we have sufficient reason for inferring, from their having been found buried with an individual, whose coffin bears an inscription, purporting that she was the minstrel of Amun, the presiding deity of Thebes.

Crotala were properly a sort of castanets, made of hollow wooden shells; and cymbals bore the name of crembala; but in some instances, as in the passage of Herodotus, the name crotala appears to signify cymbals. They were occasionally like our clappers † for frightening birds; and that Pausanias had in view something of the kind is probable, from the use to which he supposes they were once applied requiring a much more powerful sound than that produced by castanets. " The birds of Stymphalus," says that writer *, "which lived on human flesh, are commonly fabled to have been destroyed by the arrows of Hercules; but Pisander, of Camirus, affirms that they were frightened away by the noise of crotala."

That the harp was a favourite instrument in religious ceremonies, is evident from the assertion of Strabo, from the frequent mention of minstrels of Amun, and other gods, in the hieroglyphic legends placed over those who play that instrument, and from the two harpers in the presence of the god Ao, before mentioned.

The custom of approaching the holy place, and of singing the praises of the Deity, was not peculiar

* Pausan. Arcad. lib. viii.
† Represented in the Etruscan tombs.

to the Egyptians. The Jews regarded music as an indispensable part of religion, and the harp held a conspicuous rank in the consecrated band.* David was himself † celebrated as the inventor of musical instruments, as well as for his skill with the harp; he frequently played it during the most solemn ceremonies; and we find that, in the earliest times, the Israelites used the timbrel, or tambourine, in celebrating the praises of the Deity; Miriam ‡ herself, "a prophetess, and the sister of Aaron," having used it, while chanting the overthrow of Pharaoh's host.

With most nations it has been considered right to introduce music into the service of religion; and if the Egyptian priesthood made it so principal a part of their earnest inquiries, and inculcated the necessity of applying to its study, not as an amusement, or in consequence of any feeling excited by the reminiscences accompanying a national air, but from a sincere admiration of the science, and of its effects upon the human mind, we can readily believe that it was sanctioned, and even deemed indispensable, in many of their religious rites. Hence the sacred musicians were of the order of priests, and appointed to this service, like the Levites §,

---

* 2 Sam. vi. 5. " And David and all the house of Israel played before the Lord, on all manner of instruments, made of *firwood*, even on harps, and on psalteries, and on timbrels, and on cornets, and on cymbals."

† Amos, vi. 5. " Invent unto themselves instruments of music, like David;" and 1 Chron. xxiii. 5. " Praised the Lord with the instruments which I made (said David)."

‡ Exod. xv. 20.   § 1 Chron. xv. 16.

among the Jews; and the Egyptian sacred bands were probably divided, and superintended, in the same manner as among that people.

At Jerusalem "Asaph, Heman, and Jeduthun were the three directors of the music of the tabernacle, under David, and of the temple, under Solomon. Asaph had four sons, Jeduthun six, and Heman fourteen.

These twenty-four Levites, sons of the three great masters of sacred music, were at the head of twenty-four bands of musicians, who served the temple in turns. Their number there was always great, especially at the grand solemnities. They were ranged in order, about the altar of burnt sacrifices. Those of the family of Kohath were in the middle, those of Merari at the left, and those of Gershom on the right hand. The whole business of their life was to learn and practise music; and being provided with an ample maintenance, nothing prevented their prosecuting their studies, and arriving at perfection in the art. Even in the temple, and in the ceremonies of religion, female musicians were admitted as well as men; and they were generally the daughters of Levites. Heman had three daughters, who were proficients in music; and the 9th Psalm is addressed to Benaiah, chief of the band of young women, who sang in the temple.

Ezra, in his enumeration of those he brought back from the captivity, reckons two hundred singing men and singing women; and Zechariah, Aziel, and

Shemiramoth*, are said to have presided over the seventh band of music, which was that of the young women." †

In many other places, mention is made of women, who sang, and played on instruments ‡; and the fact of some of them being the daughters of priests, and of the first families, is analogous to the custom of the Egyptians, who only admitted those of the priests, and kings, into the service of the temple. Herodotus states, indeed, that women were not allowed in Egypt to become priestesses of any god or goddess, the office being reserved exclusively for men §; but though it is true that the higher functions of the priesthood belonged to these last, as far as regarded the slaying of victims, presenting offerings, and other duties connected with the sacrifices, yet it is equally certain that women were also employed in the service of the temple, and were even, according to the historian himself, so fully instructed in matters appertaining to religion, that two, who had been carried away and sold into Libya and Greece, were enabled to institute oracles in those countries.   This statement ‖ of Herodotus appears to contradict the former one above mentioned, especially as he admits them to have had

* *Vide* also 1 Chron. xv. and xvi.
† Calmet.
‡ Exod. xv. 20. Psalm lxviii. 25. " It is well seen, O God, how thou goest · · · · · in the sanctuary. The singers go before, the minstrels follow after; in the midst are the damsels playing with the timbrels." 2 Sam. xix. 35. " Can I hear any more the voice of the singing men and singing women ? "
§ Herodot. ii. 35.   ‖ Ibid. ii. 54.

access to the altars of the god * they served, the
Theban Jupiter ; but it is probable that he merely
refers to the higher offices of the priesthood, without intending to exclude them altogether from those
sacred employments.

It is difficult to decide as to the name, or the
precise rank or office they bore ; but the sculptures
leave no room to doubt that they were admitted to
a very important post, which neither the wives
and daughters of priests, nor even of kings, were
ashamed to accept. †   In the most solemn processions, they advanced towards the altar with the
priests, bearing the sacred sistrum ‡; and a queen,
or a princess, frequently accompanied the monarch,
while he offered his praise, or a sacrifice, to the
deity, holding one or two of those instruments in
her hand. §

By some the sistrum was supposed to have been
intended to frighten away Typhon, or the evil
spirit; and Plutarch, who mentions this ‖, adds,
that "on the convex surface is a cat with a human
visage; on the lower part, under the moving chords,
the face of Isis; and on the opposite side that of

* Herodot. ii. 56.
† For the offices held by women, *vide supra*, Vol. I. pp. 258, 259.
261.
‡ *Conf.* Claudian de IV. cons. Honor. 570. : —

> . . . . . " Sic numina Memphis
> In vulgus proferre solet . . . . .
> . . . . . Nilotica sistris
> Ripa sonat, Phariosque modos Ægyptia ducit
> Tibia " . . . . .

And *Vide* wood-cut, No. 8.
§ *Vide* wood-cut, No. 8. *fig.* 5.   ‖ Plut. de Iside, s. 63.

Nepthys." The bars, to which he alludes, were generally three, rarely four; and each had three or

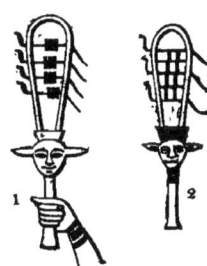

No. 230.   Fig. 1. The sistrum of four bars.   *Thebes.*
2. Of unusual form.

four rings of metal, whereby the "rattling noise made with the moveable bars" was greatly increased.

The instrument was generally from about eight to sixteen, or eighteen, inches in length, and entirely of bronze or brass. It was sometimes inlaid with silver, gilt, or otherwise ornamented; and being held upright, was shaken, the rings moving to and fro upon the bars. These last were frequently made to imitate snakes, or simply bent at each end to secure them; and I have met with one instance of their being connected with each other by cross pieces, besides the unusual addition of two intermediate bars. *

In a sacrifice to Isis, represented at Herculaneum, in company with several sistra, is an instrument, consisting of a rod and a set of moveable balls, arranged in a circle, apparently shaken by the

* *Vide* wood-cut, No. 230. *fig.* 2.

performer; who, in the other hand, holds four links
of a chain, intended, no doubt, to emit a similar
gingling sound; but as the paintings in which

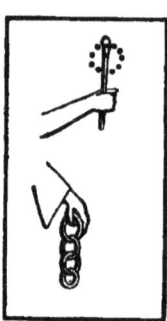

No. 231   Instrument and chain shaken by a person in a religious ceremony represented
at Herculaneum.

they occur are of a late date, and the rites only
borrowed from those of Egypt, we have no direct
evidence of their having been used by the Egyptians themselves.

The most interesting sistrum I have seen is one
brought to England by Mr. Burton, and now in
the British Museum. It was found at Thebes;
and being of a good style and of the most correct
Egyptian form, appears to indicate great antiquity,
and one of the best periods of art.

Two others, in the British Museum, are highly
preserved, but are evidently of a late epoch; and
another in the same collection is of very modern
date. They have four bars, and are of very small
size. Mr. Burton's sistrum is one foot four and a
half inches high, and was furnished with three

movable bars, which have been unfortunately lost. On the upper part are represented the goddess Pasht, or Bubastis, the sacred vulture, and other emblems; and below is the figure of a female, holding in each hand one of these instruments.

The handle is cylindrical, and surmounted by the double face of Athor*, wearing an "asp-formed crown," on whose summit appears to have been the cat, now scarcely traced in the remains of its feet. It is entirely of bronze; the handle, which is hollow, and closed by a movable cover of the same metal, is supposed to have held something appertaining to the sistrum; and the lead, still remaining within the head, is a portion of that used in soldering the interior.

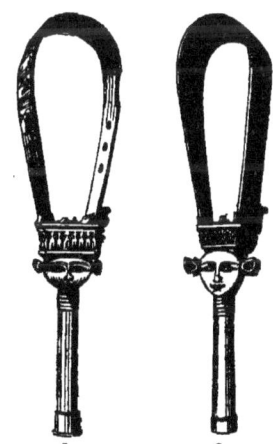

1   2

No. 232.   Sistrum in Mr. Burton's collection, now in the British Museum.

* Plutarch says, on one side the face of Isis, on the other that of Nepthys.   De Is. s. 63.

One of the Berlin sistra is eight, the other nine inches in height : the former has four bars, and on the upper or circular part lies a cat *, crowned with the disc or sun.   The other has three bars : the handle is composed of a figure, supposed to be of Typhon, surmounted by the heads of Athor ; and on the summit are the horns, globe, and feathers of the same goddess.   They are both destitute of

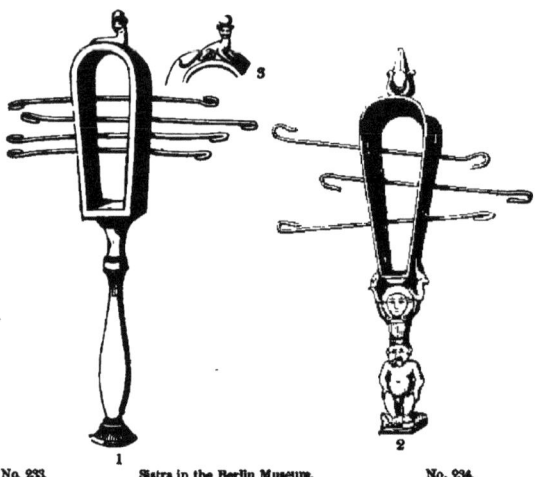

No. 233.   Sistra in the Berlin Museum.   No. 234.

rings ; but the rude Egyptian model of another, in the same collection, has three rings upon its single bar, agreeing in this respect, if not in the number of the bars, with those represented in the sculptures.

Songs and the clapping of hands may likewise be

---

* *Conf.* Plutarch, *loc. cit.*   He supposes the four bars corresponded to the four elements.

considered connected with sacred music; and they
are both noticed in the sculptures, and by ancient

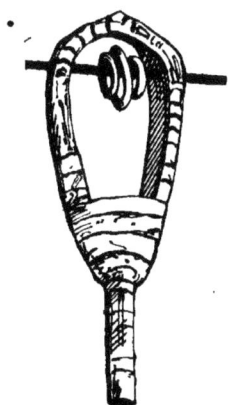

No. 235.   Rude model of a sistrum, in the Berlin Museum.

authors. Those who attended at the festival of Bubastis are said by Herodotus to have celebrated
the Deity in this manner, with the music of flutes
and cymbals; and the Jews followed the same
custom *, like the Moslem inhabitants of modern
Egypt.

The χνουη, an instrument said by Eustathius to
have been used by the Greeks, at sacrifices, to as-
semble the congregation, was reputed to have been
of Egyptian origin; but I do not believe it has
been met with in the sculptures. It was a species
of trumpet, of a round shape, and was said to have
been the invention of Osiris.

* " O clap your hands together, all ye people; O sing unto God
with the voice of melody." Psalm xlvii. 1.

THE DANCE.

The dance consisted mostly of a .succession of figures, in which the performers endeavoured to exhibit a great variety of gesture : men and women danced at the same time, or in separate parties, but the latter were generally preferred, from their superior grace and elegance. Some danced to slow airs, adapted to the style of their movement : the attitudes they assumed frequently partook of a grace, not unworthy of the Greeks ; and some credit is due to the skill of the artist who represented the subject, which excites additional interest from its being in one of the oldest tombs of Thebes.* Others preferred a lively step, regulated by an appropriate tune; and men sometimes danced with great spirit, bounding from the ground†, more in the manner of Europeans than of an Eastern people. On these occasions, the music was not always composed of many instruments, and here we only find the cylindrical maces, and a woman snapping her fingers to the time ‡ in lieu of cymbals or castanets.

Graceful attitudes and gesticulation were the general style of their dance; but, as in all other countries, the taste of the performance varied according to the rank of the person by whom they were employed, or their own skill; and the dance

---

* Of the time of Amunoph II., B.C. 1450. *Vide* wood-cut, No. 236.
† *Vide* wood-cut, No. 198.
‡ The " Lesbium servate pedem, *meique Pollicis ictum* " of Horace (Od. lib. iv. 6. 39.) might refer to this mode of marking the time.

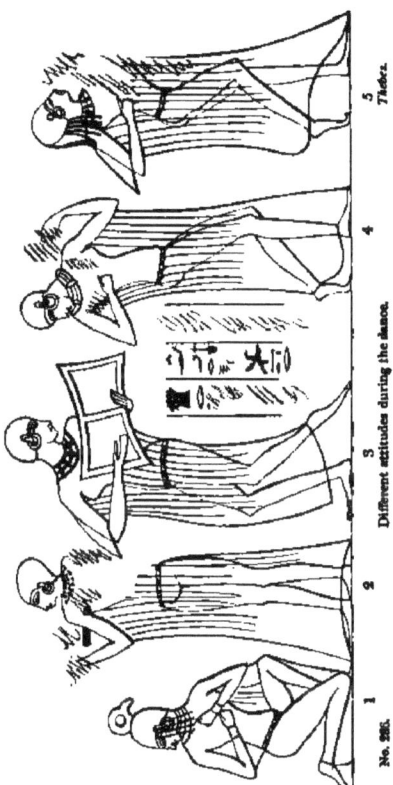

at the house of a priest differed from that among the uncouth peasantry, or the lower classes of townsmen.

It was not customary for the upper orders of Egyptians to indulge in this amusement, either in public or private assemblies; and none appear to have practised it but the lower ranks of society, and those who gained their livelihood by attending festive meetings. With the Greeks, it was also customary at feasts, to have women who professed music and dancing to entertain the guests; they even looked upon the dance as a recreation, in which all classes might indulge, and deemed it an accomplishment becoming a gentleman : it is, therefore, not surprising that, like music, it should have formed part of their education.

The Romans, on the contrary, were far from considering it worthy of a man of rank, or of a sensible person; and Cicero says *, " No man who is sober dances, unless he is out of his mind, either *when alone,* or in any decent society; for dancing is the companion of wanton conviviality, dissoluteness, and luxury." Nor did the Greeks indulge in it to excess; and effeminate dances were deemed indecent, in men of character and wisdom. Indeed, Herodotus informs us, that Hippoclides, the Athenian, who had been preferred before all the nobles of Greece, as a husband for the daughter of Clisthenes, king of Argos, was rejected on account of his extravagant gestures in the dance.

Of all the Greeks, the Ionians were most noted for their fondness of this art; and, from the wanton and indecent tendency of their songs and gesticulations, dances of a voluptuous character, like those of the modern Alméhs† of the East, were

---

* Cicero. Orat. pro Muræná.

† Alméh (Eulmeh), or Ghowázee, women in Egypt and other countries, who dance with the most indecent gestures to the sound of a

styled by the Romans " Ionic movements." * Moderate dancing was even deemed worthy of the
gods themselves.   Jupiter, " the father of gods and
men," is represented dancing in the midst of the
other deities ; and Apollo is not only introduced
by Homer thus engaged, but received the title of
ορχηστης, " the dancer," from his supposed excellence in the art.   In early ages, before the introduction of luxury, it was an innocent recreation ;
and, as Athenæus † observes, " becoming of persons of honour and wisdom ; " but extravagant
gesture corrupted its original simplicity ‡, and " no
part of the art connected with music," says Plutarch §, " has, in our time, suffered so great a de-
gradation as dancing."

Fearing lest it should corrupt the manners of
a people, naturally lively, and fond of gaiety, and
deeming it neither a necessary part of education,
nor becoming a person of sober habits, the Egyptians forbade those of the higher classes to learn it
as an accomplishment, or even as an amusement ;
and, by permitting professional persons to be in-

---

violin and tambourine, singing and repeating verses. They were formerly
learned women, whence their name Eulmeh, who rehearsed poetry,
and danced to amuse the inmates of a *haréem*.   Their general appellation
at the present day, Ghowázeh, is derived from Ghoos (warriors), a
title of the Memlooks, at whose festive meetings they used to dance,
and through whom they have lost the consideration they formerly enjoyed.

  * Hor. : — " Motus doceri gaudet Ionicos
              Matura virgo " . . . . . Od. lib. iii. 6. 21.

  † Athen. i. 19.
  ‡ Dancing was highly approved of by Socrates, as being conducive
to health. Plut. de Sanit.
  § Plut. Sympos. viii. 9. 18.

troduced into their assemblies, to entertain the guests, they sanctioned all the diversion of which it was supposed capable, without compromising their dignity.

They dreaded the excitement resulting from such an occupation, the excess of which ruffled and discomposed the mind; and it would have been difficult, having once conceded permission to indulge in it, to prevent those excesses, which it did not require the example of Asiatic nations to teach them to foresee. If those who were hired to perform, either in public or in private, transgressed the bounds of moderation, or descended to buffoonery, it might excite the contempt of those it failed to please, yet the beholders were innocent of the fault; and any word or action, offending against the rules of decency, might be checked by the veto of their superiors.

In private, in particular, they were subject to the orders and censure of the persons by whom they were employed; and, consequently, avoided any gesture or expression which they knew to be unwelcome, or likely to give offence to the spectators; and thus no improper innovations were attempted, from the caprice of a performer. They consulted the taste of the party, and adapted the style of dance and of gesture to those whose approbation they courted: it is not, therefore, surprising that excesses were confined to the inferior class of performers, at the houses of the lower orders, whose congenial taste welcomed extravagant buffoonery and gesticulation.

Grace in posture and movement was the chief object of those employed at the assemblies of the rich; and the ridiculous gestures of the buffoon were permitted there, so long as they did not transgress the rules of decency and moderation.   Music was always indispensable, whether at the festive meetings of the rich or poor; and they danced to the sound of the harp, lyre, guitar, pipe *, tambourine, and other instruments, and, in the streets, even to the drum.

Many of their postures resembled those of the modern ballet; and the *pirouette* delighted an Egyptian party upwards of 3500 years ago.†

The dresses of the female dancers were light, and of the finest texture, showing, by their transparent quality, the forms and movement of the limbs : they generally consisted of a loose flowing robe, reaching to the ankles, occasionally fastened tight at the waist; and round the hips was a small narrow girdle, adorned with beads, or ornaments of various colours.   Sometimes the dancing figures are represented without any indication of dress, and appear to have been perfectly naked ; but it is difficult to say if this is intentional, or if the outline of the transparent robe ‡ has been effaced; and it is sometimes so faintly traced as scarcely to be perceived, even when the paintings are well preserved : for we can scarcely suppose that a highly civilised

---

* Conf. Matt. xi. 17. " We have piped unto you, and ye have not danced."

† *Vide* wood-cut, No. 237.

‡ The Greeks also represented the contour of the figure, as if seen through the dress.

people, like the Egyptians, were so depraved as to admit, or to allow their artists to record, a dance of naked women, in the presence of men, or that the priesthood would permit such exhibitions.

Slaves were taught dancing as well as music; and in the houses of the rich, besides their other occupations, that of dancing to entertain the family, or a party of friends, was required of them; and that free Egyptians, who gained their livelihood by their performances, were also engaged at private parties, is evident from the paintings, where they are distinctly pointed out, by having the usual colour of their compatriots.

Some danced by pairs, holding each other's hands; others went through a succession of steps alone*, whether men or women; and sometimes a man performed a *solo* to the sound of music, or the clapping of hands. †

Feats of agility and strength were frequently exhibited on these occasions, with or without the sound of music. Some held each other by· the hand, and whirled round at arms' length, in opposite directions ‡; some lifted each other off the ground in various difficult attitudes, and attempted every species of feat, which could be performed by agility or strength; but as these enter more properly under the denomination of games, I shall not introduce them here, but shall notice them in another place, with the gymnastic exercises of the Egyptians.

* *Vide* wood-cut, No. 238.   † *Vide* wood-cut, No. 239.
‡ *Vide* wood-cut, No. 240.

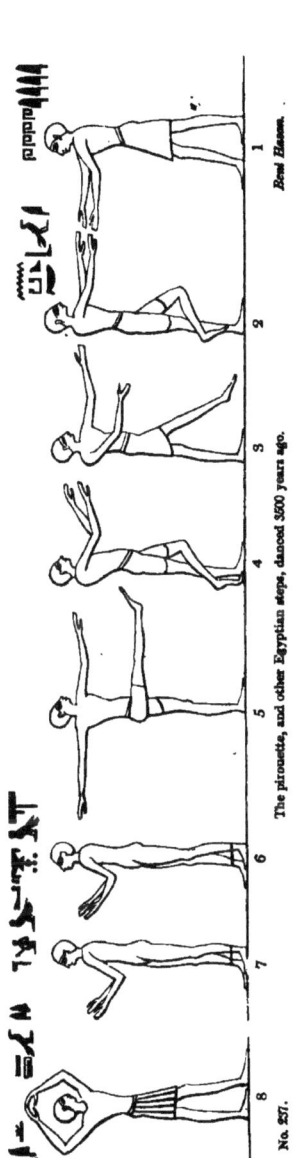

The pirouette, and other Egyptian steps, danced 3500 years ago.

Beni Hassan.

No. 271.

The dances of the lower orders appear generally to have had a tendency towards a species of pantomime; and we can readily conceive the rude peasantry to be more delighted with ludicrous and extravagant dexterity, than with those gestures which displayed elegance and grace. There is no instance of the *tripudiatio*, or dance of armed men, unless some of the figures at Beni Hassan, repre-

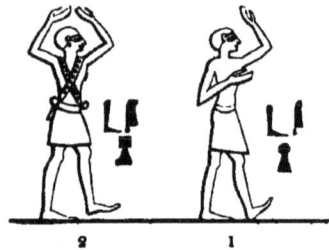

No. 238.   2   1   *Thebes.*
                    Men dancing alone.

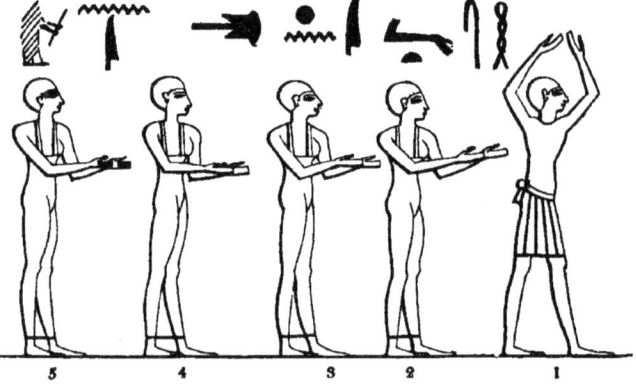

5   4   3   2   1
No. 239.   Men dancing a solo to the sound of the hand.   *Tomb near the Pyramids.*

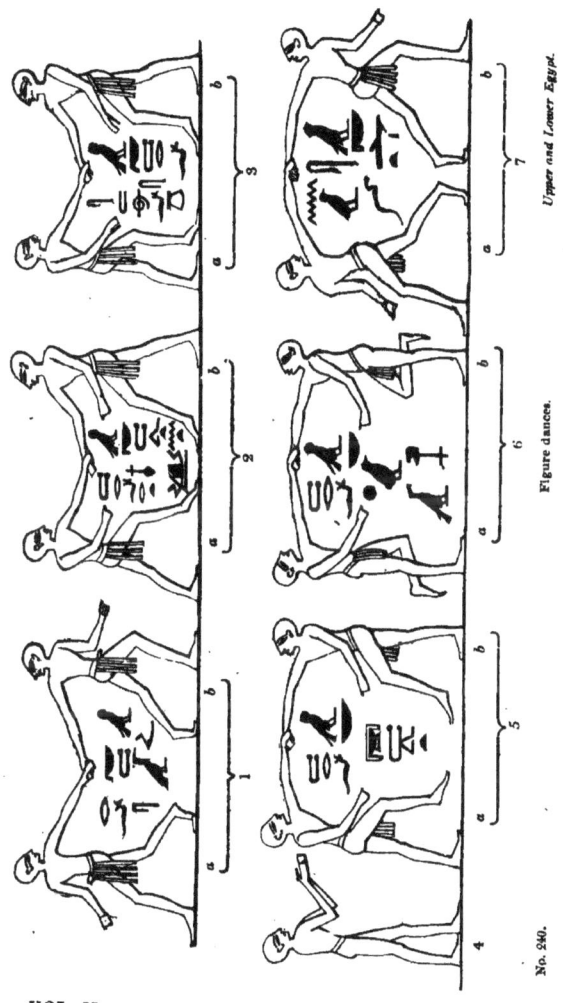

No. 240.

SACRED DANCING

That they also danced at the temples, in honour of the gods, is evident from the representations of several sacred processions, where individuals performed certain gestures to the sound of suitable music, and danced as they approached the precincts of the sacred courts. In what this differed from that of ordinary festivities, it is impossible to decide ; and, indeed, the appearance of the figures, in more than one instance, precisely the same as the usual hieroglyphic signifying dancing, may be supposed to indicate a great similarity between the ordinary dance and that of the temple.

Such a custom may at first sight appear inconsistent with the gravity of religion : but our surprise ceases, when we recollect with what feelings David himself danced * before the ark ; and the fact that the Jews considered it part of their religious duties to approach the Deity with the dance †, with tabret and with harp, suffices to remove any objection which might be offered to the probability of its introduction in the Egyptian ceremonies. And if further proof were wanting, we have their mode of worshipping the golden calf ‡, immediately derived from the country they had left, which consisted principally of songs and dancing.

* I Chron. xv. 29. 2 Sam. vi. 14.
† Psalm cxlix. 3. " Let them praise his name in the dance : let them sing praises unto him with the timbrel and harp." Conf. Exod. xv. 20.
‡ Exod. xxxii. 18, 19.

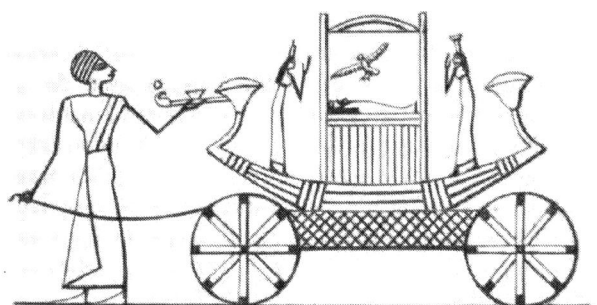

No. 243. Singular instance of a four-wheeled carriage, on the bandages of a mummy, belonging to S. D'Athanasi.

CHAPTER VII.

Vases of various Kinds. — Boxes of the Toilet and others.— Substitute for a Hinge. — Parties and Conversation. — Preparation for Dinner. — Table brought in. — Guests seated at Dinner. — Figure of a dead Man brought in. — Dancing and Entertainments. — Game of Draughts. — Various Games. — Ball. — Dwarfs. — Wrestling. — Fighting with Sticks.

HAVING concluded the preceding chapter with the arrival of a party, and the introductory custom of welcoming the guests with refreshments and music, I proceed to describe the vases placed in the apartments for the purpose of ornament, or

z 3

used on those occasions; which, as I have already observed, were of hard stone, alabaster, glass, ivory, bone, porcelain, bronze, silver, or gold : the lower classes, contented with those of humbler materials, having an inferior kind of glazed pottery, or common earthenware.

Many of their ornamental vases, as well as those in common use, present the most elegant forms, which would do honour to the skill of a Greek artist; the Egyptians frequently displaying in these objects of private luxe, the taste of a highly refined people : and so strong a resemblance do they bear to the productions of the best epochas of ancient Greece, both in their shape and in the fancy devices which adorn them, that some might even imagine them borrowed from Greek patterns. But they are purely Egyptian, and were universally adopted in the Valley of the Nile, long before the graceful forms we admire were known in Greece : a fact invariably acknowledged by those who are acquainted with the remote age of Egyptian monuments, and the period when the paintings representing them were executed in the tombs, or temples, of the Thebaïd.

Some indeed of the most elegant date in the early age of the third Thothmes, a monarch who appears to have lived about the year 1490 before our era, and whom I assume to be the Pharaoh of the Jewish Exodus : and we not only admire their forms but the richness of the materials of which they were made, the colours and the hieroglyphics themselves showing them to have been of gold and

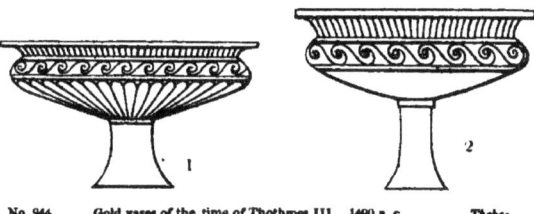

No. 944.   Gold vases of the time of Thothmes III.   1490 B. c.   *Thebes.*

silver, or of this last, inlaid with the more precious metal.

Those of bronze, alabaster, glass, porcelian, and even of ordinary pottery, were also deserving of admiration, from the beauty of their shapes, the designs which ornamented them, and the superior quality of their materials; and gold and silver cups were often beautifully engraved, and studded with precious stones. Among these we readily distinguish the green emerald, the purple amethyst, and other gems; and when an animal's head adorned their handles, the eyes were frequently composed of them, except when enamel, or some coloured composition, were employed as a substitute.

That the Egyptians made great use of precious stones for their vases, and for women's necklaces, rings, bracelets, and other ornamental purposes, is evident from the paintings at Thebes, and from the numerous articles of jewellery discovered in the tombs; they were among the presents brought by the conquered nations tributary to the Egyptians; and their value and nature are indicated by the

z 4

hieroglyphics accompanying them, as well as by the care with which they are tied up in bags, and secured with a seal.

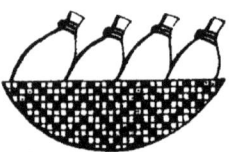

No. 245.   Bags, probably containing precious stones, tied up and sealed.   *Thebes.*

Many of the bronze vases found at Thebes, and in other parts of Egypt, are of a quality which cannot fail to excite admiration, and prove the skill possessed by the Egyptians in the art of working and compounding metals. We are surprised at the rich sonorous tones they emit on being struck, the fine polish of which they are frequently susceptible, and the high finish given them by the workmen : nor are the knives and daggers, made of the same materials, less deserving of notice ; the elastic spring they possessed, and even retain to the present day, being such as could only be looked for in a blade of steel. I believe the exact proportions of the copper and alloys, in the different specimens preserved in the museums of Europe, have not yet been ascertained ; but it would be curious to know their composition, particularly the interesting dagger of the Berlin collection, which is as remarkable for the elasticity of its blade, as for the neatness and perfection of its finish. This part of the subject, however, properly relates to the working of metals, which I shall

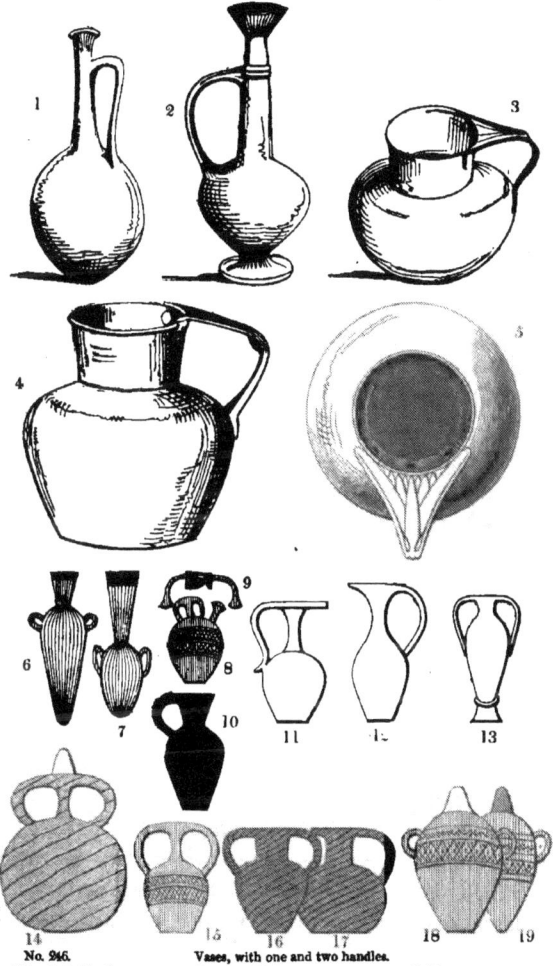

No. 246.   Vases, with one and two handles.
Figs. 1, 2. Earthenware vases found at Thebes.   3. Bronze vase.
        4. Bronze vase.
        5. The same seen from above, showing the top of the handle.
        6. to 19. From the paintings of Thebes.

were ornamented with the heads of wild animals, as the ibex, oryx, or gazelle; others had a head on either side, a fox, a cat, or something similar; and many were ornamented with horses' heads, a whole quadruped, a goose's head, figures of captives, or fancy devices. Many of these last were extraordinary and monstrous, presenting nothing to admire, except the brilliancy of their colours, when made of porcelain, or the richness of their materials, when of gold, inlaid with stones: and the head of a Typhonian * figure † sometimes served

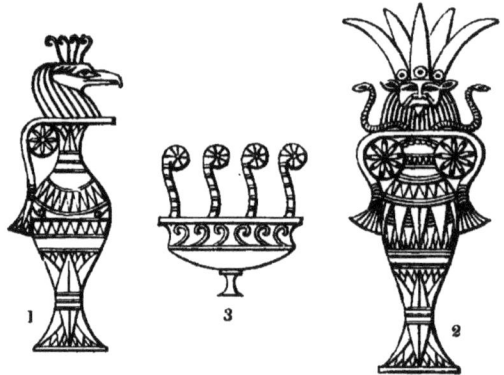

No. 249.   *Thebes.*

Fig. 1. Vase, with head of a bird as a cover.
2. With head of a Typhonian monster.
3. A golden vase, without handles.

for the cover of a vase, as it often did for the support of a mirror, which daily displayed the beauty of an Egyptian lady. Many, too, of the ordinary forms of their vases do not claim our admiration,

* It is remarkable that the name of Typhon, the evil deity, is retained in the Arabic word Tuphán, " the deluge."
† *Vide* wood-cut, No. 250., *fig.* 2.

either for neatness or symmetry, and they are occasionally as devoid of taste as the wine bottles and
flower pots of an English cellar and conservatory.

Some had a single handle fixed to one side, and
were in shape not unlike our cream jugs *, ornamented with the heads of oxen, or fancy devices :
others were of bronze, bound with gold, having

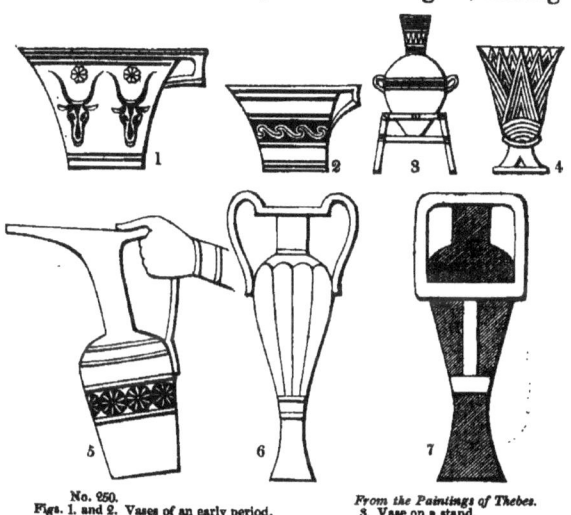

No. 250.

Figs. 1. and 2. Vases of an early period.
4. Drinking-cup of porcelain.

From the Paintings of Thebes.
3. Vase on a stand.
7. Bronze vase, bound with gold.

handles of the same metal; and many depended
on accidental caprice. Several vases had simple
handles, or rings on either side ; others were destitute of these, and of every exterior ornament:
some again were furnished with a single ring, attached to a neat bar†, or with a small knob, pro-

* *Vide* wood-cut, No. 250., *figs.* 1, 2.
† Wood-cut, No. 251. *figs.* 1, 2.

jecting from the side *; and many of those used in the service of the temple, highly ornamented with figures of deities in relief†, were attached

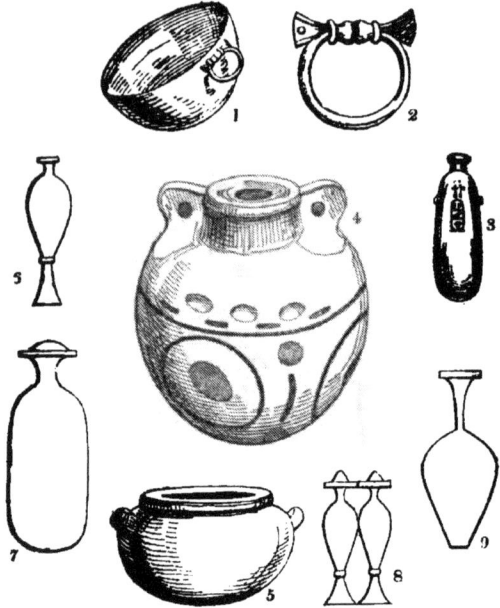

No. 251.

Fig. 1. Bronze vase brought by me from Thebes, now in the British Museum.
  2. Showing how the handle is fixed.
  3. Alabaster vase from Thebes, of the time of Naco.
  4. Vase at Berlin of cut glass   5. Stone vase.
  6. to 9. From the sculptures of Thebes.

to a movable curved handle, on the principle of, though more elegant in form than, their common culinary utensils.‡   They were of bronze, and the

---

* *Vide* wood-cut, No. 251. *figs.* 3, 4, 5.
† *Vide* wood-cut, No. 252. *fig.* 1.
‡ *Vide* wood-cut, No. 252. *fig.* 3.

style of the figures represented on them was as superior as the workmanship and quality of the materials; and while citing them, I cannot omit the notice of a vase of elongated form belonging to the late Mr. Salt *, in the manufacture of

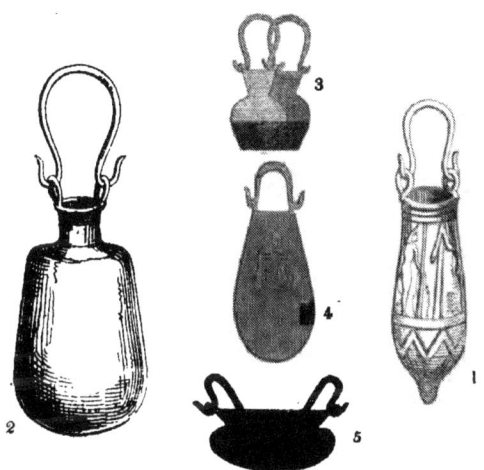

No. 252.

Fig. 1. Bronze vase 2⅔ inches high, used in the temple, in my possession.
2. A larger one in the Berlin Museum.
3, 4, 5. Culinary utensils in the sculptures at Thebes.

which, the skill of no ordinary artisan is displayed; and its cover, fitting with so much nicety, that it resembles the effect of a spring, vies with the excellent composition of the metal in claiming our admiration.

Another of much larger dimensions, and of a different form, was found by me at Thebes, and is now in the British Museum.† It is entirely of

* *Vide* wood-cut, No. 253.   † *Vide* wood-cut, No. 254.

bronze, with two large handles fastened on with pins; and though it resembles some of the caldrons in-

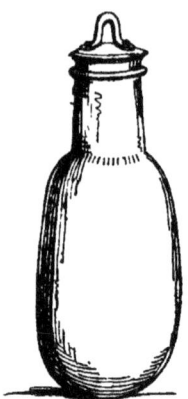

troduced in the paintings representing the Egyptian kitchen, we may doubt from its lightness whether it was used there, or intended as a basin, or for a similar purpose.

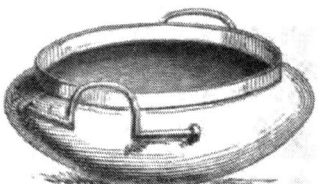

No. 254.   Large bronze vase brought by me from Thebes.

Vases, surmounted with a human head, forming the cover, appear to have been frequently used for

keeping gold and other precious objects, representations of which are met with in the small side
chambers of Medeenet Haboo, the supposed treasury of King Remeses; and it is not improbable,
that their being applied to this purpose in early
times obtained for them a name derived from
the Coptic, νουβ "gold," afterwards confounded
with Canopus; though this last, when applied to
the town, is compounded of καρι νουβ (kahi
noub), "the golden land," or χρυσεον εδαφος.
Similar vases, with human, as well as other, heads,
were also used in the ceremonies of the dead.

If Remeses III. was really the same as the
wealthy Rhampsinitus of Herodotus, these chambers may have been the very treasury he mentions,
where the thieves displayed so much dexterity *;
for though his account might lead us to infer that
it was at Memphis, we are not obliged to confine
the seat of government, and consequently the
scene of the story, to the capital of Lower Egypt,
even during the reign of his Rhampsinitus; and
the historian, who lived almost solely in the vicinity
of Memphis and Heliopolis, during his short stay
in the country, appears to speak of those cities as if
Thebes had always been a place of little consequence, and scarcely worthy of notice.   Indeed,
it may fairly be doubted if Herodotus ever visited
Thebes; though I cannot go so far as some, who
question his having been in Egypt, and suppose
he derived his information from the works of older
writers.

* *Vide* Vol. I. p. 122.

Bottles, small vases, and pots, used for holding ointment, or other purposes connected with the toilet, were of alabaster, glass, porcelain, and hard

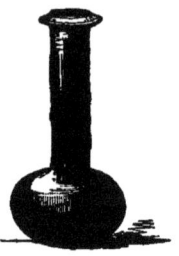

No. 255.   Glass bottle.   *Thebes.*

stone, as granite, basalt, porphyry, serpentine, or breccia: some were of earthenware *, ivory, bone, and other materials, according to the choice or means of individuals; but in a work of so limited a nature as the present it is impossible to introduce

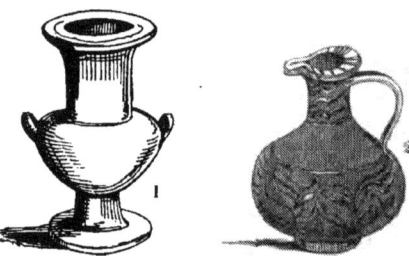

No. 256.

Fig. 1. Alabaster vase in my possession, from Thebes.
     2. Porcelain vase in Mr. Salt's Collection.

specimens of the numerous forms they present, or to illustrate the various styles of their workmanship: I have therefore only selected those which

* Conf. Athen. Deipn. ii. c. 3. " Earthenware vases, which we highly esteem, brought from Coptos."

relate more immediately to the present subject, and, if required, shall, at some future period, exa-

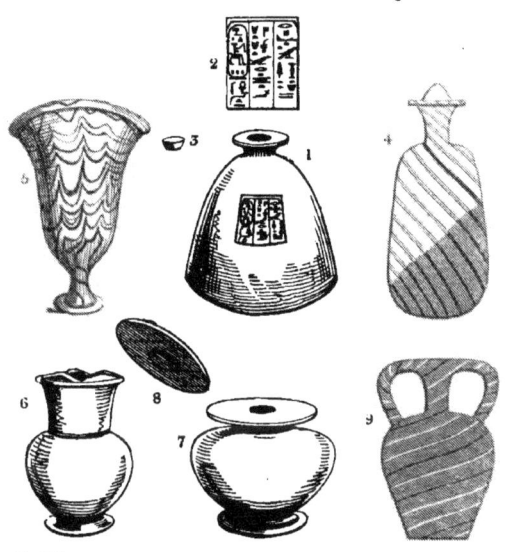

No. 257.

Fig. 1. Alabaster vase, containing sweet-scented ointment, in the Museum of Alnwick Castle.
  2. Hieroglyphics on the vase, presenting the name of a queen.
  3. The stopper.   4. and 9. Porcelain vases, from the paintings of Thebes.
  5. Porcelain cup, in my possession, from Thebes.
  6. Vase of ivory, in my possession, containing a dark-coloured ointment; from Thebes.
  7. Alabaster vase, with its lid (8), in the Museum of Alnwick Castle.

mine the vases of the Egyptians in the minute and detailed manner, which the interesting variety, found in the tombs, or painted on the monuments, deserves.

Small boxes, made of wood or ivory, were also numerous, offering, like the vases, a multiplicity of forms ; and some, which contained cosmetics of divers kinds, served to deck the dressing table, or a lady's boudoir. They were carved in various ways,

and loaded with ornamental devices in relief; sometimes representing the favourite lotus flower, with
its buds and stalks, a goose, gazelle, fox, or other
animal.   Many were of considerable length, terminating in a hollow shell, not unlike a spoon in

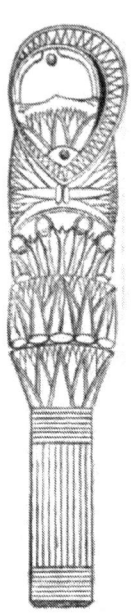
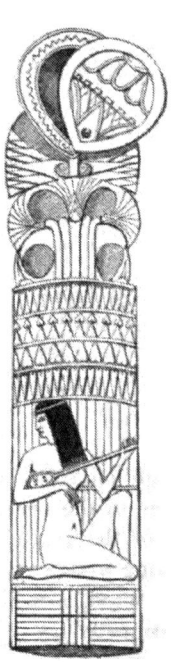

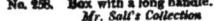

No. 258.   Box with a long handle.   No. 259.   Box in the Berlin Museum,
            Mr. Salt's Collection   showing the lid open.

shape and depth, covered with a lid turning on a
pin ; and to this, which may properly be styled the
box, the remaining part was merely an accessory,
intended for ornament, or serving as a handle.

One of these has been already noticed * for the elegance of its execution, and the grace of a female playing the guitar carved upon it; and,

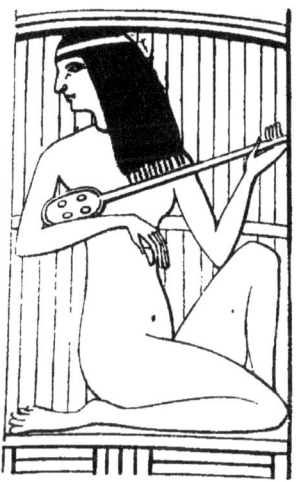

No. 260.   Figure playing the guitar on a box in the Berlin Museum.

though on so small a scale, it is difficult to do justice to the original, the reader may form some idea of the attitude of the figure from the accompanying wood-cuts.† They were generally of sycamore wood, sometimes of tamarisk‡ or sont §, and occasionally the more costly ivory or inlaid work were substituted for wood. To many, a handle of less disproportionate length was attached, representing the usual lotus flower, a figure, a Typhonian

---

* In Vol. II. p. 225.   † *Vide* wood-cuts, Nos. 259, 260.
‡ Tamarix Orientalis, *Arab.* Athul.   § Acacia, or Mimosa, Nilotica.

A A 3

monster, an animal, a bird, a fish, or a reptile; and
the box itself, whether covered with a lid or open,
was in character with the remaining part.   Some
of these shallow boxes were probably intended to
contain small portions of ointment, taken from
a large vase at the time it was wanted, or for other
purposes connected with the toilet, where greater

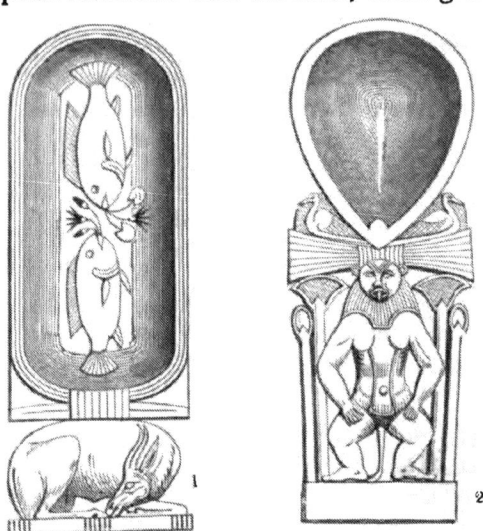

No. 261.   Wooden boxes, or saucers without covers.   *Mr. Salt's Collection.*

depth was not required; and in many instances.
they so nearly resemble spoons, that it is difficult
to decide to which of the two they ought to be.
referred.

Many are made in the form of a royal oval,
with and without a handle *; and the body of a

* *Vide* wood-cut, No. 262.

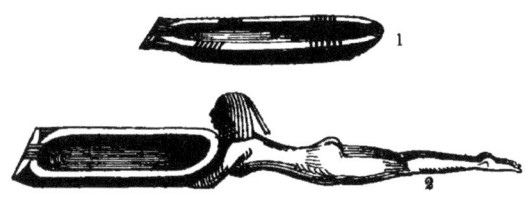

No. 262.   Other open boxes, whose form is taken from the oval of a king's name.
Alnwick Castle and Leyden Museum.

wooden fish is scooped out, and closed with a
cover imitating the scales, to deceive the eye by
the appearance of a solid mass. Sometimes a goose

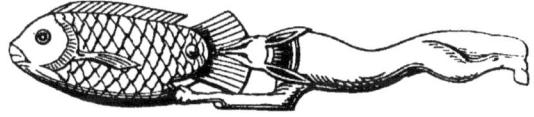

No. 263.   Box in the form of a fish, with turning lid.   *Mr. Salt's Collection.*

is represented, ready for table*, or swimming on
the water †, and pluming itself; whose head consti-
tutes the handle of a box formed of its hollow body:

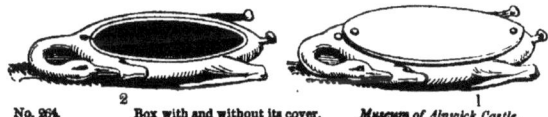

No. 264.   Box with and without its cover.   *Museum of Alnwick Castle.*

some consist of an open part, or cup, attached to
a covered box‡; others of different shapes offer
the usual variety of fancy devices, and some without covers, may come under the denomination of
saucers.   Others bear the precise form and character of a box, being deeper and more capacious,

* *Vide* wood-cut, No. 264.   † Wood-cut, No. 265. *fig.* 2.
‡ Wood-cut, No. 266.

A A 4

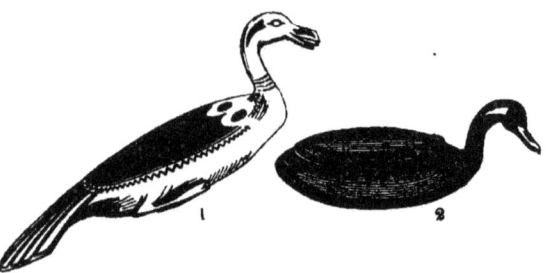

No. 265.   Boxes in form of geese.   *Mr. Salt's Collection and Leyden Museum.*

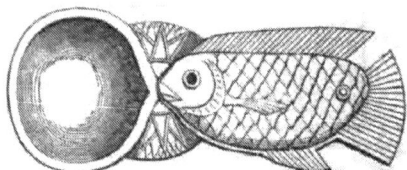

No. 266.   One part open, and one covered.   *Mr. Salt's Collection.*

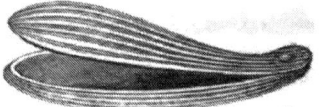

No. 267.   Box with the lid turning, as usual, on a pin.   *Mr. Salt's Collection.*

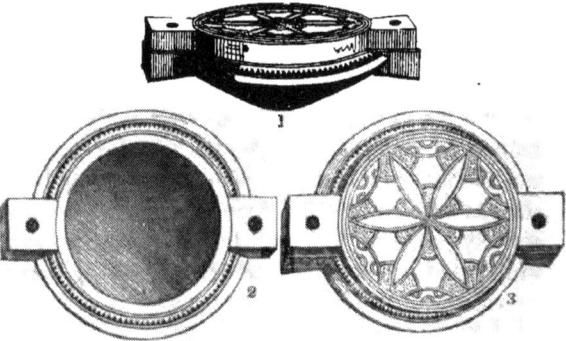

No. 268.   A box, with and without its lid.   *Mr. Salt's Collection.*

probably used for holding trinkets, or occasionally as repositories for the small pots of ointment, or
scented oils, and bottles containing the collyrium,
applied to the eyes, which I shall have occasion to
notice with the toilet of the ladies.

Some were divided into separate compartments,
covered by a common lid, either sliding in a
groove *, or turning on a pin at one end; and

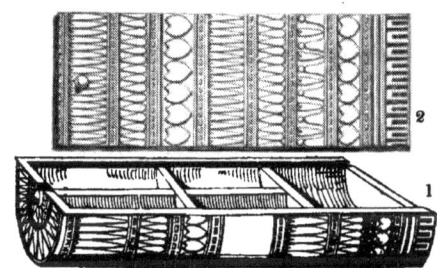

No. 269.   *Mr. Salt's Collection.*
   Fig. 1. A box, with devices carved in relief, divided into cells.
       2. The lid, which slides into a groove.

many of still larger dimensions sufficed to contain
a mirror, combs, and perhaps even some articles of
dress.

These boxes were frequently of costly materials,
veneered with rare woods, or made of ebony,
inlaid with ivory, painted with various devices, or
stained to imitate materials of a valuable nature;
and the mode of fastening some of them, and the
curious substitute for a hinge, show the lid was
entirely removed, and that the box remained open,
while used.   The principle of this will be better

* *Vide* wood-cut, No. 269.

understood by reference to the wood-cut, where *fig.* 1. represents a side section of the box, and *fig.* 2. the inside of the lid. At the upper part of the back c, *fig.* 3. a small hole E is cut, which, when

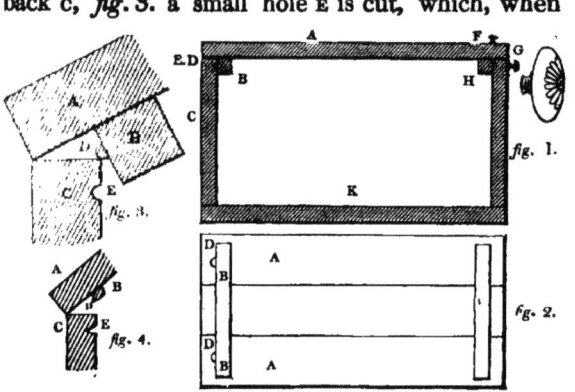

No. 270.   *Found at Thebes.*
Fig. 1.   Section of the box.   A, the lid,   K, the bottom.   C, D, the two sides.
Fig. 2.   The inside of the lid.   B, H, cross-bars nailed inside the lid.

the box is closed, receives the nut D, projecting from the cross-bar B, on the inside of the lid; and the two knobs F and G, one on the lid, the other on the front of the box itself, served not only for ornament but for fastening it, a band being wound round them, and secured with a seal. These knobs, which were of ebony, or other hard wood, were frequently turned with great care, and inlaid with ivory and silver, an instance of which is given in *fig.* 5.

Some boxes were made with a pointed summit, divided into two parts, one of which alone opened, turning on small pivots at the base, and the two ends of the box resembled in form the gable ends, as the top, the shelving roof, of a house. The sides were, as usual, secured by glue and nails, generally of wood, and dovetailed, a method of joining adopted in Egypt at the most remote period; but the description of these belongs more properly to cabinet work, as those employed for holding the combs, and similar objects, to the toilet.

Some vases have been found in boxes, made of wicker-work, closed with stoppers of wood, reed, or other materials, supposed to belong either to a lady's toilet, or to a medical man; one of which, now preserved in the Berlin Museum, has been already noticed, and introduced in a wood-cut* of the preceding volume. The vases are six in number, varying slightly in form and size: five of alabaster, and the remaining one of serpentine, each standing in its own cell or compartment.

Bottles of terra cotta are also met with, in very great abundance, of the most varied forms and

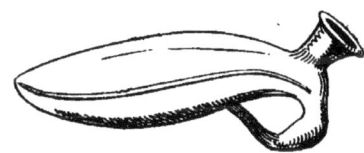

No. 271. Terra cotta bottle, perhaps used by painters for holding water, and carried on the thumb.   *Mr. Salt's Collection.*

dimensions, made for every kind of purpose of which they were susceptible; and I have met with one which appears to have belonged to a painter,

* Vol. II. page 217.

and to have been intended for holding water to moisten the colours; the form and position of the handle, suggesting that it was held on the thumb of the left hand, while the person wrote or painted with his right.

Besides vases and bottles of stone, and of the materials above mentioned, the Egyptians sometimes had them of leather, or prepared skin; and though it does not appear to what purpose they were generally applied, we may conclude, from the fact of their being imported into Egypt from foreign countries, that they were required for a particular use, or preferred on account of some peculiar quality in the leather itself.   The Egyptians, we are informed by Herodotus, like the Greeks and Romans, occasionally employed skins for holding wine, as well as water, especially when removing it from one place to another; and the fact, that the robber of Rhampsinitus's* treasury adopted the same method of carrying his wine in skins, at a time when any unusual custom would necessarily have been avoided, shows it to have been one of common occurrence.   It is, however, doubtful, if leather bottles were applied to the same' purpose; and as we do not find them introduced at parties, it may be inferred, that they were neither intended for drawing wine from the amphoræ, nor for handing it to table.

Bottles and narrow-mouthed vases, placed in the sitting room, and holding water, were frequently

* Herod. ii. 121.

closed with some light substance *, through which
the warm air could pass, as it rose, during the
cooling process, being submitted to a current of
air, to increase the evaporation : leaves were often
employed for this purpose, as at the present day,
those of a fragrant kind being probably selected ;
and the same prejudice against leaving a vase un-
covered may have existed among the ancient as
among the modern inhabitants of Egypt.

While the guests were entertained with music
and the dance, dinner was prepared ; but as it
consisted of a considerable number of dishes, and
the meat was killed for the occasion, as at the
present day in Eastern and tropical climates,
some time elapsed before it was put upon table.
During this interval, conversation was not neglected ; and the chitchat of the day, public affairs,
and questions of business or amusement, occupied
the attention of the men.   Sometimes an accident
occurring at the house afforded an additional subject for remark ; and, as at the feast of the rich
Nasidienus, the fall of a dusty curtain, or some
ill-secured piece of furniture, induced many to
offer condolences to the host, while others indulged in the criticisms of a sarcastic *Balatro*.†

A circumstance of this kind is represented in a

* *Vide infrà*, wood-cut, No. 279.
† Hor. Sat. ii. 8. 64. :

> . . . . . " Varius mappâ compescere risum
> Vix poterat. Balatro suspendens omnia naso,
> Hæc est conditio vivendi, aiebat . . . . .
> . . . . aulæa ruant si,
> Ut modo ; si patinam pede lapsus frangat agaso."

tomb at Thebes. A party, assembled at the house of a friend, are regaled with the sound of music, and the customary introduction of refreshments; and no attention which the host could show his visiters appears to be neglected on the occasion. The wine has circulated freely, and as they are indulging in amusing converse, a young man, perhaps from inadvertence, perhaps from the effect of intemperance, reclining with his whole weight against a column in the centre of the apartment, throws it down upon the assembled guests; who are seen, with uplifted hands endeavouring to protect themselves, and escape from its fall. *

Many similar instances of a talent for caricature are observable in the compositions of Egyptian artists, who executed the paintings of the tombs; and the ladies are not spared. We are led to infer, that they were not deficient in the talent of conversation; and the numerous subjects they proposed, are shown to have been examined with great animation. Among these, the question of dress was not forgotten, and the patterns or the value of trinkets were discussed with proportionate interest. The maker of an ear-ring, or the shop where it was purchased, were anxiously inquired; each compared the workmanship, the style, and the materials of those she wore, coveted her neighbour's, or preferred her own; and women of every class vied with each other in the display of " jewels

* I regret exceedingly having mislaid the copy I made of this amusing subject.

of silver, and jewels of gold *," in the texture of their "raiment," the neatness of their sandals, and the arrangement or beauty of their plaited hair. †

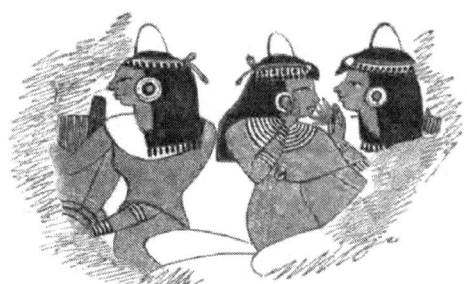

No. 272.   Ladies at a party, talking about their ear-rings.   *Thebes.*

Agreeable conversation was considered the principal charm of accomplished society: and as Athenæus says of the ancient Greeks‡, " it was more requisite and becoming to gratify the company by pleasing conversation than with variety of dishes;" and affairs of great moment were probably discussed at the festive meeting, as in the heroic ages described by Homer. §

In the mean time, the kitchen presented an animated scene; and the cook, with many assistants, was engaged in making ready for dinner: an ox, kid ‖, wild goat, gazelle, or oryx, and a quantity of geese,

---

* Exod. xii. 35. *Vide infrà,* on the dress of women.
† The Egyptian women appear to have been very proud of their hair, and locks of it, when very long, were sometimes cut off and wrapped up separately, to be buried in their tomb after death.   Conf. 1 Cor. xi. 15. and 1 Pet. iii. 3.
‡ Athen. x. 5.   § Hom. Il. i. 70.
‖ Except in the Mendesian nome.   Herod. ii. 46.

ducks, widgeons, quails, or other birds, were obtained for the occasion.   Mutton, it is supposed,
was unlawful food to the inhabitants of the Thebaïd : and Plutarch affirms * that " no Egyptians,
except the Lycopolites, eat the flesh of sheep ;"
while Strabo confines the sacrifice of this animal to
the nome of Nitriotis. †   But though we do not
find from the sculptures that sheep were killed for
the altar or the table, it is evident they abounded
in Egypt, and even at Thebes, being frequently
represented in the tombs ; and large flocks are
shown to have been kept, especially in the vicinity
of Memphis.   Sometimes they amounted to more
than 2000 : and in a tomb below the Pyramids,
974 rams are brought to be registered by his
scribes, as part of the stock of the deceased ; implying an equal number of ewes, independent of
lambs, which in the benign climate of Egypt were
twice produced within the space of one year. ‡

Beef and goose constituted the principal part
of the animal food throughout Egypt ; and by a
prudent foresight, in a country possessing neither
extensive pasture lands, nor great abundance of
cattle, the cow was held sacred, and consequently
forbidden to be eaten. §   And thus the risk of

* Plut. de Isid. s. 72.   He also says (s. 5.), " The priests abstain
from mutton and swine's flesh."
† Strabo, 17.   " Παρα μονοις τουτοις ϑυεται εν Αιγυπτῳ προβατον."
‡ This is still the case if well fed.   Diodorus says, " The sheep in
Egypt bear lambs twice, and are twice shorn."   Lib. i. 36. and 87.
§ Plutarch (s. 31.) says, red oxen were lawful for sacrifice, but not
so if they had a single white hair.   Conf. Numbers, xix. 2. " Bring thee
a red heifer without spot."— Vide Herod. ii. 38. 41.   For the table the
Egyptians killed oxen with black or red spots.

exhausting, or at least greatly lessening, their stock was effectually prevented, and a constant supply maintained for the consumption of the people.

That a considerable quantity of meat was served up at those repasts, to which strangers were invited, is evident from the sculptures, and agreeable with the customs of Eastern nations, whose *azooma*, or feast, prides itself in the quantity and variety of dishes, in the unsparing profusion of viands, and, whenever wine is permitted, in the freedom of the bowl. An endless succession of vegetables was also required on all occasions, and, when dining in private, dishes of that kind were in greater request than joints, even at the tables of the rich : we are therefore not surprised to find the Israelites, who, by their long residence there, had acquired similar habits, regretting them equally with the meat and fish *, which they " did eat in Egypt freely ; " and the advantages of a leguminous diet are still acknowledged by the inhabitants of modern Egypt. This, in a hot climate, is far more conducive to health than the constant introduction of meat, which is principally used to flavour the vegetables cooked with it ; and if at an Eastern feast a greater quantity of meat is introduced, the object is rather to do honour to the guests, who, in most countries, and all ages, have been welcomed by an encouragement of excess, and a display of such things as show a desire on the part of the host to spare no expense in their entertainment.

* Numbers, xi. 4, 5.

The same custom prevailed with the ancient Egyptians; and their mode of eating was very similar to that now adopted in Cairo, and throughout the East, each person sitting round a table, and dipping his bread into a dish placed in the centre, removed on a sign made by the host, and succeeded by others, whose rotation depends on established rule, and whose number is predetermined according to the size of the party, or quality of the guests.

Among the lower orders, vegetables constituted a very great part of their ordinary food, and they gladly availed themselves of the variety and abundance of esculent roots growing spontaneously, in the lands irrigated by the rising Nile, as soon as its waters had subsided; some of which were eaten in a crude state, and others roasted in the ashes, boiled, or stewed: their chief aliment, and that of their children, consisting of milk and cheese[*], roots[†], leguminous, cucurbitaceous, and other plants, and ordinary fruits of the country. Herodotus describes the food of the workmen, who built the Pyramids, to have been the "*raphanus* or *figl*[‡], onions, and garlic;" yet, if these were among the number they used, and, perhaps, the sole provisions supplied at the government expense, we are not to suppose they were limited to them: and it is probable that lentils, of which it is inferred from Strabo they had an abundance on this

---

* Diod. i. 87,   † Ibid. 80.
‡ Herod. ii. 125. So called by the modern Egyptians, the raphanus sativus, var. *a*. edulis of Linnæus, mistaken by the learned Larcher for horse-radish, which is not an Egyptian plant.

occasion, may be reckoned as part, or even the chief article, of their food.

The nummulite rock in the vicinity of those monuments frequently presents a conglomerate of testacea imbedded in it, which, in some positions, resemble small seeds; and the geographer, imagining them to be the petrified residue of the lentils brought there by the workmen, was led to this observation on the nature of their provisions. That he is correct in supposing lentils to have been a great article of diet among the labouring classes, and all the lower orders of Egyptians, is evident from their repeated mention in ancient authors; and so much attention was bestowed on the culture of this useful pulse, that certain varieties became remarkable for their excellence, and the lentils of Pelusium were esteemed both in Egypt and in foreign countries.* Two species of the plant† are noticed by Pliny, who shows it to have been extensively cultivated, and this, as well as the constant use of lentils among the peasants at the present day, fully justify the opinion, that they constituted a great, and even the principal, part of the aliment of the lower orders at all times.

In few countries were vegetables more numerous than in Egypt; and the authority of ancient writers, the sculptures, and the number of persons employed in selling them at Alexandria, sufficiently attest this fact. Pliny ‡ observes that the valley of

---

* " Nec Pelusiacæ curam spernabere lentis."   Virg. Georg. i. 228.
† " Duo genera ejus (lentis) in Egypto."   Plin. xviii. 12.
‡ Plin. xxi. 15.

the Nile "surpassed every other country in the abundance and spontaneous growth of those herbs, which most people are in the habit of using as food, especially the Egyptians;" and at the time of the Arab invasion, when Alexandria was taken by Amer, the lieutenant of the caliph Omer, no less than 4000 persons were engaged in selling vegetables in that city.

The lotus, the papyrus, and other similar productions of the land, during and after the inundation, were, for the poor, one of the greatest blessings nature ever provided for any people; and, like the acorn * in northern climates, constituted perhaps the sole aliment of the peasantry, at the early period when Egypt was first colonised. The fertility of the soil, however, soon afforded a more valuable produce to the inhabitants; and long before they had made any great advances in civilisation, corn and leguminous plants were, doubtless, grown to a great extent throughout the country. The palm was another important gift bestowed upon them: it flourished spontaneously in the valley of the Nile, and, if it was unable to grow in the sands of the arid desert, yet wherever water sufficed for its nourishment, this useful tree produced an abundance of dates, a wholesome and nutritious fruit, which might be regarded as

---

* Conf. Hor. s. 1. 3. 100.:—

    " Quum prorepserunt primis animalia terris,
    Mutum et turpe pecus, glandem atque cubilia propter
    . . . . atque ita porro
    Pugnabant armis."

And Jul. Pollux. Onom. lib. i. 12., who quotes Xenophon, Anab. 5.

an universal benefit, being within the reach of all classes of people, and neither requiring expense in the cultivation, nor interfering with the time demanded for other agricultural occupations.

Among the vegetables above mentioned, is one which requires some observations. Juvenal says they were forbidden to eat the onion *, and it is reported to have been excluded from an Egyptian table. The prohibition, however, seems only to have extended to the priests, who, according to Plutarch †, "abstained from most kinds of pulse;" and the abhorrence felt for onions, according to the same author ‡, was confined to the members of the sacerdotal order.

That onions were cultivated in Egypt, is proved from the authority of many writers, as well as from the sculptures; their quality was renowned in ancient as well as modern times; and the Israelites, when they left the country, regretted "the onions" as well as the cucumbers, the melons, the leeks, the garlick, and the meat § they "did eat" in Egypt. Among the offerings presented to the gods, both in the tombs and temples, onions are introduced, and a priest is frequently seen holding them in his hand, or covering an altar with a bundle of their leaves and roots. ||

* Juv. xiv. 9. " Porrum et cepe nefas violare et frangere morsu."
† Plut. de Is. s. 5 and 8.
‡ Ibid. s. 8.
§ Numb. xi. 5. and Exod xvi. 3. " In the land of Egypt, when we sat by the flesh-pots, and when we did eat bread to the full."
|| *Vide* Vol. I. p. 277., wood-cut, No. 9.

Nor is it less certain that they were introduced at private as well as public festivals; and brought to table with gourds, cucumbers, and other vegetables; and if there is any truth in the notion of their being forbidden, we may conclude it was entirely confined to the priestly order.

The onions of Egypt were mild, and of an excellent flavour, and were eaten crude as well as cooked, by persons both of the higher and the lower classes; but it is difficult to say if they introduced them to table like the cabbage, as a *hors-d'œuvre*, to stimulate the appetite, which Socrates recommends in the Banquet of Xenophon. On this occasion some curious reasons for their use are brought forward by different members of the party. Nicerates observes that onions relish well with wine, and cites Homer in support of his remark: Callias affirms that they inspire courage in the hour of battle: and Charmides suggests their utility " in deceiving a jealous wife, who, finding her husband return with his breath smelling of onions would be induced to believe he had not saluted any one while from home."

THE KITCHEN.

In slaughtering for the table, it was customary to take the ox, or whatever animal had been chosen for the occasion, into a court-yard near the house; to tie its four legs together, and then to throw it upon the ground; in which position it was held by one or more persons, while the butcher, sharpening his broad knife upon a *steel* attached to his apron, proceeded to cut the throat, as near as pos-

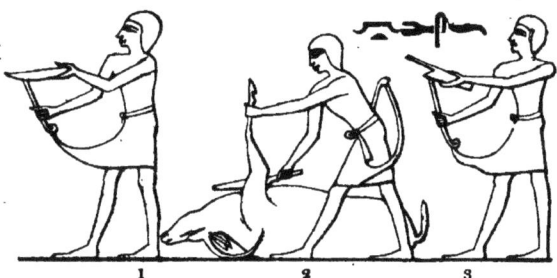

No. 273.   A butcher killing and cutting up an Ibex or wild goat : the other two sharpening their knives on a *steel.*   *Thebes.*

sible from one ear to the other; sometimes continuing the opening downwards along the throat.* The blood was frequently received into a vase or basin for the purposes of cookery †, which was repeatedly forbidden to the Israelites by the Mosaic law ‡; and the reason of the explicit manner of the prohibition is readily explained from the necessity of preventing their adopting a custom they had so constantly witnessed in Egypt. Nor is it less strictly denounced by the Mohammedan religion ; and all Moslems look upon this ancient Egyptian and modern European custom with unqualified horror and disgust.

* The Israelites sometimes cut off the head at once. Deut. xxi. v. 4. 6.
† *Vide infrà*, wood-cut No. 246.
‡ Deut. xv. 23. " Only thou shalt not eat the blood thereof : thou shalt pour it upon the ground as water." And c. xii. 16. 23. ; " be sure that thou eat not the blood, for the blood is the life." Gen. ix. 4., and Levit. xvii. 10, 11. 14, &c.

The head was then taken off, and they proceeded to skin the animal *, beginning with the leg and neck. The first joint removed was the right fore-leg or shoulder, the other parts following in succession, according to custom or convenience ; and the same † rotation was observed in cutting up the victims offered in sacrifice to the gods. Servants carried the joints to the kitchen on wooden trays‡, and the cook having selected the parts suited for boiling, roasting, and other modes of dressing, prepared them for the fire by washing, and any other preliminary process he thought necessary. In large kitchens, the *chef*, or head cook, had several persons under him, who were required to make ready and boil the water of the caldron, to put the joints on spits or skewers §, to cut up or mince the meat, to prepare the vegetables, and to fulfil various other duties assigned to them.

The very peculiar mode of cutting up the meat frequently prevents our ascertaining the exact part they intend to represent in the sculptures; the chief joints, however, appear to be the head, shoulder, and leg, with the ribs, tail, or rump, the

---

* Herod. ii. 39. — " σφαξαντες δε αποταμνουσι την κεφαλην, σωμα μεν δη του κτηντος δειρουσι."

† Levit. vii. 32.   " The right shoulder shall ye give unto the priest for an heave-offering of the sacrifices of your peace-offerings . . . . . . for the wave-breast and the heave-shoulder have I taken . . . . . . from off the sacrifices . . . . and have given them unto Aaron the priest."

‡ *Vide* Plate 12.

§ Conf. Virg. Æn. i. 215. : —

> " Tergora diripiunt costis, et viscera nudant,
> Pars in frustra secant, verubusque trementia figunt :
> Litore ahena locant alii, flammasque ministrant."

heart, and kidneys; and they occur in the same
manner on the altars of the temple, and the tables
of a private house.   One is remarkable, not only
from being totally unlike any of our European
joints, but from its exact resemblance to that commonly seen at table in modern Egypt: it is part
of the leg, consisting of the flesh covering the *tibia*,
whose two extremities project slightly beyond it;
and the accompanying drawing from the sculptures,
and a sketch of the same joint taken by me at a
modern table in Upper Egypt, show how the mode
of cutting it has been preserved by traditional
custom to the present day.

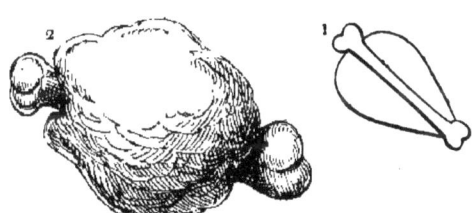

No. 274.   Peculiar joint of meat at an ancient and modern Egyptian table.

The head was left with the skin and horns, and
was sometimes given away to a poor person as a
reward for holding the walking sticks of those
guests who came on foot *; in later times when
the Greeks were settled in the country, it was sold
to them, or to other foreigners: but it was frequently taken to the kitchen with the other joints;
and, notwithstanding the positive assertion of Herodotus, we find that even in the temples themselves

* *Vide* wood-cut, No. 413. Plate 12. *fig.* 10.

it was admitted at a sacrifice, and placed with other offerings on the altars of the gods.

The historian would lead us to suppose that a strict religious scruple prevented the Egyptians of all classes from eating this part, as he affirms, " that no Egyptian will taste the head of any species of animal"*, in consequence of certain imprecations having been uttered upon it at the time it was sacrificed : but as he is speaking of heifers slaughtered for the service of the gods, we may conclude that the prohibition did not extend to those killed for table, nor even to all those offered for sacrifice in the temple ; and as with the scapegoat of the Jews, that important ceremony was perhaps confined to certain occasions and to chosen animals, without extending to every victim which was slain.

The formula of the imprecation was probably very similar with the Jews and Egyptians.   Herodotus says the latter pray the gods " that if any misfortune was about to happen to those who offered, or to the other inhabitants of Egypt, it might fall upon that head :" and with the former it was customary for the priest to take two goats and cast lots upon them, " one lot for the Lord and the other lot for the scapegoat," which was presented alive " to make atonement" for the people.   The priest was then required to " lay both his hands upon the head of the live goat, and confess over him all the iniquities of the children of Israel, and all their transgressions in all

* Herod. ii. 39.

their sins, putting them upon the head of the goat, and send him away by the hand of a fit man into the wilderness."* The remark of Herodotus should then be confined to the head, on which their imprecation was pronounced, and being looked upon by every Egyptian as an abomination it may have been taken to the market and sold to foreigners, or if no foreigners happened to be there, it may have been given† to the crocodiles.‡

The same mode of slaughtering, and of preparing the joints, extended to all the large animals; but geese, and other wild and tame fowl were served up entire, or, at least, only deprived of their feet and pinion joints: fish were also brought to table whole, whether boiled or fried, the tails and

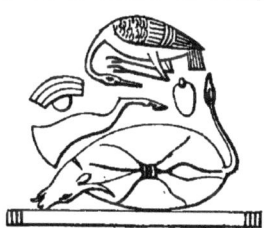

No. 275.　　　An ox and a bird placed entire on the altar.

fins being removed. For the service of religion, they were generally prepared in the same manner

* Levit. xvi. 8. 21.

† Herodotus's words are, "thrown into the river." This could only have been in places where crocodiles abounded: it would otherwise have polluted the stream they so highly esteemed. Plutarch says, a solemn curse having been pronounced upon the head, it was thrown into the river; this was in former times, but now it is sold to foreigners. De Is. s. 31.

‡ Ælian observes, " that the Ombites do not eat the head of any animal they have offered in sacrifices; they *throw it to the crocodiles.* De Nat. Anim. lib. x. c. 21.

as for private feasts; sometimes, however, an ox was brought entire to the altar, and birds were often placed among the offerings without even having the feathers taken off.

The favourite meats were beef and goose* : the ibex, gazelle, and oryx, were also in great request; but we are surprised, in a country where mutton is unquestionably lighter and more wholesome, that they should prefer the two first, and even exclude this last from the table. In Abyssinia it is a sin to eat geese or ducks; and modern experience teaches that in Egypt, and similar climates, beef and goose are not eligible food, except in the depth of winter. In Lower Egypt, or, as Herodotus styles it, the corn country, they were in the habit of drying and salting birds of various kinds, as quails, ducks, and others, a process to which I believe the sculptures themselves refer †; and fish were prepared by them in the same manner both in Upper and Lower Egypt. ‡

Some joints were boiled, others roasted : two modes of dressing their food to which Herodotus appears to confine the Egyptians, at least in the lower country § ; but, though there is no positive evidence from the sculptures that they adopted a very artificial kind of cookery, it is highly probable they had made some advances in this as in the other habits of a civilised, I may say, luxurious

---

* Conf. Herod. ii. 37.
† *Vide* wood-cut, No. 80.
‡ Herod. ii. 77., and the sculptures.
§ Loc. cit. " τους λοιπους οπτους και εφθους σιτεονται."

people, and had at a very remote period passed that state when men are contented with simplicity and primitive habits.*   And we shall at least feel disposed to allow the Egyptians as much skill in the culinary art, as was displayed by Rebekah, in the savoury meats she prepared for Isaac, where the disguise was sufficient to prevent his distinguishing the meat of kids from the promised venison.†

It is true, that in the infancy of society the diet is exceedingly plain and simple, consisting principally, if not entirely of roast meats : and as Athenæus observes, the heroes of Homer seldom " boil their meat, or dress it with sauces," the few instances, even of the former, which occur in the Iliad‡, plainly showing how unusual the custom was at the period he describes.

That the Egyptians were in early times immoderately fond of delicate living, or indeed at any period committed those excesses of which the Romans are known to have been guilty, is highly improbable, especially as the example of the priesthood, who constituted a very great portion of the higher classes, tended so much to induce moderation ; but even before the close of the 16th dynasty, or about 1600, B. C., they had already begun to indulge in nearly the same habits, as in the later Pharaonic ages ; and it appears from Diodorus and Plutarch

---

* Bocchoris complained that Menes had taught the Egyptians a luxurious mode of living, even in regard to diet.   *Vide* Vol. I. p. 129.
† Gen. xxvii. 3. 9.
‡ Iliad, Φ, 362. —

" ῾Ως δε λεβης ζει ενδον, επειγομενος πυρι πολλῳ,
Κνισσῃ μελδομενος ἁπαλοτρεφεος σιαλοιο."

that their original simplicity* gave place to luxury,
as early as the reign of their first king Menes.
Excesses they no doubt committed, especially in
the use of wine, both on private† and public oc-
casions‡, which is not concealed in the sculptures
of Thebes: and in later times, after the conquest
of Egypt by the Persians, and the accession of the
Ptolemies, habits of intemperance increased to
such an extent, and luxury became so general
among all ranks of society, that writers who mention the Egyptians at that period§, describe them
as a profligate and luxurious people, given to
an immoderate love of the table, and addicted to
every excess in drinking. They even used ex-
citants for this purpose, and *hors-d'œuvres* were
provided to stimulate the appetite; crude cabbage,
provoking the desire for wine, and promoting the
continuation of excess.||

Beyond the usual joints, which are seen on
the altars, and in the hands of the servants, it is
impossible to ascertain in what form the meat
appeared upon table, or what made dishes and
artificial viands the skill of their cooks succeeded
in devising; but as a portion of the kitchen is
occasionally represented in the tombs, and some
details of Egyptian cookery are there given, I shall
avail myself of whatever has been preserved, and

---

* Diod. i. 45.   Plut. de Is. s. 8.   *Vide* also *suprà*, p. 129. Vol. I.
† Athenæus quotes Dion on this subject. Deipn. lib. i. 25.
‡ Herod. ii. 60.
§ Josephus says the Egyptians (in his time) were abandoned to
pleasures. Antiq. ii. 9.
|| Athen. Deipn. lib. i. 25.

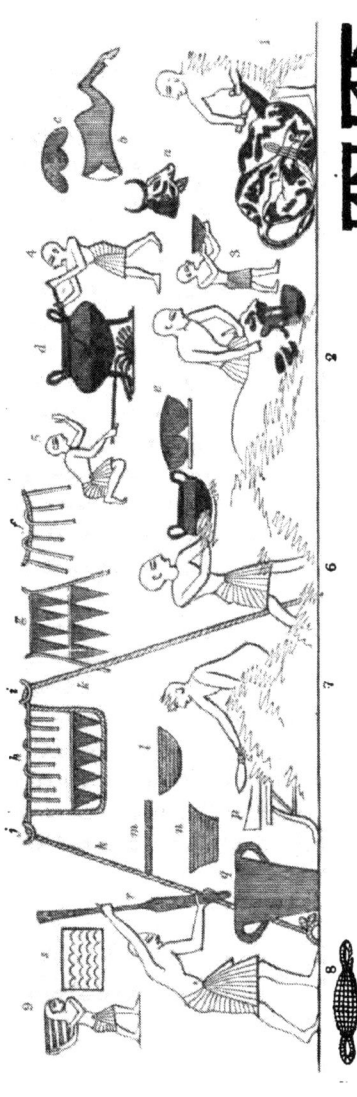

No. 276.

An Egyptian kitchen, from the tomb of Remeses III., at Thebes.

Fig. 1. Killing and preparing the joints, which are placed at a, b, c.
2. Catching the blood for the purposes of cookery, which is removed in a bowl by fig. 3.
4. and 5. Employed in boiling meat, and stirring the fire.
7. Preparing the meat for the caldron, which fig. 6. is taking to the fire.
8. Pounding some ingredients for the cook.
d. Apparently siphons.
i, j. Ropes passing through rings, and supporting different things, as a sort of safe.
j. Probably pastes.
u, v. Tables.

introduce the most interesting part of those sculptures in the accompanying wood-cuts.

The first process, as previously described, was slaughtering the ox, and cutting up the joints; the blood being sometimes caught in a vase, for the purpose of cookery*; and joints selected for the purpose were boiled in a large caldron, placed over the fire on a metal stand or tripod. One servant regulated the heat of the fire, raising it with a poker, or blowing it with bellows, worked by the feet†; another superintended the cooking of the meat, skimming the water with a spoon, or stirring it with a large fork‡, while a third pounded salt, pepper, or other ingredients, in a large mortar, which were added from time to time during this process. Liquids of various kinds also stood ready for use. They were sometimes drawn off by means of siphons §, and these appear to be represented upon a rope‖, supporting the tray which contained the things they wished to raise beyond the reach of rats or other intruders, and which answered the purposes of a safe.

Other servants took charge of the pastry, which the bakers or confectioners had made for the dinner table; and this department, which may be considered as attached to the kitchen, appears even

---

* Mentioned in p. 35. *Vide* wood-cut, No. 276. *fig.* 2.
† I shall have occasion to notice these hereafter.
‡ Wood-cut *figs.* 4 and 5.
§ This part of the picture is very much damaged, but sufficient remains to show them using the siphons, which occur again, perfectly preserved, in a tomb at Thebes. I shall introduce them among the inventions of the Egyptians.
‖ At *h* and *f*.

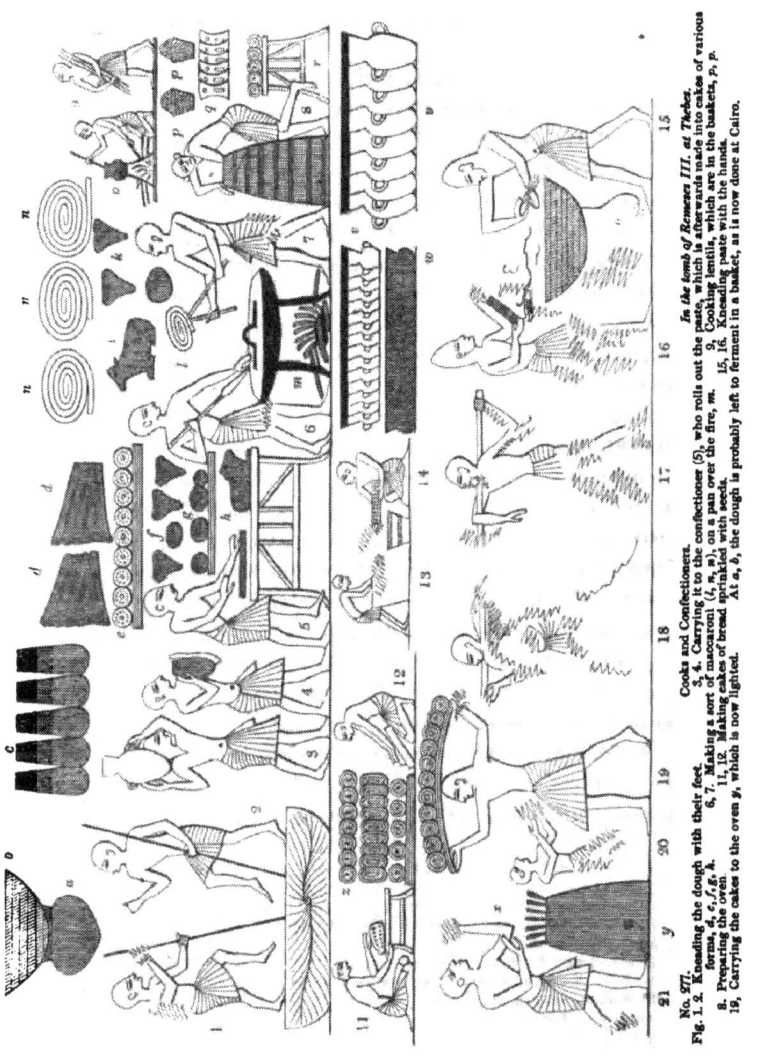

No. 977.   **Cooks and Confectioners.**   *In the tomb of Remeses III. at Thebes.*

Fig. 1, 2. Kneading the dough with their feet.   3, 4. Carrying it to the confectioner (5), who rolls out the paste, which is afterwards made into cakes of various forms, *d, e, f, g, h*.   6, 7. Making a sort of macaroni (*i, n, n*), on a pan over the fire, *m*.   9. Cooking lentils, which are in the baskets, *p, p*.

8. Preparing the oven.   11, 12. Making cakes of bread sprinkled with seeds.   15, 16. Kneading paste with the hands.

19, Carrying the cakes to the oven *y*, which is now lighted.   At *a, b*, the dough is probably left to ferment in a basket, as is now done at Cairo.

more varied than that of the cook. Some sifted
and mixed the flour *, others kneaded the paste
with their hands †, and formed it into rolls, which
were then prepared for baking, and being placed
on a long tray or board, were carried on a man's
head ‡ to the oven §. Certain seeds were previously sprinkled upon the upper surface of each
roll ||, and judging from those still used in Egypt
for the same purpose, they were chiefly the *nigella
sativa*, or *kamóon aswed*, the *simsim* ¶, and the
caraway.

Sometimes they kneaded the paste with their
feet **, having placed it in a large wooden bowl
upon the ground; it was then in a more liquid
state than when mixed by the hand, and was
carried in vases to the pastrycook, who formed it
into a sort of macaroni, upon a flattened metal pan
over the fire. Two persons were engaged in this
process; one stirred it with a wooden spatula, and
the other taking it off when cooked, with two
pointed sticks ††, arranged it in a proper place,
where the rest of the pastry was kept. This last
was of various kinds, apparently made up with
fruit, or other ingredients, with which the dough,
spread out with the hand, was sometimes mixed,

---

* Wood-cut, No. 277., *figs.* 13. and 14.   † *Fig.* 15.
‡ As at the present day. Conf. Pharaoh's chief baker, with " three
white baskets on his head." Gen. xl. 16., and Herod. ii. 35. " Men
carry loads on their heads, women on their shoulders." But it was not
the general custom.
§ Wood-cut, No. 277. *Figs.* 19. and *x.*
|| *Figs.* 11 and *z.*, called *oûk* by the Egyptians.
¶ Sesamum Orientale, Linn.
** Conf. Herod. ii. 36., and *figs.* 1. and 2.
†† *Figs.* 6. and 7., and *l.*

and it assumed the shape of a three-cornered cake, a recumbent ox, or other form *, according to the fancy of the confectioner. That his department was connected with the kitchen † is again shown, by the presence of a man in the corner of the picture, engaged in cooking lentils for a soup or porridge ‡; his companion § brings a bundle of faggots for the fire, and the lentils themselves are seen standing near him in wicker baskets. ‖

The caldrons containing the joints of boiled meat, which were often of very great size, stood over a fire upon the hearth, supported on stones ¶, having been taken from the dresser ** where they were placed for the convenience of putting in the joints; some of smaller dimensions, probably containing the stewed meat, stood over a pan †† containing charcoal, precisely similar to the *magoor*, used in modern Egypt ‡‡; and geese, or joints of meat, were roasted over a fire of a peculiar construction, intended solely for this purpose §§; the cook passing over them a fan ‖‖, which served for bellows. In heating water, or boiling meat, faggots of wood were principally employed, but for the roast meat charcoal, as in the modern kitchens of Cairo; and

---

* *Vide d, f, g, h, i, k.*   *f* and *g* appear to have the fruit apart from the pastry. I found some cakes of the form of *f* in a tomb at Thebes, but without any fruit or other addition. Many of different shapes, have been found there.

† The chief baker (שׂר האפים) of Pharaoh carried in the uppermost basket " all manner of bake-meats," not only " bread," but " all kind of food." כל מאכל. Gen. xl. 17. Anciently, the cook and baker were the same, with the Romans.

‡ *Fig.* 9.   § *Fig.* 10.   ·‖ At *p.*
¶ Wood-cut No. 278, at *d.*   ** At *b.*   †† At *c.*
‡‡ At *g.*   §§ At *e.*   ‖‖ At *f.*

the sculptures represent servants bringing this last in mats of the same form as those of the present

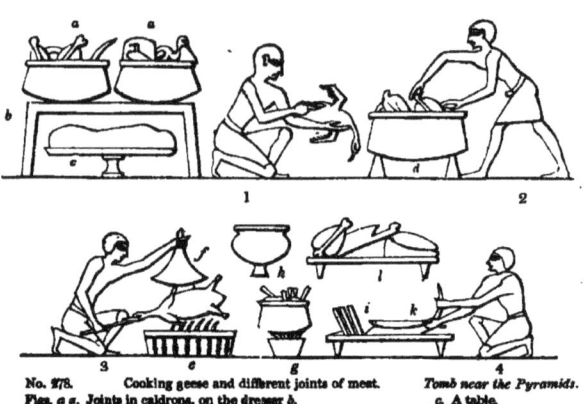

No. 278.   Cooking geese and different joints of meat.   *Tomb near the Pyramids.*
Figs. *a a.* Joints in caldrons, on the dresser *b.*   *c.* A table.
    1. Preparing a goose for the cook (*2.*), who puts them into the boiler *d.*
    3. Roasting a goose over a fire (*e*) of peculiar construction.
    4. Cutting up the meat.   *l.* Joints on a table.
    g. Stewed meat over a pan of fire, or *magoor.*

day. They sometimes used round balls for cooking, probably a composition of charcoal, and other ingredients, which a servant is represented taking out of a basket, and putting on the stove, while another blows the fire with a fan. *

THE PARTY.

At an Egyptian party, the men and women were frequently entertained separately, in a different part of the same room, at the upper end of which the master and mistress of the house sat close together, on two chairs, or on a large fauteuil; each guest,

* The same kind of fan was used by the Greeks and Romans. It is represented in the paintings of Herculaneum.

as he arrived, presented himself to receive their
congratulatory welcome *, and the musicians and
dancers, hired for the occasion, did obeisance before
them, previous to the performance of their part.
To the leg of the fauteuil a favourite monkey, a
dog, gazelle, or some other pet animal†, was tied,
and a young child was permitted to sit on the
ground at the side of its mother, or on its father's
knee.   In some instances, we find men and women
sitting together, both strangers ‡, as well as members of the same family § ; a privilege not conceded to females among the Greeks, except with
their relations ; and this not only argues a very
great advancement in civilisation, especially in an
Eastern nation, but proves, like many other Egyptian customs, how far this people excelled the
Greeks in the habits of social life.   With the
Romans it was customary for women to mix in
society, and their notions on this head are contrasted by Cornelius Nepos‖ with the scruples
of the Greeks, in these words : " Which of us
Romans is ashamed to bring his wife to an entertainment ? and what mistress of a family can be
shown, who does not inhabit the chief and most
frequented part of the house ? whereas, in Greece,
she never appears at any entertainments, except
those to which relations are alone invited, and con-

---

* *Vide* Plate 12.   † Ibid.
‡ They may be married couples.
§ *Vide* wood-cut, No. 279.
‖ Cornel. Nepos. Præfat. in Vit. Imperatorum, ad fin.

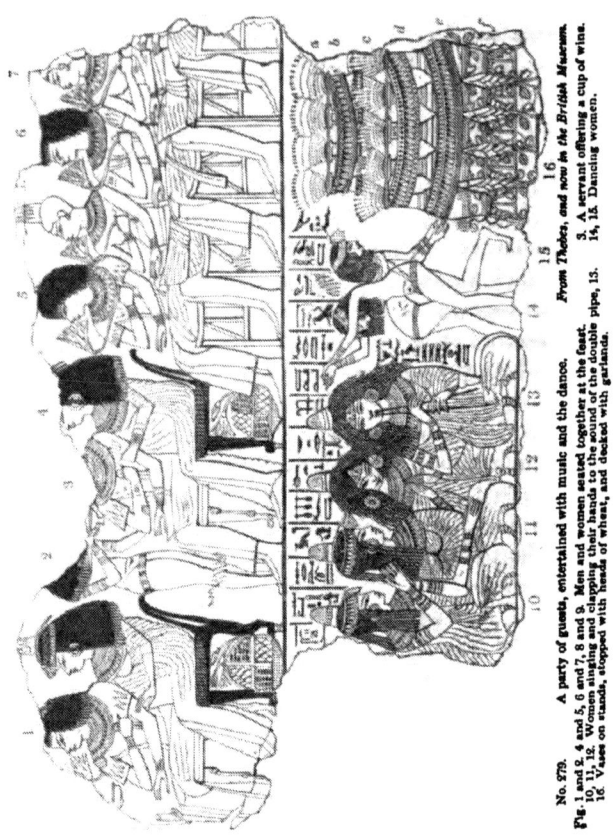

No. 278.   A party of guests, entertained with music and the dance.   *From Thebes, and now in the British Museum.*

Figs. 1 and 2, 4 and 5, 6 and 7, 8 and 9. Men and women seated together at the feast.   3. A servant offering a cup of wine.
10, 11, 12. Women singing and clapping their hands to the sound of the double pipe, 13.   14, 15. Dancing women.
16. Vases on stands, stopped with heads of wheat, and decked with garlands.

stantly lives in the uppermost part of the house, called gynæconitis *, the women's apartments, into

* Γυναικωνιτις answering to the *hareém* of the East.

which no man has admission, unless he be a near relation."

Wine, as I have already observed, was presented both to matrons and virgins at an Egyptian feast; and they were waited upon by handmaids and female slaves, as the men were attended by footmen and men slaves.   An upper maid servant, or a white slave, had the office of handing the wine, or whatever refreshment was offered them, and a black woman followed her, in an inferior capacity, to receive an empty cup when the wine had been poured from it into the goblet, or to bring and take away what it was the privilege of the other to present.   The same black slaves brought the dishes as they were sent from the kitchen, and the peculiar mode of holding a plate with the hand reversed, so generally adopted by women from the interior of Africa, is characteristically portrayed in the paintings of a tomb at Thebes, given in the

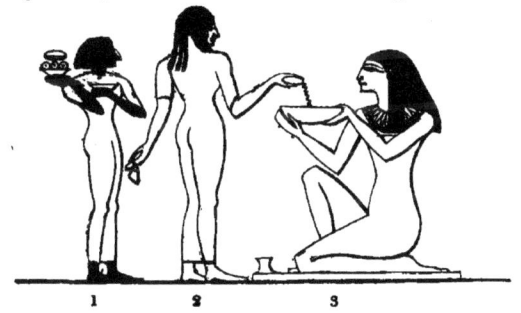

1   2   3
No. 290.   A black and white slave waiting upon a lady at a party.   *Thebes*.

accompanying wood-cut.   To each person, after drinking, a napkin was presented for wiping the

c c 4

mouth, answering to the *máhrama* of the modern
Egyptians, and other Eastern people; and the
servant who held it on his arm, while the person
was drinking, probably uttered a complimentary
wish, as he proffered it, and received the goblet; *
for the custom of saying " may it benefit you," or
some similar phrase, being so general throughout
the East, we cannot but suppose that it was adopted
by the ancient Egyptians, and that the mode of
welcoming a stranger with salt, the emblem of hospitality, was common to them, as to the Romans
and other people of antiquity.

THE DINNER.

That dinner was served up at midday, may be
inferred from the invitation given by Joseph to his
brethren†, but it is probable that, like the Romans,
they also ate supper in the evening, as is still the
custom in the East. The table was very similar
to that of the present day in Egypt, which is a
small stool, supporting a round tray on which the
dishes are placed, and it only differed from this in
being raised upon a single leg, like many of those
used for bearing offerings in the sacred festivals of
their temples.

In early times the Greeks as well as Romans,
had similar round tables‡, in imitation, as some

---

* *Vide* wood-cut, No. 281., *fig.* 12.

† Gen. xliii. 16. " Bring these men home, and slay, and make ready,
for these men shall dine with me at noon." The Hebrew expression
" slay " מבח טבח is the same as the Arabic edbah dabeëh, "kill a
killing."

‡ Whence called *orbes* by the Romans. Juv. Sat. i. 137. Plin. 13. 15.

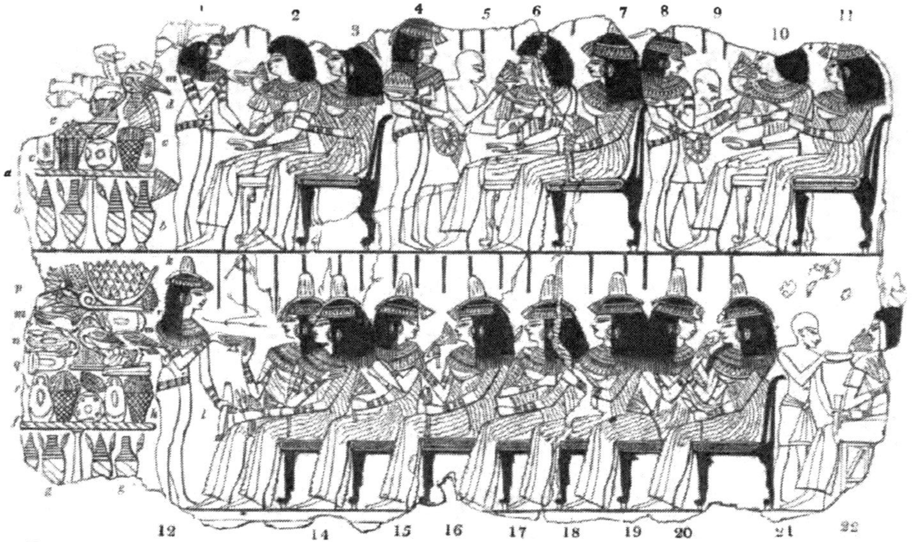

No. 281.   A party of guests, to whom wine, ointment, and garlands are brought.   From Thebes, and now in the British Museum.

Fig. 1. A maid-servant presenting a cup of wine to a gentleman and lady, seated on chairs with cushions, probably of leather.
4. Another holding a vase of ointment and a garland.
5. presents a lotus flower; and 3. a necklace or garland, which he is going to tie round the neck of the guest, 10.
12. A female attendant offering wine to a guest; in her left hand is a napkin, l, for wiping the mouth after drinking.
The tables, a, f, have cakes of bread, c, r; meat, d, v; geese, s; and other birds, m; figs, c, k; grapes in baskets, h; flower, p; and other things prepared for the feast; and beneath them are glass bottles of wine, b, g.

imagine, of the spherical shape of the world*; and, occasionally, each guest had a table to himself†; but from the mention of persons sitting in rows, according to rank, it has been supposed that they were of a long figure, which may sometimes have been the case in Egypt, even during the Pharaonic ages, since the brethren of Joseph "sat before him, the first born according to his birthright and the youngest according to his youth‡," Joseph himself eating alone at another table.§   It is not, however, certain that the table in this instance was long, or in any way different from their usual round table, since persons might, even then, be seated according to their rank, and the modern Egyptian table is not without its post of honour, and a fixed gradation of place.   No tray was used on the Egyptian table, nor was it covered by any linen ‖; like that of the Greeks, it was probably wiped with a sponge¶ or napkin, after the dishes were removed, and polished by the servants **, when the company had retired.

There has long been a question respecting the custom of reclining at meals, and its first introduction among the Greeks and Romans.   Some

---

* Myrleanus in Athen. lib. xi. c. 12.
† Athen. i. 8.
‡ Gen. xliii. 33.
§ Gen. xlii. 32. "And they set on for him by himself."
‖ Tablecloths were unknown in Rome, until the time of the emperors. Mart. xii. 29. 12.
¶ Homer Od. Λ. 112. :

" Οι δ' αυτε σπογγοισι πολυτρητοισι τραπεζας
  Νιζον, και προτιθεντο, ιδε κρεα πολλα δατευντο."

** Whether of stone or wood.   Polished wood is frequently found in the tombs of Thebes.

have supposed that it came directly to Greece from Asia, and to Rome, after the conquest of Carthage and Asia Minor: but it appears rather to have been gradually introduced, than borrowed at any particular time from a foreign people. With great reason, however, we may believe that the custom originated in Asia* ; and the only notice of it among the Greeks, in early times, is found in sacred subjects, where the deities are represented reclining on couches †, evidently with a view to distinguish their habits from those of ordinary mortals.   But when luxury increased, and men " inflated," as Aristotle observes, " with the pride of victory, laid aside their previous discrimination," new modes of indulgence were devised, their former simplicity was abandoned, and customs were introduced which their ancestors considered suited to the gods alone.

That they derived their ideas respecting the use of couches from a positive custom is certain, since all notions about the habits of the deities could only be borrowed from human analogies ; we may therefore safely ascribe to it a foreign origin, though not introduced at once, or merely adopted in imitation of an Eastern custom.   The principal person at a festival is often described as having reclined, while the others sat on chairs or on the ground.   At the Roman fête of the *Epulum Jovis,* Jupiter reposed on a couch, while the other deities were seated ; and, in Macedonia, no

* Æneas and the Trojans reclined.   Virg. Æn. i. 700.
† The *Lectisternia* of the Romans.

one could recline at meals, till he had killed a boar
without the help of nets.   It was therefore, originally, a mark of honour and distinction, and sometimes confined to men; but in process of time it
became general, and was afterwards adopted by all
ranks.   For we have evidence from many ancient
authorities, that in early times neither the Greeks
nor Romans reclined at meals.   Homer's heroes*
sat on the ground, or on chairs; Virgil†, Tacitus,
Ovid‡, Philo, and others mention the same prim-
æval custom; and Suetonius§ says that even the
grand-children of Augustus "always *sat* at the end
of the couch when they supped with him."

The ordinary Egyptian round table was similar
to the *monopodium* of ‖ the Romans, and instead
of the movable tray used by the modern Egyptians, its circular summit was fixed to the leg on
which it stood; which, as I have before observed,
frequently presented the figure of a man, generally
a captive, who supported the slab upon his head,
the whole being either of stone, or some hard
wood.   On this the dishes were placed, together
with loaves of bread¶, some of which were, apparently, not unlike those of the present day, flat and

---

* Homer, Od. i. 108., &c. " Ημενοι."
† Virg. Æn. i. 176. " Soliti patres considere mensis."
‡ Ovid. Fast. vi. 305.
§ Suet. Aug. c. 64. " Neque cœnavit unà, nisi in imo lecto *ad-
siderent.*"
‖ *Vide* Juv. Sat. xi. 122.

" Latos nisi sustinet orbeis
Grande ebur, et magno sublimis pardus hiatu."

¶ " To set on bread " was the expression used, as at present, in
Egypt, for bringing dinner. Gen lxiii. 31.   It is singular that *lahm*
should signify, in Hebrew, " bread; " and, in Arabic, " meat."

round*, as our crumpets, and others in the form of rolls or cakes, sprinkled with the seeds before noticed.

In the houses of the rich bread was made of wheat, the poorer classes being contented with barley, and flour of the *sorghum†;* for Herodotus, as I have had occasion to observe in a former work‡, has been guilty of an error in stating§ that it was considered among the Egyptians "the greatest disgrace" to live on wheat and barley, and that "they therefore made their bread of the *olyra*‖, which some call *zea.*"¶ It is doubtful whether the historian had in view the *triticum zea,* which is now no longer grown in Egypt, or the sorghum**, the *doura* of the present day; but it is probable that he gives the name of olyra to this last; and that it was grown in ancient times in Upper and Lower Egypt, particularly about the Thebaïd, is evident from the sculptures, though not in the same quantity as wheat. So far, how-

---

* These retain the form of the old "cake," baked "upon the hearth" (Gen. xviii. 6.), which are so generally used at this day by the Arabs of the desert, without leaven. The bread of Upper Egypt is more like the ancient Egyptian cake.

† Holcus Sorghum, Linn.   ‡ "Egypt and Thebes," p. 213.
§ Herod. ii. 36.

‖ Pliny (xviii. 7.) says, "Far in Ægypto ex olyra conficitur;" but not to the exclusion of any other grain; and we find in the same author, "Ægyptus . . . e tritico suo." He also observes, that the olyra had been supposed the same as rice, "olyram et oryzam eandem esse existimant;" and afterwards (c. 8.), distinguishes it from the zea, with which Herodotus has confounded it. Homer feeds horses on the olyra, as well as wheat and barley; which last is now given them in the East. Homer, Il. E. 196.

¶ Bearing no relation to the zea mays, or Indian corn.

** The Assyrian wheat and barley, he affirms, had "leaves four fingers in breadth," from which it has been conjectured that he there (lib. i. 193.) alludes to the sorghum; but the expression "wheat and barley," renders this very questionable.

ever, were the Egyptians from holding wheat and barley in abhorrence, that they cultivated them abundantly throughout the whole valley of the Nile*, offered them to the gods, and derived from them a great part of their sustenance, in common with whatever other corn the soil produced; and I fear that this, and his assertion respecting the exclusive use of brazen drinking cups†, prove Herodotus not to have lived in the best society during his stay in Egypt.‡

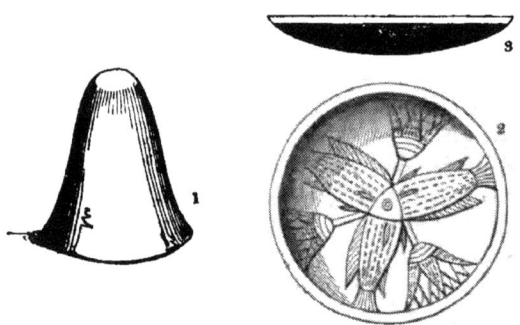

No. 282.   Drinking cups.
Fig. 1. An alabaster beaker, in the Museum of Alnwick Castle.
2. A saucer or cup of blue glazed pottery, in the Berlin Collection.
3. Side view of the same.

The drinking cups of the Egyptians, as I have already observed, were of gold, silver, glass, porcelain, alabaster, bronze, and earthenware.

* Witness the sculptures, and Exod. ix. 31, 32.; " The barley was smitten . . . . . the wheat and the rye (?) were not smitten; for they were not grown up." Wheat in Egypt is about a month later than barley.
† Herod. ii. 37. *Vide suprà*, p. 201.
‡ If Herodotus had travelled, a few years ago, in the north of our island, he might, perhaps, have made a similar remark about the English and oat cakes.

They varied greatly in their forms: some were plain and unornamented; others, though of small dimensions, were made after the models of larger vases; many were like our own cups without handles; and others may come under the denomination of beakers and saucers. Of these the former were frequently made of alabaster, with a round base, so that they could not stand when filled, and were held in the hand, or when empty, were turned downwards upon their rim: and the latter, which were of glazed pottery, had sometimes lotus or fish represented on their concave surface, which, when water was poured into the cups appeared to float in their native element. *

The tables, as at a Roman repast, were occasionally brought in and removed † with the dishes

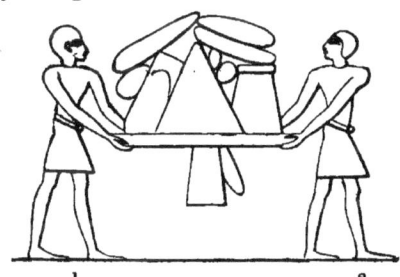

No. 283.   The table brought in with the dishes upon it.   *Tombs near the Pyramids.*

on them; sometimes each joint was served up separately, and the fruit, deposited in a plate or trencher, succeeded the meat at the close of dinner, and in

* Wood-cut, No. 282. *fig.* 2. *Vide* also the spoon in wood-cut, No. 261. *fig.* 1.
† Wood-cut, No. 283. Conf. Virg. Æn. i. 723.
    " Postquam prima quies epulis, mensæque remotæ."

less fashionable circles, particularly of the olden
time, it was brought in baskets which stood beside
the table.   The dishes consisted of fish ; meat
boiled, roasted, and dressed in various ways ; game,
poultry, and a profusion of vegetables and fruit,
particularly figs and grapes, during the season ; and
a soup, or pottage of lentils*, as with the modern
Egyptians, was not an unusual dish.   Of figs and
grapes they were particularly fond, which is shown
by their constant introduction even among the
choice offerings presented to the gods ; and figs of
the sycamore must have been highly esteemed,
since they were selected as the heavenly fruit, given
by the goddess Netpe to those who were judged
worthy of admission to the regions of eternal hap-
piness.   Fresh dates during the season, and in a
dried state at other periods of the year, were also
brought to table, as well as a preserve of the fruit,
still so common in the country, some of which I

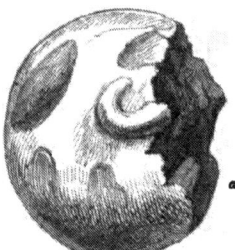

No. 284.   A cake of preserved dates, found by me at Thebes.   At *a* is a date stone.

have found in a tomb at Thebes, made into a cake
of the same form as the tamarinds now brought

* Gen. xxv. 34.   " Jacob gave Esau bread and pottage of lentils."

from the interior of Africa, and sold in the Cairo market.

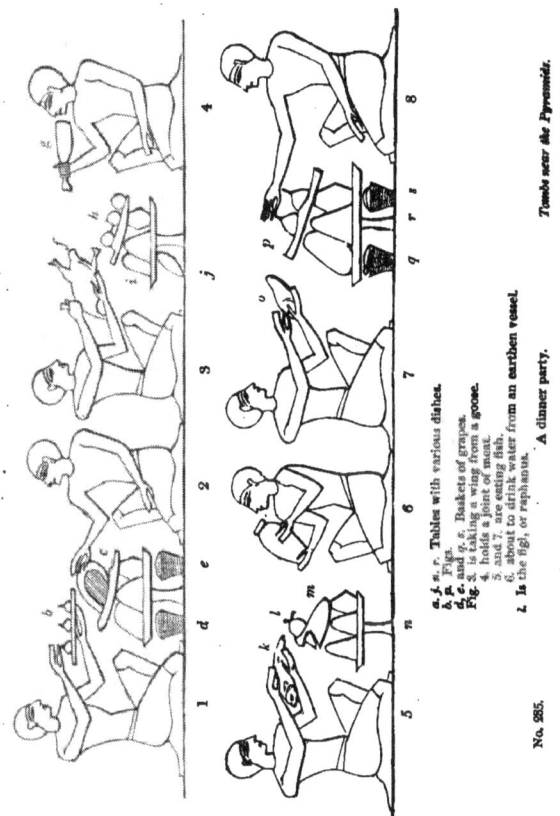

a, j, s, r. Tables with various dishes.
b, p. Figs.
d, c. and q, s. Baskets of grapes.
Fig. 3. is taking a wing from a goose.
4. holds a joint of meat.
5. and 7. are eating fish.
6. about to drink water from an earthen vessel.
i. is the fig?, or raphanus.

A dinner party.

Tombs near the Pyramids.

No. 285.

The guests sat on the ground, or on stools and chairs, and, having neither knives and forks, nor any substitute for them answering to the chopsticks

of the Chinese, they· ate with their fingers, as the
modern Asiatics, and invariably with the right hand.
Spoons were introduced at table when soup or
other liquids required their use, and, perhaps, even
a knife* was employed on some occasions, to facilitate the carving of a large joint, which is sometimes done in the East at the present day.

The Egyptian spoons were of various forms and
sizes, according to the purposes for which they
were intended.   They were principally of ivory,
bone, wood, or bronze, and other metals; and in
some the handle terminated in a hook, by which, if
required, they were suspended to a nail.†   Many
were ornamented with the lotus flower; the handles
of others were made to represent an animal, or a
human figure; some were of a very arbitrary shape;
and a smaller kind of a round form, probably intended for taking ointment out of a vase and trans-
ferring it to a shell or cup for immediate use, are
occasionally discovered in the tombs of Thebes.
One in the Museum of Alnwick Castle is a perfect
specimen of these spoons, and is rendered more
interesting from having been found with the shell,
its companion at the toilet table. ‡

Simpula, or ladles, were also common, and many
have been found at Thebes.   They were of bronze,

---

* Knives were used by the Romans at table :

        " Quin ipsa manubria cultellorum
Ossea, non tamen . .. . . . ideo pejor gallina secatur."
                            Juv. Sat, xi. 133.

though they ate with their fingers ; whence " manus unctæ," Hor.
Ep. i. 16. 23.

† Wood-cut, No. 286. *fig.* 2.   ‡ *Vide* wood-cut, No. 289.

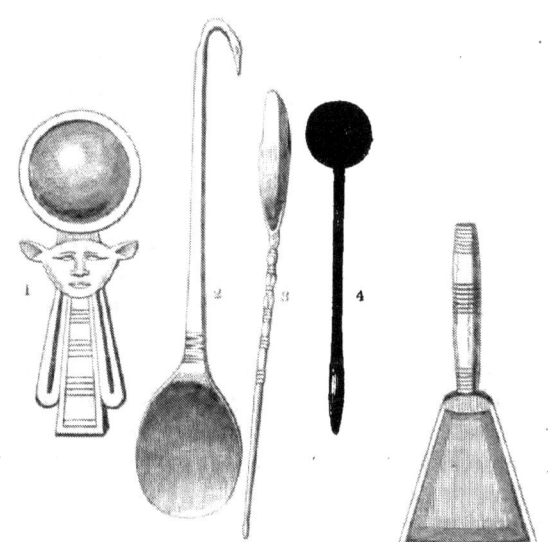

No. 286.   No. 287.   Of wood, in Mr.
    Fig. 1. Ivory spoon, about 4 inches long, in the Berlin   Salt's Collection.
            Museum, found with the vases of wood-cut, No. 181.
        2. Bronze spoon, in my possession, 8 inches in length.
        3, 4. Bronze spoons found by Mr. Burton, at Thebes.

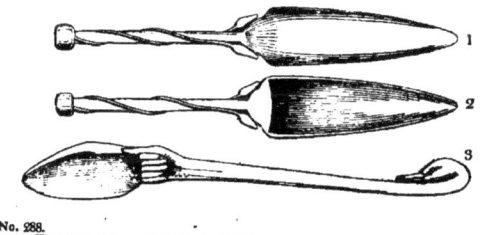

No. 288.
    Figs. 1, 2. Front and back of a wooden spoon.
        3. Ivory spoon.   Mr. Salt's Collection.

frequently gilt, and the curved summit of the
handle, terminating in a goose's head, a favourite

D D 2

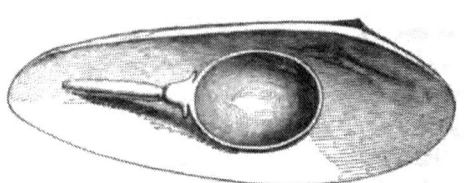

No. 289.   Alabaster shell and spoon.   *Museum of Alnwick Castle.*

Egyptian ornament, served to suspend them at the
side of a vessel after having been used for taking
a liquid from it ; and, judging from a painting on a
vase in the Naples Museum, where a priest is represented pouring a libation from a vase with the
simpulum, we may conclude this to have been
the principal purpose to which they were applied.   The gilding may either have been purely

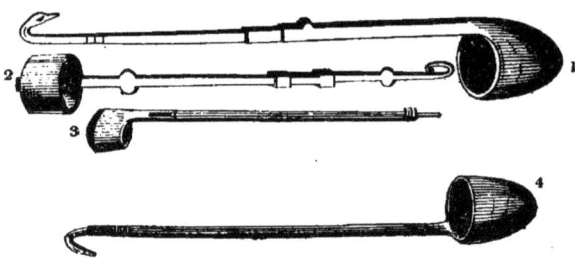

No. 290.
Figs. 1, 2. Bronze simpula in the Berlin Museum.
        3. Of hard wood in the same Museum.
        4. Bronze simpulum, in my possession, 1 foot 6 inches long. It has been gilt.

ornamental, or intended to prevent the noxious
effect of wine, or other acid liquid, after being left
in contact with it.   The length of the one in my
possession is eighteen inches, and the lower part

or ladle nearly three inches deep, and two and a half inches in diameter: but many were much smaller, and some were perhaps of a larger size.

Some simpula were made with a joint or hinge in the centre of the handle, so that the upper half either folded over the other*, or slided down behind it †; the extremity of each being furnished with a bar which held them together, at the same time that it allowed the upper one to pass freely up and down.   Two of these are preserved in the Berlin Museum, where they have also a ladle of hard wood ‡ found with the case of bottles, which, as I have elsewhere observed §, either belonged to a doctor, or to a lady's toilet table.   It is very small; the lower part, which may be properly called the handle, being barely more than five inches long, of very delicate workmanship; and the sliding rod, which rises and falls in a groove extending down the centre of the handle, is about the thickness of a needle.

Small strainers, or cullenders, of bronze have also been found at Thebes, but seldom more than five inches in diameter, one of which is in the British Museum, with several other utensils.

That they washed after as well as before dinner, we may be allowed to conclude from the invariable adoption of this custom throughout the East, and among most nations of antiquity, as the Greeks ||,

---

* Wood-cut, No. 290. *fig.* 1.   † Ibid. *fig.* 2.
‡ Wood-cut, No. 290. *fig.* 3.   § Vol. II. p. 217.
|| *Vide* the ' Banquet ' of Xenophon : " after they had done bathing and anointing, as was the custom before meals."   Hom. (Od. *δ.* v. 52.) mentions the use of water before meals ; and Aristophanes, in the Wasps, speaks of the custom, after eating.

Romans*, Hebrews†, and others: nor can we for a moment suppose that a people, peculiarly pre-possessed in favour of repeated ablutions, would have neglected so important an act of cleanliness and comfort ; and Herodotus‡ speaks of a golden basin, belonging to Amasis, which was used by the Egyptian monarch, and " the guests who were in the habit of eating at his table."

The heat of a climate, like that of Egypt, na-turally pointed out the necessity of frequent ab-lutions, and inclined them to consider the use of water an agreeable indulgence : and we frequently find many of the modern natives, who are not obliged by a religious prejudice to observe the custom of washing at meals, as particular in this respect as the Moslems themselves. §

The Greeks, at a remote period of their history, were not so scrupulous in these matters, and were contented to wipe their fingers, after meals, on pieces of bread-crum (απομαγδαλιαι), which they threw to the dogs‖; but it is probable, that the refreshing habits of cleanliness always existed in

---

* Virg. Æn. i. 701. : —

　　" Dant manibus famuli lymphas."

and Georg. iv. 377.

　　——— " Manibus liquidos dant ordine fontes
　　Germanæ, tonsisque ferunt mantilia vittis."

† The Pharisees " marvelled that he had not first washed before dinner." Luke, xi. 38.

‡ Herod. ii 172. He calls it a foot basin, ποδανιπτηρ.

§ I allude to the Copts of Cairo: I cannot, however, say that the monks of their convents are always so scrupulous or so cleanly, mis-taken zeal leading them to construe the censure, pronounced by Christ against the Pharisees, into a prohibition.

‖ Whence the απομαγδαλια was called κυνας by the Lacedæmonians.

Egypt, even when society was in its earliest stage. In later times the Greeks used an absorbent, to scour the hands, for which purpose nitre and hyssop* were employed; and though we have no evidence of its prevailing among the Egyptians, we may infer they had a similar custom; and, from lupins having been so long adopted in the country for the same purpose, that the *doqáq*† of modern Egypt is an old invention, handed down to, and imitated by, the present inhabitants.

Soap was not unknown to the ancients, and a small quantity has even been found at Pompeii. Pliny‡ mentions it as an invention of the Gauls, and says it was made of fat and ashes; and Aretæus, the physician of Cappadocia, tells us, that the Greeks borrowed their knowledge of its medicinal properties from the Romans. But there is no evidence of soap having been used by the Egyptians; and if accident had discovered something of the kind, while they were engaged with mixtures of natron or potash, and other ingredients, it is probable that it was only an absorbent, without oil or grease, and on a par with steatite, or the argillaceous earths, with which, no doubt, they were long acquainted.

We know that this scrupulously religious people were never remiss in evincing their gratitude for

* Conf. Psalm li. 7.; the Jews only used it as a sprinkler. Numb. xix. 18.

† Pounded lupins, purposely prepared for washing the hands after eating. *Termes* is the name of the lupin in Arabic, and the ancient Egyptian, or Coptic, word is θαρμος.

‡ Pliny, xxviii. 12.

the blessings they enjoyed, and in returning thanks to the gods for that peculiar protection they were thought to extend to them and to their country, above all the nations of the earth. It cannot, therefore, be supposed, that they would have omitted a similar acknowledgment, previous to and after meals * ; and even if the impulse of their own feelings had not dictated its propriety, the assiduous zeal of their spiritual pastors, who omitted nothing which could inspire the people with due respect for the Deity, would not have failed to impose upon them so important a duty. But on this point there is no need of conjecture: Josephus expressly states, that the custom of saying grace before meals was practised by the Egyptians ; and when the seventy-two elders were invited by Ptolemy Philadelphus to sup at the palace, Nicanor requested Eleazar to say grace for his countrymen, instead of those Egyptians, to whom that duty was committed on other occasions.† The Greeks, and other nations of antiquity, offered a part of what they were about to eat, as *primitiæ*, or first fruits‡, to the gods ; and it is probable, that besides a thanksgiving, the religious Egyptians commenced their repasts with a similar ceremony.

We cannot suppose that this people were so ad-

---

* The Moslems, before eating, say " Besmillah," or " Besm Allah é'rahman é'raheem," " In the name of the kind and merciful God." On rising from table, each repeats the " El hamdoolillah," " Praised be God." From this use of the word besmillah, they say, " Besmillah mâna," " Will you in the name of God (*i. e.* eat) with us."
† *Vide* Joseph. Antiq. xii. 2. 12.
‡ Hom. Il. κ. 219. Odys. ι. 231. Athen. iv. 27.

dicted to the pleasures of the world *, as to depre-
ciate in their conviviality all moral and religious
feelings, or to have been more disposed than the
generality of men on similar occasions, to forget
futurity in the pleasures of the moment; though
this has been frequently urged against the Egyptians; and because they were guilty of excesses † at
the table, some have not scrupled to consider them
immoral and depraved. But if they were fond of
luxury, and all the mirth in which a lively people
naturally indulge, if they banished religious thoughts
during the hour of festivity, and allowed themselves
to give way to occasional intemperance, it is unjust
to throw the stigma of immorality upon the whole
nation; and few civilised communities of modern
Europe would desire to be judged with the same
severity.

It was a custom of the Egyptians, during, or
according to Herodotus, after their repasts, to introduce a wooden image of Osiris‡, from one foot
and a half to three feet in height, in the form of a
human mummy, standing erect, as Plutarch informs
us, in a case, or lying on a bier, and to show it to

---

* Josephus says "The Egyptians are a peevish, lazy set of people,
abandoned to their pleasures, and their very souls set upon profit, let
it come which way it will." Antiq. ii. 9. This was in the late age of
Vespasian, when they were a very different people from the Egyptians
of a Pharaonic period, and no longer a nation.

† The Romans, under the emperors, committed unheard-of excesses.
Seneca says, " Vomunt ut edant, edunt ut vomant."

‡ The Egyptians made their mummies in the form of Osiris, and the
deceased, as soon as he had passed the ordeal of his final judgment,
was admitted into the presence of the deity, whose name was then pre-
fixed to his own.

each of the guests *, warning him of his mortality, and the of transitory nature of human pleasures.

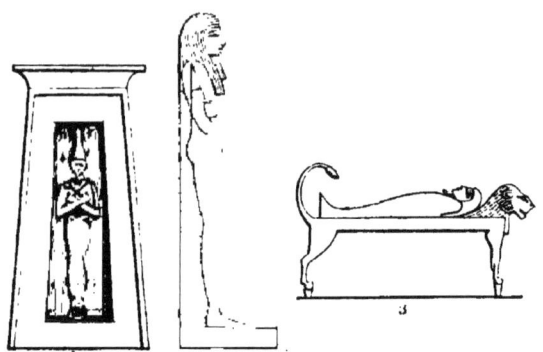

No. 290. a.   Figure of a mummy in form of Osiris, brought to an Egyptian table, and
shown to the guests.

He was reminded that some day he would be like that figure; that men ought " to love one another, and avoid those evils which tend to make them consider life too long, when in reality it is too short;" and while enjoying the blessings of this world, to bear in mind that their existence was precarious, and that death, which all ought to be prepared to meet, must eventually close their earthly career. Thus, while the guests were permitted, and even exhorted to indulge in conviviality, the pleasures of the table, and the mirth so congenial to their lively disposition, the prudent solicitude of the priests did not fail to watch over their actions, and, by this salutary hint, to show

* Herod. ii. 78. Plut. de Is. s. xv., and Sept. Sapient. Conv. p. 153.
Vide Dr. Young, Hier. Lit. p. 104.

them the propriety of putting a certain degree of
restraint upon their conduct; and, by avoiding
any indiscreet prohibition of those amusements, in
which men will indulge, in spite of mistaken zeal,
(too often dictated by a mind devoid of experience,
and frequently of sincerity,) these guardians of
morality obtained the object they had in view,
without appearing to interfere.

If, as was necessarily the case, all the guests were
not impressed with the same feelings, by the introduction of this moral sentiment, the custom was
not thereby rendered in any degree objectionable,
since a salutary lesson neglected loses not its merit:
and however it may have been corrupted by others,
who adopted the external form without the true
feeling of the original, it must be confessed that the
object was good and deserving of commendation.
Perverted by the Greeks, this warning of the temporary pilgrimage of man served as an inducement to
enjoy the pleasures of life, while in this world, as if
death closed the scene, and no prospect was held out
of a future existence ; a notion directly at variance
with the maxims of the Egyptians, and the constant
mindfulness they were exhorted to cherish of an
hereafter ; and we find that the Greeks advocated
the principle " Live while you may," with unblush-
ing earnestness.   The beauties of poetry * were

---

* Anacreon, Od. 4. εις εαυτον.

" Ο δ' Ερως χιτωνα δησας	" In decent robe, behind him bound,
Υπερ αυχενο ςπαπυρφ	Cupid shall serve the goblet round :
Μεθυ μοι διηκονειτω·	For fast away our moments steal,
	Like the swift chariot's rolling wheel ;

summoned to assist in its recommendation, and every lover of excess welcomed and adopted it, with sentiments evincing the same spirit as the exhortation of Trimalchio; which is thus given by Petronius: " To us, who were drinking, and admiring the splendour of the entertainment, a silver model of a man was brought by a servant, so contrived that its joints and moveable vertebræ could be bent in any direction.   After it had been produced upon the table two or three times, and had been made, by means of springs, to assume different attitudes, Trimalchio exclaimed *, ' Alas, unhappy lot, how truly man is nought! similar to

---

Τροχος αρματος γαρ οια
Βιοτος τρεχει κυλισθεις,
Ολιγη δε κεισομεσθα
Κονις, οστεων λυθεντων·

Τι σε δει λιθον μυριζειν ;
Τι δε γη χεειν ματαια;
Εμε μαλλον, ως ετι ζω,
Μυρισον, ροδοις δε κρατα
Πυκασον, καλει δ' εταιρην.

Πριν, Ερως, εεει μ' απελθειν
Υπο νερτερων χορειας,
Σκεδασαι θελω μεριμνας."

The rapid course is quickly done,
And soon the race of life is run.
Then, then, alas! we droop, we die,
And sunk in dissolution lie :
Our frame no symmetry retains,
Nought but a little dust remains.
Why o'er the tomb are odours shed ?
Why pour'd libations to the dead ?
To me far better, while I live,
Rich wines and balmy fragrance give.
Now, now, the rosy wreath prepare,
And hither call the lovely fair.
Now, while I draw my vital breath,
Ere yet I lead the dance of death,
For joy my sorrows I 'll resign,
And drown my cares in rosy wine."

And Hor. 2 Od. iii. 13. :

" Huc vina, et unguenta, et nimium brevis
Flores amœnos ferre jube rosæ,
Dum res, et ætas, et sororum
Fila trium patiuntur atra."

* Petron. Satyric. c. 34. ad finem :

" Trimalchio adjecit;

" Heu, heu nos miseros, quam totus homuncio nil est !
Sic erimus, cuncti, postquam nos auferet Orcus:
Ergo vivamus, dum licet esse, bene."

this shall we all be, when death has carried us away : therefore, while we are allowed to live, let us live well.'"

The same sentiments were used by the Jews in the time of Solomon*, and " the ungodly" of his time thus expressed themselves : " Our life is short and tedious, and in the death of a man there is no remedy ; neither was there any man known to have returned from the grave.   For we are born at all adventure, and we shall be hereafter as though we had never been, ... come on, therefore, let us enjoy the good things that are present, ... let us fill ourselves with costly wine and ointments; and let no flower of the spring pass by us; let us crown ourselves with rosebuds, before they be withered; let none of us go without his part of our voluptu- ousness; let us leave tokens of our joyfulness in every place."

The intent, however, of this custom, with the Egyptians, was widely different, and even if from long habit, and the increase of luxurious manners, the good warning it was intended to convey was disregarded, or failed in its effect, still the original intention was good, and cannot, in justice, be con- demned as tending to immorality : and though He- rodotus, who merely says, that the guests were re- quested to " observe that man, whom they would all resemble after death," and were exhorted " to drink and enjoy themselves," omits to inform us, if it was intended to convey a moral lesson, Plu-

* Book of Wisdom, ii. 1. et seq.   Conf. Is. xxii. 13., and lvi. 12. Eccles. ii. 24.   Luke xii. 19., and 1 Corinth. xv. 32.

tarch expressly asserts this, and removes all doubt respecting the object they had in view. The idea of death, among the ancients, was less revolting than among Europeans and others, at the present day; and so little did the Egyptians object to have it brought before them, that they even introduced the mummy of a deceased relative at their parties, and placed it at table, as one of the guests; a fact, which is recorded by Lucian*, in his " Essay on Grief," and of which he declares himself to have been an eyewitness.

After dinner, music and singing were resumed; men and women performed feats of agility, swinging each other round by the hand; or throwing up and catching the ball; and the numerous tricks of jugglers, both in the house and out of doors, were introduced to amuse the company.

Part of a similar scene, at a Greek entertainment, is described in the 'Banquet' of Xenophon. A little boy, two dancing girls, and a jester named Philip, were present on that occasion, and one of the former began by displaying her skill, in throwing up her cymbals, and catching them, to the tune of a flute played by her companion. A hoop was then brought, round which a number of swords were fixed, and the same dancing girl jumping in and out of the hoop with perfect confidence, and without receiving any injury, afforded infinite delight and satisfaction to the guests; and gave occasion to Socrates, who was present, to make

* And by Damascenus, Orat. i.

some general remarks on the courage of women, and to observe that they " are capable of learning any thing you will they should know." Then standing upright, she bent backwards, and touching her heels with her head, flung herself round swiftly three or four times, in imitation of a wheel; occasionally reading and writing at the same time that she was going through this rotatory movement. Every one expressed his delight at this exhibition of her agility; and Philip pretending to imitate her, by throwing himself in the same manner forwards, offered a striking contrast to the grace she had exhibited, and excited the ridicule of the party.

The singular feat here described is more interesting, as it bears some resemblance to one of those indicated in the paintings illustrating the customs of the Egyptians, at an era far more remote, dating no less than 1300 years before the age of Socrates; where women are represented turning over backwards, either singly or in pairs. In the latter case, the head of one was placed between the legs of the other, front to front, but in such a manner that when one was standing, the head of the other was downwards, and the feet over her neck; and in this position they turned over, the feet of each alternately reaching the ground.*

The most usual games† within doors were, odd and even, *mora*, and draughts. The first of these was played also by the Romans, and called " lu-

* There is no appearance of the Cottabus, so fully described by Athenæus, which was supposed to have passed from Sicily into Greece.
† Wood-cut, No. 291.

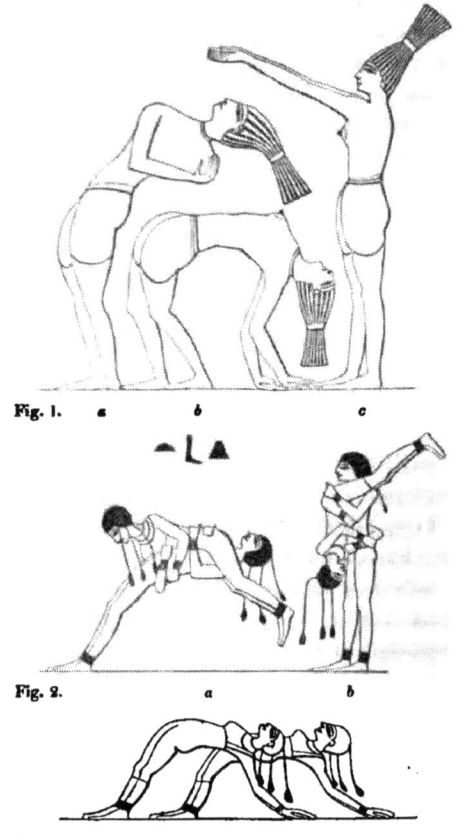

Fig. 1.   *a*   *b*   *c*

Fig. 2.   *a*   *b*

Fig. 3.   *a*   *b*

No. 291.   Women tumbling, and performing feats of agility.   *Beni Hassan.*

dere par et impar," but considered better suited to the levity of young persons * than to the gravity of

* And to the lower orders.

a more advanced age; and Horace* looked upon it in the same light as the trifling amusements of building children's houses, yoking mice to carts, and riding on a stick.† According to J. Pollux they used bones (*astragali*), beans, nuts, almonds, or coins, in the game of odd and even, and any indefinite number was held between the two hands.‡

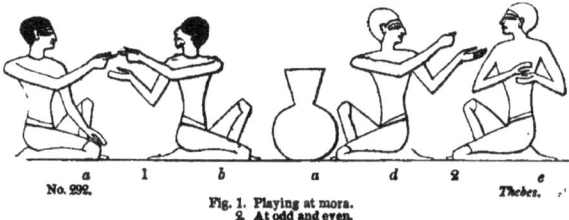

No. 292.

Fig. 1. Playing at mora.
2. At odd and even.

Thebes.

The second was common in ancient as well as modern Italy, and was played by two persons who each simultaneously threw out the fingers of one hand, while one party guessed the sum of both. They were said, in Latin, "micare digitis §," and it is remarkable that a game still so common among the lower orders of Italians, with whom

---

* Hor. 2 Sat. iii. 247.:

" Ædificare casas, plostello adjungere mures,
    Ludere par impar, equitare in arundine longâ,
    Si quem delectat barbatum, amentia verset."

† Agesilaus is mentioned by Plutarch making " a hobby-horse of a reed, and riding with his children." Plut. Life of Agesilaus.

‡ J. Poll. Onom. ix. 7. He describes another game, which was throwing the same bones, or coins, within a ring, and also into a hole, well known in modern times : this last was called τροπα.

§ Juv. Sat. Cicero de Divin. lib. ii. says " Quid enim sors est ? idem propemodum quod micare, quod talos jacere, quod tesseras." Offic. iii. 23. Suet. Aug. 13. The " sortiri digitis," επαλλαττειν τους δακτυλους," was different.

it bears the name I have adopted, should be found
to have existed in Egypt from the earliest periods
of which their paintings remain, even in the reign
of the first Osirtasen.*

The same antiquity may be claimed for the game
of draughts, or, as it has been erroneously called,
chess. As in the two former, the players sat on
the ground †, or on chairs, and the pieces, or men,
being ranged in line at either end of the table,
probably moved on a chequered board, as in our
own chess and draughts; but, the representations
being always given in profile, it is impossible to
ascertain the exact appearance, or the number, of
squares it contained.

The pieces were all of the same size and form,
though they varied on different boards, some being

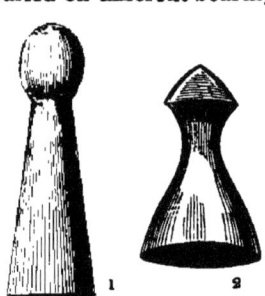

No. 293.   Draughtmen.
          Fig. 1. From the sculptures of Remeses III.
                2. Of wood, in my possession.

small, others large with round summits: many
were of a lighter and neater shape, like small nine-
pins, probably the most fashionable kind, since they
were used in the palace of king Remeses. These

---

* *Vide* Vol. I. p. 44.   † Ibid.

last seem to have been about one inch and a half high, standing on a circular base of half an inch in diameter; and one in my possession, which I brought from Thebes, of a nearly similar taste, is one inch and a quarter in height, and little more than half an inch broad at the lower end. It is of hard wood, and was doubtless painted of some colour, like those occurring on the Egyptian monuments.

They were all of equal size upon the same board, one set black, the other white or red, standing on opposite sides *, and each player raising it with the finger and thumb advanced his piece

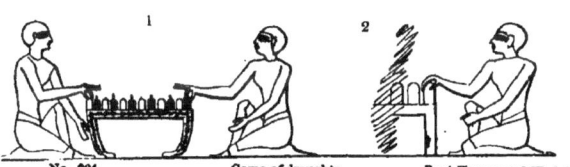

No. 294.   Game of draughts.   Beni Hassan and Thebes

towards those of his opponent; but though we are unable to say if this was done in a direct or a diagonal line, there is reason to believe they could not take backwards, as in the Polish game of draughts, the men being mixed together on the board.†

It was an amusement common in the houses of

* *Vide* Jul. Pollux, Onom. ix. 7. on a game of tessera ($\psi\eta\phi\omicron\iota$) of this kind, where the men, or dogs, as they called them, on the two opposite sides were of a different colour. Another similar game, called $\delta\iota\alpha\gamma\rho\alpha\mu\mu\iota\sigma\mu\omicron\varsigma$, is there mentioned. It is remarkable that the name dog (kelb) is applied also by the Arabs to their draughtmen. J. Pollux was a Greek writer who lived about the year 185, A. D. Some suppose the Roman game of Duodecim Scripta to have resembled draughts, but the moves were generally determined by throwing dice.

† As in wood-cut, No. 294. *fig.* 1.

E E 2

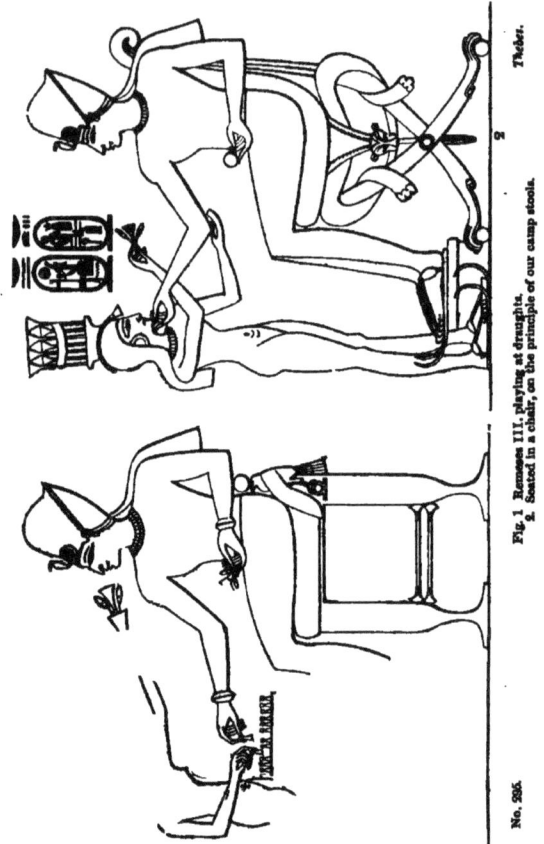

Fig. 1 Remeses III. playing at draughts. 2. Seated in a chair, on the principle of our camp stools. *Thebes.*

No. 295.

the lower classes and in the mansions of the rich;
and king Remeses is himself portrayed on the walls
of his palace at Thebes, engaged in the game of
draughts with the favourites of his *haréem.*

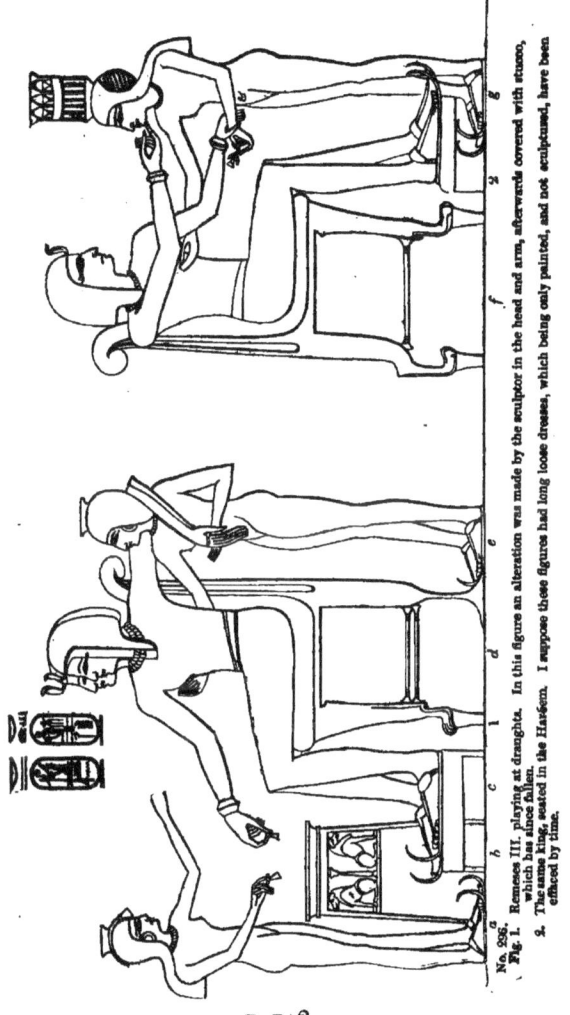

No. 286.

a b c Rameses III. playing at draughts.
Fig. 1.   which has since fallen.

d e f g In this figure an alteration was made by the sculptor in the head and arm, afterwards covered with stucco,

Fig. 2. The same king, seated in the Harēem.   I suppose these figures had long loose dresses, which being only painted, and not sculptured, have been effaced by time.

E E 3

The modern Egyptians have a game of draughts, very similar, in the appearance of the men, to that of their ancestors, which they call *dámeh*, and play much in the same manner as our own.

Analogous to the game of odd and even was one, in which two of the players held a number of shells or dice in their closed hands, over a third person who knelt between them, with his face towards the ground, and who was obliged to guess the combined number[*] ere he could be released from this

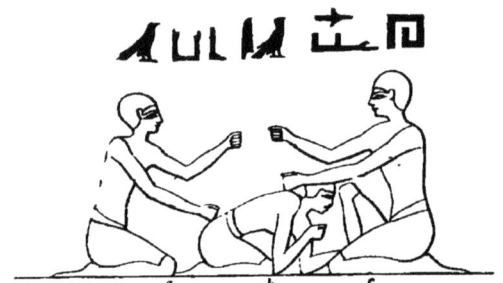

No. 297.   A game perhaps similar to the Greek *kollabismos.*

position; unless indeed it be the *kollabismos* (κολλαβισμος) of the Greeks[†], in which one person covered his eyes, and guessed which of the other players struck him.

Another game consisted in endeavouring to snatch from each other a small hoop, by means of hooked rods, probably of metal; and the success of a player seems to have depended on extricating his own from the adversary's rod, and then snatching up the hoop, before he had time to stop it.[‡]

[*] This I conjecture from the mode of representing it.
[†] Jul. Poll. Onom. ix. 7.
[‡] It is taken from Prof. Rosellini's work. I suppose this to be their mode of playing with the hoop.

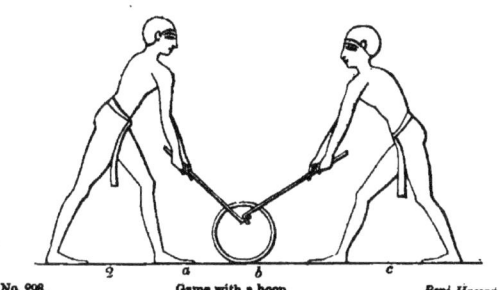

No. 298.   Game with a hoop.   *Beni Hassan.*

Some other games are represented in the paintings, but not in a manner to render them intelligible; and many, which were doubtless common
in Egypt, are omitted both in the tombs, and in the
writings of ancient authors.   It is, however, evident that dice were already used by the Egyptians
in the reign of Rhampsinitus; that monarch according to Herodotus, being reported to have
played* with the goddess Ceres; for the allegorical
meaning of the story in no way militates against
the fact of such a game having been known at the
period in question, and the Egyptians, his inform-
ants, were necessarily persuaded that it dated at
least as early as his era.

I do not suppose that the dice discovered at
Thebes, and other places, are of a very remote
epoch; they may not even be of a Pharaonic period,
but the simplicity of their form, and mode of notation, may lead us to suppose them similar to those
of the earliest age, in which too the conventional

* Herod. ii. 122. " συγκυβευειν τῃ Δημητρι."

E E 4

number of six sides had probably always been adopted.* They were marked with small circles, representing units, generally with a dot in the centre; and those I have seen were of bone or ivory, varying slightly in size.

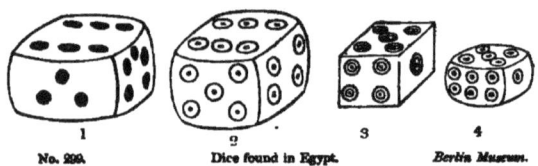

No. 299.   Dice found in Egypt.   *Berlin Museum.*

Plutarch† would lead us to believe that dice were a very early invention in Egypt, and acknowledged to be so by the Egyptians themselves, since they were introduced into one of their oldest mythological fables; Mercury being represented playing at dice with the moon, previous to the birth of Osiris, and winning from her the five days of the epact, which were added to complete the 365 days of the year.

The modern Egyptians have a game called in Arabic *mùngala*, which is traditionally reported to have been borrowed from their ancient predecessors; but as a full description of it has been given by Mr. Lane, in his curious and accurate account of the customs of modern Egypt‡, it is unnecessary here to repeat it.

It is probable that several games of chance were

* *Vide* J. Poll. Onom. lib. 9. c. vii. The Romans and Greeks had another kind of *tali*, or αστραγαλοι, with four sides only marked, the 2 and 5 being omitted. J. Poll. Ibid.
† Plut. de Is. s. xii. " παιξαντα πεττια προς Σεληνην."
‡ Lane's " Modern Egyptians," vol. ii. p. 47.

known to the Egyptians, besides dice and *mora*, and as with the Romans, that many a doubtful mind sought relief in the promise of success, by having recourse to fortuitous combinations of various kinds; and the custom of drawing or casting lots, to decide a disputed question, was common at least as early as the period of the Hebrew Exodus. *

Among the various methods adopted by the Romans for ascertaining the probable accomplishment of a wish, one of the most singular, was that of shooting up the fresh pips of an apple†, by squeezing them between the finger and thumb, and endeavouring to strike the ceiling, while seated at table; and the success or failure of the attempt augured in favour or against their good fortune, in obtaining the affections of a favourite, or whatever object they had in view.   Such scenes cannot of course be looked for among the subjects of the Egyptian sculptures; but that they were superstitious observers of accidental occurrences, and inferred from them the chance of certain results, is proved to us by the testimony of those who visited the country: for "whenever," says Herodotus‡ "any thing extraordinary occurs, they note it down in writing, and pay particular attention to the events

* Conf. Leviticus xvi. 8. "And Aaron cast lots upon the two goats."   The Hebrew word is גורל Górel; as in Joshua xviii. 10.
† Hor. 2 Sat. iii. 273.:

> " Quid cum Picenis excerpens semina pomis,
>   Gaudes si cameram percusti forte, penes te es ?"

and J. Poll. ix. c. 7.
‡ Herod. ii. 82.

which follow it, and if at a subsequent period some thing of a similar kind happens to take place, they feel persuaded it will be attended with the same result."

The games and amusements of children were such as tended to promote health by the exercise of the body, and to divert the mind by laughable entertainments. Throwing and catching the ball, running, leaping, and similar feats, were encouraged, as soon as their age enabled them to indulge in them ; and a young child was amused with painted dolls, whose hands and legs, moving on

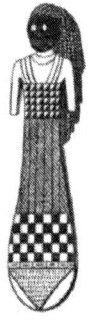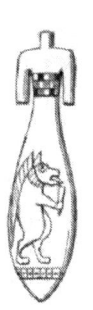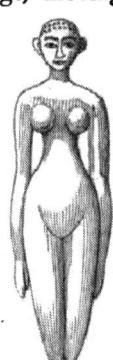

No. 300.   Wooden dolls.

pins, were made to assume various positions by means of strings.* Some of these were of rude and uncertain form, without legs, or with an imperfect representation of a single arm on one side. Some had numerous beads, in imitation of hair,

* Conf. Herod. ii. 48., who mentions another kind of figure carried at " the fête of Bacchus."

hanging from the doubtful place of the head ; others exhibited a nearer approach to the form of a man ; and some, made with considerable attention to proportion, were small models of the human figure. They were coloured according to fancy ; the most informous had usually the most gaudy appearance, being intended to catch the eye of an infant ; but a show of reality was deemed more suited to the taste of an older child ; and the nearer their resemblance to known objects, the less they partook of artificial ornament.   Sometimes a man was figured washing, or kneading dough, the necessary

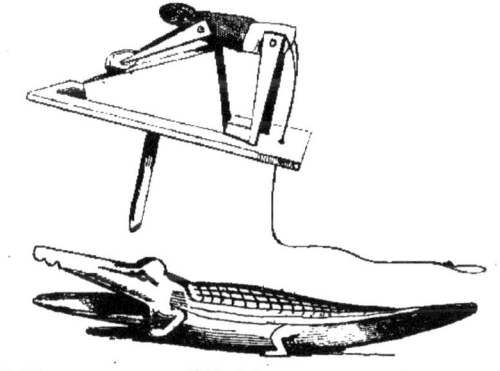

No. 301.   Children's toys.   *Leyden Museum.*

movement indicative of the operation being imitated by pulling a string ; and a typhonian monster, or a crocodile, amused a child by its grimaces, or the motion of its opening mouth ; plainly showing that children, in all ages, delight in the frightful, and play with objects which, if real, they would

shudder to behold.   In the toy of the crocodile,
we have sufficient evidence that the erroneous notion of Herodotus, who states that this animal
"does not move the lower jaw, and is the only
creature which brings the upper one down to the
lower*," did not originate with the Egyptians:
but we are not surprised at this assertion, when we
recollect how easily the motion of the head of the
crocodile is mistaken for that of the upper jaw.
Like other animals, it moves the lower jaw *only*,
but when seizing its prey, the head being thrown
up, gives the appearance of motion in the upper
jaw, and readily leads those who see it into this
erroneous conclusion.

The game of ball † was not confined to children,
or to either sex, though the mere amusement of
throwing and catching it appears to have been
considered more particularly adapted to females.‡
They had different methods of playing. §   Sometimes a person unsuccessful in catching the ball
was obliged to suffer another to ride on her back,
who continued to enjoy this post until she also
missed it: the ball being thrown by an opposite
party, mounted in the same manner, and placed
at a certain distance, according to the space previously fixed by the players ; and, from the position
and office of the person who had failed, it is not

* Herod. ii. 68.
† Pliny says painting and the game of ball were invented in Egypt:
" Pythus pilam lusoriam, Gyges Lydius picturam in Ægypto."
Lib. vii. 56.
‡ Not so with the Romans.
§ J. Poll., Onom. ix. c. 7., describes various games of ball; and a
sort of cockfight with quails.

improbable that the same name was applied to her as to those in the Greek game, who were called *ovoi* (asses), and were obliged to submit to the commands of the victor.*

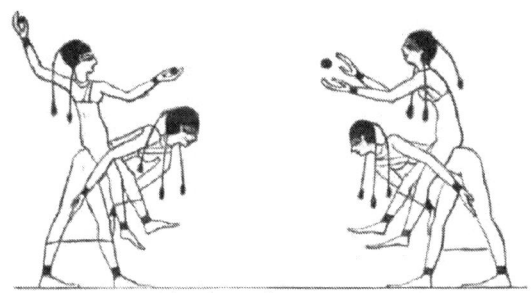

No. 302.   Playing the game of ball mounted on each others backs.   *Beni Hassan.*

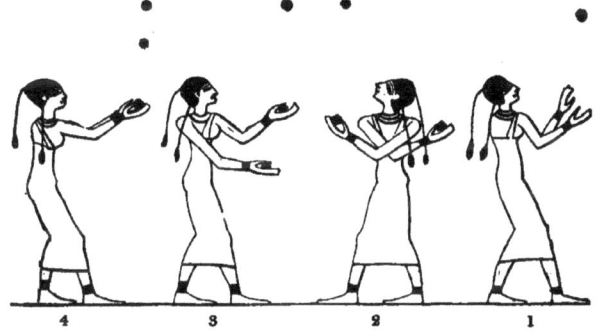

No. 302. *a.*   Throwing up and catching one, two, and three balls.   *Beni Hassan.*

Sometimes they showed their skill in catching three or more balls in succession, the hands occasionally crossed over the breast; and the more

* J. Poll. ix. 7. " Ο μεν ηττωμενος ονος εκαλειτο, και παν εποιει το προσταχθεν." *Vide* wood-cut, No. 302.

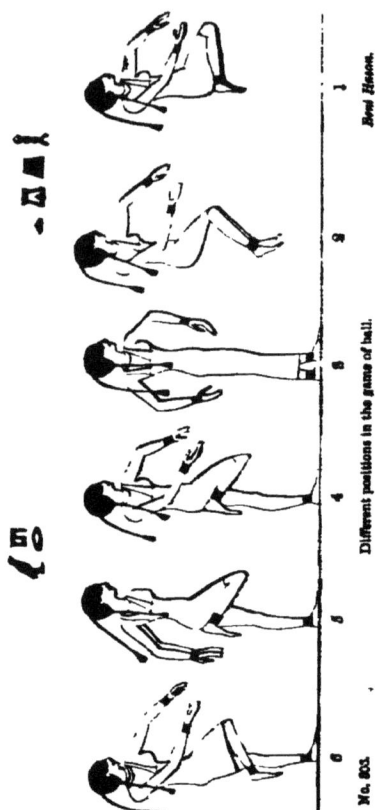

simple mode of throwing it up to a height, and
catching it, known to the Greeks by the name of
ουρανια *, was common in Egypt.   They had also

* From being thrown up ως τον ουρανον, " to the sky."

the game described by Homer * to have been played by Halius and Laodamas, before Alcinöus, in which one party threw the ball as high as he could, and the other, leaping up, caught it on its fall, before his feet again touched the ground.

When mounted on the backs of the losing party, the Egyptian women sat sidewise. Their dress consisted merely of a short petticoat, without a body, the loose upper robe being laid aside on these occasions : it was bound at the waist with a girdle †, and was supported by a strap over the shoulder, nearly the same as the undress garb of mourners, worn during the funeral lamentation on the death of a friend.

There is no appearance of any thing resembling rackets ; nor is the Roman game of striking the ball with the hand ‡ represented in the Egyptian sculptures : but we can draw no inference from their absence ; and, considering the remote antiquity of the paintings, it is singular that any should have been preserved to this late period, to give us an insight into their customs and amusements.

The balls were made of leather or skin, sewed

---

* Homer Od. θ. 374. : —

" Την ετερος ριπτασκε ποτι νεφεα σκιοεντα
Ιδνωθεις οπισω· ο δ'απο χθονος υψος αερθεις
Ρηϊδιως μεθελεσκε, παρος ποσιν ουδας ικεσθαι"

Vide J. Poll. ix. 7.; and wood-cut, No. 303. *fig.* 1.

† As the women in mourning, επεζωσμεναι, και φαινουσαι τους μαζους. Herod. ii. 85.

‡ One of these was the follis, inflated like our football, called also pila, or pila velox, and struck with the arms ; the other was smaller, and struck with the hand, on which they wore a sort of gauntlet ; whence it was called follis pugillatorius.

with string, crosswise, in the same manner as our
own, and stuffed with bran or husks of corn; and
those which have been found at Thebes are about
three inches in diameter. Others were made of

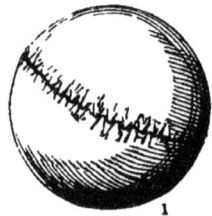
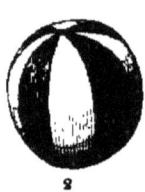

No. 304.   *From Mr. Salt's Collection.*

Fig. 1. Leather ball, three inches in diameter.
2. Of painted earthenware.

the stalks of rushes, platted together so as to form
a circular mass, and are, like the former, covered
with leather; instances of both which occur in the
British Museum. They appear also to have had a
smaller kind of ball, probably of the same materials,
and covered, like many of our own, with slips of
leather of a rhomboidal shape, sewed together lon-
gitudinally, and meeting in a common point at
both ends *, each alternate slip being of a different
colour †; but, as these have only been met with in
pottery, it is uncertain whether they were really
imitations of leather balls, or solely made of those
materials, and used for some other purpose connected with the toys of children.

Sometimes, in their performances of strength

* Wood-cut, *fig.* 2.
† Homer describes one of a purple colour, Od. θ. 372.: —

    " . . . . . . σφαιραν καλην μετα χερσιν ελοντο
    Πορφυρεην."

and dexterity, two men stood together side by
side, and, placing one arm forward and the other

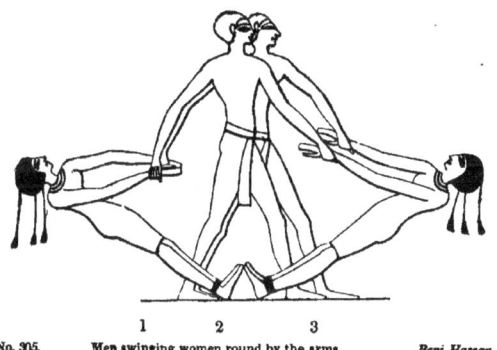

behind them, held the hands of two women, who
reclined backwards, in opposite directions, with
their whole weight pressed against each other's
feet, and in this position were whirled round; the
hands of the men who held them being sometimes
crossed, in order more effectually to guarantee the
steadiness of the centre, on which they turned.

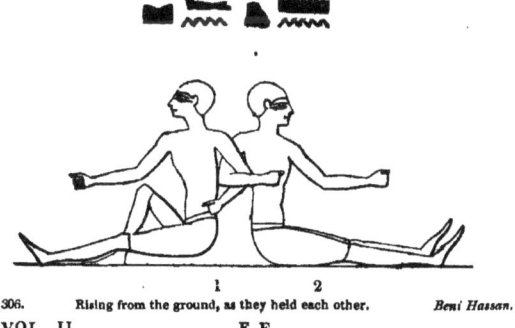

No. 306.   Rising from the ground, as they held each other.   *Beni Hassan.*

Sometimes two men *, seated back to back on the ground, and passing the elbows of the opposite arms within each other, endeavoured to rise in

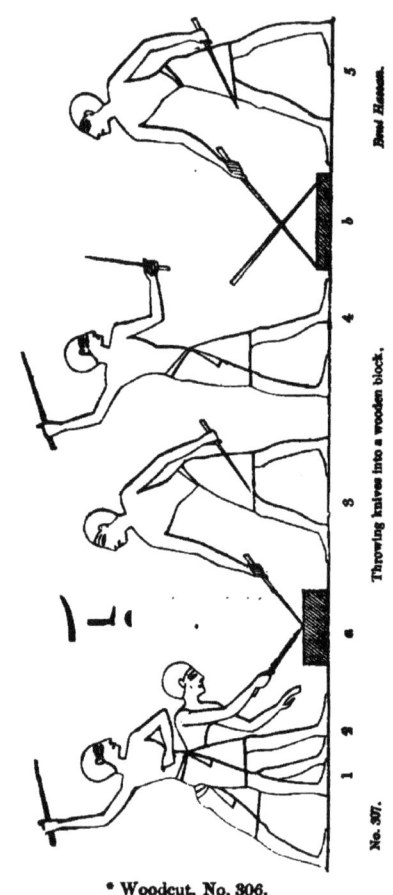

* Woodcut, No. 306.

that position, without touching the ground with
the disengaged hand; each, probably, trying to
rise before his companion, and striving to prevent
his success, in order to obtain the merit or the
reward of superior dexterity.

Another game consisted in throwing a knife, or
pointed weapon, into a block of wood, in which
each player was required to strike his adversary's,
or more probably to fix his own in the centre of a
ring painted on the wood; and his success depended on being able to ring his weapon most frequently, or approach most closely to the centre.

Conjuring appears also to have been known to
them, at least, the game of cups, in which a ball

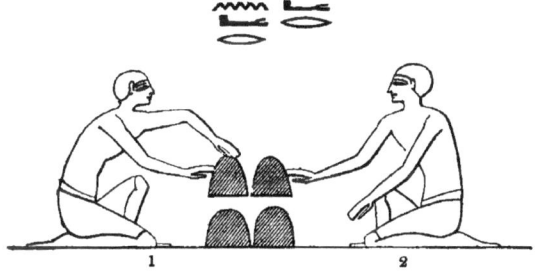

No. 308.   Conjurors, or thimble rig.   *From the work of Professor Rosellini.*

was put, while the opposite party guessed under
which of four it was concealed.

The Egyptian grandees frequently admitted
dwarfs and deformed persons into their household,
originally, perhaps, from a humane motive, or
from some superstitious regard for men who bore
the external character of one of their principal

gods, Pthah-Sokari-Osiris, the misshapen Deity of
Memphis; but, whatever may have given rise to

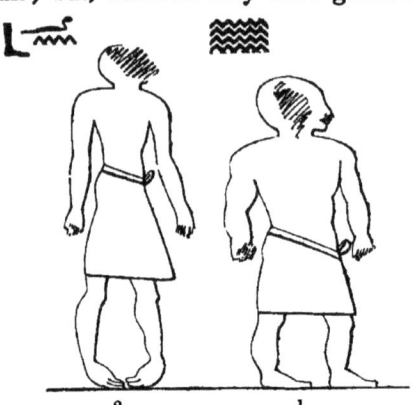

No. 309.   Dwarfs and deformed persons in the service of the Egyptian grandees.
Beni Hassan.
The stone is broken in that part where the hands should be.

the custom, it is a singular fact, that, already as
early as the age of Osirtasen, more than 3500
years ago, the same fancy of attaching these persons to their suite existed among the Egyptians,
as at Rome, and even in modern Europe, till a late
period.

GAMES AND AMUSEMENTS OF THE PEOPLE.

The games of the lower orders, and of those who
sought to invigorate the body by active exercises,
consisted of feats of agility and strength.   Wrestling was a favourite amusement; and the paintings
of the grottoes at Beni Hassan present all the
varied attitudes and modes of attack and defence
of which it is susceptible. And, in order to enable

the spectator more readily to perceive the position of the limbs of each combatant, the artist has availed himself of a dark and light colour, and even ventured to introduce alternately a black and red figure. It is not, however, necessary to give an instance of every position indicated in those varied subjects; and a selection of the principal groups will suffice to convey some idea of their mode of representing the combatants, and of their general system of attack and defence.

It is probable that, like the Greeks, they anointed the body with oil, when preparing for these exercises, and they were entirely naked, with the exception of a girdle, apparently of leathern thongs.

The two combatants generally approached each other, holding their arms in an inclined position before the body; and each endeavoured to seize his adversary in the manner best suited to his mode of attack. It was allowable to take hold of any part of the body, the head, neck, or legs; and the struggle was frequently continued on the ground, after one or both had fallen; a mode of wrestling common also to the Greeks, by whom it was denominated ανα-κλινοπαλη. I do not find that they had the same sign of acknowledging their defeat in this game as the Greeks, which was by holding up a finger, in token of submission, and it was probably done by the Egyptians with a word.

They also fought with the single stick, the hand being apparently protected by a basket, or guard projecting over the knuckles; and on the left arm they wore a straight piece of wood, bound

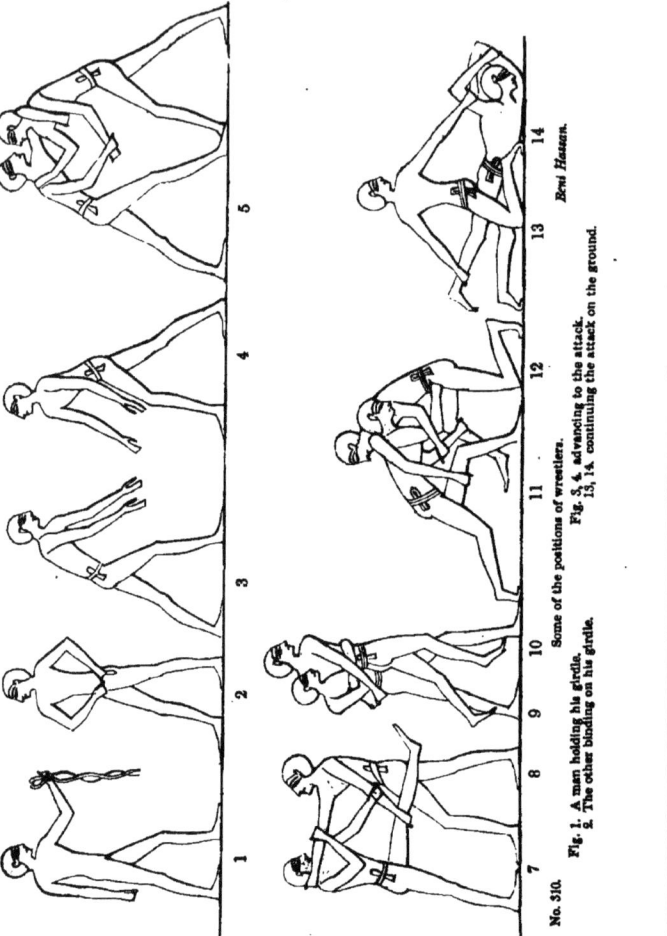

No. 310.   Some of the positions of wrestlers.   Beni Hassan.

Fig. 1. A man holding his girdle.
2. The other binding on his girdle.   Fig. 3, 4. advancing to the attack.
13, 14. continuing the attack on the ground.

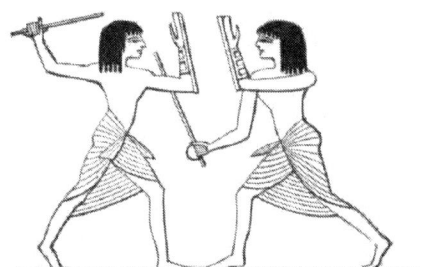

No. 311.   Singlestick.   *From the work of Professor Rosellini.*

on with straps, serving as a shield to ward off their adversary's blow. They do not, however, appear to have used the *cestus*, or to have known the art of boxing * ; nor was throwing the discus, or quoit, an Egyptian game.

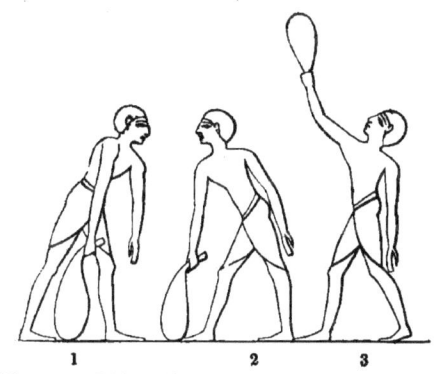

1   2   3

No. 312.   Raising weights.   *From the work of Professor Rosellini.*

Among their feats of strength or dexterity may be mentioned that of lifting weights; and bags full

---

* In one group alone, at Beni Hassan, the combatants appear to strike each other.

of sand were raised with one hand from the ground, and carried with a straight arm over the head, and held in that position.

Mock fights * were also an amusement, particularly, I imagine, among those of the military class, who were trained to the fatigues of war, by these manly recreations. One party attacked a temporary fort, and brought up the battering ram†, under cover of the testudo; another defended the walls and endeavoured to repel the enemy; others, in two parties of equal numbers, engaged in single stick, or the more usual *neboot*‡, a pole wielded with both hands; and the pugnacious spirit of the people is frequently alluded to in the scenes portrayed by their artists.

The use of the *neboot* seems to have been as common among the ancient, as among the modern, Egyptians; and the quarrels of villages were often decided or increased, as at present, by this efficient weapon. Crews of boats are sometimes represented attacking each other with the earnestness of real

* The Ludus Trojæ of the Romans. *Vide* Virg. Æn. v. 560. Hor. 1 Ep. xviii. 61.

† The battering ram (protected by the covering of the testudo, or χελωνη), is supposed by Pliny to have been first mentioned as the wooden horse of Troy; and the *aries*, or ram, is said by him to have been originally called a "horse." Lib. vii. 56. In early times it was merely a pike, τρυπανον, or terebra. The χελωνη is the same as the testudo, and both may be applied exclusively to that part which covered the men. The testudo arietaria includes the covering and the pike or ram. *Vide* Vitruv. x. c. 19, 20, 21, and 22.

‡ It was not a short club, but a pole of considerable length, longer than those now used in Egypt, which are about eight or nine feet. In mentioning the arms of the African enemies of Egypt, at the end of Vol. I., I omitted a remark of Pliny, that "the Africans were the first people who used clubs, called "phalangas," during their wars with the Egyptians. Lib. vii. 56.

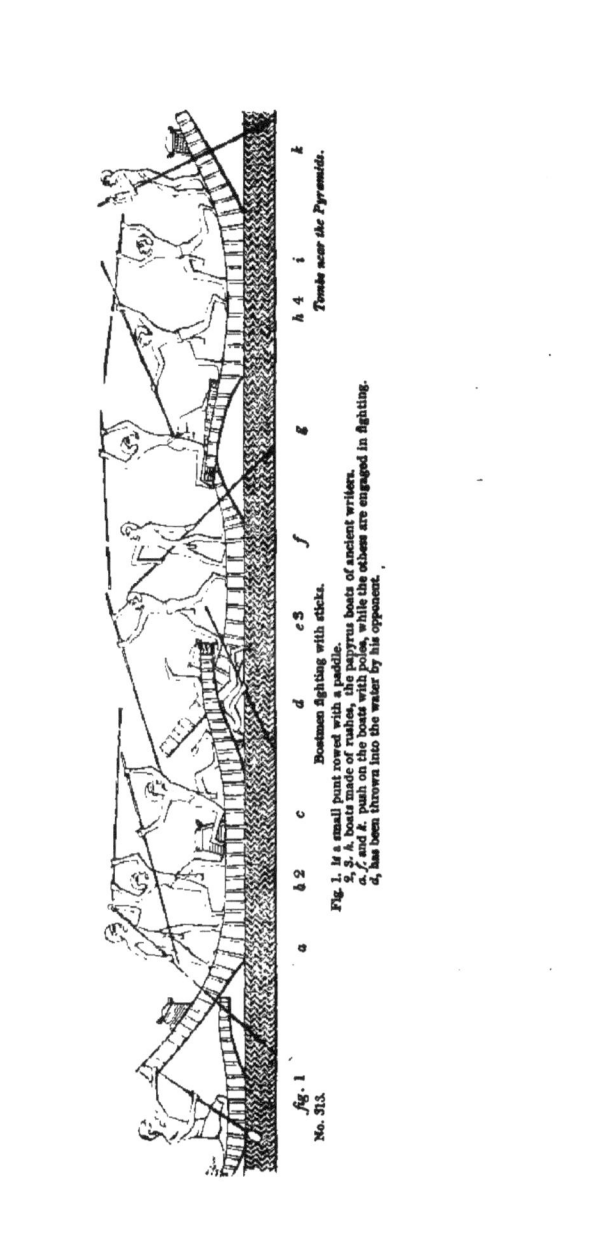

fig. 1

No. 313.

a   b 2   c   d   e 3   f   g   h 4   i   k

Tombs near the Pyramids.

Boatmen fighting with sticks.

Fig. 1. is a small punt rowed with a paddle.
2, 3. 4. boats made of rushes, the papyrus boats of ancient writers.
a, f, and k. push on the boats with poles, while the others are engaged in fighting.
d, has been thrown into the water by his opponent.

strife. Some are desperately wounded, and, being felled by their more skilful opponents, are thrown headlong into the water; and the truth of Herodotus's assertion, that the heads of the Egyptians [*] were harder than those of other people, seems fully justified by the scenes described by their own draughtsmen; and that this peculiarity has been inherited by their successors is abundantly proved by modern experience.

Many singular encounters with sticks are mentioned by ancient authors; among which may be noticed that described by Herodotus, at Papremis, the city of Mars.[†]   When the votaries of the deity presented themselves at the gates of the temple, their entrance was obstructed by an opposing party; and all being armed with sticks, they commenced a rude combat, which ended, not merely in the infliction of a few severe wounds, but even, as the historian affirms, in the death of many persons on either side.[‡]

In buffoonery they also took great pleasure, and in witnessing the performances of those who danced in the streets to the sound of a drum [§], decorated with whatever could add to the extravagance and ridicule of their appearance, as ribands, long pendent tassels, or fool's caps; and, judging from a custom still common in Egypt, it

---

[*] Herod. iii. 12.   [†] Herod. ii. 63.

[‡] Though, he adds, the Egyptians assured him the contrary. The modern Egyptians used to have the same kind of fatal encounters. *Vide* Egypt and Thebes, p. 237. note §.

[§] *Vide* wood-cut, No. 201.

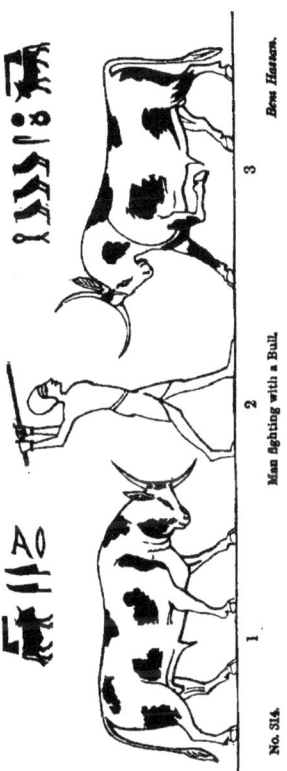

No. 314. 1.   2. Man fighting with a Bull.   3.   Beni Hassan.

is probable that these jesters passed impromptu remarks on the spectators, abounding either in the wit of satire, or the flattery of praise. For, besides professional dancers and musicians, who were hired at entertainments, many ambulant bands went from village to village to amuse the lower

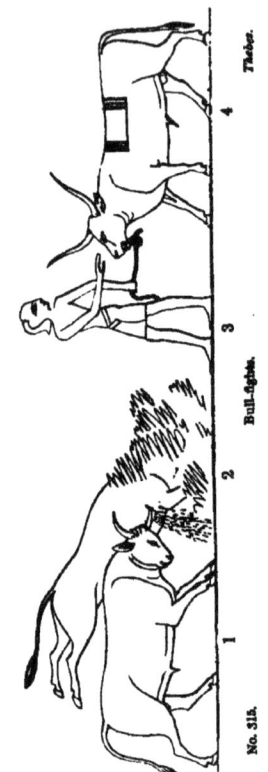

orders, gaining a livelihood by their occupation;
and all the tricks and gestures were resorted to on
those occasions, which the ingenuity of a sprightly
people could suggest, to excite the generosity of
the bystanders, and contribute to their amusement.

Bull-fights were also among their sports, and

men appear occasionally to have courted the approbation of their friends, and displayed their courage and dexterity, in attacking a bull single-handed, and baffling his attacks.*

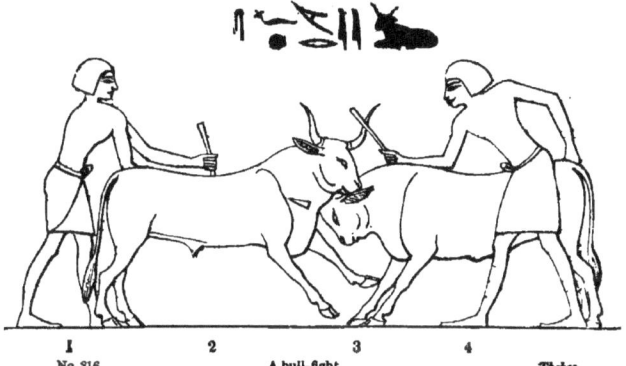

No. 316.   A bull-fight.   *Thebes.*

It does not, however, appear that the Egyptians condemned culprits, or captives taken in war, to combat with wild beasts, for the amusement of an unfeeling assembly, as in ancient Rome ; nor did they compel them to fight as gladiators, to gratify a depraved taste, which delighted in exhibitions revolting to humanity ; and, though we may feel disposed to blame them for compelling prisoners of war to labour at public works, it must be recollected that the usages of society, in those early ages, tolerated a custom which modern civilisation has abandoned ; and it is evident that neither the refined Greeks nor Romans can vie with the Egyptians in their manner of treating slaves : a remarkable proof of which is evinced in the behaviour of

* Wood-cut, No. 314.

Potiphar towards Joseph; for in few countries, even at the present day, would the crime, of which he was supposed guilty, have been visited with more lenient punishment.

Bull-fights appear sometimes to have been encouraged by the higher classes, and to have been held in the dromos, or avenue, leading to their large temples; as Strabo describes * at Memphis, before the temple of Vulcan; and prizes were awarded to the owner of the victorious combatant. Great care, he adds, was taken in their mode of training the animals for this purpose, as much as is usually bestowed on horses, and from their being customary in the metropolis of Lower Egypt, we may conclude that bull-fights were not a Greek or Roman introduction, but of early Egyptian date, particularly since we see them noticed, at the most remote period, at Thebes and Beni Hassan.

* Strabo, lib. xvii.

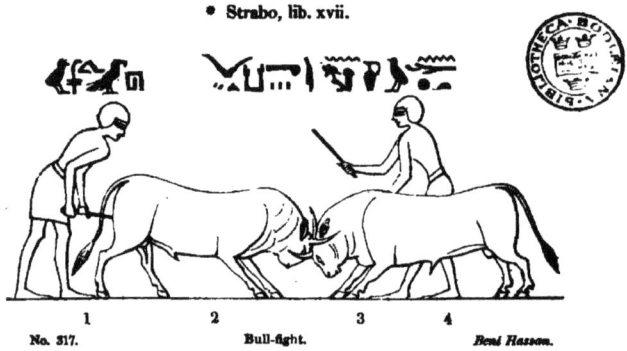

1   2   3   4

No. 317.   Bull-fight.   Beni Hassan.

END OF THE SECOND VOLUME.

LONDON:
Printed by A. SPOTTISWOODE,
New-Street-Square.

Milton Keynes UK
Ingram Content Group UK Ltd.
UKHW051555051223
433765UK00025B/1057